W9-BXP-234

# THE PLACE OF CHRIST IN LITURGICAL PRAYER

Josef A. Jungmann

Foreword by
BALTHASAR FISCHER

THE LITURGICAL PRESS
Collegeville, Minnesota 56321

Published throughout the world except North America
by **Geoffrey Chapman**
an imprint of Cassell Publishers Limited
Artillery House, Artillery Row, London SW1P 1RT

Published in North America
by **The Liturgical Press**,
St John's Abbey, Collegeville, MN 56321

Translation copyright © Geoffrey Chapman,
an imprint of Cassell Publishers Limited, 1965, 1989

All rights reserved. No part of this publication may be reproduced or
transmitted in any form or by any means, electronic or mechanical including
photocopying, recording, or any information storage or retrieval system
without prior permission in writing from the publishers.

Originally published 1925 as
*Die Stellung Christi im liturgischen Gebet*
(*Liturgiewissenschaftliche Quellen und Forschungen* 19/20)
by Aschendorffsche Verlagsbuchhandlung, Münster Westfalen
Revised German edition 1962

First published in English 1965 by Geoffrey Chapman
This edition, with new Foreword, first published 1989

ISBN 0-225-66528-X (Geoffrey Chapman)
0-8146-1916-9 (The Liturgical Press)

**British Library Cataloguing in Publication Data**
Jungmann, Josef A. (Josef Andreas), *1889–1975*
The place of Christ in liturgical prayer.
1. Christian church. Public worship. Prayer
I. Title   II. Die Stellung Christi im liturgischen
Gebet. *English*
264'.1

Printed in Great Britain at the
University Press, Cambridge

# CONTENTS

PART TWO: HISTORY OF THE CHRISTOLOGICAL THEME
IN LITURGICAL PRAYER

# ABBREVIATIONS

| | | |
|---|---|---|
| AAA | = | Acta apostolorum apocrypha. |
| Ap. Const. | = | Apostolic Constitutions. |
| BKV | = | Bibliothek der Kirchenväter. |
| Br. | = | Brightman. |
| CSEL | = | Corpus scriptorum ecclesiasticorum latinorum. |
| DACL | = | Dictionnaire d'archéologie chrétienne et de liturgie. |
| GCS | = | Die griechischen christlichen Schriftsteller der ersten drei Jahrhunderte. |
| JL | = | Jahrbuch für Liturgiewissenschaft. |
| JThSt | = | The Journal of Theological Studies. |
| LF | = | Liturgiegeschichtliche Forschungen. |
| LQ | = | Liturgiegeschichtliche Quellen. |
| MEL | = | Monumenta ecclesiae liturgica. |
| PG | = | Migne, Patrologia graeca. |
| PL | = | Migne, Patrologia latina. |
| Mur. | = | Muratori. |
| Ren. | = | Renaudot. |
| TU | = | Texte und Untersuchungen. |
| ZkTh | = | Zeitschrift für katholische Theologie. |

# BIBLIOGRAPHY

*Full titles of works referred to in abbreviated form*

Assemani Jos. Al., *Codex liturgicus ecclesiae universae*. 13 Vols. Romae 1749—1766.
Bardenhewer Otto, *Geschichte der altkirchlichen Literatur*. 4 Vols. 2. Aufl. Freiburg i. B. 1913—1924.
Baumstark Anton, *Geschichte der syrischen Literatur*. Bonn 1922.
—, *Die Messe im Morgenland*. Kempten 1906.
—, *Vom geschichtlichen Werden der Liturgie* (Ecclesia Orans X). Freiburg i. B. 1923.
Bishop Edm., *Liturgica historica*. Oxford 1918.
Brightman F. E., *Liturgies Eastern and Western*. I. *Eastern Liturgies*. Oxford 1896.
ΧΡΥΣΟΣΤΟΜΙΚΑ. *Studi e ricerche intorno a s. Giovanni Crisostomo a cura del comitato per il 15° centenario della sua morte*. Roma 1908.
Connolly, R. H., O.S.B., *The so-called Egyptian Church Order and derived documents* (Texts and Studies VIII, 4). Cambridge 1916.
—, *The liturgical homilies of Narsai*. With an appendix by Edm. Bishop (Texts and Studies VIII, 1). Cambridge 1909.
Diettrich G., *Die nestorianische Taufliturgie ins Deutsche übersetzt und unter Verwertung der neuesten handschriftlichen Funde historisch-kritisch erforscht*. Giessen 1903.
Dölger Fr. J., *Sol salutis. Gebet und Gesang im christlichen Altertum. Mit besonderer Rücksicht auf die Ostung in Gebet und Liturgie*. 2. Aufl. (LF 4/5). Münster i. W. 1925.
Duchesnel L., *Origines du culte chrétien. Étude sur la liturgie latine avant Charlemagne*. 4. éd. Paris 1908.
Feltoe Ch. L., *Sacramentarium Leonianum*. Cambridge 1896.
Férotin M., O.S.B., *Le liber ordinum en usage dans l'église wisigothique et mozarabe d'Espagne du V. au XI. siècle* (MEL V). Paris 1904.
—, *Le liber mozarabicus sacramentorum et les manuscrits mozarabes* (MEL VI). Paris 1912.
Funk Fr. X., *Didascalia et Constitutiones Apostolorum*. 2 Vols. Paderbornae 1905.
Gerbert Mart., O.S.B., *Monumenta veteris liturgiae alemannicae*. 2 Vols. S. Blasien 1777—1779.
Goltz Ed. von der, *Das Gebet in der ältesten Christenheit*. Leipzig 1901.

Hahn A., *Bibliothek der Symbole und Glaubensregeln der alten Kirche*. 3. Aufl. Breslau 1897.

Hauler Edm., *Didascaliae Apostolorum fragmenta Veronensia latina; accedunt Canonum qui dicuntur Apostolorum et Aegyptiorum reliquiae*. Lipsiae 1900.

Hennecke E., *Neutestamentliche Apokryphen in deutscher Übersetzung und mit Einleitungen*. 2. Aufl. Tübingen 1924. (English trans. edited by R. McL. Wilson, *New Testament Apocrypha*, London, Vol. I 1963, Vol. II 1965.)

Jungmann J.A., *Missarum sollemnia. Eine genetische Erklärung der romischen Messe*. 2 Vols. 5 Aufl. Wien 1962. (Engl: *The Mass of the Roman Rite*. New York 1950/55.)

Kellner K. A. Heinr., *Heortologie oder die geschichtliche Entwicklung des Kirchenjahres und der Heiligenfeste*. 3 German editions 1901, 1906, 1911. (English trans. from 2nd ed. by a priest of the diocese of Westminster, *Heortology: A History of the Christian Festivals from their Origin to the Present Day*. International Catholic Library, Vol. VII, Kegan Paul, London 1908.)

Klawek A., *Das Gebet zu Jesus. Seine Berechtigung und Übung nach den Schriften des Neuen Testaments* (Neutestamentliche Abhandlungen VI, 5). Münster i. W. 1921.

Lebreton Jules, *Les origines du dogme de la Trinité*. Paris 1910.

Lietzmann H., *Das Sacramentarium Gregorianum nach dem Aachener Urexemplar* (LQ 3). Münster i. W. 1921.

Maltzew Al. v., *Liturgikon. Die Liturgien der orthodox-katholischen Kirche des Morgenlandes*. Berlin 1902.

Margreth J., *Das Gebetsleben Jesu Christi, des Sohnes Gottes*. Münster i. W. 1902.

Mercer Sam. A. B., *The Ethiopic Liturgy. Its sources, development and present form*. Milwaukee 1915.

Muratori L. A., *Liturgia Romana vetus*. 2 Vols. Venetiis 1748.

Pamelius Jac., *Liturgica latina*. 2 Vols. Coloniae Agripp. 1571.

Prat F., S. J., *La théologie de s. Paul*, II., 6. éd. Paris 1923.

Probst Ferd., *Liturgie des 4. Jahrhunderts und deren Reform*. Münster i. W. 1893.

—, *Die abendländische Messe vom 5. bis zum 8. Jahrhundert*. Münster i. W. 1896.

Rahmani Ign. Ephr., *Testamentum Domini nostri Jesu Christi*. Moguntiae 1899.

Renaudot Eus., *Liturgiarum orientalium collectio*. 2 Vols Parisiis 1716.

Rücker Adolf, *Die syrische Jakobosanaphora nach der Rezension des Ja'qob(h) von Edessa. Mit dem griechischen Paralleltext* (LQ 4). Münster i. W. 1923.

Schermann Theodor, *Ägyptische Abendmahlsliturgien des ersten Jahrtausends in ihrer Überlieferung dargestellt* (Studien zur Geschichte und Kultur des Altertums VI, 1/2). Paderborn 1912.

—, *Die allgemeine Kirchenordnung, frühchristliche Liturgien und kirchliche Überlieferung*. 3 Parts (Studien zur Geschichte und Kultur des Altertums, 3rd supplementary volume). Paderborn 1914—1916.

Schmidt C., *Zwei altchristliche Gebete: Neutestamentliche Studien für G. Heinrici* (Untersuchungen zum Neuen Testament edited by H. Windisch). Leipzig 1914. S. 66—78.

Storf R., *Griechische Liturgien übersetzt, mit Einleitungen von Th. Schermann* (BKV 5). Kempten 1912.

Swainson C. A., *The Greek Liturgies chiefly from original authorities*. Cambridge 1884.

Thalhofer V.-Eisenhofer L., *Handbuch der katholischen Liturgik*. 2 Vols. Freiburg i. B. 1912. (Engl: Eisenhofer-Lechner, *The Liturgy of the Roman Rite*. Freiburg 1961.)

Vetter P., *Chosroae Magni episcopi monophysitici explicatio precum missae e lingua armeniaca in latinam versa*. Friburgi B. 1880.

Wilson H. A., *The Gelasian Sacramentary*. Oxford 1894.

# ADDENDA TO BIBLIOGRAPHY

Perhaps the most significant piece of liturgical research which develops Jungmann's original, as mentioned in the 1989 Foreword, is Albert Gerhards' doctoral thesis:

Gerhards, A., *Die griechische Gregoriosanaphora. Ein Beitrag zur Geschichte des Eucharistischen Hochgebets* (Aschendorffsche Verlagsbuchhandlung, Münster Westfalen 1984). He offers a very full bibliography (pp. XV–XXIV), which includes the following key works or items of English-language interest:

Baumstark, A., Review of 1925 edition of this book: *Oriens christianus* 27 (1930) 247–50.

Bouyer, L., *Eucharistie. Théologie et spiritualité de la prière eucharistique* (Tournai 1966); *Eucharist: Theology and Spirituality of the Eucharistic Prayer* (Notre Dame, IL 1973).

Burmester, O. H. E., *The Egyptian or Coptic Church. A detailed description of her liturgical services and the rites and ceremonies observed in the administration of her sacraments* (Cairo 1967).

Casel, O., Review of 1925 edition of this book: *Jahrbuch für Liturgiewissenschaft* 7 (1927) 177–84.

Cutrone, E. J., 'The Anaphora of the Apostles: Implications of the Mar Ěsa'ya text': *Theological Studies* 34 (1973) 624–42.

—, 'Cyril's Mystagogical Catecheses and the evolution of the Jerusalem Anaphora': *Orientalia christiana periodica* 44 (1978) 52–64.

Dix, G., *The Shape of the Liturgy* (London 1945, 1975).

Fischer, B., 'Vom Beten zu Christus' in J. G. Plöger (ed.), *Gott feiern. Theologische Anregung und geistliche Vertiefung zur Feier von Messe und Stundengebet* (Festschrift Th. Schnitzler; Freiburg-Basel-Vienna 1980) 94–9.

Gerhards, A., 'Zu wem beten? Die These Josef Andreas Jungmanns über den Adressaten des Eucharistischen Hochgebets im Licht der neueren Forschung': *Liturgisches Jahrbuch* 32 (1982) 219–30.

—, 'Prière adressée à Dieu ou au Christ? Relecture d'une thèse importante de J. A. Jungmann à la lumière de la recherche actuelle' in A. M. Triacca and A. Pistoia (eds), *Liturgie-Spiritualité-Cultures. Conférences Saint-Serge 1982* (Bibliotheca EL, Subsidia 29; Rome 1983) 101–14.

Jones, C., Wainwright, G. and Yarnold, E. (eds), *The Study of Liturgy* (London, 1978).

Lebreton, J., Review of 1925 edition of this book: *Recherches de science religieuse* 16 (1926) 370–3.

Pollard, T. E., *Johannine Christology and the Early Church* (Society for New Testament Studies, Monograph Series 13; Cambridge 1970).

Talley, T. J., 'The Eucharistic Prayer of the Ancient Church according to recent research: results and reflections': *Studia Liturgica* 11 (1976) 138–58.

Also:

Fischer, B., 'La place du Christ dans la liturgie' in *Sacrements de Jésus Christ:* Collection 'Jésus et Jésus Christ', ed. J. Dore, no. 18 (Paris 1983) 185–98.

# FOREWORD

## TO THE SECOND ENGLISH EDITION (1989)

I was delighted to hear that the publishers of the English language edition of *The Place of Christ in Liturgical Prayer* intended to reprint it. I cannot think of a more appropriate way to mark the 100th anniversary of Josef Andreas Jungmann's birth (16 November 1889). I am honoured that they should invite me to offer a few introductory remarks, and I am pleased to do so because it gives me the opportunity to pay tribute to my revered professor.

Looking back now, it is even clearer what a milestone in twentieth-century liturgical studies this thesis (first published in 1925) represents. It showed clearly for the first time that *per Christum*, the characteristic presidential prayer-ending in the Roman liturgy, was a precious legacy from early times. Every liturgical action culminates in the great trinitarian perspective of salvation in which Christ assumes the role of mediator: 'there is one mediator between God and man, the man Christ Jesus' (1 Tim 2:5).

This was a most influential insight. Firstly, as Jungmann himself would have wanted, it helped to give a more secure, a more genuinely traditional theological basis to liturgical piety. Secondly, since it clarified the nature of liturgical presidential prayer (as we would say today, though the term was not current in 1925), especially the Eucharistic Prayer, it paved the way for key elements of the post-conciliar reform.

Jungmann was aware, and indeed never sought to minimize (*pace* many of his adherents), that the *per Christum* presidential prayer represented a 'summit'; that there were 'valleys' around this summit where the people's liturgical prayer could be and indeed was addressed differently. In particular, we have evidence from hymnody that from the beginning Christians addressed not only the Father directly, but also (nourished by Johannine piety) Christ: prayer was directed *ad Christum*. It was important to establish this, for sound liturgical piety depends on both the *ad Christum* and the *per Christum*.

One particular, and important, example of this concerns the postconciliar insertion of the Memorial Acclamation into the Eucharistic Prayer. Unlike many of his adherents, Jungmann did not question but expressly welcomed this liturgical reform. His thesis does not mean either that *per Christum* has held good for the people's liturgical prayer, or that it should do so.

The essence of Jungmann's thesis is that up until the fourth century liturgical presidential prayer (*a fortiori* the Eucharistic Prayer) did not address Christ directly, but used the *per Christum* form. The years of intensive liturgical research since the thesis was first published in 1925 now offer some refinements: in particular, alongside the principal Pauline strand rightly identified by Jungmann, there was a not insignificant secondary Johannine strand, characterized by the form *ad Christum* (even in the Eucharistic Prayer). This can be seen especially in the work of my pupil, the young Bochum liturgical scholar, Albert Gerhards: his study of the fourth-century Anaphora of Gregory of Nazianzus confirmed the co-existence of the two basic forms (*per Christum* and *ad Christum*) in the liturgical presidential prayer, especially in the Eastern Church.[1]

*The Place of Christ in Liturgical Prayer* represents what was a major breakthrough in liturgical theology, whose importance is not diminished by discovering that the total picture has turned out to be more nuanced than was supposed in the first flush of discovery. If anything, this is proof of the value of Jungmann's thesis, a seminal work whose fruitfulness has been confirmed by the refinements that subsequent research has brought to it.

Trier, 6 January 1969.
BALTHASAR FISCHER

---

[1] Albert Gerhards, *Die griechische Gregoriosanaphora. Ein Beitrag zur Geschichte des Eucharistischen Hochgebets* (Aschendorff'sche Verlagsbuchhandlung, Münster Westfalen, 1984).

# PREFACE

TO THE FIRST ENGLISH EDITION (1965)

The main difference between the present edition and the second German impression of 1962 is that the Addenda, which previously formed a twenty-page section on their own, have now been incorporated into the text. This naturally made it necessary to modify the relevant portions of the text and in the end to look through the work as a whole. But it also provided an opportunity to make minor corrections in many places, to amend outdated opinions, to delete superfluous observations and occasionally, mainly in the notes, to refer to later developments.

It was not intended, even had it been possible, to revise the work completely, and so the book remains a product of 1925. The source references are to editions available at the time, though new editions have occasionally been introduced into the notes. The same applies, by and large, to the various works referred to, unless any of their ideas have been superseded as a result of later studies. There was no need to make any alteration to the book's essential thesis, which since the time of writing has not only retained its validity but has also proved fruitful in the present liturgical and religious revival. This may perhaps serve as justification for a new edition.

Innsbruck, 20 January 1965

Jos. A. Jungmann S.J.

# PREFACE

TO THE SECOND GERMAN EDITION (1962)

The kind offer of the house of Aschendorff and the editor of the
*Liturgiewissenschaftliche Quellen und Forschungen* to publish a new
edition of my first work, which thirty-seven years ago gained me my
university lectureship in pastoral theology, was one which I could
only accept with many thanks—in spite of some misgivings. It is
obvious that the work has considerable shortcomings, which, with
all fundamental appreciation, were properly brought out by several
reviewers, especially Jules Lebreton and Odo Casel, and which I
myself see more clearly today. The task indicated in the title would
merit a much more thorough treatment than was given it here, and
this in regard both to the assembling of the pertinent material,
especially for the first centuries of the Church, and its elucidation
with the aid of dogmatic history. In particular, the limits of the
proposed subject should have been more distinctly outlined and
strictly adhered to. The liturgical prayer could not be treated in its
full compass, which indeed embraces the popular and poetic elements of the acclamation and the hymn, and attention had to be
limited to the liturgical priestly prayer, the official prayer of the
leader of the liturgical assembly. The further limitation to the
eucharistic liturgy seemed legitimate, since the preparatory parts of
the eucharistic celebration could at least represent the divine
office.

However, the treatment of the subject seemed already at that time to be demanded by the religious situation. In fact very soon no less a person than Karl Adam, in a much-noticed essay, 'Durch Christus unsern Herrn'—first published in the periodical *Seele*, 8(1926)321–9; 355–64—referred to the book and to the importance of the questions raised therein. After all, the main thing was the essential thesis of the book, the evidence for the decisive influence which the Arian crisis exerted on the development, firstly of liturgical prayer and then of Western piety in general. And this evidence has finally been acknowledged on all sides as valid.

For this new edition, I have added to those points which have been affected by the interval of time since the first edition was published, in the light of the discussion on many questions which has since ensued—discussion for which there is reason to be grateful. I have limited myself to points already treated in the book—in particular to the new light thrown on the kind of piety evident in oriental liturgies.

Innsbruck, 1 February 1962.
Jos. A. Jungmann S.J.

# PREFACE

TO THE FIRST GERMAN EDITION (1925)

If the promising movement to renew and deepen our religious life through the liturgy is not to become the sport of moods and feelings, and end in disappointments, the scientific treatment of the liturgy must, besides its perennial tasks, increasingly attend to the questions, and throw light on the areas, which can provide a response to the yearning of our time and satisfy its thirst. And these are without doubt the questions which, if we ask them, bring us nearer to the spirit and to the ideas embodied in the words and actions of the liturgy. Only this understanding brings the full reward to detailed and critical literary research. The results of years of this devoted scholarship and research are in themselves a clarion call to further work, to the attempt, based on these results, to advance to the point where the liturgy, in its manifold shape, makes vital contact with the entire life of the Church, but especially with her central beliefs.

It was in view of giving some modest help in this task that the present work was undertaken and carried through. It offers no grand solutions. Rather, it would help a little to clarify something in which there is a certain evident contrast between the older, traditional way of liturgical piety (or, perhaps better, biblical-liturgical piety) on the one hand, and on the other our current forms of popular devotion: the relation of the individual and of the community at prayer to Christ. This work is limited to an outline of the development connecting these two types, and that only in so far as it can be traced in the prayers of the liturgy. The way in which the struggle against Arianism, especially in the West, affected the spirit of liturgical prayer, promoting *inter alia* the custom of addressing prayers to Christ, should thus appear for the first time in some detail.

Obviously the same current of ideas that is here pursued in the liturgical field, with the same diminution of references to Christ the Mediator in favour of a more reverential attitude towards him, will appear in other departments of the Church's life. Treatment of this aspect, in Part Two of this volume, which deals with the historical development, has had to be severely restricted. All that could be done was to synthesize the liturgical material, previously assembled analytically, against the background of the history of dogma; while for all other movements only the starting-point could occasionally be remarked. Nor could the liturgical field itself claim exhaustive treatment. For the Western liturgies, only the more important documents were used, as these seemed sufficient to mark the main stages of development. For the eastern non-Greek liturgies, a limit was set at once by the extent of the formularies and texts available in Western languages; thanks to the work of recent decades, they should go back sufficiently far. Finally, the theological characteristics of the different liturgies had to be treated only as far as seemed called for in the context of the particular question under discussion.

Innsbruck, September 1925
Jos. A. Jungmann S.J.

# INTRODUCTION

Prayer, the intercourse of man with God, is of its nature not bound by clearly determined forms and methods; there are, rather, in the words of Cassian, 'as many kinds of prayer as in a soul, or, better, in all souls together, there are different states and moods'.[1] For in prayer is reflected not only the essence of the immutable God, but still more the behaviour of the creature, which is mutable a thousand ways, according to time and place, ability and lot.

This is true not only for the individual, but also to a lesser degree for the prayer of the Christian community, or liturgical prayer. Of course, from its nature as prayer of the community, the latter is more permanent and uniform; its character, also, is determined chiefly by the fixed body of religious beliefs that unites all its adherents and finds expression in praise, thanksgiving and supplication. Yet this body of Catholic dogma possessed by the faithful has again its own history, in the course of which its outline only gradually becomes clearer. Besides, liturgical prayer is not simply a confession of faith, whose only object is to define the area of dogma as precisely as possible, or to divide truth from error ever more sharply. It is rather that a spontaneous use is made, with God in view, of the deposit of faith; a joyful use of Revelation, in which at different times, among the fixed and basic facts, those traits are brought out which are nearest to the religious atmosphere, the experiences and interests

[1] Collat. IX, 8. CSEL 13, p. 259.

of that period and people which has been the matrix of the liturgical prayer-formula. Hence the use of Christian doctrine in liturgical prayer may have a history; and this inner liturgical history, which is part of the history of religious life in general, may in places become the main line governing the history of outward liturgical forms.[1]

At the centre of the Christian faith stands Jesus Christ, the Son of God. His personality, as presented by Scripture and Tradition, at once historical and actual and, while of the earth, far surpassing all things earthly, is not to be taken in by the human mind at one glance. Divinity and humanity are here in a unique manner united. The manner of this union, this marriage of heaven and earth in Christ, on which our whole hope hangs became in the course of the Church's history the object of heated struggles. Indeed, the fact of the question being put and the consequent need to protect a threatened point of doctrine could influence the simple attitude of the ordinary man at prayer, and could even in liturgical compositions of such times call attention to that threatened point. Thus the use made in prayer of the idea of Christ and the position assigned to him in it could change.

How far this actually occurred we are here concerned to enquire. We are not therefore concerned in the present work to establish in its finer details the image of Christ that hovers over the different parts of the liturgy, as it may appear from a comparison of lessons, foreshadowing in the Old Testament and fulfilling in the New; or from hymns and canticles, which may praise him as conqueror and king, or as the intimate friend of the soul. The enquiry is confined to *the prayer* alone, and even the prayer, apart from the earliest period, is pursued only in so far as it belongs to the liturgy of the Mass—on the one hand, because the text material for the history of the sacraments and the divine office is even less accessible; on the

---

[1] This truth and the importance of studies related thereto, as well as of the investigation of the liturgical forms and the full use in dogma and apologetics of the liturgical texts, was pointed out some years ago by the notable English Catholic liturgiologist, E. Bishop (d. 1917), in his supplement to R. H. Connolly, *The liturgical homilies of Narsai* (Cambridge, 1909), 93: 'Yet it would seem true that a true appreciation and exact knowledge of different types of piety as manifested in various parts and the successive ages of the Christian Chruch, in a word, a knowledge of the history of religious sentiment among Christians, is a necessary condition for understanding the origin or rise even of rites and ceremonies themselves.'

other, because the Mass liturgy after all occupies the first place in all liturgies and suffices to typify the individual liturgical creations.

The subject has up to now been treated, so to speak, only marginally and in passing. Nevertheless, the liturgy manuals contain no little material pertaining to our subject in the sections on the essence of the liturgy, the place of the performer of the liturgy, doxologies and liturgical prayer endings.[1] A superficial attempt to arrange the known facts into an outline history has been made by F. Heiler.[2] As is only to be expected, it needs a lot of correction.

It will put the enquiry itself into a clearer light to distinguish at this point the most important ways in which a distinct relation to Christ can be shown. They are all comprised in the form of address of the prayer, the attitude taken to the heavenly powers under consideration in the Christian prayer. The simplest case is that of the liturgical prayer directly addressed to *Christ*. This has a certain affinity with the prayer to God the Father in which Christ also is expressly *named* and prayed to. Then the prayer can be directed to God in such a way that there is *no mention* of the Son, or the Redeemer, but he may be included more or less in the address (e.g. 'Lord'). We also meet cases in which Christ is spoken of as a third element between God and the one who prays, as the Mediator between God and men. This can happen in such a way that Christ is brought in only remotely in connexion with the *subject-matter*: thanksgiving for salvation, to which we have access through him; petition for the good things which he has promised; the prayer dwells in meditation or confession on the facts which Scripture or Tradition relate of the Redeemer. The reference is internal, when Christ in the prayer itself is relied on in any way for assistance. The Redeemer with all that he has done and willed for our advantage is cited as a *motive* on account of which God should be merciful to us: hear us for the sake of thy Son! But this case is important only for the prayer of petition. By way of contrast, another kind of reference to our Lord which

---

[1] For example, V. Thalhofer–L. Eisenhofer I, 6–15, 311–36. English edn: Eisenhofer–Lechner, *The Liturgy of the Roman Rite* (Freiburg, 1961).

[2] F. Heiler, *Das Gebet* (Munich, 1923), 463–7, in the section on the liturgical communal prayer: doxology, prayer invocation. English version: *Prayer* (London, 1932), 317–22; 333–5.

strengthens the prayer brings him into intimate union with the prayer itself and is important for all types of prayer: he is referred to as high priest and advocate before God, who with a kind of complicity assists our prayer at the throne of God; the prayer is offered 'through Christ our Lord'.

Our study will have to concentrate mainly on the first and the last of these ways. Prayer *to* Christ and prayer *through* Christ—or Christ as receiver of prayer and Christ as Mediator of prayer[1]—are clearly two poles between which the other ways of referring to Christ in the wording of the prayer may be classified. There are, therefore, two main types of liturgical prayer. Each of them, in so far as it seems to be preferred in a particular class of liturgical works, may be referred to a particular religious viewpoint, to a particular attitude towards Christ and therefore to a particular cast of thought concerning Christ. When, therefore, the relevant facts are established they will have to be explained, as far as possible, historically.

The work falls, accordingly, into two parts. In the *first* part, it will be our task to enquire into the place of Christ in the liturgical prayer, by going through the different liturgies as they appear in the course of the Church's history. Many of these liturgical growths soon disappeared again and frequently only a few documents witness to them. Others, since their origin in the early Church, have gone through a long evolution, and have formed new layers round the ancient kernel, in which one finds evidence of the religious characteristics of the different periods. In the latter case, when possible, distinct phases of the same liturgy have to be considered in order to find how far the evolutionary process touches on our point of enquiry. Then in the *second* part the results will be assembled and arranged, added to and elucidated by data drawn from a wider field, and drawn up into a more coherent whole, to provide a historical outline of the place occupied by the idea of Christ in liturgical prayer through the ages.

---

[1] Christ can appear as Mediator in the further sense, as he who has reconciled us to God, without his being thought of or referred to as Mediator of the prayer.

# PART ONE

# THE DIFFERENT LITURGIES
# EXAMINED

# I

# THE ANCIENT CHURCH ORDERS

THE regulation of the liturgy is an important element in the oldest
extant books of Church law. In these too the earliest liturgical texts
are preserved. In the earliest period, as is even expressly remarked
from time to time, they were not thought of as a binding norm to
which the liturgy must be held but rather as suggestions and aids for
it. The collection of *Hippolytus* confirms the words of E. v. d. Goltz:
'Spontaneous prayer apparently remains predominant right into
the third century'.[1]

## 1. THE DIDACHE

We meet the first liturgical prayer-collection about the end of the
first century in chapters nine and ten of the *Didache*.[2] The question
whether the formularies are prescribed for the celebration of the
Eucharist or for the agape we can here leave unanswered.[3] The

---

[1] *Das Gebet in der ältesten Christenheit* 181; cf. p. 193.—R. H. Connolly, *The
So-Called Egyptian Church Order* (Cambridge, 1916), 64–6, 179 f. This freedom survived longest in Rome; cf. A. Baumstark, *Vom gesch. Werden der Liturgie* 95 f.

[2] Funk, *Patres apostolici I*, pp. 20–4; J. P. Audet, *La Didaché* (Paris, 1958), 221–43.

[3] In DACL, H. Leclercq in the art. 'Didache' (4, 777–94) defends the latter,
F. Cabrol in art. 'Eucharistie' (5, 689) the former view.

prayers of the *Didache* are directed to God, who is addressed confidently as 'our Father' (9: 2, 3), 'holy Father' (10: 2), but then also as 'almighty Lord' and 'Lord' (10: 3, 5). Their subject is principally thanksgiving for the goods which he has bestowed on us through Christ, διὰ ('Ιησοῦ) τοῦ παιδός σου, e.g. 9:3: 'We thank thee, our Father, for the life and the knowledge which thou hast made manifest to us through Jesus, thy Son; thine is the glory for ever.' Here Jesus, the envoy of the Father, is matter for thanks. To the prayer of thanks which is recited before and after the meal, always in two parts, is attached on both occasions a prayer of petition for the Church which just as the former closes with the doxology just quoted. Only 9: 4 refers also to Christ as Mediator in this doxology: ὅτι σοῦ ἐστιν ἡ δόξα καὶ ἡ δύναμις διὰ 'Ιησοῦ Χριστοῦ εἰς τοὺς αἰῶνας.[1] The acclamations to Christ (10: 6), 'Hosanna to the God of David', 'Maranatha', not being formal prayers, do not concern us here.

Most of the prayers of chapter nine of the *Didache* appear in Athanasius: *De Virginitate*, chap. 13,[2] as grace before and after meals, but with the διὰ 'Ιησοῦ Χριστοῦ of the doxology left out. On the other hand, we meet the prayers of both chapters of the *Didache* in somewhat altered form, with more precise adaptation to the celebration of the Eucharist, in the seventh book of the *Apostolic Constitutions*.[3] Here Christ is not only the one through whom praise is offered (chap. 25:4) and through whom God on his side has performed the work of redemption, for which he is thanked in a lengthy account; he is also the medium between God and the world in the creation.[4] In fact, even the simple 'Remember, Lord, thy Church' becomes the somewhat involved combination 'Through him remember. . .'.

---

[1] The phrase διὰ 'Ιησοῦ Χριστοῦ in Did. 9: 4 is considered by J. P. Audet, *La Didaché*, 234.403 who refers to the parallel 10: 5 as a later addition. Likewise thinks E. Peterson, 'Über einige Probleme der Didache-Überlieferung': *Rivista di Archeologia cristiana* 27 (1951, 37–68) 38.

[2] Ed. von der Goltz, TU 29, 2a, p. 47.

[3] VII, 25 f. (Funk I, 410 ff.).

[4] c.25, 2: Εὐχαριστοῦμέν σοι, πάτερ ἡμῶν, ὑπὲρ τῆς ζωῆς ῆς ἐγνώρισας ἡμῖν διὰ 'Ιησοῦ τοῦ παιδός σου, δι' οὗ καὶ τὰ πάντα ἐποίησας.

## 2. THE CHURCH ORDER OF HIPPOLYTUS

In recent years the study of the liturgy of Christian antiquity has been enriched by a new source of the first rank. E. Schwartz and, independently, in a still more thorough investigation, R. H. Connolly have shown that in the so-called Egyptian Church Order we have a work of *St Hippolytus of Rome* (d. 235), the ἀποστολικὴ παράδοσις, which is listed among the titles of his works on his well-known statue, and hitherto was taken as lost.[1] Hippolytus intended by this work to make regulations for his separated community when, about the year 220, he started a schism, which he seems to have given up, however, before he died. As the title indicates, his main intention was to fix in writing the existing tradition. This title and the Roman provenance won for the work a wide circulation in the East.[2] The parts which matter most to us are mainly preserved in, firstly, a Latin translation which is accepted as a literal rendering of the Greek and, according to its editor, must belong to the time of St Ambrose;[3] and, secondly, an Ethiopian translation which for the most part agrees with remarkable exactness with the Latin text, although it is deemed to go back to the Greek via an Arabic and a Coptic version. The combined witness of both is therefore of the

[1] E. Schwartz, 'Über die pseudoapostolischen Kirchenordnungen', in *Schriften der wissenschaftlichen Gesellschaft in Strassburg*, VI (Strassburg, 1910). R. H. Connolly, *The So-Called Egyptian Church Order* (Cambridge, 1916).

[2] *Bardenhewer II* (2nd Edn), 555 f. 596-9. On the personal share of Hippolytus in the prescriptions and texts of the church order, cf. P. Galtier in *Recherches de science religieuse* 13 (1923) 511-27. The wording of the anaphora itself belongs evidently to Hippolytus: R. H. Connolly, JThSt 24 (1924) 458.

[3] E. Hauler, *Didascaliae apostolorum fragmenta Veronensia*; 'accedunt canonum qui dicuntur apostolorum et Aegyptiorum reliquiae' (Leipzig, 1900). The trinitarian formula attached to the end of the anaphora is to be understood (*pace* A. Stuiber, *Doxologie: Reallexikon f. Antike u. Christentum* IV, 219, 223 f.) such that Hippolytus wished the two phrases 'tibi gloria Patri et Filio cum Sancto Spiritu' and 'in sancta Ecclesia' (personally proper to him) to be inserted every time in the traditional doxology (δι' οὗ). The διά is thus missing in the seven formulas of the doxology only once, in the prayer after Baptism, where the ending fails to mention Christ. When therefore Lebreton (loc. cit. 372) and Casel (loc. cit. 179) in their reviews stress that we have a later insertion in the trinitarian address, one can only agree in the sense that Hippolytus here wants his own ideas inserted deliberately in the traditional formulation.

highest value. For other parts, the Coptic and Arabic translations, as well as fragments in other languages, have to be called upon.[1]

In Hippolytus's church order, we find the following prayers: the formulary for the celebration of Mass—which, following Greek terminology, one may briefly term the anaphora—one prayer each for the consecration of a bishop, the ordination of a priest and of a deacon, and one for Baptism; also, a prayer for the lamp-lighting at the evening Agape, and a prayer for the blessing of fruits. Besides these, following the anaphora is a rubric that prescribes a similar thanksgiving on occasion over oil or cheese and olives, the blessing to end with the prescribed doxology.

What position is given to Christ in these prayers? All the liturgical prayers are directed to God and, as the endings to some extent declare, to God in his three persons. However Christ always stands as Mediator in the foreground, though in different ways. Where the occasion suggests it, he stands predominant in the context of the prayer: lamp-lighting—the true Light; episcopal consecration—the powers bestowed by Christ; diaconate—Christ also came to serve διακονεῖν;[2] the anaphora, finally, praises in solemn fashion the incarnation of the Logos, as also his triumph in death and resurrection.[3] But elsewhere Christ comes in usually at the beginning and regularly at the end of the prayer, denoting the Mediator of the prayer. A typical case is that of the priest's ordination:

'Deus et Pater Domini nostri Jesu Christi, respice super servum tuum istum et inpartire spiritum gratiae et consilii praesbyterii, ut adiuvet et gubernet plebem tuam in corde mundo, sicuti respexisti super populum

---

[1] The only sufficient text at the time of first publication of this book (1925) was Connolly's: in the supplement to his work, pp. 174–94, he gives the Latin text after Hauler, so far as it is extant, and fills the gaps with the English translation of the Ethiopian text in G. Horner, *The Statutes of the Apostles* (London, 1904). In the meantime two critical editions have appeared: G. Dix, Ἀποστολικὴ παράδοσις, *The treatise on the Apostolic Tradition of St Hippolytus* (London, 1937); B. Botte, *La Tradition Apostolique de Saint Hippolyte* (Münster, 1963). They involve no change in the picture outlined. Unfortunately in both, the reconstruction of the doxologies is unacceptable; cf. J. A. Jungmann, 'Die Doxologien in der Kirchenordnung Hippolyts', ZkTh LXXXVI (1964) 321—6.

[2] An allusion to this idea probably underlies the expression which even the later Greek liturgies have preserved, to denote the status of the deacon: ἡ ἐν Χριστῷ διακονία.

[3] For the wording, see below: Ethiopian liturgy.

electionis tuae et praecepisti Moysi, ut eligeret praesbyteros, quos replesti de spiritu tuo, quod tu donasti famulo tuo; et nunc, Domine, praesta indeficienter conservari in nobis spiritum gratiae tuae et dignos effice, ut credentes tibi ministremus in simplicitate cordis, laudantes te per puerum tuum Christum Jesum, per quem tibi gloria et virtus, Patri et Filio cum Spiritu Sancto, in sancta ecclesia et nunc et in saecula saeculorum. Amen.'[1]

The mode of address used here is proper to all three ordination prayers: God and Father of our Lord Jesus Christ;[2] the anaphora and the prayer at the lamp-lighting have instead, in common with the beginning of the thanksgiving, Christ as Mediator of the prayer: 'Gratias tibi referimus, Deus, per dilectum puerum tuum Jesum Christum'.[3]

The end of the above prayer in praise (present or desired for the future) of God *per puerum tuum Jesum Christum* is found in at least five of the seven prayers.[4] In every case, then, the ending still consists of a doxology.[5] The solemn form, as found in the priest's ordination prayer, where the triune God is praised through Christ in the holy Church, returns in the anaphora and in the episcopal consecration prayer, and was probably also in the deacon's ordination prayer.[6]

A shorter doxology ends the blessing of fruits, and is here—

---

[1] Hauler 108 f.; Connolly 178.

[2] At the deacon's ordination expanded to: *Deus, qui omnia creasti et verbo preordinasti, Pater Domini nostri Jesu Christi.* Hauler 110.

[3] Hauler 106; Connolly 176; 188.

[4] The only exception is the baptismal prayer, and perhaps the blessing of fruits. In the latter, the phrase *per puerum tuum* could also refer to Christ as the one through whom God adorns the creation with various fruits; but by analogy the sense above is more likely. On the other hand, in the baptismal prayer Christ is not named.

[5] Its form is not in every case equally certain, as the Latin version fails in two passages (at the deacon's ordination and at the lamp-lighting); the Egyptian, however, testifies here to a form of doxology such as we shall find in use in Egypt towards the middle of the first millennium: '(Through thy son Jesus Christ our Lord) through whom to thee with him be glory and power and praise with the Holy Spirit.' The 'with him', which Connolly 189 omits (against Horner 160; 384), belongs in this old Egyptian doxology.

[6] This is also the view of Connolly: JThSt 24 (1923) 146. He reconstructs here the original text of this doxology, which is supported for the given passages also by the Ethiopian wording and by the end of Hippolytus's work *contra Noetum*. His reconstruction is as follows: διὰ τοῦ παιδός σου Ἰησοῦ Χριστοῦ, δι' οὗ σοὶ ἡ δόξα καὶ ἡ τιμή (or τὸ κράτος), πατρὶ καὶ υἱῷ σὺν ἁγίῳ πνεύματι, ἐν τῇ ἁγίᾳ ἐκκλησίᾳ.

together with the rest of the prayer, coinciding with the Latin—also extant in Greek: διὰ τοῦ παιδός σου Ἰησοῦ Χριστοῦ τοῦ κυρίου ἡμῶν, δι' οὗ (καὶ) σοὶ ἡ δόξα.[1] The elements of the solemn doxology, missing in this shorter form, with the naming of the three divine Persons and the holy Church, are the basis of another short formula of praise, which ends the prayer after Baptism: 'Quoniam tibi est gloria, Patri et Filio cum Spiritu Sancto, in sancta ecclesia et nunc et in saecula saeculorum.'[2] This ending would, according to the rubric mentioned above, also conclude the remaining blessings, for which no proper formulary is provided.[3] In this last form, Christ is not expressly named. But the reference to the holy Church, which in the solemn doxology at first glance is almost a pleonasm with the mention of Christ ('per quem tibi gloria—in sancta ecclesia'), here represents the christological member by bringing out the sanctified nature, worthy of God, which the praise of God has acquired in Christianity. A certain freedom reigns, therefore, in the naming or otherwise of Christ expressly as Mediator of the prayer; yet it shines out from them all that the user of the prayer has a lively awareness of him as such.[4]

The church order of Hippolytus became important, not only as such, especially in Egypt; from the fourth century, it also became the basis for several other works regulating the liturgy, which afterwards won recognition in Syria and its ambit. Some of Hippolytus's

---

[1] R. H. Connolly, 'An ancient prayer in the medieval euchologia', JThSt 19 (1918) 132–44; esp. 134 ff. We may put this same form, probably also in the prayer at the lamp-lighting, in the place of the Egyptian doxology given both here and at the blessing of fruits in the Ethiopian text. Cf. Jungmann, *Die Doxologien* (footnote 10) 325. Thus we would have here already the custom still in use today in the Roman liturgy whereby, depending on the solemnity of the rite, a longer or shorter conclusion is employed.

[2] Hauler 111.

[3] 'In omni vero benedictione dicatur: Tibi gloria, Patri et Filio cum Sancto Spiritu, in sancta ecclesia et nunc et semper . . .' Hauler 108.

[4] It is worth noting that even the private prayer to which the faithful are exhorted (at the third, sixth and ninth hour in memory of the Passion, then at bed-time and at midnight, and lastly in memory of the Resurrection in the morning) is always to take the form of praise of God, praise above all for the benefits of the redemption; the basis for this: '(Haec) itaque omnes fideles agentes . . . neque temptari neque perire poteritis, cum semper Christum in memoriam habetis.' Hauler 120 f.

liturgical texts reappear in them, although generally in suitably developed and expanded forms; for this reason they must be considered now. The genealogy of these writings may be represented thus:

Church Order of Hippolytus

Canons of Hippolytus/Apostolic Constitutions VIII/Testament of
Our Lord

Epitome

## 3.  THE CANONS OF HIPPOLYTUS

The Canons of Hippolytus[1] take over from Hippolytus, besides the bishop's consecration prayer (which is also intended for priestly ordination), only that for the diaconate, Baptism and the blessing of fruits. They show in these prayers no great change in the theological structure of the prayer as found in Hippolytus. Only the ending of the prayer in a doxology '*per puerum tuum Jesum Christum, per quem* . . .', in which therefore the prayer was raised to God through Christ, is just once roughly retained:[2] 'Accipe omne servitium eius (diaconi) per Dominum nostrum Jesum Christum.' In the other cases it is, according to the context, the benefits requested—the overcoming of Satan,[3] the possession of the kingdom of heaven[4]— which are to be bestowed 'through Christ', and therefore to come down on those who are praying.[5] The doxology which follows runs: '(per D. n. J. Chr.) per quem tibi gloria cum ipso et Spiritu Sancto in saecula saeculorum.' This form will reappear in Egyptian texts.

---

[1] They are extant in Arabic. Their origin is obscure. Latin with parallels in H. Achelis, *Die Canones Hippolyti* (TU 6, 4), (Leipzig, 1891), 38–137. Additional manuscripts are used in the German version by W. Riedel, *Die Kirchenrechtsquellen des Patriarchats Alexandrien* (Leipzig, 1900), 193–230. The texts in question here contain no variants.

[2] Achelis 67.      [3] P. 46.      [4] Pp. 99; 113.

[5] P. 113 (blessing of fruits) has a striking ending without any other doxology: fac ut hereditate accipiat id, quod est in coelis, per Dominum nostrum Jesum Christum Filium tuum dilectum et Spiritum Sanctum in saecula saeculorum. Amen.

Although it cannot stem from Hippolytus, the only essential difference from his doxology is the omission of the 'holy Church'. The 'holy Church' is likewise omitted in the doxology with which the freely improvised prayers over the first fruits are to end and which, together with the connected rubric, seems actually to have been taken from Hippolytus: 'Gloria tibi, Patri et Filio et Spiritui Sancto, in saecula saeculorum. Amen.'[1] The influence of Hippolytus appears also in the postscript added by the author: they who observe these rules may rest at peace in the kingdom of our Lord Jesus Christ, 'per quem gloria Deo, Patri et Filio et Spiritui Sancto, et nunc . . .'.[2] Hence the position of Christ as high priest is preserved in a few doxologies, in part independent of Hippolytus, while otherwise his mediatorship is hardly recognized except in the wider sense.

## 4. THE APOSTOLIC CONSTITUTIONS

The work of ancient Church law most mentioned in the history of the liturgy is the *Apostolic Constitutions*, a compilation in Greek, in eight books, of the end of the fourth century, from the region of Antioch.[3] The first six books are a recension of the Syrian *Didascalia*, of about one and a half centuries earlier, and in the second book (chapter 57) have a description of the liturgy, but in the way of prayer formularies only a short blessing: 'Save thy people, O Lord, and bless thine inheritance, which thou hast won with the precious blood of thy Christ and hast called to be a royal priesthood and a holy nation.' On the other hand, half of the seventh book is a collection of prayers of more or less liturgical character; of these, the *Didache* prayers have already been mentioned. The great majority of the rest (ch. 33 ff.), W. Bousset[4] has shown, are based on Jewish prayers adapted for Christian use.

The eighth book, finally, is a recension and enlargement of Hippolytus's church order. The prayers of Hippolytus are greatly altered and expanded. The prayer after Baptism and that at the

[1] P. 56.   [2] P. 137.

[3] F. X. Funk, *Didascalia et Constitutiones Apostolorum* I (Paderborn, 1905).

[4] 'Eine jüdische Gebetssammlung im 7. Buch der Apostolischen Konstitutionen' in *Nachrichten der kgl. Gesellschaft der Wissenschaften in Göttingen, phil.-hist. Klasse* (1915), 435–89.

lamp-lighting are entirely missing. In their place, many new prayers are introduced. The formulary for the celebration of Mass, the so-called Clementine Liturgy, occupies ten chapters (VIII, 6-15). However, from the length of the Preface, *inter alia*, one would conclude that we have here in part an ideal formulary, intended to be rather a collection of suitable material than an official Church book. On the other side, many points of similarity with the Antiochene usage, of which there is witness elsewhere, show that the compiler introduced into Hippolytus's work much matter from the liturgical practice of his environment.[1] It is disputed whether the whole is the work of one author. The latest answer, that of O. Bardenhewer,[2] is in the affirmative.

The mode of address of the prayers is here in general the same as in Hippolytus. Among the prayers of different lengths (in Funk, occupying about sixty pages), which are all directed to God, one exception stands out, viz. the prayer with which the energumens are dismissed before the Mass of the faithful;[3] this prayer is addressed to Christ. The address repeatedly emphasizes his power over the evil spirits, which at the same time probably explains the exception: it is a kind of exorcism, meant to show the power of Jesus' name 'Thou who hast bound the strong man and wrested from him his whole armoury . . ., only-begotten God, Son of the august Father, threaten the wicked spirits . . ., for to thee (belongs) honour, glory and worship, and through thee to thy Father in the Holy Spirit for ever. Amen'. Thus we find also in the prescriptions for Baptism (VII, 43, 3): Then (after the priest has thanked God the Father for sending his Son to redeem us) 'he adores the only-begotten God for and on account of himself (δι' αὐτὸν, not δι' αὐτοῦ), by thanking him for undergoing death on the Cross for all men, and as its symbol instituting the Baptism of rebirth'. Here the prayer to Christ is assigned a place according to a deliberate plan: it serves as conclusion to a rite which the author clearly depicts as burial and Resurrection with Christ.[4] The short acclamations immediately before the Com-

---

[1] Cf. Brightman, *Liturgies*, xvi ff.      [2] IV, 268 f.

[3] VIII, 7, 5-8; cf. VIII, 7, 2.

[4] VII, 22, 6; 43, 5; 44, 2. The Resurrection accomplished with Christ is also the reason why the newly baptized is to stand during the prayer: VII, 45, 1.

munion (VIII, 13, 13), as in the *Didache*, belong more to the sphere of the hymn.

All the other prayers are directed to God. The addresses, mostly very solemn and wordy, often contain such expressions as 'God and Father of thy Christ'[1] or 'Creator and Preserver of all through Christ' (VIII, 37, 2), which refer to the Mediator. Thus the character of the prayers is shown by the ever-recurring phrase 'through Christ'.[2]

It is Christ through whom God made the world;[3] through him, he restores the dead to life (VII, 34, 8); through him he gives the Holy Spirit (VIII, 5, 5, 7), and in the divine mysteries (VIII, 6, 13) he threatens the evil spirits (VIII, 7, 2) and consoles those at prayer (VIII, 36, 2). The author is clearly anxious to stress that God distributes all good things only through Christ as his mediator,[4] and, *vis-à-vis* God, to emphasize in the prayer that we expect to be heard only for the sake of Christ, who is our hope.[5]

However, not only the descent of grace, but also the ascent of prayer, through Christ's mediation, is often expressed—indeed in most of the prayers and frequently in the instructions.[6] Thus, the summons to prayer of the deacon (VIII, 10, 2) corresponding roughly to our *oremus*, runs: 'Let us ask God through his Christ . . .'; 10, 22: 'In instant prayer let us submit ourselves and each other to the living God through his Christ'; 13, 3: 'Let us further beg God through his Christ; let us beg on account of the gifts that have been offered to the Lord our God, that the good God through the media-

---

[1] VIII, 6, 11; cf. 12, 8; 13, 10.

[2] This is true in part even of the doctrinal sections, including the other books comprising the work. In the interpolations in the text of the *Didascalia* (I–VI)—underlined in Funk—expressions recur frequently in which Christ's position as Mediator is emphasized. Sometimes there is a simple insertion of διὰ Ἰησοῦ Χριστοῦ (e.g. II, 14, 11; 26, 2; cf. 55, 2; 56, 2); often, however, it is a matter of the relation, in the prayer, of man to God, to whom we have access only 'through Christ'—a theme to which, besides, the author of the *Didascalia* himself was no stranger (II, 28, 6). By interpolations of this kind the Jewish prayer-material of the seventh book also was christianized.

[3] E.g. VII, 25, 2; 34, 1; 35, 10; 36, 1. Only rarely is he mentioned in his pre-existence—concerned in the creation—with other titles which do not involve his humanity; thus, VIII, 12, 7 f.

[4] διὰ μεσίτου: VII, 35, 10; cf. VII, 36, 6; VIII, 5, 5; 48, 3.

[5] VIII, 6, 13; cf. 12, 42; 29, 3.        [6] II, 26, 2; 56, 1; VI, 14, 2; VII, 39, 1.

tion of his Christ will accept them on his heavenly altar.' It is the same, with changes in expression only, before nearly every longer or more solemn prayer of the eighth book. Also the prayer itself repeatedly shows the same idea, e.g. VIII, 12, 38: 'We offer thee, King and God . . . this bread and this chalice, for we give thee thanks through him'; VII, 35, 6: 'Wherefore must everyone send up to thee from his heart through Christ the hymn above everything.'[1]

Nevertheless, here also the mention of Christ towards the end of the prayer in the formularies found also in Hippolytus has only perhaps at VIII, 5, 7 and 16, 5 the sense of praise offered through Christ; but the doxology following the name of Christ offers homage, at least up to VIII, 12, always through Christ: (διὰ τοῦ ἁγίου παιδός σου 'Ιησοῦ Χριστοῦ τοῦ θεοῦ καὶ σωτῆρος ἡμῶν), δι' οὗ σοὶ δόξα, τιμὴ καὶ σέβας ἐν ἁγίῳ πνεύματι νῦν καὶ ἀεὶ . . . .[2] After VIII, 12 the manuscripts begin to falter. At least one of the manuscripts (Vat. 1506) noted by Funk in the apparatus retains the doxology form unchanged. The majority—followed by Funk—from that point onwards change from praise of God through Christ in the Holy Spirit to praise to the three divine Persons: Christ, μεθ' οὗ σοὶ δόξα, τιμὴ καὶ σέβας και τῷ ἁγίῳ πνεύματι εἰς τοὺς αἰῶνας.[3] Has the author himself here bowed to the custom already at that time adopted in Antioch? Or is in fact the single manuscript genuine and is the adaptation of the doxology to the new custom then spreading through Antioch only the work of later copyists?[4] That the difference between the formulas was no light matter to the author, nor to go before God 'through Christ' an empty phrase, appears from the relatively frequent use he makes of Christ's title of high priest. Funk has thirteen references in the index under ἀρχιερεὺς Χριστός.

Also the addition 'in the Holy Spirit', which is generally joined to

---

[1] Cf. VII, 38, 4, 8; VII, 47, 2, 3: in the *Gloria*, to be discussed later; see Part Two, Ch. II.

[2] VIII, 5, 7; the divergences in other passages are unimportant, e.g. VIII, 6, 13: δι' οὗ σοὶ δόξα καὶ τὸ σέβας ἐν ἁγίῳ πνεύματι εἰς τοὺς αἰῶνας. Cf. VII, 45, 3; 48, 3 and also the above-quoted prayer to Christ, VIII, 7, 8.

[3] An exception, VIII, 37, 3.

[4] Cf. C. H. Turner, 'A primitive Edition of the Ap. Const.', JThSt 15 (1914) 53–62. He defends the single manuscript with the form διὰ—ἐν.

'through Christ' in the doxology, occurs without it, with the same meaning.[1]

The form of the pure trinitarian praise,[2] which in the majority oᵢ manuscripts appears for the first time at VIII, 12, 50, varies somewhat, according as it follows or not a mention of Christ: 12, 50: ὅτι σοὶ πᾶσα δόξα . . . καὶ προσκύνησις τῷ πατρὶ καὶ τῷ υἱῷ καὶ τῷ ἁγίῳ πνεύματι καὶ νῦν . . .;[3] on the other hand, if Christ has just been mentioned: μεθ' οὗ σοὶ δόξα . . . εὐχαριστία καὶ τῷ ἁγίῳ πνεύματι εἰς τοὺς αἰῶνας.[4] In the text there also occurs at times the expression, may something redound 'to the praise of thy Christ',[5] an attempt to insert the praise of Christ expressly into the prayer without abandoning the usual mode of address, as in the above-quoted examples, i.e. to God direct.

## 5. THE EPITOME

The offshoot from the eighth book of the *Apostolic Constitutions*, the fifth-century *Epitome*,[6] contains in its second part, under the title Διατάξεις τῶν ἁγίων ἀποστόλων διὰ Ἱππολύτου, newly returned to honour, the prayers at the χειροτονία of bishop, priest, deacon, deaconess and subdeacon, the first taken direct from Hippolytus's church order and so in the original tongue, the others from the eighth book with small variants or contractions. The only point of significance is that here the doxology everywhere and unfalteringly takes the form: (through thy Christ) μεθ' οὗ σοὶ δόξα . . . σὺν ἁγίῳ πνεύματι,[7] while outside the doxology the passages in which

---

[1] VI, 14, 2; VII, 37, 5. Besides this, there occurs also a short doxology in which neither the Holy Spirit nor Christ are named, VII, 27, 2.

[2] 'Trinitarian' is always used in this book in the sense of praise *to* the three divine Persons.

[3] In this form it is difficult to see the influence of the doxology of Hippolytus (end of the anaphora) with its address to the three divine Persons. The doxologies of the Ap. Const., in other words, are independent of the particular form of doxology found in Hippolytus. The element 'in the holy Church', for example, does not occur at all. The manuscript favoured by Turner has here: ὅτι δι' αὐτοῦ σοὶ πᾶσα ἡ δόξα, σέβας καὶ εὐχαριστία, καὶ διὰ σὲ καὶ μετὰ σὲ αὐτῷ τιμὴ καὶ προσκύνησις ἐν ἁγίῳ πνεύματι; similarly, 15, 9.

[4] VIII, 13, 10; cf. 15, 5; 16, 5; 18, 3 etc.       [5] VIII, 12, 39. 44; 20, 2.

[6] F. X. Funk, *Didascalia* II, pp. 72–96.       [7] c. 4–12; Funk II, pp. 79–82.

Christ appears as Mediator or as high priest, including Mediator of the prayer, are retained throughout.[1]

## 6. THE TESTAMENT OF OUR LORD

Another recension of the church order of Hippolytus and of its liturgical formularies, combined with an apocalypse not otherwise extant, is the *Testament of Our Lord Jesus Christ*. This also was written in Greek, in the second half of the fifth century in Monophysite circles, probably in Syria.[2] The Syrian version of the year 687 is extant, and was first published by I. E. Rahmani, patriarch of the Syrian Uniates.[3] This work, too, circulated widely. In appropriately developed forms, it also—or at least part of its liturgy—exists in Ethiopian,[4] Coptic[5] and Arabic,[6] i.e. in languages of areas accepting Monophysitism. The prayers of the various recensions are in great part printed, mainly in parallel columns, in T. Schermann.[7] The latest, according to him, is the Arabic form of the prayers; he would place them 'not before the eighth to ninth century'.[8] Our description follows mainly the text of Rahmani.

The basis of the liturgical prayers of the *Syrian Testament* is the formularies, taken from Hippolytus, for a bishop's consecration, priest's and deacon's ordination, the celebration of Mass, Baptism

---

[1] c. 12, 2: ποιεῖν τὸ θέλημά σου διὰ παντὸς διὰ τοῦ Χριστοῦ σου, μεθ' οὗ. c. 28, 14: πρῶτος τοίνυν τῇ φύσει ἀρχιερεὺς ὁ μονογενὴς Χριστός. Cf. c. 4, 4; 6, 1. 2; 8, 3; 17, 1; 28, 4. 12.

[2] Bardenhewer IV, 274.

[3] I. E. Rahmani, *Testamentum Domini nostri Jesu Christi* (Mainz, 1899); Syrian and Latin.

[4] The anaphora in Job Ludolf, *Ad suam historiam Aethiopicam commentarius* (Frankfurt, 1691), 341–5; English by J. M. Harden in JThSt 23 (1922) 44–8.

[5] A few prayers in H. Hyvernat, 'Fragmente der altkoptischen Liturgie'; *Röm. Quartalschrift*, 1 (1887) 335–7, 2 (1888) 26 f., fragment A and n. CX.

[6] A. Baumstark, 'Eine ägyptische Mess- und Taufliturgie vermutlich des 6. Jahrhunderts': *Oriens christianus* 1 (1901) 1–45, introduction, Arabic and Latin text.

[7] *Ägyptische Abendmahlsliturgien* 121–44.

[8] P. 190; cf. 129 f. 144. The Ethiopian edition is closer to the Syrian of Rahmani; in certain passages it gives the impression of having kept to the original more faithfully than the Syrian; the same may be said of the Coptic fragments. Cf. P. Drews' discussion: *Theol. Studien und Kritiken* 74 (1901) 160–2 and A. Baumstark: *Röm. Quartalschrift* 14 (1900) 28 ff.

and the blessing of fruits,[1] which, however, are not only expanded but also considerably altered, including their mode of address.

This is evident, for example, at the end of the episcopal consecration prayer. The bishop appears indeed, as in Hippolytus, at the end of the prayer as the one who will offer to God worship and prayers *in odorem suavitatis per Dominum nostrum Jesum Christum Filium tuum dilectum*, and the doxology that follows is similarly joined to the phrase by *per quem*, but in the striking form: *per quem tibi gloria honor et imperium una cum Spiritu Sancto ante saecula . . .* (p. 31). God the Father appears with the Holy Spirit as receiver of the honour and dominion which is offered through Christ. The same peculiar form of the doxology, which is proper to the Syrian Testament alone, recurs in the other prayers taken from Hippolytus,[2] except that for the diaconal ordination.[3] This wording makes the expression an apparently mechanical shortening of the doxology of Hippolytus: '*Per quem tibi gloria . . .*, Patri et Filio *cum Spiritu Sancto* in sancta ecclesia.' In the prayers, which are remarkable for their number and length and constitute the special property of the Syrian *Testament*, this doxology appears in only two further passages.[4] Another christological ending is found also in the morning prayer of the Church widows.[5] The remaining prayers show only a short concluding doxology: *. . . Deus, quoniam fortis et gloriosus es per omnia saecula saeculorum,*[6] or the three divine Persons are simply put on the same footing: *quoniam tu, Domine, es Deus noster et benedictum et laudatum regnum tuum, Pater, Fili et Spiritus Sancte, et ante saecula et nunc. . . .*[7]

The mention of Christ introducing the doxology in these six

---

[1] P. 29 f., 69 f., 93; 39 ff., 131, 139; only the prayer at the lamp-lighting is missing.

[2] Pp. 13, 45, 71, 139.

[3] P. 93; this closes with the wish: 'dignus fiat ordine hoc . . . per voluntatem tuam et te laudet indesinenter per Filium tuum unigenitum Jesum Christum Dominum nostrum, per quem tibi gloria et imperium in saecula saeculorum'.

[4] P. 79 in the *Collaudatio quotidiana* and p. 119 in the prayer over the catechumens.

[5] '. . . Te laudo, Deus, qui lumine tuae scientiae mihi illuxisti per Filium tuum unigenitum Dominum nostrum Jesum Christum, per quem tibi gloria, imperium in saecula saeculorum.' P. 105.

[6] P. 125; cf. p. 47; 49 at the foot, 57.

[7] P. 55; similarly p. 49, top. On the contrary, with the address to only one Person, p. 103: 'quoniam in tuo Patre, in te et in Spiritu Sancto est spes nostra in saecula saeculorum'; cf. p. 99.

Hippolytus prayers of the Syrian *Testament* has the meaning of praise offered to God through Christ probably only in the two quoted passages—in the episcopal and diaconal prayers. In the other two passages, viz. the presbyteral ordination prayer and the Mass, in which the Hippolytus model has this theme, it is omitted. The latter had in Hippolytus[1] the transitional 'ut te . . . glorificemus *per* puerum tuum Jesum Christum'; in contrast, in the Syrian Testament (p. 45): 'ut tribuant tibi semper doxologiam *et* Filio tuo dilecto Jesu Christo'. A similar changing of the idea of Christ as Mediator of the prayer is found also at the beginning of the Preface:

HIPPOLYTUS (Hauler 106):

*Gratias tibi referimus, Deus, per dilectum puerum tuum Jesum Christum, quem in ultimis temporibus misisti*[2]

SYR. TESTAMENT (Rahmani 39):

*Gratias tibi agimus, Deus sancte, . . . Pater Unigeniti tui, salvatoris nostri, quem ultimis temporibus misisti*

If Christ hardly appears as Mediator of the prayer in the formularies that are the special property of the *Testament*, apart from the two or three concluding doxologies just quoted, which are formed on an outside model[3]—yet the redemptive mediatorship of Christ is also broadly described and praised in odd thanksgiving prayers outside the texts derived from Hippolytus;[4] while in general, nevertheless, consideration of the attributes of God-in-the-abstract predominates.

A number of prayers occur in the Syrian *Testament* which either from the beginning or in the course of the prayer are addressed to Christ. Of the three longish prayers which make up the *Laudatio aurorae*, at least the third is directed wholly to Christ;[5] of the *Collaudatio finalis*, which follows the latter and is similarly constructed,

---

[1] Hauler 107.

[2] The mediatorship of the Logos at the creation, on the other hand, is present in the immediately following passage in both cases. Hauler 106; Rahmani 41.

[3] Yet Christ himself is introduced as praying on the day of his Resurrection, in the *Mystagogy*, a catechesis held in solemn manner, which the bishop sometimes conducted at the start of the Mass of the faithful (p. 65 f.). This *Mystagogy* is, however, also found outside the *Testament*, in a more ancient form. F. X. Funk, *Didascalia* II, 133–6. Cf. P. Drews loc. cit. 164–6.

[4] E.g. pp. 77, 121 ff.       [5] *Fili Dei*, 53.

the second and third.[1] The people respond uniformly, without
regard to the differences of address: *Te laudamus, tibi benedicimus, tibi
confitemur (Domine), teque supplicamus, Deus noster*.[2] The long list of
prayer intentions for the deacon to announce begins with the summons: *Supplicemus Dominum Deum salvatoremque nostrum Jesum
Christum*.[3]

In the middle of the Preface from Hippolytus, of which the
beginning has just been quoted, a passage is inserted addressed
to Christ: *Tu virtus Patris, gratia gentium . . . Filius Dei vivi*.[4] What is
most worthy of remark, however, is the phraseology which Hippolytus's anamnesis has retained:

| HIPPOLYTUS (Hauler 107): | SYR. TESTAMENT (Rahmani 43): |
|---|---|
| *Memores igitur mortis et resur-rectionis eius, offerimus tibi panem et calicem gratias tibi agentes, quia nos dignos habuisti adstare coram te et tibi ministrare.* | *Memores ergo mortis tuae et resurrectionis tuae, offerimus tibi panem et calicem, gratias agentes tibi, qui es solus Deus in saeculum et salvator noster, quoniam nos dignos effecisti, ut staremus coram te et tibi sacerdotio fungeremur.*[5] |

This anamnesis prayer is recited in the Syrian *Testament* by the
bishop and by the people. The prayer that follows, which is in large
part special to the *Testament*, begins with the address: offerimus tibi
hanc gratiarum actionem, aeterna Trinitas, Domine Jesu Christe,
Domine Pater, a quo omnis creatura et omnis natura contremiscit in
se confugiens, Domine Spiritus Sancte, adfer potum hunc. . . .[6] The
reason why Christ here precedes the other two Persons—*pace* the
editor's explanation[7]—is simply that he is addressed in the foregoing
prayer. This address recurs in the middle of the same prayer: *Da*

---

[1] *Domine Jesu; Domine Sancte*, p. 57.    [2] Pp. 51, 53, 57.

[3] More precisely in the Syriac: Let us beseech *the* Lord and God and Saviour
Jesus Christ. P. 84 or 85.

[4] P. 41; also in the Ethiopian edn., see Schermann 126.

[5] Likewise in the Ethiopian, Schermann 131; ibid. p. 142 a case in which the
Ethiopian has changed from addressing God, as in the Syrian, Coptic and Arabic,
to addressing Christ: 'qui accepimus corpus tuum et proprium tuum sanguinem',

[6] P. 43.    [7] P. xlviii.

*igitur, Domine, ut oculi nostri ... te intueantur ... quoniam in te uno portionem habent, Fili et Verbum Dei,* in order to be dropped again at the end; for the conclusion returns again to the Hippolytus mode and ends in that special doxology: through Christ to God the Father with the Holy Spirit.

This passing from one address to another within the same prayer is in general a peculiarity of the (Syrian, and, with regard to the Mass liturgy, also the Ethiopian) *Testament*; usually, first God the Father—(*Domine*) *Deus*; (*Domine*) *Pater*, then the Son is addressed— *Fili Dei*; *O Verbum*, etc. The transition is found in the first and second of the three prayers of the *Laudatio aurorae*,[1] in the *Laus nocturna viduarum*[2] and in the exorcism before Baptism.[3] In certain passages it is hard to say whether it is God the Father who is first addressed, or whether it is simply that another title is being used for Christ, who is thus addressed in the whole prayer.[4] In the mind of the author, evidently, the two forms of address are equivalent; he has, however, wittingly or not, opposed the idea that the Son is in any way subordinate to the Father. A noteworthy pendant to this twofold style of address is an expression towards the end of several prayers: 'fiant (diaconi) in gradum isto superiorem per sanctum nomen *tuum* dilectique *Filii tui* Jesu Christi, per quem[5] ... ingrediantur (neophyti)

---

[1] P. 51. For the second, the Greek author must have had in front of him an older prayer that was directed to God throughout. Drews gives for comparison (l.c. 152) the parallels from the (non-Monophysite) Mark Liturgy, Br. 135, 11 ff., and from the Basil Liturgy of the (Monoph.) Copts, Ren. I, 20, in both of which it serves as a transition to the Pater noster. For the character of the model and the work of the editor, the following comparison suffices:

| MARK LITURGY | SYR. TESTAMENT |
|---|---|
| Θεὲ φωτὸς γεννῆτορ ... εὐχῶν καθαρῶν δοχεῦ, ψυχῆς εὐεργέτα, ὁ τοῖς ὀλιγοψύχοις εἰς σὲ πεποιθόσι διδοὺς εἰς ἃ ἐπιθυμοῦσιν ἄγγελοι παρακύψαι ... ὁ τὸ ἐν ἡμῖν σκότος τῆς ἁμαρτίας διὰ τῆς παρουσίας τοῦ μονογενοῦς σου υἱοῦ λύσας. | *Deus genitor lucis ... susceptor orationum purarum; te laudamus, Fili unigenite, primogenite et Verbum Patris ... Tu qui habes essentiam nesciam laedi, ubi neque caries neque tinea corrumpunt, qui iis, qui toto corde in te confidunt, largiris, quae angeli cupierunt inspicere ... qui tenebras, quae erant in nobis, voluntate Patris tui illustrasti. ...* |

[2] P. 103.   [3] P. 121 ff.
[4] *Domine Deus*: in the prayer at the blessing of oil, p. 49.   [5] P. 119.

in tabernacula tua aeterna *per te et per dilectum Filium tuum* Jesum Christum.'[1] By the use of the preposition *per* in the closing phrases of this prayer in a different sense from that of mediation of the prayer, equally for God the Father and for Christ, the author gives at least the impression that the 'through Christ' kept in some doxologies is also free from dangerous innuendo.

It is further remarkable that the address to Christ prefers to denote his divinity alone (*Verbum*); also, in the course of the passages of praise, this aspect is prominent in comparison with his humanity, which the consistent Monophysite will naturally underplay.[2] Praise is given to the share of the Logos in creation, his eternal origin from the Father, and so on. The idea now suggested itself to introduce the third Person too now and then into the address of the prayer, either expressly or by including him in the word *Trinitas*. But this happens only in a few passages of the Syrian *Testament*, and these do not appear to belong to the original version. Thus, we have, following the first sentences of the Preface: *super nos veniat, Domine, gratia tua ad assidue te collaudandum Filiumque tuum unigenitum ac Sanctum Spiritum tuum.*[3] This addition to the Hippolytus Preface is found only in the Syrian text; it is missing in the Ethiopian and the Arabic.[4] The same applies to the address in the epiklesis prayer, which we have already met: *aeterna Trinitas, Domine Jesu Christe, Domine Pater . . . Domine Spiritus Sancte,*[5] and to the address *Sancta, sancta, sancta Trinitas* before the communion.[6]

A further word is demanded by the *Arabic* version of the *Testament*, which by its greatly expanded prayers betrays the activity of a thoroughgoing reformer. In all the prayers of the Mass (preface,

---

[1] P. 131; cf. 79, 125.    [2] Pp. 51 f, 57, 77.    [3] P. 39 f.

[4] Schermann 125 f; Drews 160. In the Arabic, however, it is added in another form: *Oriens christ.* 1 (1901) 11, 11.

[5] P. 43; Schermann 132, 137; Drews 149, 161. Ethiopian: 'aeterna Trinitas, Domine Pater Jesu Christi'; Coptic: 'Domine, Domine'; Arabic (*Oriens christ.* I (1901) 17, 28): 'Domine noster.'

[6] P. 47; cf. Schermann 140. This last prayer with this address also passed into the Coptic and the Ethiopian liturgy: Br. 185, 27; 251, 8. With this placing of the mystery of the Trinity in the prayers of the Syrian *Testament* compare the emphasis on the *dogmata fidelia Trinitatis* (p. 29) and the instruction to offer three loaves on the Saturday *in symbolum Trinitatis* (p. 35) and on the same grounds to provide the church with three entrances (p. 23).

anamnesis, epiklesis), again, the address to Christ is suppressed and the prayer directed uniformly to God (*Domine Deus omnipotens; Pater Domini nostri Jesu Christi*). On the other hand, the glorification of the Son (in the third person) is given plenty of scope, especially in the Preface, where he is praised under about twenty titles, relating as much to his redemptive work as to his divinity.[1] As Mediator of the prayer, however, Christ appears only in a pair of specifically Coptic or Egyptian end-formulas,[2] which we shall meet again elsewhere. The normal doxology is addressed to God the Father, Son and Spirit being embraced on the same level: *glorificatio tibi debetur et Filio tuo unico et Spiritui tuo Sancto in saecula saeculorum.*[3]

---

[1] *Oriens christ.* 1 (1901) 11 f.; pp. 25, 24 he is called *Omnipotens Dominus Deus noster.*

[2] 'Per Jesum Christum Dominum nostrum, illum, per quem gloria . . . tibi debetur cum ipso et Spiritu Sancto' (p. 33, 14; cf. p. 27, 12); or: 'per gratiam Unici tui, illius, per quem . . .' (p. 45, 18; cf. 39, 24). A similar doxology is also in the Coptic fragments: *Röm. Quartalschrift* 1 (1887) 337; 2 (1888) 27.

[3] P. 37, 17 etc. In the *Coptic* fragments, likewise, in general the address to God the Father is retained; this rule is broken by a passage in the embolism of the (only inserted later) Pater noster (*Röm. Quartalschrift* 1 (1887) 336; cf. Schermann 138 f. Cf. Br. 136, 11): 'Ita Domine Jesu Christe, . . . ne (permittas) spiritum nostrum declinare a te in servitutem (passionum). Fuga autem a nobis eum qui nos tentat . . . Te enim decet omnis gloria cum Patre tuo bono et Spiritu Sancto in saecula saeculorum'. The change to the address to Christ precisely in this passage was suggested by the last petition in the Our Father, ἀλλὰ ῥῦσαι ἡμᾶς ἀπὸ τοῦ πονηροῦ which was understood, as elsewhere in the East, as referring to protection against the wicked adversary. His conqueror Christ was placed in opposition to him. It is the same as in Ap. Const. VIII, 7, top of p. 12. Cf. Fr. J. Dölger, *Die Sonne der Gerechtigkeit und der Schwarze; eine religionsgeschichtliche Studie zum Taufgelöbnis* (LF 2), (Münster i. W., 1918), p. 9.

# II

# REMAINS OF EARLY EGYPTIAN LITURGY

## 1. THE EUCHOLOGIUM OF SERAPION

A valuable insight into the liturgical prayer of an Egyptian episcopal city of the fourth century is given us by the *Euchologium* of Bishop Serapion of Thmuis. The single extant manuscript was discovered in the Athos monastery of Hagia Laura in 1894 by Dimitrievski, and in 1898 by G. Wobbermin, and afterwards published in various editions.[1] Serapion is also well-known as the friend of St Athanasius and of St Antony the Hermit; there is evidence that he was Bishop of Thmuis at least from 339 to 362. That the *Euchologium* incorporates older material is self-evident; to what extent it does so, however, is hard to determine.[2]

The *Euchologium* contains in its thirty items prayers for the

[1] G. Wobbermin, 'Altchristliche liturgische Stücke aus der Kirche Ägyptens' (TU 17, 3b), (Leipzig, 1898); with commentary in F. X. Funk, *Didascalia* II, 158–203. I cite the prayers after Funk's numbering and add in brackets Wobbermin's.

[2] According to A. Baumstark (*Röm. Quartalschrift* 18 (1904) 123–42: 'Die Messe im Morgenland' 69), Serapion would have made only a few alterations, principally in the Canon of the Mass, and these would have been rearrangements of words rather than insertions of new material into the text. On the contrary, E. von der Goltz (in E. Hennecke, *Neutestam. Apokryphen*, 2nd edn., 613), probably with greater reason, would prefer to see unaltered ancient tradition precisely in the Mass formulary.

celebration of Mass, as well as for various sacramental rites and church blessings. All prayers are addressed to God, and indeed apparently to the Person of the Father; the address, often very solemn, varies considerably in expression.[1] Certain blessing-formularies are preserved in the optative form and only towards the end pass into the address to God. Christ the Mediator is not lacking in any prayer. If God is not already named in the address as Father of the Only-begotten,[2] the prayer frequently has further on an appeal to the loving-kindness of God shown in the work of redemption, or to the salvation made manifest in Christ.[3] At other times, the blessing derived from Christ[4] or the worthy, or efficacious, Communion[5] is itself the subject of the prayer. Only occasionally is the 'Only-begotten' named expressly for the first time in the conclusion of the prayer,[6] but here he is never missing. This conclusion runs in most cases, with unimportant variations, as in the following 'Prayer after Baptism and ascent (from the water)',[7] which is also a good example of the shorter prayers of Serapion:

> O God, thou God of truth, Creator of the universe, Lord of all creation, bless this thy servant with thy blessing, make him clean in re-birth, give him fellowship with the angelic powers, so that he may be called no longer flesh, but spirit, since he has received a share in divine and profitable gifts. May he be preserved until the end to thee, the Creator of the universe,

---

[1] δέσποτα, φιλάνθρωπε θεέ, πάτερ τοῦ μονογενοῦς, θεὲ τῆς ἀληθείας etc.

[2] 1 (19); 2 (20); 12 (26); 13 (1); 26 (12); 27 (13); 29 (17). It seems also that the title θεὲ τῆς ἀληθείας (Ps. 30: 6) is taken in the same sense as πάτερ τοῦ μονογενοῦς. It occurs 5 (27) 3; 13 (1) 13; 14 (2) 1; 18 (6) 1; 20 (8) 1; 22 (15) 1; 24 (11) 1; 28 (14) 1. For evidence, cf. 15 (3) 1: δέομαι ἐκταθῆναι τὴν τῆς ἀληθείας χεῖρα with 6 (29) 1: ἡ χεὶρ τοῦ μονογενοῦς... ἐκταθήτω; similarly, the epiklesis 13 (1) 15, where the descent of the Logos is implored, that the bread may become σῶμα τοῦ λόγου and the wine αἷμα τῆς ἀληθείας. Hence ἀλήθεια is a name for the Son parallel to the term Logos, which (cf. veritas) also occurs frequently in other Fathers, and the use of which in Serapion is on the same footing as the reflexions on the knowledge of the Father through the Son and of the Son through the Father (Luke 10:22) at the beginning of the Preface. In general, the appellations of Christ show throughout the same strong preference for bringing out his divinity, and it is not easy to attribute to Serapion only such passages as that in the Preface—as does Baumstark —and not also regularly the titles of Christ and God in nearly all the prayers.

[3] 3 (21); 5 (27) 4; 19 (7); 25 (16).      [4] 6 (29); 15 (3); 17 (5).

[5] 14 (2); 16 (4); 18 (6).      [6] 8 (30); 9 (23); 7 (22).      [7] 24 (11).

through thy Only-begotten, Jesus Christ, through whom is to thee honour and power in the Holy Ghost, now and for ever and ever. Amen.[1]

The mention of Christ denotes here, and in most of the prayers, him through whom the aid and blessing, blameless conduct and final election are to be bestowed, as also elsewhere Christ's redemptive mediation is a favourite theme of these prayers. Often the Holy Spirit is added here before the doxology as one in whom the Christian lives; he is missing then—[2] and also occasionally in other cases —in the doxology itself: 'Grant us to expound the divine Scriptures ... with truth and dignity, so that all present may profit through thy Only-begotten, Jesus Christ, in the Holy Spirit, through whom (δι' οὗ) (is) to thee honour and power now and for ever and ever'.[3] Only very occasionally in this transition to the doxology is Christ found as Mediator of an act of homage or petition: 'Thee have we invoked for all things through thy Only-begotten, Jesus Christ, through whom . . .'.[4] Now and then, the link with the doxology takes a freer form: ὅτι δι' αὐτοῦ,[5] ὅτι διὰ τοῦ μονογενοῦς σοὶ ἡ δόξα.[6] The doxology itself contains uncontaminated the idea: to God the honour through Christ (in the Holy Ghost). Indeed, the incidental slight variation of the connexion and of the wording itself shows that the theme is very much alive and by no means hardened into a rigid formula. This appears yet more clearly from similar expressions in the course of several prayers; thus, in the Preface:[7] 'There speaks in us the Lord Jesus and the Holy Spirit, and they praise thee through us'; or when the sanctifying descent of the Logos is implored over the baptismal water, so that the baptized may be no longer flesh and blood, 'but spiritual, and may be able to worship thee, the uncreated Father, through Jesus Christ in the Holy Spirit'.[8]

---

[1] διὰ τοῦ μονογενοῦς σου 'Ιησοῦ Χριστοῦ, δι' οὗ σοὶ ἡ δόξα καὶ τὸ κράτος ἐν ἁγίῳ πνεύματι . . .
[2] In fact the omission is only apparent, for the connecting δι' οὗ unites Son and Spirit together, just as both are combined in one unity in other passages, e.g. 13 (1) 7: λαλησάτω ἐν ἡμῖν ὁ κύριος 'Ιησοῦς καὶ ἅγιον πνεῦμα καὶ ὑμνησάτω σὲ δι' ἡμῶν. By this means, it is intended to express the unity of essence in God.
[3] 1 (19); likewise 2 (20); 3 (21); 19 (7); cf. 23 (10).
[4] 5 (27) 11; similarly, 7 (22) 2; 19 (7) 4.    [5] 8 (30); 20 (8); 22 (15); 29 (17).
[6] 14 (2); cf. 23 (10).    [7] 13 (1) 7.
[8] 19 (7) 4. Cf. also 2 (20) 2; 4 (28) 1; 13 (1) 13, 16; 20 (8) 2; 23 (10) 2.

## 2. THE PAPYRUS OF DÊR-BALYZEH

Another document witnessing to early Egyptian liturgy, now dated in the 6th century, is the Dêr-Balyzeh, first published by P. de Puniet.[1] The prayers in it, in part in very fragmentary condition, may be listed as follows: intercessory prayer, Preface with sanctus, epiklesis, institution account, anamnesis, prayer for the fruits of the Communion; at the end, a Creed follows. All the prayers are directed to God, except for the anamnesis, which is addressed to Christ with the words: Τὸν θάνατόν σου κ⟨αταγγέλλ⟩-ομεν, τὴν ἀνάστασίν ⟨σου ὁμολογοῦμ⟩εν καὶ δεόμεθα τ⟨...⟩, where the text breaks off. But the latter text is to be regarded not as a sacerdotal anamnesis prayer but as an acclamation of the people;[2] the Christ-address thus loses all its striking character. Christ appears in the Communion prayer as mediator of the benefits sought: εἰς ἐλπίδα τῆς... ζωῆς διὰ τοῦ κυρίου ἡμῶν Ἰησοῦ Χριστοῦ; whether he is also represented as Mediator of the prayer in the doxology following is more than doubtful.[3] The further doxology, still preserved after a fashion, in the intercessory prayer does not name Christ; it runs, according to Brightman, simply: ὁ ὢν ⟨εὐλογητὸς εἰς⟩ τοὺς αἰῶνας; elsewhere, too, Christ is not named, outside the institution account, except at the beginning of the Preface, in the address to God the Father: ὁ θεὸς καὶ πατὴρ τοῦ ⟨κυρίου ἡμῶν Ἰησοῦ Χριστοῦ⟩.[4]

## 3. THE HYVERNAT FRAGMENTS

Of great antiquity, also, are the *Fragments of the Old Coptic Liturgy*,[5] published by H. Hyvernat. The manuscript is dated to the ninth or

[1] *Report of the XIXth Eucharistic Congress*, (London, 1909), pp. 367—401, and in *Revue Bénédictine* 26 (1909) 34–51. Newly published with augmented text by C. H. Roberts and B. Capelle, *An Early Euchologium* (Lyons, 1949).

[2] Cf. Brightman 52.

[3] The text that follows here was given as follows by the first editions: ⟨δι’ οὗ⟩ σοὶ τῷ πατρὶ ἡ δόξα σὺν ἁγίῳ πνεύματι εἰς τοὺς αἰῶνας. ἀμήν. But the addition δι’ οὗ is not justified together with the σὺν ἁγίῳ πνεύματι. From all we know of older doxologies, it should much rather run μεθ’ οὗ, so that Christ receives the glory along with the Father and the Holy Spirit. See my more detailed argument on this point: ZkTh 48 (1924) 468–71. This restoration of the text has won the approval of the editors Roberts and Capelle (1962 postscript).

[4] Schermann restores the text towards the end of the intercessory prayer as follows: ⟨σ⟩ῶσον (⟨πλήρ⟩ωσον) δέ⟨σποτα⟩... καὶ τὰ αἰτήματα τῶν ⟨δούλων σου ὅπως χα⟩ρίσηται. By the δέσποτα, according to him (*Ägyptische Abendmahls-liturgien* 47), is meant Christ as mediating Person. However, over such 'texts' it is probably best not to dispute.

[5] *Röm. Quartalschrift* 1 (1887) 330–45; 2 (1888) 20–27. For the part of these fragments furnished with Greek parallel passages the modern edition of H. Lietzmann

tenth century; the text, part Greek, part Coptic (Sahidic), would, according to Hyvernat, go back to the fifth century. Of the nine fragments, however, the first and the last belong to the Coptic *Testament of our Lord* and were considered above.[1] Fragments B and F are from the Coptic anaphoras of Gregory and Basil.[2] Fragment G contains praises of the Redeemer in hymn-form, not proper prayers.[3] Fragments C, D and E have intercessory prayers in a long series, each beginning with the words, *Memento Domine*; the occasional mention of Christ in the third person shows that 'Domine' here is God the Father;[4] some of these intercessory prayers belong to the Coptic Cyril–(Mark–) anaphora. There remains the fragment H,[5] with two blessing prayers and a thanksgiving prayer after the Communion, all three addressed to God, and in their themes and form close to the corresponding formularies of Serapion, without having the same wording; even the doxology at the end is at the most only once in the same words as Serapion:[6] *per . . . Christum Dominum nostrum, per quem etc.*, while the indications in the two other passages (*per gratiam*) point to the type we are now to meet in the liturgy of St Mark.

is now available: 'Sahidische Bruchstücke der Gregorios- und Kyrillosliturgie': *Oriens christ.* 2nd edn., 9 (1920) 1–19.

[1] 16 A. 57; 21 A. 93.    [2] T. Schermann, *Ägyptische Abendmahlsliturgien* 72, A. 4.
[3] T. Schermann, ibid. 230.    [4] *Röm. Quartalschrift* 1 (1887) 339–45.
[5] *Röm. Quartalschrift* 2 (1888) 24–6.    [6] II, 26.

# III
# THE MAIN EGYPTIAN LITURGIES

Just as we distinguish in the Roman liturgy between the Mass and fore-Mass, so we may make a distinction in the liturgical formularies of the East, and also of Egypt, between the anaphora and what we will call the fore-anaphora. The anaphora begins with the Preface and continues to the Last Blessing. In many formularies, however, it is taken as beginning with the Kiss of Peace, which follows the Gospel (the Offertory—the prothesis—is generally situated at the beginning of the Mass). In nearly all oriental liturgies, a number of anaphoras are extant; on the other hand, the fore-anaphora, in the course of centuries much elaborated, and to which in most cases several prayers inside and at the end of the Mass belong, forms a fixed framework, not subject to variation. In the following, we shall, as a rule, consider first the anaphora formularies, and only then go into the extra-anaphora *ordo*.

The metropolis of Egyptian Christianity is *Alexandria*. Here lies the starting-point of the common heritage in originally Greek liturgical material which then, particularly after the Monophysite schism, from 451 developed independently in three liturgical regions: that of the Catholic and Orthodox Greeks; of the Monophysite Copts; and of the likewise Monophysite Ethiopians of the Abyssinian highlands. This common core of the liturgy of the three regions is no longer discernible in any document; we therefore adopt instead the formulary of Serapion, which most probably was close to the liturgy of Alexandria—probably already in existence at that time— known from the sixth to seventh century as that of St Mark. The oldest texts already show the diverging branches of the development, but show also, in the essential agreement of the Coptic and Greek St Mark liturgies especially, the common stem from which they derive.[1]

## 1.  THE ST MARK LITURGY

Among the Orthodox Greeks in Egypt, there was, together with the corresponding fore-anaphora *ordo*, only one anaphora in use, named after St Mark, whence we can speak in summary fashion of the St Mark liturgy. Towards the end of the middle ages, the St Mark liturgy was completely displaced by the Byzantine; in fact, it is now extant in only a few manuscripts, and these go back only to the twelfth century.[2]

Various fragments of the St Mark anaphora, which in part derive from the fourth century, have since been discovered and published: see A. Raes, 'Liturgie' VI B: LThK VI (1961) 1087. And also, the very oldest fragment of the papyrus of Strasbourg, ed. M. Andrieu and P. Collomp, in *Revue de Science religieuse* 8 (1928) 489–515, makes no change in the picture given above. (Postscript, 1962.)

[1] Cf. Ren. I, p. xxxv f.; A. Baumstark, *Röm. Quartalschrift* 18 (1904) 126 f.

[2] T. Schermann, *Ägyptische Abendmahlsliturgien* 157 ff. Modern edn. of text in Brightman 113–43. Lately, S. A. B. Mercer, *The Ethiopic Liturgy* 115–37, believes that, by the extraction of those parts of the St Mark liturgy which, according to other sources, correspond to the structure of the Egyptian Mass of the fifth century, he has ascertained 'pretty nearly' that wording which would give the condition of the St Mark liturgy of the fifth century as the Ethiopian Church took it over from the Alexandrian mother Church. Unfortunately, Mercer is not here a reliable guide, since he not only foregoes any serious attempt at textual comparison, but also proceeds too mechanically in the acceptance of many prayers. E.g., the prayer at the incensation after the Gospel, Θυμίαμα προσφέρομεν (Br. 118, 26), has striking Byzantine parallels (Br. 410, 24; 359, 34). According to E. G. C. F. Atchley, *A History of the Use of Incense in Divine Worship* (London, 1909) 125, it was composed as a censing prayer in the ninth to tenth century. Similar considerations speak against the age adopted by Mercer for the εὐχὴ τῆς εἰσόδου καὶ εἰς τὸ θυμίαμα, Br. 115 f., particularly in the existing form. For the prayer of blessing at the end of the Mass, cf. below, p. 32, n. 4. For the elements from the later period, cf. the descriptive account (synopsis of the individual prayers and ceremonies) of T. Schermann, 'Der Aufbau der ägyptischen Abendmahlsliturgien vom 6. Jahrhundert an', in *Der Katholik* 92 (1912) I, 229–54; 325–54; 396–417.

We can distinguish the prayer-type of the oldest layer of the St Mark liturgy in an example which, by its partial verbal repetition in the Coptic and Abyssinian liturgies, itself bears witness to its existence before the schism. Our example is the 'threefold' prayer for peace, for the clergy and for the Church, at the beginning of the Liturgy of the Faithful, of which there is also evidence elsewhere by the fourth century.[1] It suffices to quote the beginning and end of the priest's prayer.[2]

(Master, Lord,) almighty God, Father[3] of our Lord [and Saviour] Jesus Christ,[4] we beg and call upon thee [. . .], grant the peace of heaven to the hearts of us all and bestow on us also the peace of this life . . . Bless thy loyal and orthodox people, (make it) a thousand thousand and ten thousand times ten thousand (and may the death wrought by sin have no power over us and over thy whole people)—through the grace, mercy and loving-kindness of thy only-begotten Son [our Lord and God and Saviour Jesus Christ], through whom and with whom [be] to thee together with thy (all)-holy, (good) and life-giving Spirit honour and power now and always and for all eternity.

The prayer-address to God the Father is, in the text of the St Mark liturgy as we now have it, predominant throughout; and it clearly reigns alone in those prayers that constitute the basic material of the liturgy. It governs the prayers of the Enarxis[5]—derived from the former morning office—the prayer of the faithful, and that at the Kiss of Peace, then from the anaphora all the prayers inclusively up to the blessing before the Communion,[6] and finally, after some impetratory formulas and chant texts during the Communion, again the sacerdotal prayer of thanksgiving after the latter.[7]

[1] A. Baumstark, Die Messe im Morgenland 106 f.

[2] Br. 121 f.; Coptic Br. 160 f. (cf. the Egyptian-Greek St Basil anaphora Ren. I, 58 ff.); Ethiopian Br. 223 ff. In [ ] the common majority of the Coptic and Ethiopian liturgies, in ( ) the minority.

[3] 'And again let us beg the almighty God the Father': Coptic, Ethiopian.

[4] + δι' οὗ (sc. δεόμεθα): St Basil anaphora.

[5] Br. 113 ff.; cf. Coptic Br. 147 f.; Eth. Br. 202 f.—A. Baumstark, Die Messe im Morgenland 80 ff.

[6] Br. 125–37; cf. Copt. Br. 164 ff.

[7] Br. 141. 143.—The form of the address varies: Δέσποτα κύριε παντοκράτορ (Br. 123. 137), δέσποτα κύριε ὁ θεὸς ἡμῶν. (Br. 128, 23; 129, 11; 141, 10; cf. Eth. Br. 194 ff.), often lengthened: ὁ πατὴρ τοῦ κυρίου καὶ θεοῦ καὶ σωτῆρος ἡμῶν 'Ιησοῦ Χριστοῦ (Br. 113 ff.; cf. Copt. Br. 147. 160 f.).

The endings of these prayers directed to God take various forms. The majority of the independent prayers end as in the above example with the χάριτι formula: through the grace . . . of thy only-begotten Son. . . .[1] In two cases we find also the other method, which takes any title of Christ in order to link to it the doxology.[2] Comparable with the latter method, there is in the χάριτι formula, a certain independence of the prayer-ending in a type of elliptical ending sentence: Preserve us for the sake of this thy Son, who enjoys thy favour and is full of mercy towards us. The doxology itself retains the idea that it is Christ through whom God the Father receives due honour; but with the δι' οὗ there now appears the μεθ' οὗ as a constant companion: as much as Christ as divine-*human* Redeemer and Mediator bends in homage before God, he is nevertheless as second Person of the *Godhead* of the same rank and worthy of the same honour as the Father and the Holy Spirit. Christ as Mediator and as sharer of the honour of the triune God—both are thus jointly expressed.

However, in another group of prayers directed to God, outside the anaphora, the ending dispenses completely with the theme of Christ; these end somewhat in this fashion: thou it is whom we praise, and to thee we send up praise and thanks, to the Father and to the Son and to the Holy Spirit. . . .[3] What is remarkable is that parallels can be found for nearly all these prayers with the ending quoted, without mention of the Mediator and with direct address to the three divine Persons, in foreign liturgies but not, it seems, in indigenous ones; but on the other hand the parallel does not always extend to

---

[1] χάριτι καὶ οἰκτιρμοῖς καὶ φιλανθρωπίᾳ τοῦ μονογενοῦς σου υἱοῦ, δι' οὗ καὶ μεθ' οὗ σοὶ ἡ δόξα καὶ τὸ κράτος σὺν τῷ παναγίῳ καὶ ἀγαθῷ καὶ ζωοποιῷ σου πνεύματι . . . Br. 114, 8. 29; 115, 17; 120, 24; 122, 2; 137, 15; inharmoniously also 116, 15; 124, 31.

[2] Br. 123, 29, prayer at the Kiss of Peace: ἐν Χριστῷ 'Ιησοῦ τῷ κυρίῳ ἡμῶν, μεθ' οὗ (the simple μεθ' οὗ appears in the St Mark liturgy only here); Br. 141, 28, Communion thanksgiving prayer: ἐπὶ τοῦ φοβεροῦ βήματος τοῦ Χριστοῦ σου, δι' οὗ καὶ μεθ' οὗ.

[3] Br. 118, 29 at the incensation before the Gospel; Br. 122, 22b at the incensation at the Great Entrance (cf. Byz. Br. 377 f.); Br. 123, 8 first offertory prayer (cf. West Syr. Br. 61, 22); Br. 143, 15 thanksgiving prayer in the sacristy (cf. West Syr. Br. 68, 15). Similarly also Br. 124, 2 at the incensation after the Kiss of Peace (cf. West Syr. Br. 36, 5). An ending of the same kind is found also in the prayer, directed at the start to Christ, in the trisagion Br. 118, 4.

this precise end-formula. Also, all these prayers evidently belong to a later enlargement of the liturgy which added accompanying prayers to the incensations that came into use with the end of paganism. Whence it appears that these end-formulas with the abandonment of the Christ theme together belong to a period in which indeed foreign formularies were admitted and perhaps independently edited, but in which the predilection for the old Egyptian christological ending had by then been lost.

At first sight it might appear strange that the solemn doxological ending of the ancient kernel of the Mass, the Canon part, seems not to contain the theme of Christ the Mediator. But it is found there in another way: in the epiklesis the Holy Spirit was besought to descend, in order to turn the bread and wine into the body and blood of Christ, 'so that they may prove to be for all of us who partake of them . . . to the glory of thy most holy name and to the forgiveness of sins, in order that in this as in all things thy . . . name may be praised with Jesus Christ and the Holy Spirit'. The reception of the body of Christ should lead to the glory of God.[1] The christological theme comes through strongly, and indeed in the sense of the mediation of prayer, at the thanksgiving for creation and redemption in the Preface. 'All things hast thou made through thy wisdom . . . thy only-begotten Son, our Lord . . .; through him ($\delta\iota$' $o\tilde{\upsilon}$) we thank thee with him and the Holy Spirit [the holy, consubstantial, undivided Trinity] and offer thee these spiritual [gifts] and this unbloody homage, which all peoples offer to thee (O Lord) from the rising of the sun to its setting. . .'.[2] The theme is taken up again in

[1] Br. 134; cf. Copt. Br. 180. Disengaged from its christological eucharistic starting-point, this doxology seems to have migrated from the Copts to the Syrian Jacobites, where, as the ending of the intercessory prayer inserted after the epiklesis, it belongs to the general anaphora pattern: 'Preserve us for a hallowed end, so that in this as in all things thy name may be praised with that of our Lord Jesus Christ and of the Holy Spirit.' Cf. A. Rücker, *Die syrische Jakobosanaphora* 45.

[2] Br. 126. In [ ] the majority, in ( ) the minority of the Coptic text after Br. 165. The redemption is really praised only in the *Greek* St Mark liturgy and here the passage is derived from the (Greek) St James liturgy of Syria: Br. 125, 29 and 51, 13. The Coptic form of the $\delta\iota$' $o\tilde{\upsilon}$ is given by Br. 165, 10 in agreement: 'through whom (we give thanks)'. If in Ren. I, 40 it runs instead: 'propter quod (gratias agimus tibi)', as if a $\delta\iota$' $\ddot{o}$ were translated, this is an oversight by Renaudot. (According to reliable information from Prof. A. Rücker, who compared for me the Coptic and Arabic texts.)

the connexion to the *sanctus*: 'For truly full is heaven and earth of thy [holy] glory by virtue of (the epiphany) [of thy only-begotten Son] our Lord and God and Saviour [and King of us all] Jesus Christ. Fill, O God, also this sacrifice, through the descent of thy Holy Spirit, with thy blessing [. . .]; for in the night. . . .'[1]

If the prayer-address to God entirely predominates especially in the basic material of the St Mark liturgy, nevertheless there are also prayers later on that are addressed *to Christ*. But they belong to secondary parts of the Mass liturgy and furthermore often bear traces of a later origin. They are the following:

1. A Communion thanksgiving prayer to which the deacon summons the people 'after the reception of the divine, unspotted, undying, awful, fearful and heavenly mysteries';[2] 2. a prayer at the elevation of the sacred host before the Communion, to the 'holy, most high, awful . . . Lord', the Logos, for the acceptance of the (Kyrie?) chant;[3] 3. a longer prayer at the blessing at the end of Mass;[4] 4. further, the same mode of address is found in three longer prayers in the fore-anaphora, parts of which are similar in style to each

---

[1] Br. 132; Copt. Br. 176. Christ as source of the glory appears to have more primitive expression in the Coptic: 'through thine only-begotten Son', than in the Greek: διὰ τῆς ἐπιφανείας τοῦ κυρίου.

[2] Br. 140, 13a; not contained otherwise in the majority of manuscripts.

[3] Br. 137, 31; possibly the prayer to Christ is to be drawn in the first place from Br. 138, 2: κύριε ὁ θεὸς ἡμῶν, ἀκατάληπτε θεὲ λόγε τῷ πατρὶ καὶ τῷ ἁγίῳ πνεύματι ὁμοούσιε, πρόσδεξαι τὸν ἀκήρατον ὕμνον. The prayer appears in the Greek St James liturgy Br. 61, 22, while in the non-Greek sister liturgies it is lacking to both the latter and the St Mark liturgy. It has in the Greek St James at any rate its more primitive place; for it gives a good sense, since after it, as response to the cry Τὰ ἅγια τοῖς ἁγίοις follows immediately the hymnic passage of praise: Εἷς ἅγιος, εἷς κύριος Ἰησοῦς Χριστός. On the contrary, in the St Mark liturgy there would be no other ἀκήρατος ὕμνος offered to Christ the Lord than the inserted Kyrie; for the following verse has kept the form of a *trinitarian* praise: εἷς πατὴρ ἅγιος, εἷς υἱὸς ἅγιος ἐν πνεῦμα ἅγιον.

[4] Br. 142, 11, apparently without parallel: Ἄναξ μέγιστε καὶ τῷ πατρὶ συνάναρχε, ὁ τῷ σῷ κράτει τὸν ᾅδην σκυλεύσας . . . τῇ θεουργικῇ σου δυνάμει καὶ φωτιστικῇ αἴγλῃ τῆς σῆς ἀρρήτου θεότητος; after the request for a blessing, the prayer closes: ὅτι διὰ σοῦ καὶ σὺν σοὶ τῷ πατρὶ καὶ τῷ παναγίῳ πνεύματι πᾶς ὕμνος πρέπει. . . . The style, especially in this prayer, gives the impression of not so great age. E. A. Sophocles, *Greek Lexicon of the Roman and Byzantine Period* (Cambridge, 1914), quotes as evidence for the word θεουργία and its derivatives, outside neo-Platonists, only Pseudo-Dionysius (end of the fifth century). Cf. the repeated use of this word in the Pseudo-Dionysius quotations Br. 488 f.

other, of which two are at the Little Entrance (with the Gospel-book),[1] and the third at the prothesis (Offertory prayer after the Credo).[2] Of these three prayers, the first and the third show a note-worthy peculiarity. Although the train of thought after the address to Christ regularly runs on further without any distinct break or new start being perceptible, the prayer closes as if it were addressed to God the Father, with the christological mediator-phrase: χάριτι . . . τοῦ μονογενοῦς σου υἱοῦ. Has there been here earlier, perhaps, another prayer which, addressed to God, ended with this formula which, because it was spoken aloud[3] and had become a recognized formula, later at the substitution of the old by the new prayer showed a greater resistance to change?

Finally, we find in the St Mark liturgy, as also in most of the liturgies from the middle period, texts which are addressed simply to the 'Lord', so that whether God the Father or Christ is meant one cannot tell. To these belong especially the prayers which deacon and people recite together, then various shorter blessing texts.[4] Also, the remembrance of the saints occurs here in a more pro-nounced fashion, viz. in the intercessory prayer which after the old Egyptian custom is inserted in the Preface. In it is named St Mark and 'our most holy immaculate blessed Lady, the Mother of God and ever-virgin Mary'; the priest precedes her mention with the greeting of the angel: 'Hail, full of grace. . .'.[5]

---

[1] Br. 115, 36: Δέσποτα Χριστὲ ὁ θεὸς ἡμῶν; then, after the singing of the troparion 'Ο μονογενής, derived from Justinian I, the 'Prayer of the trisagion' Br. 117, 17: Δέσποτα κύριε 'Ιησοῦ Χριστὲ ὁ συναίδιος λόγος. The trisagion itself comes from the fifth century, apparently.

[2] Br. 124, 22: Δέσποτα 'Ιησοῦ Χριστὲ κύριε, ὁ συνάναρχος λόγος. The first part of this prayer—and only of this one— is demonstrable also in the Coptic and in the Ethiopian liturgy: Br. 148, 8; 204, 10. But no trace remains in the prayer of the offerings of gifts by the faithful, which is to be assumed at this point for the early period.

[3] ἐκφώνως, Br. 116, 17.

[4] Br. 119 f. 141 (Kyrie eleison); Br. 118, 23; 129, 7; 138, 23b; 143, 24.

[5] Br. 128 f. In the Coptic and Ethiopian parallel texts Br. 169. 230 the *Ave* is missing; instead, there is attached to the mention of the Mother of God a longish list of saints' names. The *Ave* is found, however, in the same connexion in the Greek St James liturgy Br. 56, 25.

## 2.   THE COPTIC LITURGY

The Copts gradually united after 451 on account of their Mono-physite creed to form a separate church, and soon went over in the liturgy to the use of the Coptic and later the Arabic tongue—except for a small remnant of Greek formulas, in particular for short acclamations and greetings, which they retained. At this time, not only was the received liturgical material expanded according to need. For together with the St Mark anaphora, here usually called the St Cyril anaphora, went two further formularies of Syrian provenance,[1] the St Basil and the Gregorius anaphoras, both still preserved in Greek in a manuscript of the fourteenth century. Both formularies are connected with the same fore-anaphora *ordo* as the St Mark anaphora, which *ordo* will therefore be discussed separately at the end.

The Coptic St Mark (Cyril) anaphora demands our attention only in so far as it diverges from the Greek.[2] All sacerdotal prayers of this anaphora, the text of which begins after the Gospel, are uniformly directed to God; the Communion prayer is no exception. Even the very long intercessory prayer inserted in the Preface is not necessarily an exception.[3] The case is otherwise, however, with the prayers which deacon and people contribute. The deacon's summons to prayer between the different sections of the intercessory prayer, as yet lacking in the Greek St Mark liturgy, which usually takes the pattern 'Pray . . ., that God the Lord. . .', is on one occasion made more precise with the invitation to implore the blessing in question of 'Christ our true God'.[4] His summons is pointed the same way

---

[1] T. Schermann, *Ägypt. Abendmahlsliturgien* 165. There will be an opportunity to elucidate their origin in the further course of our enquiry. Their treatment at this point might be justified by the fact that both anaphoras gained practical significance among the Copts and consequently characterize the theological character of *their* liturgical prayer.

[2] Br. 158–88 in English translation.

[3] Br. 165–75; the separate sections begin, as in most liturgies, 'Remember, Lord', and have no special end-formula.

[4] Br. 167, 24: Pray for the rising of the rivers of waters in this year: that Christ our true God bless them,

before the beginning of the Preface.[1] Likewise, the acclamations of the people, which here are far more plentiful than in the Greek St Mark anaphora, regularly take the form of an appeal to Christ, when the plain address 'Lord' does not leave it uncertain whether God or Christ is meant.[2]

All sacerdotal prayers keep the address to God, and their conclusion regularly embodies the christological mediator idea, which opens the doxology. But we find with the χάριτι formula another—clearly equally indigenous and likewise become an independent ellipsis—which leads to the doxology with the words: in Christ Jesus our Lord.[3] The christological Mediator is entirely lacking only in the ending of the prayer at the Kiss of Peace[4] and in a silent Communion prayer of the priest which derives from the Syrian *Testament of our Lord.*[5]

It should also be mentioned that in the sacerdotal prayers God is relatively often addressed as 'Father of our Lord Jesus Christ', as 'almighty Father' or even as 'our holy Father', *inter alia.*[6] A rather long passage from the great thanksgiving of St Paul for the salvation poured out on us in Christ (Eph. 1: 3 ff.) opens the prayer at the breaking of the Host.[7]

---

[1] Br. 164, 6.

[2] Br. 177, 35 anamnesis: Τὸν θάνατόν σου κύριε καταγγέλλομεν καὶ τὴν ἁγίαν σου ἀνάστασιν καὶ ἀνάλημψιν ὁμολογοῦμεν: cf. Br. 178, 13. The Greek preserved here witnesses to a considerable antiquity. Contrariwise, in the vernacular, after the epiklesis Br. 180, 31: 'We worship thine holy body—and thy precious blood'. An exception (West Syrian in origin) with the address to God the Father, *vide* Br. 179, 7; cf. Br. 53, 17; 88, 7.

[3] Br. 182, 29; 184, 12; 186, 29; 188, 8: in Christ Jesus our Lord through whom. These prayers appear to be of later origin. They show also, at least in so far as the cross-references in Brightman 561 are an indication, no parallels in the Egyptian sister-anaphoras, apart from the Embolism Br. 182, 24; however, Br. 136, 11, lacks just this ending. This suggests the hypothesis that the prayer-ending with the phrase 'in Christ Jesus our Lord' first came into use among the Coptic Monophysites.

[4] Br. 163, 31: . . . 'and to thee we send up the glory . . . the Father and the Son and the Holy Ghost . . .'—Cf. Br. 183, 18 (Prayer after the Pater noster, 'of John of Bostra'), where, however, there is a christological transition to the similar trinitarian ending.

[5] Br. 185, 27; see above, p. 20, n. 6.

[6] Br. 160 f., 164, 178 ff.       [7] Br. 181.

The rule of addressing all prayers to God the Father is followed
also by the *St Basil anaphora* of Egypt.[1] Only the epiklesis has in the
Coptic text changed to the address to Christ.[2] The address to God is
as a rule simple and more often than not uses the name of Father.
The transition to the doxology is regularly christological, be it with
any title of Christ with the continuation δι' οὗ καὶ μεθ' οὗ[3]—or be it
with the χάριτι[4] formula or with the words ἐν Χριστῷ 'Ιησοῦ τῷ
κυρίῳ ἡμῶν, δι' οὗ καὶ μεθ' οὗ,[5] once also διὰ τοῦ κυρίου...
'Ιησοῦ Χριστοῦ, δι' οὗ καὶ μεθ' οὗ.[6] Only rarely a doxological
ending appears in which Christ is not named, and then the prayers
concerned obviously do not belong to the ancient stock of the

---

[1] The Greek text in Ren. I, 57–89; Latin version of the Coptic ibid. 9–25. The
Egyptian St Basil anaphora is identical neither with the Syrian nor with the
Byzantine anaphora of the same name. But it represents the primitive form of the
latter; H. J. Schultz, *Die byzantinische Liturgie* (Freiburg, 1964) 22. A prayer at the
Kiss of Peace is common to the Syrian and the Egyptian: Ren. I, 62 f. and II,
548; a prayer at the breaking of bread is common to all three: Ren. I, 74; II, 559 f.;
and Br. 338. Several prayers of the Greek text, especially duplicates, are not found
in the Coptic text. Others show a noticeable elaboration, as will now be demonstrated.

[2] P. 16: 'Rogamus te, Christe Deus noster, nos peccatores... ut adveniat
Spiritus Sanctus tuus... Et panem quidem hunc faciat corpus... Jesu Christi';
on the other hand, in the Greek, p. 68: παρακαλοῦμέν σε, φιλάνθρωπε, ἀγαθὲ κύριε,
ἡμεῖς οἱ ἁμαρτωλοί...

[3] Greek p. 57, 84 (the call of the deacon before the Communion: ἐν εἰρήνῃ καὶ
ἀγάπῃ 'Ιησοῦ Χριστοῦ ψάλλωμεν Br. 185, 24, here continued: δι' οὗ καὶ μεθ' οὗ
πρέπει πᾶσα δόξα... τῷ πατρὶ καὶ τῷ ἁγίῳ πνεύματι; on the contrary, in the Coptic,
p. 24:'Omnis honor... debetur Trinitati sanctae, Patri, Filio et Spiritui Sancto').
85 (Communion thanksgiving prayer: 'Our mouths are filled with joy'; in the
Coptic, p. 24 bottom, again the christological Mediator has dropped out; likewise
in the Ethiopian liturgy, which also contains the prayer Br. 241, 26–242, 6).

[4] Greek p. 79: χάριτι καὶ οἰκτιρμοῖς καὶ φιλανθρωπίᾳ κτλ. and p. 86, where the
formula is continued: φιλανθρωπία τοῦ Χριστοῦ 'Ιησοῦ, μεθ' οὗ εὐλογητὸς εἶ;
similarly p. 62. All three prayers are missing with the Copts. This fact, together
with the doxology-form μεθ' οὗ (without the δι' οὗ and εὐλογητὸς εἶ, concludes to
the later derivation of these prayers from West Syrian sources; ; cf. e.g. Br. 31, 12;
32, 21.

[5] Greek pp. 63, 64, 80, 82; in the Coptic text pp. 12, 13, 22, 23 after Renaudot:
per Jesum Christum Dominum nostrum. Of these, the last passage belongs to an
Absolution prayer before the Communion, which recurs also in the Coptic St Mark
anaphora; here the conclusion goes, according to Br. 184, 12: 'in Christ Jesus our
Lord through whom'.

[6] Greek p. 77; Coptic p. 21.

anaphora.[1] On the contrary, we meet the christological Mediator theme even outside the prayer-ending. at the beginning of each member of the 'threefold prayer': 'We beseech the almighty and merciful God, the Father . . . of Jesus Christ; through him ($\delta\iota$ $o\tilde{v}$) we beseech thee. . .'.[2] It is not as Mediator acting of himself, but as a motive for God, that Christ appears in the phrase $\delta\iota\dot{\alpha}$ $\tau\dot{o}\nu$ $\upsilon\dot{\iota}\acute{o}\nu$ $\sigma o\upsilon$: 'God, for the sake of thy Son who has taken away the sins of the world, condescend now to accept the repentance of thy servants'.[3] The mediatory position of Christ is finely expressed in the reflections on salvation history which are also found in the West Syrian anaphoras at the Kiss of Peace and after the *sanctus*. In the latter case, the priest speaks as representative of humanity in the first person plural: 'When we had broken thy commandment . . . and were driven out of the garden of delight, thou didst not cast us off . . . but didst appear to us, who sat in darkness and in the shadow of death, through thy only-begotten Son'.[4] As an example of how in other

[1] Greek pp. 88, 89. In the Coptic, in the first passage, there is missing also the doxology $\kappa\alpha\dot{\iota}$ $\sigma o\dot{\iota}$ $\tau\dot{\eta}\nu$ $\delta\acute{o}\xi\alpha\nu$ . . . $\dot{\alpha}\nu\alpha\pi\acute{e}\mu\pi o\mu\epsilon\nu$ $\tau\tilde{\omega}$ $\pi\alpha\tau\rho\dot{\iota}$ $\kappa\alpha\dot{\iota}$ $\tau\tilde{\omega}$ $\mu o\nu o\gamma\epsilon\nu\epsilon\tilde{\iota}$ $\sigma o\upsilon$ $\upsilon\dot{\iota}\tilde{\omega}$ $\kappa\alpha\dot{\iota}$ $\tau\tilde{\omega}$ $\dot{\alpha}\gamma\dot{\iota}\tilde{\omega}$ $\sigma o\upsilon$ $\pi\nu\epsilon\dot{\upsilon}\mu\alpha\tau\iota$; in the second passage, the (second dismissal) prayer entirely; likewise p. 86 bottom: '$O\tau\iota$ $\dot{\alpha}\gamma\iota o\nu$ $\dot{\upsilon}\pi\acute{\alpha}\rho\chi\epsilon\iota$ $\tau\dot{o}$ $\ddot{o}\nu o\mu\acute{\alpha}$ $\sigma o\upsilon$ $\tau o\tilde{\upsilon}$ $\pi\alpha\tau\rho\dot{o}s$ $\kappa\alpha\dot{\iota}$ $\tau o\acute{\upsilon}$ $\upsilon\dot{\iota}o\tilde{\upsilon}$ $\kappa\alpha\dot{\iota}$ $\tau o\tilde{\upsilon}$ $\dot{\alpha}\gamma\dot{\iota}o\upsilon$ $\pi\nu\epsilon\dot{\upsilon}\mu\alpha\tau os$ 19. Further, p. 73 (Copt. p. 19), the trinitarian doxology at the end of the epiklesis ('so that in this as in all things may be glorified . . . thy most holy . . . name with Jesus Christ and the Holy Spirit'; see above p. 29 f.) is separated from this its eucharistic starting-point by the insertion of the intercessory prayer, as with the West Syrian Jacobites. Finally, two prayers, which derive from the West Syrian St James liturgy, viz. that at the Kiss of Peace and that over the chalice veil (Ren. I, 13 [Copt.], and I, 9 [Copt.] I, 57 f. [Greek]; cf. A. Rücker, *Die syr. Jakobosanaphora* p. 3, 7, XVI, f.n. 1), have lost the christological transition to the trinitarian doxology. From here the latter prayer has passed into the Ethiopian liturgy, with further shortening of the ending however, Br. 205, 4: 'Glory and honour be to thine holy name both now and ever and world without end'.

[2] P. 58 ff.; see above p. 27; in the Coptic text p. 10 f. the $\delta\iota$ $o\tilde{v}$ is missing.—P. 80 (Copt. p. 21 f.) apparently the transition itself contains the praise through Christ: $\delta o\xi o\lambda o\gamma o\tilde{\upsilon}\nu\tau\acute{e}s$ $\sigma\epsilon$ $\pi\acute{\alpha}\nu\tau o\tau\epsilon$ $\dot{\epsilon}\nu$ $X\rho\iota\sigma\tau\tilde{\omega}$ $'I\eta\sigma o\tilde{\upsilon}$ $\tau\tilde{\omega}$ $\kappa\upsilon\rho\dot{\iota}\omega$ $\dot{\eta}\mu\tilde{\omega}\nu$ ($\delta\iota$ $o\tilde{v}$ $\kappa\alpha\dot{\iota}$ $\mu\epsilon\theta$' $o\tilde{v}$).

[3] P. 81; in the Coptic p. 22 it runs instead: 'Deus qui tollis peccata mundi, praeveni eos suscipiens poenitentiam servorum tuorum'; cf. Br. 183, 33. On the other hand, in the prayer of blessing after the Communion again in the Coptic a sentence is inserted which stresses the Mediator theme: 'Da illis ut vivant . . . intelligantque, quae tua sunt, per Filium tuum unigenitum Jesum Christum Dominum nostrum, ad quem nos et omnis populus tuus clamamus dicentes: Domine miserere nostri, O Salvator'. P. 25.

[4] P. 65 f. (Copt. p. 14). But also God has created the world through Christ: $\dot{o}$ $\pi\alpha\tau\dot{\eta}\rho$ $\tau o\tilde{\upsilon}$ . . . $X\rho\iota\sigma\tau o\tilde{\upsilon}$ $\delta\iota$' $o\tilde{v}$ $\tau\dot{\alpha}$ $\pi\acute{\alpha}\nu\tau\alpha$ $\dot{\epsilon}\pi o\dot{\iota}\eta\sigma\alpha s$. P. 65; Copt. p. 13.

prayers also Scripture themes are harmoniously combined with elements of the older prayer style, the short thanksgiving-prayer after Communion may serve:

> Our mouths sound forth joy, our tongues jubilation for partaking of thy holy mysteries, Lord. What eye hath not seen nor ear heard nor hath entered into the heart of man, that hast thou prepared for them that love thy holy name, that hast thou revealed to the little ones of thy holy Church. Yes, Father, so was it pleasing to thee. Blessed art thou, God, the Father of our Lord and God and Saviour Jesus Christ, through whom. . . .[1]

The liturgy, or, more correctly, the *Anaphora of St Gregory the Theologian* stands out, by reason of its individuality, from all other liturgies, not only of Egypt, but of Christendom as a whole; it is celebrated by the Copts on feast-days.[2] This individuality consists in the fact that all prayers are directed to Christ. A sole exception in the Greek text, apart from the Pater noster, is an 'Egyptian' prayer over the chalice veil,[3] which presumably was only received from an Egyptian model foreign to the original. In the Coptic recension, where it comes at the beginning of the formulary, there is also a Communion thanksgiving prayer at the end of the text, likewise addressed to God the Father. They frame the anaphora proper, which therefore in other respects preserves the uniform address to Christ as a strict rule

---

[1] P. 84 f.: δι’ οὗ κτλ. Contrariwise in the Coptic p. 24: 'Ita Pater fuit bene-placitum ante te, quia tu misericors es, et mittimus tibi sursum gloriam, honorem et adorationem Patri, Filio et Spiritui Sancto . . .'

[2] The Greek text from the manuscript of the fourteenth century in Ren. I, 90–126; Latin trans. of Coptic ibid. I, 26–38. That the anaphora is also extant in Greek probably indicates a considerable age, not, however, the use of the anaphora among the Orthodox, since the Greek text shows a breaking-prayer which openly supports Monophysitism: μία ἐνέργεια . . . μία θέλησις, μία φύσις (p. 115), not to speak of further traces of the same outlook. The difference between Greek and Coptic text consists in general only in that the Greek contains some fore-anaphora prayers (p. 90–3) as well as duplicates of chalice-veil, breaking- and absolution-prayers (before the Communion), (pp. 93 f., 114–7, 120–2), which in the Coptic were eliminated by practical use. On the other side, the Coptic text, corresponding to the Coptic individuality, is often punctuated with cries from the people or the deacon, while the more restrained use which the Greek makes of the anaphora tallies with its Syrian origin.

[3] P. 95: Εὐχὴ ἄλλη καταπετάσματος παρ’ Αἰγυπτίοις.

of style. It would seem worth while to set out the most important passages from the core of the anaphora.[1]

Vere (enim) dignum est et justum te laudare . . . solum verum Deum, humani generis amatorem ineffabilem . . . factorem universorum, liberatorem omnium; qui propitiaris omnibus iniquitatibus nostris . . . (Tu qui es), O Deus [aeterne], Domine vere ex Deo vero, qui Patris lumen nobis demonstrasti, qui nobis Sancti Spiritus cognitionem veram concessisti: qui magnum hoc vitae mysterium ostendisti. . . . Te enim circumsistunt [Cherubim et] Seraphim . . . Triumphalem hymnum salutarium nostrorum voce clara (et nitida celebrant, canunt) clamant [alter ad alterum], laudant clamantes et dicentes: Sanctus, sanctus, sanctus . . .

Sanctus, sanctus es Domine et omnino sanctus . . . Nullus sermo dimetietur benignitatis tuae erga homines pelagus. Fecisti me[2] hominem . . . propter me naturam animalium creasti omnia subjecisti sub pedibus meis . . . comedi . . . praeceptum neglexi, ego autem sententiam mortis rapui. Tu mihi Domine poenam transtulisti [in salutem]; tu velut pastor bonus ad errantem concurristi . . . prophetas misisti, propter me aegrotantem legem ad auxilium dedisti . . . in virginalem uterum venisti. Incircumscriptus Deus existens non rapinam arbitratus es esse aequalem Deo, sed temetipsum exinanivisti . . . Tamquam ovis ad immolationem venisti . . . in coelum primitias meas elevasti, adventus tui praesentiam mihi significasti, in quo venturus es judicare vivos et mortuos et reddere unicuique secundum opera eius. Istius meae libertatis offero tibi symbola . . . Tu mihi mysticam hanc tradidisti carnis tuae in pane et vino participationem. Ea enim nocte, qua ipse tradidisti te . . .

Igitur Domine memores [sumus] tuae super terram descensionis et mortis vivificae . . . tua ex tuis donis tibi offerentes secundum omnia, per omnia et in omnibus.[3]

Ipse (igitur) Domine tua voce haec proposita transmuta, ipse praesens mysticam hanc liturgiam perfice, ipse nobis tuae adorationis (et cultus) memoriam conserva. Ipse Spiritum tuum Sanctum mitte ut . . . faciat

---

[1] After Renaudot's Latin version of the Greek text. In ( ) the minority, in [ ] the majority of the Coptic is indicated, likewise following Renaudot's Latin text.

[2] The first person singular, retained for a long space from here on, in which the liturgist appears as representative of humanity, is found also in the West Syrian anaphora of John of Bosra, Ren. II, 423.

[3] This phrase τά σά ἐκ τῶν σῶν σοὶ προσφέρομεν is witnessed quite early in Syria, but also in Byzantium, to whose liturgy it belongs: Br. 329, 7; see Rücker, Die syr. Jakobosanaphora 19, 11, note.

panem quidem istum fieri sanctum corpus tuum.[1] . . . Memento Dom ine
. . . Populus enim tuus et ecclesia tua deprecatur te (et per te) atque
tecum Patrem tuum dicens: Miserere nobis Deus salvator noster . . . ut in
hoc sicut et in omnibus glorificetur . . . benedictum nomen tuum cum
immaculato tuo Patre et Sancto Spiritu.

One has to allow that in the treatment of the economy of salvation, especially in that which follows on the *sanctus*, there is much
fervour, humility and gratitude; also that the idea of the proximity
of Christ is often vividly expressed. On the other hand, one is struck
by the view of certain Fathers that makes Christ in his pre-existence,
i.e. the Logos, the subject of the entire salvific action under the old
covenant. Because the special activity—urged in this view—of a
particular divine Person is not compatible with the unity of essence
and activity in God, the view was soon generally abandoned; but it
was perfectly consistent with the Monophysite conception, since
here only one (divine) will was recognized in Christ, that of the
Logos. Christ is, indeed, in his work of redemption brought in once
also expressly as Mediator between us and the Father;[2] in the
prayers of the Greek text, also, as high priest, yet, as it appears, only
because, as at the Last Supper, he performs the Consecration by
blessing and sanctifying.[3] In prayer and doxology a high-priestly
mediatorship is unrecognized. The only passages (from the Syrian-
Jacobite anaphora order) in which prayer through Christ to the
Father was expressed is, as indicated above, deprived of this idea in
the Coptic text: 'Populus tuus et ecclesia tua te obsecrant et Patrem

---

[1] In this passage, the Coptic diverges somewhat widely, but without altering the
meaning essentially. For *faciat*: *facias*. There follows here in the Syrian manner the
intercessory prayer, which in the Greek text partly becomes a litany, in which the
people respond with κύριε ἐλέησον, pp. 106–13, and Copt. 31–4. The regular Syrian
phrase at the end of the anamnesis, 'Thy people and thy inheritance beg thee and
through thee and with thee thy Father' (Br. 88, 4), which has found a place there,
is on the other hand preserved more faithfully in the Greek text than in the Coptic
—as is immediately evident above.

[2] P. 96 (Copt. 26), prayer at the Kiss of Peace.

[3] ὁ μέγας ἀρχιερεύς p. 115, 116; cf. the words reproduced above from the
epiklesis; similarly the *Prooemium fractionis*, p. 114 (Copt. 34 f.): ὁ τότε εὐλογήσας
καὶ νῦν εὐλόγησον, ὁ τότε ἁγιάσας καὶ νῦν ἁγίασον, ὁ τότε κλάσας καὶ νῦν διάθρεψον, ὁ
τότε διαδοὺς τοῖς ἑαυτοῦ μαθηταῖς καὶ ἀποστόλοις καὶ νῦν, δέσποτα, διαδὸς ἡμῖν καὶ
παντὶ τῷ λαῷ σου . . .

tuum *tecum*, dicentes.'[1] The sense of the phrase διά σου καὶ σύν σοι is, moreover, reversed even in the Greek text[2] by the sacrifice itself being offered only to Christ.[3]

If the three Coptic anaphora formularies show on the whole the strict stylistic rule of uniform prayer-address, whether to God or to Christ, we see instead, in the *fore-anaphora*,[4] prayers with the one and the other mode of address alternating with each other without any recognizable rule. Five prayers are addressed to Christ: One at

[1] P. 35.

[2] The Gregory anaphora is newly edited and fully discussed by E. Hammerschmidt, *Die koptische Gregorios-anaphora* (Berlin, 1957). Pp. 85–92 establish for εὐχὴ ἄλλη καταπετάσματος (not Prayer over the chalice-veil, as commonly supposed but: Prayer at the [altar-] curtain), which alone is directed to the Father: it does not belong to the original text. The Communion prayer also directed to the Father (Renaudot 38) is not given at all. On the other hand, the phrase διά σου above, in the intercessory prayer is retained as an authentic part of the text (Hammerschmidt 51: Thy people and thy Church beg thee and through thee the Father with thee). The Syrian origin of the anaphora is confirmed (176 ff.; p. 179 reference to the Syrian community of the Sketis). The exclusive Christ-address is understood by H. as the expression of a strong devotion to Christ, 'which can probably also be seen as a reaction to the denial of the divinity of Christ by the Arians' (178). The author is assigned to 'the last phase of the Arian struggle' (179). For the time of origin, the period between 350 and 400 is suggested (178 f.), to which, it must be admitted, *inter alia*, the Benedictus here already following on the Sanctu spresents a grave difficulty. The indefinite phrase 'about the sixth century' chosen by me on p. 227 may still correspond better to the situation.

[3] See above, anamnesis, Ren. I, 105 (Copt. p. 31); further p. 90, 92 ff., 103 (Copt. p. 30). With particular emphasis Christ is celebrated as receiver of the eucharistic sacrifice in the prayer over the chalice veil (p. 93), which, to judge from its whole character, has here in the St Gregory anaphora its original position, but already in the ninth century is found in the Byzantine liturgy (Br. 318), and in somewhat altered form has remained there (Br. 377 f.), thus to enter also into the Armenian liturgy (Br. 430 f.). It begins: Οὐδεὶς ἄξιος... λειτουργεῖν σοι, βασιλεῦ τῆς δόξης, then praises the Incarnation and priesthood of the Lord, whence he has left us this unbloody sacrifice, and closes with the request for the removal of one's own unworthiness: ἀξίωσόν με προσενεχθῆναί σοι τὰ δῶρα ταῦτα ὑπ᾽ ἐμοῦ τοῦ ἁμαρτωλοῦ καὶ ἀναξίου δούλου σου. Σὺ γὰρ εἶ ἁγιάζων καὶ ἁγιαζόμενος, προσφέρων τε καὶ προσφερόμενος, ὁ δεχόμενος καὶ δεκτός, ὁ διδούς καὶ διαδιδόμενος. καὶ σοὶ δόξαν ἀναπέμπομεν μετὰ τοῦ πατρὸς καὶ τοῦ ἁγίου πνεύματος. Thus Christ is not only sacrificing priest and sacrificial gift, but also the one who receives the sacrifice. The last theme permeates the whole prayer. It is remarkable that Br. 318, 36 in the final sentence of the older Byzantine text lacks the decisive δεχόμενος, while it re-appears in the later texts Br. 378, 7 (προσδεχόμενος) and 431, 8; indeed, it is already in a manuscript of the eleventh century which C. A. Swainson reproduces (*Greek Liturgies*, p. 123, cf. p. 78 and p. xxiii).

[4] Br. 144–58; less complete and with some variants Ren. I, 1–9.

the first offering of the gifts, one at the absolution (perhaps corresponding to our prayers at the foot of the altar), a censing prayer
and two prayers at the first and fourth lesson respectively. At each,
the rubric has the remark: to the Son. Four prayers so addressed
are found also in the Ethiopian fore-anaphora.[1] The censing prayer
before the lessons appears to be proper to the Coptic, or at any rate
not taken over by the Ethiopian liturgy:[2]

> O Christ our God, great, faithful and true, only-begotten Son and
> Word of God the Father . . . let our prayer be before thy face as incense
> and the raising of our hands as an evening sacrifice; for thou art the true
> evening sacrifice that itself was offered for our sins on the precious cross
> at the behest of thy good Father, thou who art praised with him and the
> Holy Spirit, the Giver of life consubstantial with thee, now and always
> and for all eternity.

The prayers addressed to God the Father, or simply to the Lord,
are represented by various types. Two, of which parallels exist in the
Ethiopian, close there as here in the Coptic with a pure trinitarian
doxology;[3] three others, likewise recurring in the Ethiopian liturgy,
close with the Coptic formula: 'In Christ Jesus our Lord, through
whom and with whom be honour to thee. . .', which, however, seems
to have been taken over with the rest into the Ethiopian only in the
first two cases.[4] On the other hand, the χάριτι formula proves also

[1] Br. 148 f., 153, 155, or 204 f., 212, 219. Most of them begin with the address:
Master, Lord Jesus Christ', and end with a trinitarian doxology. The first (Br. 148
or 204) is also in the prothesis of the St Mark liturgy (Br. 124), here however with
the different type of ending, χάριτι.

[2] Br. 152.

[3] Thou art he to whom we send up the glory and the honour and the worship,
the Father and the Son and the Holy Ghost, for ever: Br. 144, 16, similarly 149, 33;
th. 197, 26; 206, 15. In both, Severus (of Antioch, d. 538) is named, in the one as
author, in the other as holy patriarch, who will assist the prayer of absolution.
Here belong also various shorter trinitarian prayer-texts which are interspersed in
the fore-anaphora part: thus during the procession round the altar: Glory and
honour unto honour and glory to the all holy Trinity the Father and the Son and
the Holy Ghost, Br. 145, 34; cf. 146, 12 ff.; 152, 3; 154, 20 etc. But these texts,
frequent in all later oriental liturgies, do not belong any longer to the prayer-stock
in the narrower sense.

[4] Br. 145, 3; 154, 15; 157, 8; or 198, 9; 215, 29; 221, 5. The first of the three
prayers, a prayer of preparation for the priest, is also in the Byzantine St Basil
liturgy (Br. 316 f., 400 f.), but here, instead of the christological ending, the
doxology customary in Byzantium is inserted.

here to be old Egyptian; with it end three prayers which, belonging to the old form of the Egyptian liturgy, recur in the Greek St Mark liturgy as in the Ethiopian liturgy: the prayer that closes the former morning service; then in the Mass of the Catechumens a shorter duplicate of the 'threefold' prayer of the faithful; finally, the general prayer for the Church after the Gospel.[1]

## 3. THE ETHIOPIAN LITURGY

The Church of Abyssinia, which was founded in the fourth century from Alexandria and after the end of the fifth century lapsed into Monophysitism, acquired its basic liturgical heritage from the Alexandrian mother Church. This applies in the first place to the structure and to the most important constituents of the invariable *Ordo missae*, especially of the fore-anaphora part. But also among the twenty anaphora formularies of the Abyssinian Church[2] are included the three Egyptian: the St Mark (Cyril) anaphora, the St Basil and the St Gregory. Also, direct Syrian models are represented. The anaphora of the *Testament of Our Lord* has already been considered;[3] the St James anaphora will be treated briefly with the Syrian St James anaphora. The greater part of the remaining indigenous Ethiopian anaphoras appeared in Abyssinia only after the turn of the millennium.

But none of these formularies have much importance compared

---

[1] Br. 147 f., 151, 157 ff.; or Eth. Br. 202 f., 220 ff.; or Greek St Mark Lit. Br. 113 ff., 119 ff.—Cf. A. Baumstark, *Die Messe im Morgenland* 80 f., 99 f., 106 f.

[2] Br. p. lxxiii f.; T. Schermann, *Ägyptische Abendmahlsliturgien* 182 ff., also lists existing translations. Two further formularies have been made available by S. Euringer: 'Die äthiopische Anaphora unserer Herrin Maria': *Der Katholik* 95 (1916) I, 241–66; 'Die äthiopische Jakobusanaphora': *Oriens christ.* (2 edn.) 4 (1914) 1–23. Then S. A. B. Mercer has translated individual anaphoras: see JL4 (1924) p. 375. Finally, of the known anaphora formularies of the Ethiopic Liturgy, thirteen have since been made accessible in English, partly in the form of extracts, by J. M. Harden, *The Anaphoras of the Ethiopic Liturgy* (London, 1928). Still more important are the critical editions of the Ethiopic texts, unfortunately distributed over several periodicals, appearing in the years 1925–37, prepared in part by O. Löfgren and in part by S. Euringer, to each of which Euringer has contributed a German translation and a commentary.

[3] Above, p. 15; p. 18 notes 4 and 5; pp. 20–1.

with the Ethiopian normal anaphora, the *Anaphora of the Apostles*, which alone was ordinarily used for the celebration of Mass and only exceptionally gave place to one of the others. Here very ancient liturgical material is organically joined to later and very late liturgical growths. The kernel of this anaphora is the Eucharistic prayer from *Hippolytus'* church order, only slightly modified but, by the insertion of intercessory prayer and *sanctus* as well as by enlargement of the epiklesis, considerably broken up. In the following, for easier comparison, the Latin text from the Apostles' anaphora in Renaudot[1] is placed alongside Hippolytus's text, which is best preserved in the old Latin version.

<table>
<tr><td align="center">HAULER 106f.</td><td align="center">RENAUDOT I, 513f.</td></tr>
<tr><td>Gratias tibi referimus, Deus, per dilectum puerum tuum Jesum Christum, quem in ultimis temporibus misisti nobis salvatorem et redemptorem et angelum voluntatis tuae; qui est verbum tuum inseparabile[m], per quem omnia fecisti et bene placitum tibi fuit;</td><td>Gratias agimus tibi Domine per dilectum Filium tuum unigenitum Dominum, Deum et salvatorem nostrum Jesum Christum, quem ultimis diebus misisti nobis, Filium tuum, salvatorem, redemptorem, Angelum consilii tui, qui est verbum a te prodiens et in quo omnia fecisti per voluntatem tuam.</td></tr>
</table>

At this point there follows in the Ethiopian liturgy the intercessory prayer. After the deacon has read out a series of names of saints, the priest begins:[2] '*Holy Trinity*, Father and Son and Holy Spirit, bless thy people . . .'; after naming the various conditions and concerns: '. . . And of all those who have charged us to remember them, *Christ our God*, be mindful in thy heavenly kingdom . . . through the intercession and prayer that the Mistress of us all, thy Mother, the holy and spotless Mary, offers on our behalf'; there follows a long list of saints, then the closing request to Christ, the King of Peace, 'that we may come and go in peace'. The Preface follows immediately:

---

[1] I, 513 ff. At the same time, I remark the most important variants of Brightman 228 ff., and Mercer, *The Ethiopic Liturgy* 322 ff.

[2] After Br. 229 ff.

*misisti de caelo in matricem Virginis, quique in utero habitus incarnatus est et Filius tibi ostensus est ex Spiritu Sancto*

*(Nobis et omnibus qui quietem acceperunt miserere) tu qui misisti Filium tuum in sinum Virginis. Gestatus est in utero, et caro factus est Filius tuus manifestatusque est a Spiritu Sancto.*

Here, after a suitable introduction (*'Before thee stand a thousand thousands . . .'*), the Sanctus is inserted. Then: '*Truly heaven and earth are full of the holiness of thy majesty in our Lord . . . Jesus Christ thy holy Son.*'[1]

*et Virgine natus; qui voluntatem tuam complens et populum sanctum tibi adquirens extendit manus, cum pateretur, ut a passione liberaret eos qui in te crediderunt; qui cumque traderetur voluntariae passioni, ut mortem solvat et vincula diaboli dirumpat et infernum calcet et iustos inluminet et terminum figat et resurrectionem manifestet, accepit panem gratias tibi agens dixit: Accipite, manducate; hoc est corpus meum, quod vobis confringetur. Similiter et calicem dicens: Hic est sanguis meus qui pro vobis effunditur. Quando hoc facitis, meam commemorationem facitis.*

*Qui venit et natus est ex Virgine, ut voluntatem tuam perficeret populumque sanctum tibi constitueret. Extendit manus suas ad passionem; passus est, ut passiones solveret eorum qui sperant in te: qui tradidit se ipsum voluntate propria ad patiendum, ut mortem destrueret et vincula satanae dissolveret, infernum calcaret, testamentum suum constitueret et resurrectionem suam manifestaret.* Ea ipsa nocte qua traditus est, *accepit panem . . .* aspexit in coelum *ad* te Patrem suum, gratias egit . . .

The institution account is greatly extended and accompanied with acclamations from the people.

---

[1] Br. 232, 3; cf. 176, 5.

3

*Memores igitur mortis et resur-rectionis eius offerimus tibi panem et calicem gratias tibi agentes, quia nos dignos habuisti adstare coram te et tibi ministrare.*

*Et petimus, ut mittas Spiritum tuum Sanctum in oblationem sanctae ecclesiae;*

*in unum congregans des omnibus, qui percipiunt, sanctis in repletionem Spiritus Sancti ad confirmationem fidei in veritate, ut te laudamus et glorificemus per puerum tuum Jesum Christum, per quem tibi gloria et honor, Patri et Filio cum Sancto Spiritu, in sancta ecclesia tua et nunc et in saecula saeculorum. Amen.*

*Nunc etiam Domine memoriam agentes mortis et resurrectionis* tuae[1] *offerimus tibi hunc panem et hunc calicem; gratias agentes tibi, quod per ea dignos fecisti nos standi coram te tibique sacerdotale mini-sterium exhibendi.* Rogamus te Domine *et deprecamur te, ut mittas* Sanctum Spiritum *et virtutem super hunc panem et super hunc calicem* faciatque utrumque corpus et sanguinem Domini et Salvatoris nostri Jesu Christi in saecula saeculorum. Amen ... *Da, ut omnibus illa sumentibus fiant ad sanctificationem et plenitudinem Spiritus Sancti et ad roborationem fidei, ut te sanctificent per* Dominum et Salvatorem nostrum[2] Jesum Christum *cum Spiritu Sancto in saecula saeculorum. Amen.*

If these prayers stem from the Roman Church of the early third century, then some further prayers that serve as preparation for the Communion and as thanksgiving, and that follow on the above-quoted Eucharistic prayer in the Ethiopian form of Hippolytus' church order, should go back at least to the origin of the Ethiopian

---

[1] Also Mercer 355: 'remembering *thy* death'; contrast Br. 233, 5: 'his death'.

[2] Br. 233, 28; 'praise thee *and* the beloved Son'; Mercer 356: 'praise thy beloved Son'.

Church.[1] Typical of these is the prayer of thanks after the Communion.[2]

> [And again we beseech thee,] almighty Lord, Father of the Lord, of our Saviour Jesus Christ: we give thee thanks that thou hast preserved us to partake of thy holy mystery; let it not be the occasion of our guilt or judgment, but of the renewal of soul, body and mind: through thy only Son, through whom be to thee with him and with the Holy Spirit honour and power now and for ever and ever.

The end-formula recurs unaltered in the other three prayers, partly also the address. Thus the Mediator phrase 'through thy only Son' appears just as independent of the words preceding it as elsewhere the χάριτι formula.[3]

Outside these texts from the earliest period, the same manner of prayer, through Christ to God, is found again in two absolution prayers before the Communion, of which one belongs also to the Coptic liturgy,[4] while the other clearly presupposes the conditions of early Christian penitential discipline;[5] and again in another Communion prayer for whose age there is no surviving evidence.[6]

[1] Funk, II, 101, 7 ff.; Br. 190, 37 ff. There are four prayers and a preceding summons to prayer. The last prayer excepted, they have passed into the Apostles' anaphora almost unaltered: Br. 234, 15 ff. They no longer belong to the church order of Hippolytus; for while the other prayers of the same recur little altered, only greatly expanded, in the corresponding formularies of *Ap. Const.* VIII and *Testament of our Lord*, there is scarcely a reminiscence of these. They were obviously, therefore, not in front of the editors concerned. Schermann (p. 137 ff.) discusses them as the 'Ethiopian addition' and establishes a partial connexion with the Arabic *Testament of our Lord (Oriens christ.* 1 [1901] 25 ff.).

[2] Br. 192, 10 or 243, 11 Apostles' anaphora; in [ ] the majority of them.

[3] Only the first prayer has a transitional phrase: 'bless every one in Christ, through whom.' The ending of the second is contracted in the Apostles' anaphora (Br. 235, 23) to the form '(increase to them . . . the fear of thy name) through thine only Son world without end'. From the last prayer, a request for blessing, which as a whole has not been taken into the Apostles' anaphora, seems at least to have determined the address and conclusion for the later text; Br. 192, 25 and 243, 20: 'Lord eternal . . . protect . . . through thine only Son through whom' (or 'join us in Christ through whom'); perhaps also for the related prayer of blessing of the deacon Br. 242, 7: 'Lord eternal . . . bless . . . through our Lord Jesus Christ through whom.'

[4] Br. 237, 1; Copt. Br. 184, 4.

[5] Br. 238, 3: 'Upon them that are in penitence, thy people, have mercy . . . join them with thine holy church: through the grace and might of thine only Son . . .'

[6] Br. 240, 18b.

Hence the Ethiopian anaphora of the Apostles has, with the ancient text, on the whole preserved also the mode of address of the prayer. Nevertheless, the small interest in the matter betrays itself occasionally in that sometimes in the course of the tradition the christologically developed doxology was dropped,[1] and at other times, in the middle of the prayer, the address to Christ seems to be assumed.[2] The latter characteristic of the unnoticed slipping to and fro of the address is strengthened by a part of the later insertions, a fact evident especially in the intercessory prayer outlined above. Apart from this feature and the acclamations of the people, the address to Christ is the choice of only a few other prayers, which are related to the Communion.[3] The preceding confession 'that this is the body and the blood of our Lord and our God and our Saviour Jesus Christ' closes with a similar blending of Christ and triune God: 'That is the one to whom all honour and glory and worship are due, to the holy Trinity, the Father and the Son and the Holy Spirit. . .'.[4]

If in the anaphora of the Apostles liturgical treasures are faithfully preserved to us from patristic times, it is equally certain that later forms of Ethiopian liturgy have gained recognition for their own religious approach. It suffices to give details of two of these anaphoras.

The *anaphora of St John Chrysostom* is thought to be the work of an Abyssinian theologian of the fifteenth century.[5] The author in the

---

[1] See above p. 36, n. 3; p. 43. According to Mercer 367, also in the present text of the above-mentioned prayer of blessing of the deacon the whole christological end-formula Br. 242, 11 is omitted. A certain tendency to abandon the doxology or to shorten it appears frequently: Br. 233, 31; 244, 10. 26.

[2] See above, p. 46, the anamnesis; then Br. 243, 23.

[3] Br. 239, 15; 240, 15; 244, 19. The first runs as follows: 'O Lord, Lord, it in no wise beseemeth thee to come under the roof of my polluted house, for I have provoked thee . . . but for the sake . . . of thy precious cross and thy lifegiving death and Resurrection . . . have mercy . . . through the petition of our lady Mary and of John the Baptist and for the sake of all the saints and martyrs world without end'.

[4] Br. 239, 10. This ending is missing in the similar confession of the Copts, Br. 185, 15. On the other hand, there occurs after the Communion an acclamation of the people that clearly separates God and Christ: 'Glory be to the Lord who hath given us the body of our Lord Jesus Christ'. Br. 242, 3; cf. Br. 242, 29 ff.

[5] T. Schermann, *Ägypt. Abendmahlsliturgien* 184–7. German trans. by A. Schulte: *Der Katholik* 68 (1888) I, 417–25. The likewise frequently printed anaphora of Dioscorus is closely related to it. Schermann 188 f.

composition of his work kept quite independent of tradition, pro-
ducing instead a homogeneous, unbroken, flowing text, which later
editors, by virtue of its strongly rhetorical character, sought to use
even as homilies. The anaphora opens in the Preface with a spirited
panegyric on 'the existence of the Father, which was, before time
began . . . before the lightning flashed and the thunder rolled', and
on his redemptive plan after the fall of man; and then goes on to
praise in detail the work and nature of the Son. Only at the very
end of the long Preface appears for the first time for a short space the
second person singular applied to Christ, to whom even the *sanctus*
is addressed: 'Never therefore will we also cease to sound in our
hearts thy holy praises and will cry out, saying: "Holy, holy, holy
thou who art in truth Jesus Christ. . .".' The institution account is
spun out into a remarkable anamnesis in fervent contemplation of
the chief phases of the Passion, and continues to the Ascension: 'With
his body, together with the power of the Godhead, he ascended
towards heaven to his former state of being.' Then only recom-
mences the prayer-style directed, as it seems, to Christ:

> We beg thee, O God . . . send to us also thy Holy Spirit, to sanctify our
> souls, our bodies and our minds. But to thee be honour and glory for ever.
> Amen. Remember, O God, thy promise of the covenant which thou
> madest with our fathers and thy holy Apostles, so that to us may come thy
> Holy Spirit, which the world cannot comprehend. Take us as thy spoil,
> as we invoke thee, while we say:[1] Our Father. . . .

Thereafter contemplative passages follow again. Even the epi-
logue, in other respects summons to prayer rather than prayer itself,
shows afresh that in the thought of the author God the Father and
Christ are deeply interfused. Of the prayer through Christ, of the
appeal to his priesthood, naturally no mention is made, although he is
distinctly termed a sacrificial offering: 'He it is whom we offer, our
Redeemer, as he was offered on the hill of Calvary.'[2]

---

[1] That up to the Pater Noster, indeed in the Pater Noster itself, the address to
Christ betrays a shadowy presence, is all the more significant if here the translation
of Euringer mentioned by Schermann, 186, f.n. 1 is right: 'Thou hast also taught
us how we should invoke thee.'
[2] Schulte, 424.

Likewise of strongly homiletic character, but in other respects a type on its own, is the perhaps equally old *anaphora of our Lady Mary*.[1] By far the greatest number of the prayers proper to it are addressed to Mary. After a few introductory words, in which the liturgist announces his intention to celebrate the sacrifice which is consuming fire, the Preface continues: 'And therefore we love thee, O Mary, and praise thee; for thou hast borne for us the true food of righteousness and the true drink of life' (n. 3). Here is inserted the intercessory prayer, which after the quoted introductory words (O holy Trinity etc.) is the same as above in the Apostles' anaphora. Then the text resumes: 'For these, therefore, and for all, intercede with thy Son, O Lady our advocate . . . so that all their souls will be refreshed' (n. 7). There follows the proper praise of Mary, which sets the keynote for the greatly expanded Preface.[2] Quite half a hundred titles of honour, mostly figures from the Old Testament (promise of Adam, ladder of Jacob, bush of Sinai, etc.) glorify her virginal purity, which finally moved the Father to send down his shining angel Gabriel with the great announcement (n. 8–20). 'There came to thee the Word, without his being separated from the bosom of the Father: thou hast received it, without its being contracted; it was enclosed in thy womb, without its being diminished above or increased below.'[3] There is now inserted a rather long exposition of the essence of the Godhead, which is not limited in human fashion, and on the Trinity of Persons: 'Three names, one God . . . the Father reflects, the Son speaks, the Holy Spirit confirms; the Father decrees, the Son proclaims, the Holy Spirit performs . . . one is the dawn, before whose brightness the darkness fades . . .' (n. 21–30).[4] And again arises the praise of the Virgin and her Son, to end finally in the *sanctus* chant, which resounds to him (n. 31–7). Even after the

[1] Schermann, 187 f. German by S. Euringer after the *Editio princeps* of the year 1548, preceded by an introduction: *Der Katholik* 96 (1916) I, 241–66.

[2] Pp. 249–58.

[3] Euringer remarks on this: 'i.e. without the Logos becoming less God and more man. This sentence, orthodox in itself, probably came to be written down with Monophysite overtones.'

[4] Although afterwards again the unity of the divine essence is decidedly stressed, there is revealed here the other complex of ideas, according to which a proper divine activity is allotted to each of the divine Persons; see above, p. 40.

*sanctus* recurs the praise of Mary, who ripens for us the bread that is redemption, and mingles the cup that is the source of wisdom (n. 38).

It must be allowed that Mary in this entire panegyric in no way appears as isolated greatness—much more her whole worth is derived from her place in the history of salvation. Then comes the institution account (n. 41-3), framed by shorter prayers to Christ, which later get longer. Thus: 'O Lord, as at that time, so bless, break and give (now) this bread. Amen. O Lord, as at that time, so seal and sanctify and present (now) this cup. Amen' (n. 44).[1] The Canon part of the anaphora now finishes with the words: 'When thou unitest thyself (in holy Communion), grant to all that receive of it that it may be to them for sanctification, for the fullness of the Holy Spirit and for the strengthening of faith, so that they may hallow and praise thee through our Lord and Saviour Jesus Christ with the Holy Spirit for ever and ever' (n. 45, 46). Here, therefore, at the end of a prayer obviously addressed to Christ, to find the closing words of *Hippolytus'* Mass with their doxology through Christ, and roughly in the hybrid form as in the *Testament of our Lord*,[2] provides two indications that little understanding of the formula remained,[3] indeed that there was no longer any knowledge of how to use it fittingly. A final series of petitions to and praises of Mary the Virgin, addressed to her, begin after the Communion: that she might remind her Son of the privations of his childhood, be merciful with sinners (n. 60). The end of the anaphora consists of the summons: 'We will thank God for every gift which he has bestowed, and that by which he has given his Mother power over this Mass . . . according to his good pleasure, to whom as to the wise be praise for ever and ever. Amen' (n. 62). The juxtaposition of

---

[1] This passage is apparently modelled on the St Gregory anaphora, which indeed also belongs to the Ethiopian anaphora stock; see above, p. 39. The prayer-style of the St Gregory anaphora, which directs all prayers to Christ, also may have prompted the author to compose an anaphora which, going a step further, is addressed primarily to Christ's Mother. A Syrian quality is presented also by n. 14 and 41. But naturally even indirect Syrian models suffice to account for these traits; cf. Euringer 241 f., 247.

[2] See above, p. 16.

[3] Since Euringer's text, moreover, takes cognizance of several manuscripts and/ or edns., a mere oversight of the copyist is excluded.

'God' and 'his Mother'[1] show how much here the concepts of God and Christ flow into one another; whence we perceive that the few prayers and passages that speak simply of 'Lord, our God' *et sim.* are not intended to constitute a passing to another prayer-address;[2] the Godhead is regularly in Christ himself in the foreground. Thus it is also comprehensible that Mary is invoked as advocate vis-à-vis him, while he himself nowhere appears in the role of the Mediator of our prayers—apart from the inharmoniously employed doxology of Hippolytus. Although in all these pecularities there is as yet no sort of heretical avowal to be found, nevertheless the Monophysite view that makes the humanity of our Lord vanish in his divinity offers the most obvious explanation of this development.

In the case of most other anaphoras, only short extracts have been published. They might, for the rest, be in some manner represented already in the types discussed. How much the address to Christ is favoured in the Ethiopian liturgy is shown by the fact that in four anaphoras it appears even inside the institution account: in the anaphora (of the Testament) of our Lord, in the anaphora of James of Serug, in that of St Athanasius and in that of Gregory the Armenian. In the latter it runs: Conjunge Domine, humanitatem nostram cum divinitate tua . . . ut offeramus istud sacrificium quod dedisti discipulis tuis dicens: Accipite, manducate: hic panis est corpus meum.[3]

The *fore-anaphora* has grown to a great length in the Ethiopian Mass: it is easily twice as long as the Apostles' anaphora itself.[4] The basis is provided with slight changes by the Coptic fore-anaphora, whose core again consists of the old Egyptian prayers at the end of

---

[1] 'Mother of God' as a title of honour for Mary is only a natural consequence of the fact that Christ is true God, whence everyone knows that the motherhood of the title relates to the humanity of him who is God and man. Since, however, the word 'God' in itself does not in the first instance indicate the God-man, the above manner of speaking is, to say the least, confusing.

[2] n. 48, 50, 53, 54, 55.—Also the Trinity is in some acclamations (n. 6, 56, 61) praised or besought; yet at least the first two passages belong quite as little to the proper stock of the Marian anaphora as the passage of praise n. 47.

[3] M. Chaine, 'La Consécration et l'épiclèse dans le missel éthiopien': *Bessarione* 14 (1909–10) 195, and 181–209. Also in Mercer 258–64.

[4] Br. 194–227.

the morning service, the 'threefold' prayer of the faithful and the general prayer for the Church. In this last, older layer, already discussed above,[1] the manner of prayer in which God is addressed through Christ is retained,[2] as well as in the later Coptic layer, in so far as this prayer-style was dominant there.[3] Of the prayers, however, which comprise the extended Ethiopian heritage, none strictly speaking belong to this type.[4] But prayers directed to God which go on to the trinitarian end-doxology without any christological Mediator phrase are not only derived from the Coptic liturgy but also are found among those which are proper to the Ethiopian.[5] Others abandon in their endings any mention of the Trinity, indeed even any doxology.[6]

Also, to the prayers directed to Christ, which belong to the common heritage of the Ethiopian and Coptic fore-anaphoras,[7]

---

[1] Pp. 28 ff.; 41 ff.

[2] Br. 202 f, 223 ff, and the shorter duplicates pp. 210 f. and 214, 220 ff. The χάριτι formula is in the second case replaced by that of the 'Ethiopian addition': through thine only Son through whom to thee with him and with the Holy Ghost be glory . . . Br. 224, 33; 214, 20; 211, 14.

[3] Br. 197, 30; 215; 227 (cf. Ren. I, 62 f., and 12: Egn. St Basil anaphora. The prayer at the Kiss of Peace, on account of its being found here, is headed 'of Basil'). Also, there is inserted here in the two latter cases the formula with 'through Jesus Christ' instead of the ending 'in Christ Jesus' of the Coptic.—The prayer over the chalice-veil native to the St James anaphora of Syria, likewise taken over from the St Basil anaphora and headed 'of Basil', Br. 204, 31, had lost its christological ending earlier; see above, p. 37, n. 1.

[4] This is true at least as far as the text of Brightman (from the seventeenth century) is concerned. Only one prayer directed to Christ has unfittingly the ending: 'through whom . . .' Br. 213, 22. In the modern text given by Mercer a prayer of blessing before the Gospel also ends: '. . . Christ the Son of the living God, through whom to thee be glory . . .' (p. 340; cf. on the contrary Br. 222, 8). But this seems to be pure chance. For the rest, the numerous insertions and variants of this text never contain this theme; probably however they displace it in certain passages of the anaphora (p. 353, cf. Br. 232, 3; p. 367, cf. Br. 242, 11), just as also the uncertainty of the address increases.

[5] E.g. Br. 194, 15: 'Lord our God . . . make them (the church equipment) such, that on them may be wrought the mystery of the Father and the Son and the Holy Ghost both now and ever and world without end'. Cf. also the attached prayer Br. 195, 13: 'Lord our God . . . defend thy people. To thee and to thine only good and merciful Son and to the Holy Ghost the lifegiver be glory world without end.'

[6] E.g. Br. 199, 19: 'Lord our God . . . recompense him . . . in this world.'

[7] See above, pp. 41-2: 'and in that which is to come both now and ever and world without end.'

several have been added. They are interspersed without recognizable order. Sometimes the address here is simply 'Lord our God'; or
indeed the thanksgiving following on the address is more concerned
with the general divine being and activity, and only as if by chance
in certain cases can one recognize from this or that word that the
prayer is directed to Christ; e.g.: 'Lord our God, who art enthroned
above the angels and archangels . . . thou hast revealed to us a new
way for our deliverance . . . make us worthy of this thy holy mystery
. . . to thee with thy good heavenly Father . . . will we send up
praise. . . .'[1]

There is increase also in the number of short praises and petitions
that are interspersed between the prayers or serve as companion
texts to various ceremonies, especially incensation. Mostly they are
applied to the Trinity or to the individual divine Persons in succes-
sion;[2] sometimes to Christ the Lord[3] or even to the Mother of God,[4]
as often in the mouth of the people as in that of the priest. Just as
here Mary's intercession, so too elsewhere[5] that of the saints is
occasionally pleaded in texts and prayers.[6]

---

[1] Br. 196, 28; more precisely: Br. 196, 14; 199, 32; 200, 5. 13. In the preparatory
prayer Br. 195, 27 the address changes twice; the prayer begins: 'Lord our God
and our creator who hath made all things through his word'; then 'O our Lord
and our God and our Saviour Jesus Christ'; finally, after the petition for the
acceptance of the sacrifice again: 'let it be to the glory of thine only Son . . .'
Similarly in another prayer in Mercer, 301 f.; cf. ibid. 356 a breaking-prayer.

[2] Br. 200 f.; 209, 17; 213 etc.

[3] E.g. Br. 216, 6; 220, 26; 227, 29.

[4] Br. 211 f., 216 f. Increased in number in the present liturgy: Mercer 320, 321,
326, three passages in which every time an acclamation to Mary follows the praise
to the Father, the Son and the Holy Spirit.

[5] Br. 214, 25; 215, 34; 206, 4 (Copt. 149, 24); cf. the intercessory prayer Br.
228 ff. (see above, p. 44).

[6] A style of prayer like that found in the fore-anaphora *ordo*, uniting and
even mixing the different types, is shown by the Ethiopian ritual, published by
M. Chaine: *Bessarione* 29 (1913) 38–71, 249–83, 420–51; 30 (1914) 12–41, 212–31.
The separation of the different prayer-types might here be a useful aid to the
elucidation of the textual history.

# IV
# WEST SYRIAN LITURGY

IF here again we look first at the anaphora formularies, we find as kernel of the West Syrian liturgy, as the normal form of its Mass celebration, the *anaphora of St James*, the brother of the Lord. The name appears at the Synod of Trulles (692) and points to Jerusalem as its home. After the Council of Chalcedon (451), at which Jerusalem received patriarchal rights over the greater part of Syria, its liturgy also held sway over a growing area embracing, by the middle of the sixth century, the whole of non-Nestorian Syria.[1] From the local variations of liturgical practice which had arisen in the meantime, there came into being about this time in connexion with the new revival of Monophysitism, still within the common Greek language, three mutually exclusive recensions of the anaphora: one in *Greek*,[2] which was then translated into Georgian, on the Catholic side; a second, which was in use among the moderate phthartolatrian Monophysites—called 'Jacobites' after their organizer Jacob Baradai (d. 578)—and which, translated soon after into *Syrian*, still survives today;[3] the Ethiopian translation is related to this recen-

---

[1] Cf. A. Baumstark, *Die Messe im Morgenland*, 38–42.      [2] Br. 49–68.

[3] The Monophysites started from the thesis that the human nature of Christ was absorbed by the divine, so that one could speak in fact of only one nature, μία φύσις. As a result of the ensuing disputes a large section, led by the Patriarch Severus of Antioch (d. 538), which shied at the consequences of Monophysite

sion;[1] finally a third which, according to A. Baumstark, must originally have been proper to the schismatic Monophysite-aphthartodocetic Church of Julian of Halicarnassus, which came to an end in the ninth to tenth century; this recension passed into the *Armenian* liturgy.[2]

The basic form, of which only the quotations of *St Cyril of Jerusalem* give us direct knowledge,[3] is given as nearly as possible in the edition of A. Rücker. Parallel with the Syrian text as, according to the oldest manuscripts (eighth to tenth century), it appears to have come from the pen of *Jacob of Edessa* (d. 708) when he set out to improve the Syrian text of the time after the Greek original, Rücker gives as translation a reconstruction of the Greek text that Jacob must have used. We now see from this edition that in the common original form of the St James anaphora, i.e. in the fifth century, all prayers must still have been directed to God. Rücker's text indicates *two prayers addressed to Christ*: the one as the last prayer of blessing after the Communion, which prayer ends the anaphora,[4] the other as anamnesis after the institution account.[5] But in both cases our recension of the Syrian has opposing it the Greek with the address to God, although this on its side betrays hardly more than other derivatives an inclination to give the Godward direction to prayers eventually addressed to Christ, indeed rather the opposite.[6]

teaching, defended the thesis: up to the Resurrection of the Lord the special characteristics of his human body, in particular its corruptibility, continued to exist in his one divine-human nature. They were called by the more extreme school, at the head of which was Julian of Halicarnassus (d. after 518), φθαρτολάτραι. Whence the radicals, who were forced to the denial of all physical weaknesses of the corporeality of the Lord, indeed in the end to the acceptance of a mere apparent body, received the name ἀφθαρτοδοκῆται. The St James anaphora of the moderate party is in English in Br. 83–106. It now exists also in a separate edition: A. Rücker, *Die syrische Jakobusanaphora nach der Rezension des Ja'qob(h) von Edessa. Mit dem griechischen Paralleltext* (Münster, 1923).

[1] German by S. Euringer in *Oriens christ.*[2] 4, II (1915) 1–23.
[2] Latin with introduction and apparatus by A. Baumstark: *Oriens christ.*[2] 7/8 (1918) 1–32.
[3] Br. 464–70.                    [4] P. 57, 2.
[5] P. 17, 11—not to mention the immediately preceding cry of the people (p. 65, 19): 'Thy death, O Lord, we recall and thy Resurrection we acknowledge and thy second coming we await; thy mercy be on us all'.
[6] Cf. Rücker 55, 1 = Br. 64, 32a.

The prayer of blessing goes, according to Rücker:[1]

O God, so great and wonderful [who lowered heaven and came down for the deliverance of the human race], look down on us [in mercy and grace] and bless thy people, protect thy inheritance, so that we always and everywhere may praise thee, our only true God,[2] [with the Father, who begat thee, and thy Holy Spirit, now . . .][3]

The quotation of John (17:3) shows clearly enough the original mode of address of the prayer. Yet clearer is the stance of the anamnesis prayer, as the following contrast shows:

SYRIAN-JACOBITE (Rücker 17f. Br. 87 f.):

As we now, Lord, recall *thy* death and *thy* Resurrection from the dead on the third day and *thy* Ascension into heaven and *thy* sitting at the right hand of God and Father and *thy* fearful and glorious coming . . ., we offer thee this awful and unbloody sacrifice, that thou mayest deal with us not according to our sins . . ., but according to thy graciousness and ineffable loving-kindness blot out the sins of those who implore thee; for thy people and thy inheritance beg thee and through thee and with thee the Father, while it says: Have mercy on us, God almighty Father!

GREEK (Br. 52 f.)

As now also we sinners recall *his* life-giving Passion, the redeeming cross and the death and burial and the Resurrection from the dead on the third day and the Ascension into heaven and the sitting at *thy* right hand, of God and Father, and *his* second glorious and fearful coming . . ., we offer thee this awful and unbloody sacrifice, while we pray that thou dealest with us not according to our sins . . ., but according to thy graciousness and ineffable loving-kindness ignore and efface the bond of those who implore thee . . ., for thy people and thy Church beg thee: Have mercy on us, Lord God almighty Father!

[1] [ ] indicates a majority of the Syrian or of its model over against the Greek; cf. Br. 105, 17.
[2] John 17: 3.
[3] The Greek has instead: ‘Ο θεός, ὁ μέγας καὶ θαυμαστός, ἔπιδε ἐπὶ τοὺς δούλους σου . . . ἵνα ἀεὶ καὶ διὰ παντὸς δοξάζωμεν σὲ τὸν μόνον ζῶντα καὶ ἀληθινὸν θεὸν ἡμῶν, τὴν ἁγίαν καὶ ὁμοούσιον τριάδα, πατέρα καὶ υἱὸν καὶ τὸ ἅγιον πνεῦμα νῦν . . . Br. 67, 2.

Here the Syrian (and the Ethiopian) is in contrast not only with the above-quoted Greek (and the Georgian)[1] but also with the Armenian, all of which direct the ᴄnamnesis to God. That the latter was the original form follows—apart from the fact that precisely the texts concerned vary widely in the Syrian manuscripts[2]—from the incongruity of offering the sacrifice to Christ, as in the Syrian above, an idea we first meet in the Syrian *Testament of our Lord*.[3] Thus at first in all prayers of the anaphora the address to God predominated in the same way. The prayers then regularly closed with a christo-logical phrase, in which, nevertheless, it is preferred to refer to Christ with respect to his divinity, and which serves as a bridge to a trinitarian passage of praise: '(Bless, aid, grant) through the favour, mercy and benevolence of thy only-begotten Son, with whom to thee glory . . . is due, together with thy all-holy . . . Spirit. . .'.[4] In this doxology, Christ appears exclusively as Son of God, as fellow-receiver of praise ($\mu\epsilon\theta$ $o\hat{v}$). In contrast, he comes into his own in the transitional phrase ($\epsilon\nu$ $\chi\acute{a}\rho\iota\tau\iota$) as *Mediator* in the broader sense: one on whose account God is to be gracious to us. This general mediator-ship of the Lord, his whole position in the history of salvation, is thrown into relief by the prayer between the *sanctus* and the institu-

---

[1] The Georgian St James liturgy published by M. Tarchnisvili in the *Eph. liturg.* 62 (1948) 49–82 agrees in the prayer-address of the anamnesis with the Greek text, from which it is derived.

[2] See Rücker's Syrian apparatus at p. 16, 11 ff.; 18, 8 ff; cf. p. 58 ff.

[3] So also the final prayer, which *inter alia* a manuscript of the thirteenth century has added to our anaphora: Rücker 61 f. Other examples from the Syrian St James liturgy: Br. 73, 9; 80, 26. Also, the Armenians, in a somewhat later passage of this anaphora with a sudden change of direction inside a prayer, give expression to the presentation to Christ (*Oriens christ.*[2] 7/8 [1918] 19, 7), which Baumstark calls 'a very late "Text-retouche" '.

[4] $\epsilon\nu$ $\chi\acute{a}\rho\iota\tau\iota$ $\kappa\alpha\grave{\iota}$ $\grave{\epsilon}\lambda\acute{\epsilon}\epsilon\iota$ $\kappa\alpha\grave{\iota}$ $\phi\iota\lambda\alpha\nu\theta\rho\omega\pi\acute{\iota}\alpha$ $\tauο\hat{\upsilon}$ $\mu\ono\gamma\epsilon\no\hat{\upsilon}\varsigma$ $\sigmaο\upsilon$ $\upsilon\grave{\iota}ο\hat{\upsilon}$, $\mu\epsilon\theta$' $o\hat{\upsilon}$ $\sigmaο\grave{\iota}$ $\pi\rho\acute{\epsilon}\pi\epsilon\iota$ $\delta\acute{ο}\xi\alpha$ $\kappa\alpha\grave{\iota}$ $\tau\iota\mu\grave{\eta}$ $\kappa\alpha\grave{\iota}$ $\kappa\rho\acute{a}\tauο\varsigma$ $\sigma\grave{\upsilon}\nu$ $\tau\hat{\omega}$ $\pi\alpha\nu\alpha\gamma\acute{\iota}\omega$ $\grave{a}\gamma\alpha\theta\hat{\omega}$ $\kappa\alpha\grave{\iota}$ $\pi\rhoο\sigma\kappa\upsilon\nu\eta\tau\hat{\omega}$ $\kappa\alpha\grave{\iota}$ $\zeta\omegaο\pi\oiο\hat{\omega}$ $\kappa\alpha\grave{\iota}$ $\grave{ο}\muοο\upsilon\sigma\acute{\iota}\omega$ $\sigmaο\upsilon$ $\pi\nu\epsilon\acute{\upsilon}\mu\alpha\tau\iota$ $\nu\hat{\upsilon}\nu$ . . . Rücker 5, 9; 7, 10; similarly 37, 12; 51, 9; 55, 8. At least the wording brought out in the text may belong to the original form. Again, at 51, 9 the expression: $\phi\iota\lambda\alpha\nu\theta\rho\omega\pi\acute{\iota}\alpha$ $X\rho\iota\sigma\tauο\hat{\upsilon}$ $\sigmaο\upsilon$ is noteworthy. Cf. 25, 6: 'these holy places (of Jerusalem), which thou hast glorified $\tau\hat{\eta}$ $\grave{\epsilon}\pi\iota\phi\alpha\nu\epsilon\acute{\iota}\alpha$ $\tauο\hat{\upsilon}$ $X\rho\iota\sigma\tauο\hat{\upsilon}$ $\sigmaο\upsilon$'. This simple title 'thy Christ', by which the humanity and the Mediator position of Christ is put more to the fore, was especially frequent in the prayers of the *Ap. Const.* VIII and will also have been more frequent in our anaphora earlier. On p. 49, 3 there is mention of the consecration of the sacrificial gifts $\tau\hat{\eta}$ $\chi\acute{a}\rho\iota\tau\iota$ $\tauο\hat{\upsilon}$ $\mu\ono\gamma\epsilon\no\hat{\upsilon}\varsigma$ $\sigmaο\upsilon$ $\upsilon\grave{\iota}ο\hat{\upsilon}$ $\kappa\alpha\grave{\iota}$ $\grave{\epsilon}\pi\iota\phiο\iota\tau\acute{\eta}\sigma\epsilon\iota$ $\tauο\hat{\upsilon}$ $\pi\alpha\nu\alpha\gamma\acuteiο\upsilon$ $\sigmaο\upsilon$ $\pi\nu\epsilon\acute{\upsilon}\mu\alpha\tauο\varsigma$.

tion account, which is rather a continuation of the thanksgiving prayer, going into detail.[1] But also his high-priestly mediation of the prayer is still occasionally recognizable, and with distinct marks of a greater age: (a) twice in the doxology-form: δι' οὗ καὶ μεθ' οὗ σοὶ πρέπει δόξα . . .[2]; (b) at the end of the intercessory prayer that is here inserted towards the end of the Canon part of the Mass, comprises over a third of the whole anaphora and contains many later additions[3]—in the *Memento* for the dead: give (their souls rest) 'as thou dost not charge to their account all their false steps . . ., there is indeed no-one free of sin and spotless, of all men on earth, except our Lord and God and Saviour alone, Jesus Christ, thy only-begotten Son, through whom also we hope to find mercy and forgiveness of sins, for his sake both for us and for those';[4] (c) finally, the theme is also strikingly expressed at the end of the anamnesis prayer already quoted, which has taken on the address to Christ.

[1] Rücker 13, cf. also 7, 3.

[2] 3, 9; 49, 12. The δι' οὗ καὶ is both times bracketed in Rücker, as it is lacking in these passages in the Greek, but is not any the more for that a later interpolation; cf. below Pt. II, ch. III and IV.

[3] Rücker 24–43 and appendix pp. 66–73; cf. p. xv: even a ninth century commentator sees here much which is later, superfluous interpolation. Precisely the parts considered chiefly as such, the first, second, third and fifth spoken texts of the priest, are also distinguished from the rest by the complete disappearance of the Mediator theme from their end-formulas. Thus the recited text after the *memento* for the royal house runs: 'For thou art the refuge of salvation and the helping power and the giver of victory for all who cry to thee and hope on thee, Lord. And to thee we offer praise and to thy only-begotten Son and thy all-holy . . . Spirit now. . . .' (p. 35).

[4] Rücker 43. Although the wording varies from one form to another of the St James anaphora, the great age of the present theme is particularly well verified in this passage. The text of the Greek is somewhat wider, Br. 57, 21: 'Grant us a Christian end . . . διὰ τοῦ μονογενοῦς σου . . . 'Ιησοῦ Χριστοῦ · αὐτὸς γάρ ἐστιν ὁ μόνος ἀναμάρτητος φανεὶς ἐπὶ τῆς γῆς · δι' ὃν καὶ ἡμῖν καὶ αὐτοῖς ὡς ἀγαθὸς καὶ φιλάνθρωπος ἄνες ἄφες . . . τὰ παραπτώματα ἡμῶν . . . The prayer then ends again with the χάριτι formula. The high-priestly Mediator position finds expression probably already in the first phrase, διὰ τοῦ μονογενοῦς . . . ἐπὶ τῆς γῆς: it is because of his sinlessness that we rely on him (αὐτὸς γάρ). The following expressions δι' ὃν and χάριτι again make Christ appear expressly as God's motive for hearing us. The passage is even drawn on by *Jerome*, to whom, when in Palestine, the St James liturgy must have been familiar, *Adv. Pel.* 2, 23: 'Quae omnia sacerdotum quotidie ora concelebrant: ὁ μόνος ἀναμάρτητος, quod in lingua nostra dicitur: qui solus est sine peccato'. Cf. related passages from the Catecheses of *Cyril* in Br. 469, 50.

The plea for mercy—that is at the Last Judgment—ends: 'Thy people . . . implore thee [and *through thee* . . . the Father, while they say] have mercy on us, God almighty Father!'[1] Although this passage in the text of Jacob of Edessa is the result of later editing, probably nevertheless it serves only to re-adapt the text of the anamnesis subsequently to the traditional form of address, from which it had departed.

So there follows as the state of the St James anaphora at the beginning of its advance beyond its native sphere (fifth century): the prayers are directed to God. In varying form they regularly contain towards the end the reference to Christ as Mediator, chiefly in the wider sense, in that God must be gracious to us on his account ($\chi\acute{\alpha}\rho\iota\tau\iota$), but also sometimes in the narrower sense of the mediation of the prayer, in that he will recommend our prayer with God.

At the end of the seventh century, in the text of Jacob of Edessa, the Mediator theme before the ending doxology in the new-grown prayers (audible texts of the intercessory prayer) is no longer in use; two prayers have assumed the address to Christ; in other respects, the order of address of the anaphora prayers has remained the same.

If we now go a step further and look at this same Syrian St James anaphora as it is in the manuscripts from the thirteenth century onwards and still is in use today,[2] a single alteration really strikes the attention. While hitherto as a rule Christ was named as Mediator only before the doxology, as our title for a hearing, in order to appear in the doxology itself merely as co-receiver of the praise with Father and Holy Spirit ($\mu\epsilon\theta$' $o\hat{\delta}$), now the doxology in the anaphora, apart from the audible texts of the intercessory prayer, runs— corresponding to a Greek $\delta\iota$' $o\hat{\delta}$ $\kappa\alpha\grave{\iota}$ $\mu\epsilon\theta$' $o\hat{\delta}$—in every case: (through the grace . . . of thy Son) *through whom and* with whom to thee . . . honour is due.[3] We have here, therefore, a clearly retrograde movement in the sense that the theme of Christ's position as Mediator of prayer, often suppressed in the earlier period, is again brought out.

On the model of the St James anaphora a considerable number of

---

[1] Rücker 19, 7; cf. above p. 57.

[2] Textus receptus; see Rücker p. xvii ff, xxxii; Br. 83–106.

[3] Not only Br. 83, 28 and 100, 15 as in Jacob of Edessa, but also Br. 84, 15. 34; 89, 22; 93, 26; 105, 1.

*further anaphoras*, of which the oldest were likewise originally Greek, were composed among the Syrian Jacobites in the period up to the fifteenth century. There are about sixty of them, of which perhaps two-thirds, the more important, are accessible in Western languages.[1] However, it suffices here to discuss them briefly as one. In contrast to the bold freedom that reigns in the Ethiopian new creations, there grew up among the Syrian Jacobites a fixed rule, a strict plan, to which all new formularies apparently cling. The same prayer-passages are followed, the same processes of thought, which are treated only in different forms and with varying fullness of detail. From our point of view, the following common traits probably deserve to be underlined.

In the first place, the West Syrian anaphoras are distinguished in general by Christ's position as Redeemer—especially in the further course of the eucharistic prayer—being brought warmly and vividly before our eyes. Thus the *sanctus* is as a rule carried on so that it acts as basis to a following short survey of the divine economy of salvation, reaching its climax in the Passion of Christ, suitably followed by the institution account.[2] In later anaphoras, the consideration of the history of salvation, of the divine work of atonement, also gives its imprint in most cases to the prayer at the Kiss of Peace.[3]

---

[1] Mostly in Ren. II, 126–565. For the dating of the different anaphoras, see A. Baumstark, *Geschichte der syrischen Literatur* (Bonn, 1922), in which, with the help of the index (see under 'anaphora'), the abundant but widely-scattered data are to be found. Also the existing editions and translations are there accurately listed for each anaphora. The chief data are also given already in *Die Messe im Morgenland* 44–6. Postscript 1962: The number of West Syrian anaphoras is now given as 'about eighty'; A. Raes, 'Liturgie' VI B: LThK VI (1961) 1089. A number of them have meanwhile gone through a critical edition: *Anaphorae syriacae* (Rome, 1939 ff.).

[2] In spite of its particular brevity, a typical example is provided by the Anaphora of Eustathius, Ren. II, 235–40: 'Trinas sanctificationes offerimus tibi, Deus Pater, et unigenito Filio tuo et Spiritui tuo Sancto: neque enim mensurabilis est sanctitas tua, Domine: qui cum indigni essemus, misisti Filium tuum in mundum pro salute nostra, ortusque est ex Virgine et per mortem suam vitam praestitit mortalitati nostrae. Qui, cum voluntate sua quasi succidaneus pro nobis peccatoribus venit ad mortem, accepit panem', etc. Likewise in the St James Anaphora itself. Only rarely, instead of this survey, a kind of epiklesis follows on the 'Thrice-holy': 'Make us holy also'; e.g. Ren. II, 146 (anaphora of Peter). 277 (of Cyril).

[3] E.g. Ren. II, 176 (of Mark). 456 (of Gregory Jacob). 492 (of Dioscurus). 512 (of Johannes bar Madani). 528 (of Ignatius bar Wahib). These formularies are dated in Baumstark 13th–14th century.

In regard to the order of address, it has become the unbreakable rule that all prayers are addressed to God the Father, with the exception of the anamnesis and the last prayer of blessing—exactly as in the Syrian St James anaphora.[1]

The idea that Christ mediates our prayer appears to some extent in every formulary. In the anamnesis prayer itself, which is directed to Christ, an appropriate concluding phrase belongs to the unchanging elements of every formulary, which vary only in their wording. After the liturgist has pondered the glorification of the Lord and then, often at great length, the terrors of his second coming at the Last Judgment, he passes to the request: 'On that day do not repel us; thy Church begs thee and through thee and with thee thy Father: have mercy on us.'[2] Similarly, the reference to the one Redeemer from sin, 'through whom and for whose sake we hope for mercy', at the end of the sixth audible text (for the dead) of the intercessory prayer after the Consecration, is one of the fixed points at which every formulary makes contact with the Syrian anaphora of St James.[3] Outside these two passages, there occurs, only by way

---

[1] To this rule there are just one or two exceptions, which may very well relate to a primitive period in which the rule had not yet been elaborated. Thus deviations exist to some extent in the anaphora of Cyril (Ren. II, 275–85: only anamnesis recognizably to Christ), in that of the twelve Apostles (Ren. II, 170–4: also Preface to Christ), and in that of John of Bosra (Ren. II, 421–34: a further prayer before the anamnesis: *O Verbum Deus*; cf. Rücker p. xv).—In fact, A. Baumstark (*Geschichte der syrischen Literatur* 266 f.) puts these three formularies with the oldest, which go back again to Greek originals. The additional Christ-addressed prayers of the anaphora of Xystus (Ren. II, 134–41) belong to the *Ordo communis*. (Cf. Br. LVI, 31.)

[2] Deviations from the usual wording: '(Ecclesia tua) deprecatur te et per te atque tecum Patrem tuum dicens', i.e. from the text of the St James anaphora in the recension of Jacob of Edessa (see above p. 57), are rare. Thus the ancient anaphora of Cyril (Ren. II, 278) has, blunting the meaning again: 'clamat ad te, Patrem tuum, Spiritumque Sanctum dicens'. Similarly, however, also the later anaphora of the Patriarch Michael (d. 1199; Ren. II, 441): 'clamat ad te et ad Patrem tuum dicens'. Whence the anaphora of John of Harran (thirteenth century) is so much the more distinct: 'deprecationem tibi offerimus et te mediante Patrem etiam tuum interpellamus dicentes' (Ren. II, 257).

[3] See above p. 58 ff. Only rarely is the mediator theme obscured, as in the anaphora of Gregory the Younger (d. 1214; Ren. II, 466): 'Secundum promissiones eius ad nos factas speramus misericordiam consequi'. On the other hand, other formularies are all the more at pains in this passage to lay great stress on the Mediator idea. The anaphora of the Patriarch John XIV (d. 1220), e.g., has (Ren.

of exception, a similar reference to the mediatorship of our Lord within the prayers of several anaphora formularies.

With regard to the doxology, the majority of the anaphoras bear a closer resemblance to the older text of the St James anaphora in the recension of Jacob of Edessa than to the *textus receptus* with its formula 'through him and with him'. The pure trinitarian doxology, which is retained in the first five audible texts of the intercessory prayer almost throughout (as in the St James anaphora), is in individual formularies also used elsewhere almost exclusively: 'And to thee we offer praise and to thy only-begotten Son and to the Holy Spirit'. If then in others the naming of our Lord, or the χάριτι formula or the phrase 'through Christ' frequently comprises the transition to the doxology and thus makes felt his mediation for the prayer so ended, Christ nevertheless appears in the doxology itself in a great number of cases only as receiver (μεθ' οὗ), not also as Mediator (δι οὗ καὶ μεθ' οὗ), of the glory. Beside these, however, there do occur anaphoras which, outside the intercessory prayer, yet more often employ the latter's full christological formula, and indeed such anaphoras come from the earlier[1] as well as the later period.[2]

We must now cast a glance at the other forms of the St James anaphora. A descendant of the Syrian form is the *Ethiopian*. It displays the characteristics which have marked the development of its mother form, but is somewhat further removed—in the same direction—from the basic form than the recension of Jacob of Edessa. According to Rücker,[3] an older Syrian text lies behind it. To the two prayers addressed to Christ, has been added a third, the prayer of blessing *before* the Communion.[4] The Mediator theme

---

II, 484): 'Quia nemo est immunis a peccato, etiamsi una hora tantum in terra habitaverit, nisi solus Dominus Deus et Salvator noster Jesus Christus unigenitus Filius tuus, quem tibi offerimus, deprecantem te pro nobis, ipsum, per quem speramus misericordiam consequi et remissionem peccatorum tam nobis quam ipsis propter eum.'

[1] E.g. anaphora of Clement (Ren. II, 186–99), of Ignatius (Ren. II, 215–26), of Basil (Ren. II, 548–62; agreeing word-for-word, in places, with the Byzantine of the same name); also the liturgy of the Presanctified of John Chrysostom (Χρυσοστομικά 721–9).

[2] E.g. anaphora of Mark (thirteenth cent., Ren. II, 176–83), of Peter (13th cent., Ren. II, 145–52), of the Patriarch John XIV (d. 1219/20; Ren. II, 474–88).

[3] P. xxvi ff.      [4] *Oriens christ.*[2] 4, II (1915) 21, 11.

is further suppressed: the anamnesis prayer—also, it is true, considerably altered in other parts—does not end as in the Syrian: 'thy people . . . implore thee and *through thee* . . . thy Father', but with 'the holy Church . . . appeals to thee and *to* thy Father'.[1] The high-priestly position of Christ is nowhere recognizable; also, the christological transition to the trinitarian doxology with χάριτι as reference to the Redeemer is kept in only two places.[2]

The *Armenian* St James anaphora has developed in basically the same way. Already the Greek form of its Syrian model was different, as remarked, from the recension which Jacob of Edessa had in front of him, and A. Baumstark holds that it is more primitive than its two sister recensions.[3] In fact, here we find retained the address to God, not merely in the anamnesis prayer;[4] in the prayer over the chalice-veil, which in Rücker's text[5] ends with the formula ἐν χάριτι, we here read[6] the ending: et petimus expiationem . . . *interventione* unigeniti Filii tui Domini nostri et salvatoris Jesu Christi, quocum tibi Patri omnipotenti, et Spiritui Sancto gloria, potestas et honor. Baumstark notices the ancient character of this doxology (δόξα, κράτος καὶ τιμή); so much the more does the Mediator phrase prove to be a survivor from an older prayer-style. Baumstark himself quotes as a parallel: διὰ μεσιτείας τοῦ Χριστοῦ, Ap. Const. VIII.[7] Besides this, in the intercessory prayer[8] the Passion of the Son still occurs as a motive for God to hear the prayer. In other respects, however, the Armenian shows in fact a strong recession from the older prayer-style, although this is apparent at other points than in the Syrian and the Greek. Thus the address to Christ has made its way here into three other passages;[9] in a fourth prayer of the anaphora, there is a transition of a striking character to the address to the Holy Spirit,[10] such as frequently occurs in the Armenian liturgy. The address to Christ dominates also the proper fore-anaphora, which is firmly tied to the St James anaphora in Armenia and betrays a relatively great age.[11]

The concern to stress in particular the divinity of Christ, a further common reason for the naming of Christ,[12] was most probably promoted in

---

[1] P. 9, 32; cf. above, p. 62, note 2.    [2] Pp. 17, 11; 21, 33; cf. 11, 25.
[3] *Oriens christ.*[2] 7/8 (1918) 7 f.    [4] P. 17, 10.
[5] Rücker 7.    [6] P. 13, 4.
[7] Br. 23, 16 f (= c. 13, 3; cf. c. 5, 5; c. 48, 3).    [8] Pp. 23, 4. 11.
[9] P. 19, 7 (at the end of the epiklesis); 31, 5 and 31, 14 (Communion thanksgiving prayer and Last Blessing).
[10] P. 29, 3.    [11] Pp. 9–11; cf. p. 2 f.
[12] Cf. also in the fore-anaphora the name Θεοπάτωρ for David and the 'haec est victima divina' repeated litany-wise, p. 10.

part by the Monophysite sect of strict observance.[1] The outlook of this school is most effectively expressed in the editing of the institution account of our anaphora: while in the Syrian and the Greek it says of the chalice that the Lord mixed the drink from wine and water: κεράσας ἐξ οἴνου καὶ ὕδατος, here the mention of the water is omitted.[2] For the non-Uniate Armenians are even now the only church body in the East that in the Mass uses wine without the admixture of water—because, as was said later on, the water would indicate that in Christ the human nature has continued as such together with the divine—a practice which the Trullanum of 680 condemned in despite of them.[3]

For the *Greek* recension of the St James anaphora, a few words will now suffice.[4] Here the universal prayer-address to Christ is seen at its purest in the sacerdotal prayers. Of the prayers of ancient standing, only the first half of the Communion thanksgiving prayer is provided with the address to Christ, but it is spoken by deacon and people.[5] On the other hand, the christological transition to the doxology is present in only a few passages;[6] the doxology itself then always begins with εὐλογητὸς εἶ.[7]

---

[1] Aphthartodocetists: see above, p. 55, note 3.

[2] Baumstark gives for the old form, completing it: '⟨miscuit⟩ vino ⟨et aqua⟩ et ostendit tibi,' p. 16, 9.

[3] V. Thalhofer—L. Eisenhofer II, 116. Cf. also the *Decretum pro Armenis* from the Bull of Union of 1439: H. Denzinger—C. Bannwart, *Enchiridion* (14th edn.) n. 698. Cf. H. Engberding, 'Das chalkedonische Christusbild und die monophysitischen Kirchengemeinschaften': *Das Konzil von Chalkedon* II (Würzburg, 1953) 697–733. According to this, there is no evidence that the use of unmixed wine was understood as an expression of Monophysite views before the eighth century. At the Council of Constantinople, 692, the custom was condemned, but without reference to Monophysitism. Cf. J. A. Jungmann, *Missarum Sollemnia*[5] (Vienna, 1962) II, 50.

[4] The whole Greek St James liturgy according to a manuscript of the fourteenth century in Br. 31–68. The anaphora begins with the Preface, Br. 49, but here, in order to extract the full parallelism with the Syrian text, it is regarded, as in the latter, as starting with the Kiss of Peace, Br. 43. For older texts, see Rücker p. xii f.

[5] Br. 64, 32; cf. Rücker 55. The litanies recited by the deacon and answered by the people with κύριε ἐλέησον, are addressed to the 'Lord', who finally seems to be identified with Christ: Br. 59, 12; 66, 14.

[6] Br. 43, 16; 49, 6; 66, 6.

[7] The preference thus shown for the pure trinitarian doxology can also be due to Byzantine influence (cf., e.g., Br. 44, 13 ὑπερένδοξον ὑπάρχει τὸ πανάγιον ὄνομά σου τοῦ πατρὸς καὶ τοῦ υἱοῦ καὶ τοῦ ἁγίου πνεύματος, with 310, 5; 67, 10 with 310, 28), which is also revealed by later prayers derived from thence and which in the end led to the complete suppression of the Greek St James liturgy; the predilection can, however, equally point to an old Antiochene usage, which, starting from Antioch originally, made its way also into Byzantium. Cf. below Part Two, Ch. XII.

There is still the *fore-anaphora* of the West Syrian liturgy to consider, more precisely the extra-anaphora *ordo Missae* in general,
which also has here its own history, albeit still little investigated.[1]
In this connexion, there is only the Syrian-Jacobite and Greek-
Orthodox St James liturgy to treat.

The fore-anaphora of the *Greek* St James liturgy is quite different
from that of the Syrian. On the contrary, it has points of contact
with the Byzantine liturgy and also with the Greek St Mark
liturgy;[2] it has apparently undergone much the same development
as the Greek St James anaphora just discussed, which it approaches
also in the order of address of its prayers. The prayer is addressed in
general to God.[3] To the trinitarian doxology, which here normally
also ends the prayers, there is in about half the cases a transition by
way of the christological Mediator theme.[4] The doxology itself then
always begins with μεθ᾽ οὗ εὐλογητὸς εἶ. In other prayers, this
christological link being missing, the ending is roughly: For blessed
art thou and to thee belongs the honour, to the Father and to the
Son and to the Holy Spirit now and always and for evermore.[5] This
applies particularly to the texts which belong to the mentioned
points of contact with the other Greek liturgies and probably to the
later layer.[6]

---

[1] Cf. Rücker p. xv.      [2] Br. 31 ff.; cf. Br. 555 ff. (cross-references).

[3] Exception: the first censing-prayer Br. 32, 3 (Δέσποτα κύριε ᾽Ιησοῦ Χριστέ).
Apart from this, the Christ-address is met only in the chant. Short blessing-texts
derive the blessing mostly from the 'Lord', Br. 32, 36 from Christ. Likewise the
petitions of the diaconal litanies, cf. Br. 40, 7. In the course of the Mass, again, a
silent prayer at the elevation of the Host (θεὲ λόγε: Br. 61, 25; cf. above, p. 32,
n.3) and one before the Communion (Br. 63, 62b) have the address to Christ.

[4] ἐν Χριστῷ ᾽Ιησοῦ τῷ κυρίῳ ἡμῶν (Br. 31, 12; 40, 11; 68, 3b)—χάριτι καὶ
οἰκτιρμοῖς καὶ φιλανθρωπίᾳ τοῦ μονογενοῦς σου υἱοῦ (Br. 33, 28; 36, 10 at the end
of a prayer common to the Greek St Mark liturgy, which there, however, does not
end christologically). Once, Christ occurs as Mediator of the praying Church at the
beginning, Br. 32, 16: Εὐεργέτα βασιλεῦ... πρόσδοξαι προσιοῦσάν σοι διὰ τοῦ
Χριστοῦ σου τὴν ἐκκλησίαν σου. The prayer, as εὐχὴ τῆς εἰσόδου, passed for a short
time also into the Byzantine liturgy (Barberini manuscript, Br. 312, 15b; cf., on
the other hand, the later texts Br. 368 and C. A. Swainson, *Greek Liturgies* 114,
where it is replaced by another); but there the very phrase διὰ τοῦ Χριστοῦ σου is
omitted.

[5] Br. 32, 31; cf. 35, 18; 40, 32 (here, however, at the beginning of the thanks for
the sending of Christ); 41, 20.

[6] Br. 38, 5 (Byz. 371, 35); 41, 25b (Byz. 309, 8a); 68, 11 (St Mark liturgy 143, 11).

A totally different picture appears, on the other hand, of the extra-anaphora ordo of the *Syrian-Jacobite* liturgy,[1] different, too, from the prayer-type of the Jacobite anaphoras themselves. Only in part is this explicable from the outset from the fact that the kernel of the Jacobite fore-anaphora goes back to indigenous Syrian practice (in contrast to the manner of Jerusalem and probably also of Antioch) and that for that reason the fore-anaphora is the end-product of an evolution stretching into the late Middle Ages.[2] Of the most important group of the texts here concerned, the so-called sedro prayers,[3] the Patriarch John I (631–48) is considered to be the author. These are Preface-type prayers sung by the priest, of uniform structure, always with an incensation, and they have taken the place of an older intercessory prayer. After the 'Prooemium' with the statement of the theme, the priest offers adoration and thanks to Christ, that they may rise to him like the sweet-smelling incense, in order then to pass on to the petitions: for gracious acceptance, for pardon and blessing for living and dead, for the intercession of the holy Mother of God and of the martyrs and confessors—or he even begins at once with these petitions. The address made to Christ sometimes merges into praise of the Father, Son and Holy Spirit, of the holy and glorious Trinity; this is its invariable end. In this, Christ is conceived exclusively as divine receiver of prayer and homage, as 'the creator and Lord of the universe', as receiver, even, of the sacrifice.[4] Of similar type, though not of the same regular structure, are the majority of the other extra-anaphora prayers. Nowhere in them is the theme of mediation through Christ expressed. Sometimes the address begins: 'Lord, (almighty) God', but in

[1] Fore-anaphora Br. 69–83; prayers at the breaking and at the Communion Br. 97–9; 102–4; at the end of the Mass Br. 106–10. In Ren. II, 1–11 still another Mass ordo is reproduced, which for the most part appertains to the Maronites (Rücker p. xv, n. 1). The order of address of its prayers is on the whole the same as in the text here discussed.

[2] According to A. Baumstark, *Geschichte der syrischen Literatur* 328, the extra-anaphora ordo is found as a whole only from the thirteenth century. Cf. *Die Messe im Morgenland* 42–4.

[3] Br. 71 f. (Prothesis); 74 ff. (before the lessons); 80 f. (after the same); 108 f. (end of the Mass). Cf. A. Baumstark, *Die Messe im Morgenland* 11 f.

[4] Br. 80, 25: 'Be we accounted worthy to *offer to* the high-priest of our confession, even Jesus Christ, a holy and righteous sacrifice'; cf. 73, 8; 74, 3 etc.

longer prayers it is later resumed as an address to Christ.[1] In such and similar cases, it is evident that Christ and God are simply made one. Thus especially the first Offertory prayer runs, without another address such as 'God' or 'O my Lord' having preceded it, 'O kind and gracious God . . . remove far from him (who honours Mary) temptations and punishments . . . through the prayers of thy Mother and of all thy saints'.[2] However, there also occur some prayers which are in form harmoniously constructed, addressing the 'Lord' in the beginning and in the final portion solemnly expanding this address either as: '. . . Creator of the universe, to whom worship is due from all, Father and Son and Holy Spirit, for ever',[3] or more shortly, perhaps derived from it: '. . . To the praise of thy holy name, O our Lord and our God, for ever'.[4]

---

[1] Br. 72, 26; 78, 2.

[2] Br. 74, 1. Similarly Br. 83, 7: 'O holy and glorious *Trinity*, receive this offering from my weak and sinful hands. O *God*, in thy mercy make rest and good remembrance on thine holy and heavenly altar for *thy mother*. . . .' Obviously, the conceptions of God and Christ on occasion become more clearly distinct again in didactic meditative passages, e.g., Br. 73, 8. 21; 106, 10; but this is not so much the case when we consider the structure of the prayer itself. The contrast of Father and Son is at its clearest in a second breaking prayer 'of mar Jacob the doctor', Br. 98.

[3] Br. 69, 5; cf. 72, 12.    [4] Br. 70; cf. 106 ff.

# V

# EAST SYRIAN LITURGY

When the teaching of Nestorius was condemned at the Council of Ephesus in 431 and some time later banned from the Roman Empire, its adherents gained admission to the Persian Empire of the Sassanids, where they found protection. Here then arose the Nestorian schismatic Church with its own liturgy, which in succeeding years was little influenced from outside, and whose basic material, leaving aside ancient variations due to locality, probably represents the common Syrian heritage from an older period which in West Syria was largely displaced by the liturgy of Jerusalem. To the East Syrian liturgical sphere of influence belong today, beside the Nestorians of Mesopotamia, Uniate Chaldeans and St Thomas Christians of the Malabar Coast of India also. However, that which distinguishes the two latter bodies from the Nestorians does not demand any special treatment here.

The East Syrian main formulary is the 'liturgy of the Apostles', (i.e. of the legendary proto-missionaries of that eastern region, Addai and Mari).[1] Beside the anaphora of the Apostles built into it, two more are still in use: the anaphora of Theodore of Mopsuestia and that of Nestorius.[2] Fragments of a fourth formulary are extant,

---

[1] English in Br. 247–305.
[2] Latin in Ren. II, 616–21, and 626–38 respectively. On the origin of the anaphora of Nestorius see A. Baumstark, *Liturgie Comparée*[3] (Chevetogne, 1953) 63.

inscribed in the sixth century on two parchments, which at the same time provide the oldest direct knowledge of East Syrian liturgy.[1] For the rest, older texts for the East Syrian rite are either inaccessible or not extant.

In spite of their, as it seems, very different origins, these four anaphoras, as they are at present, on the whole show *common characteristics*. The prayer is directed almost throughout to (the triune) God. This is true without exception for the anaphora of the two parchments and for that of Theodore; also for that of Nestorius if we consider only the older core (from the Preface to the end of the Canon portion);[2] and finally for the same section of the Apostles' anaphora, with one exception.[3] Also, all of them, like the West Syrian liturgy, attach to the *sanctus* a passage of praise of the three divine Persons and then pass to a grateful, contemplative survey of the history of salvation, in which are interwoven for preference Pauline themes and expressions in praise of the work of redemption. 'Accessit ad passionem [et mortem . . . ut] passione sua liberaret nos . . . [et per] ascensionem suam gloriosam [ad regnum] supernum elevaret nos gloriose'.[4] Also Jesus' sacrificial death as such is interwoven here in the anaphora of Theodore: 'Eam quoque (sc. dispensationem) complevisti . . . per Filium tuum . . . ipseque est caput ecclesiae et primogenitus ex mortuis . . . ipse per Spiritum aeternum seipsum obtulit immaculatum Deo et sanctificavit nos per oblationem corporis sui semel factam'.[5] In addition, not only in two cases does the anamnesis assemble once again the facts of salvation;[6] also, in the course of the prayers this mediatory position of Christ occasionally appears, thus, e.g., when the Lord's words are quoted in the form: 'Thou hast said to us through thy Son.'[7]

---

[1] Latin in Br. 511–8. Critical edition of the text with corrected translation by R. H. Connolly, *Oriens christ.*[2] 12 (1922/24) 99–128.

[2] Cf. A. Baumstark, 'Die Chrysostomosliturgie und die syrische Liturgie des Nestorios': Χρυσοστομικά 771–857.

[3] Br. 283, 1–288, 7. Only Br. 285, 5 has a phrase (probably only Nestorian) which presupposes the address to Christ: '(we give thanks to thee, O my Lord . . . for that thou hast given us great grace past recompense in that) thou didst *put on* our manhood, that thou mightest quicken it by thy godhead'.

[4] *Oriens christ.*[2] 12, 112 f.; cf. Br. 515, 14–20.      [5] Ren. II, 618.

[6] Ren. II, 619. 630.      [7] Ren. II, 631. 633 f. Cf. also Br. 253, 6; 266, 8.

It is all the more remarkable that the theme of Christ as Mediator of the prayer strictly understood does not appear at all. The clearest passage occurs characteristically every time at the end of the ancient Canon part of the Mass, i.e. within the oldest layer. In the anaphora of Theodore: 'Dignos etiam fac nos omnes per gratiam Domini nostri Jesu Christi, ut cum omnibus illis qui placuerunt voluntati tuae . . . laetemur in regno coelorum . . . et hic et illic . . . laudabimus Patrem et Filium et Spiritum Sanctum nunc et semper et in saecula saeculorum.'[1] In that of Nestorius, the same petition, with the final words: 'per gratiam et miserationes Unigeniti tui, cum quo tibi . . . exaltatio cum Spiritu tuo. . .'.[2] Similarly, or else from the theme of sanctification through the Eucharist, the fragment seems to evolve its trinitarian doxology.[3] Lastly, the Apostles' anaphora joins to the consecration of the gifts besought in the epiklesis the promise of never-ending thanks 'in thy Church redeemed by the precious blood of thy Christ'.[4] As is evident, Christ appears in none of these cases as the Mediator who himself offers prayer and homage to God; rather, his grace here only creates the possibility that *we* may praise God worthily. This last theme is also found in another form elsewhere.[5] The other doxologies occurring in the area mentioned praise the name of God or the three divine Persons, without further mention of Christ.

It only remains to complete these remarks for the later layers of the *Nestorius anaphora*, in which the kernel, taken over, as is now generally

[1] Ren. II, 621. In this anaphora the first prayer also has a similar ending: 'gratiam et miserationes inveniamus coram te cum omnibus illis qui a saeculo placuerunt tibi, per gratiam et miserationes Unigeniti tui, et tibi ipsique et Spiritui Sancto . . . adorationem referamus [referemus?] nunc et semper.' Ren. II, 616.

[2] Ren. II, 634; cf. A. Baumstark, *Die konstantinopolitanische Messliturgie vor dem 9. Jahrhundert*, p. 14, 42; the same author, Χρυσοστομικά 843.

[3] Br. 517, 39.          [4] Br. 288, 1.

[5] Ren. II, 627 (Nestorius anaphora, Preface): 'Pater . . . Jesu Christi spei nostrae . . . per quem accepimus cognitionem Spiritus Sancti . . . Ipse est per quem naturae omnes rationabiles . . . sanctificantur et perficiuntur. Et tibi Filioque tuo unigenito et Spiritui tuo Sancto laudes perpetuas offerunt.' Similarly, admittedly without naming Christ as revealer of the Holy Spirit, Ren. II, 617 (Theodore anaphora, Preface): 'qui per Filium tuum . . . constituisti coelum et terram et omnia quae in eis sunt. Et per Spiritum Sanctum . . . omnes naturae rationales . . . sanctificantur dignaeque fiunt referendi laudem divinitati tuae adorandae.'

assumed, in the fifth century from Constantinople, became enveloped; and in like manner for the *Apostles' anaphora*. Here the prayer-style is less uniform. In both, the Pater noster is introduced by a prayer to Christ with the request: 'Praesta nobis Domine ut cum fiducia, quae a te sit, pronuntiemus coram te orationem istam . . . quam docuit os tuum vivificum.'[1] Also, annexed Communion prayers are directed to him. Here the Christ-address is inserted harmoniously, whereas we find in the prayer of blessing that follows in the Nestorius anaphora Christ and God again treated as one: 'Ipse sit vobiscum et inter vos, sicut fuit cum Joseph in terra Aegypti, parcatque . . . sicut pepercit delictis David . . . dignosque vos efficiat Dominus et Deus noster illa promissione non fallaci quam in evangelio suo pronuntiavit discipulis suis dicens: . . . quicumque manducat corpus meum . . . in me manet . . . simusque obsignati et custoditi signo vivo crucis . . . per orationem Dominae Mariae beatae at per orationem omnium sanctorum.'[2] The intercession of the saints also closes in the same way as other prayers of this type.[3] In the Apostles' anaphora, prayers addressed to Christ are also interspersed elsewhere; but they often have this address only as if by chance, for then as occasion serves it is resumed as an address to the triune God.[4]

The attitude is similar in the *fore-anaphora*.[5] Also, the diaconal intercessory prayer to the 'Lord' gains here on occasion the more precise limitation to Christ.[6] He appears a few times as receiver of the sacrifice.[7] But as basic type there stands out here more clearly

[1] Ren. II, 634; Br. 295, 21.    [2] Ren. II, 635.

[3] Ren. II, 638; cf. Br. 250, 42; 264, 34; 304, 17.

[4] Br. 288, 13. 34; 290, 5b; 292, 43b. Br. 304 f. four Communion prayers follow the pattern: '(For that we have received of thy body openly, let thy power dwell in us secretly . . .), O Christ the hope of our nature: Lord of all, Father and Son and Holy Ghost, for ever.' The later origin of the majority of these prayers is clear from their omission from a liturgical commentary ascribed to *Narsai* (end of the fifth century); the psalm *Miserere* with the inserted refrain 'O king Christ, have mercy upon me', or 'glory to thy name' before the breaking is missing again in one ascribed to *George of Arbela* (tenth century). Cf. R. H. Connolly, *The Liturgical Homilies of Narsai* 75–7.

[5] Br. 247–82. A large part is here taken up by the diptychs and by poetical passages. These mostly praise the Redeemer; cf. A Rücker, 'Die wechselnden Gesangstücke der ostsyrischen Messe': JL 1 (1921) 61–96.

[6] Br. 263, 18. The earlier style of address of this prayer (to God) is shown in Br. 262, 33.

[7] Br. 268, 4b; 272, 35; 273, 34.

the prayer to the 'Lord our God', closing with an acclamation of praise to Father, Son and Holy Spirit. So runs even the very first prayer:

> Grant us, our Lord and our God, to advance in good works, which are pleasing to thy majesty, so that our pleasure may be in thy law and we may abide therein day and night, Lord of the universe, Father and Son and Holy Spirit, for ever.[1]

In this prayer-pattern, not only is the theme of Christ's Mediatorship entirely left out, but also the question of to whom the prayer is directed is by-passed. Christ appears simply as second Person of the Godhead together with Father and Holy Spirit. And at bottom, also, in most of the prayers which are directed to him, only this his divinity is in mind. Although the Mass from the outset appears as a commemoration of his redeeming death, and although his Mediatorship is mentioned now and again,[2] and it is even occasionally stated in chants that the Word of the Father has 'put on' human nature and has returned to heaven, 'in order to exercise his priestly office for the human race'[3]—yet this his priestly position nowhere makes itself felt in the prayer. But there are at least signs that an older custom has used more often a kind of χάριτι formula, as found in the anaphoras.[4] For here there is inserted into the prayer more often than in the liturgies discussed hitherto the phrase: 'In thy grace and mercy'—an obsecratory phrase similar to the χάριτι formula, but which could be used also in prayers addressed to Christ.[5]

---

[1] Br. 247, 5; cf. 249 f., 253 f., 266, 282, 289. Prayers of this type also govern the Nestorian baptismal liturgy, which was re-ordered by Ischojabh III (seventh century): G. Diettrich, *Die nestorianische Taufliturgie* (Giessen, 1903). Blessing texts mostly end analogously to the baptismal form: 'In the name of the Father and of the Son and of the Holy Spirit'. Br. 248, 251 f., etc.

[2] Br. 249, 251 f., 267 f.; and 266, 8; 271, 41b.    [3] Br. 260, 11; 261, 9.

[4] Br. 272, 3: also outside the anaphora an offering prayer implores gracious acceptance 'by the grace of Christ'.

[5] E.g. Br. 266, 32; 267, 13; 268, 9b; 275, 29; cf. Ren. II, 632, 636 f.

# VI
# LITURGIES OF THE BYZANTINE REGION

## 1. BYZANTINE LITURGIES

While older local liturgies of episcopal cities of Asia Minor and Greece vanished without trace, the liturgy of the new capital of the East Roman Empire rapidly gained in importance. Roughly from the second half of the seventh century,[1] it began to displace the former—in general, all foreign—liturgies, at first within the frontiers of the then Byzantine Empire. In the end it extended its sway over all the countries of the Greek Orthodox Church and became, from the ninth century, at first in the Old Slavonic tongue, the liturgy of the greater part of the Slav peoples.

The liturgical prayer-collection for the Mass consists—apart from the Missa Præsanctificatorum, ascribed to Pope Gregory I—of two formularies, each at first drawn on for the whole Mass, anaphora and fore-anaphora. The two were the liturgies of St John Chrysostom and of St Basil respectively, which were used alternately on fixed days. While the latter is now attributed with certainty to the celebrated Cappadocian doctor, there can only be probability in ascribing the former to Chrysostom as author or editor.[2] The oldest

[1] A. Baumstark, *Die Messe im Morgenland* 58.
[2] On the liturgy of St Basil see H. Engberding, *Das eucharistische Hochgebet der Basileos-liturgie* (Munster, 1931), and B. Capelle *Un Témoin Archaïque de la Liturgie*

manuscripts giving the full text of either Byzantine formulary take us back to the beginning of the ninth century.[1] It was only the later development that added a common stock of further prayers. These belong chiefly to the ever-expanding Fore-Mass—up to the beginning of the Mass of the Faithful.

The *liturgy of St Basil* of the ninth century, which by that time begins with prayers at the prothesis and enarxis, has only four shortish prayers—not belonging to the ancient core of the liturgy—which are addressed to Christ: 1. The last of the 'antiphon prayers'. 2. A prayer recited silently by the priest during the singing of the Cherubic hymn at the Great Entrance (with the offerings). 3. The likewise silently spoken prayer 'at the Elevation of the Bread'. 4. A second thanksgiving prayer in the sacristy.[2]

In the rest of the liturgy it is always God who is addressed, usually with the formula: Κύριε ὁ θεὸς ἡμῶν.[3] The normal ending is the doxology addressed to the three divine Persons, e.g. 'for to thee belongs all glory, honour and worship, to the Father and to the Son

---

*copte de St Basile* (Louvain, 1960). It is now clear that St Basil in the Byzantine liturgy of St Basil has adapted an older form of the text, which is preserved in essentials in the Egyptian St Basil anaphora.

Information on the origin of the East Syrian Nestorius anaphora and the Byzantine Chrysostom liturgy and their mutual relation is now to be found in A. Baumstark, *Liturgie Comparée*[3] (Chevetogne, 1953), 63. He affirms that Nestorius found the Chrysostom liturgy and enlarged it to form the Nestorius anaphora. Cf. H.-J. Schultz, *Die byzantinische Liturgie* (Freiburg, 1964), 18–28.

[1] Br. 309–44 gives first the text of both liturgies in parallel after the so-called Barberini manuscript (ca. 800); he gives the modern text of both according to the Orthodox Εὐχολόγιον τὸ μέγα (Venice, 1869).

[2] Br. 311, 22; 318, 4; 341, 7; 344, 22. This *last* prayer arose from a later addition due to private devotion. Also the *second* is more of a private nature; its later origin, besides, is suggested by the Emperor Justin II (565–78) being named as author of the hymn sung at the same time. (Cf. A. Baumstark, *Die Messe im Morgenland* 113). The prayer itself, Οὐδεὶς ἄξιος, to all appearances derives from the Egyptian Gregory anaphora; see above, p. 41, n. 3. Of a private character, also, is the *third* prayer, at the elevation of the Host, which likewise appears to be taken from the Gregory anaphora (Ren. I, 120). In Byzantium, it already belongs to those texts which are common to the Basil and Chrysostom liturgies, and is lacking, moreover, in several old manuscripts (Χρυσοστομικά 346). Probably still later are the *'antiphons'* with their prayers; P. de Meester allots them to the eighth century. (Cf. Χρυσοστομικά 320, 357/8).

[3] In the Preface, the Father's name also occurs: Br. 321, 28 Ὁ ὢν δέσποτα κύριε θεὲ πατὴρ παντοκράτωρ; Br. 322, 25 πατὴρ τοῦ . . . Χριστοῦ.

and to the Holy Ghost, now and for ever and ever'; or, 'for thou art a merciful and bounteous God, and to thee we offer praise, to the Father and to the Son and to the Holy Ghost. . .'.[1]

Over against these dozen or more pure trinitarian endings, there are two cases only, in which the christological idea of mediation— at least in a weakened form ($\chi\acute{a}\rho\iota\tau\iota$)—forms a transition to the doxology: in the Offertory prayer, probably of foreign origin, after the Great Entrance; and in the prayer of Blessing before the Communion.[2] The doxology itself follows with the simple $\mu\epsilon\theta$' $o\tilde{v}$ formula; thus, in the prayer of Blessing: '. . . make us worthy to partake without blame of these pure and life-giving mysteries, for the remission of sins, for the imparting of the Holy Spirit, through the grace ($\chi\acute{a}\rho\iota\tau\iota$) and mercy and bounty of thy only-begotten Son, with whom ($\mu\epsilon\theta$' $o\tilde{v}$) thou art praised, together with thy all-holy and good and lifegiving Spirit. . .'.[3] The idea that only through Christ are we empowered to praise God worthily finds an echo in the Preface, which primarily glorifies God's creative power and his triune nature: '. . . Right . . . is it, to praise thee . . . and to offer thee this spiritual service . . . Lord . . . Father of our Lord Jesus Christ . . . who is the image of thy goodness . . . the true Light, through whom the Holy Ghost appeared . . . the source of sanctification, through whom ($\pi\alpha\rho$' $o\tilde{v}$) every intelligent creature . . . pays thee homage and raises to thee endless worship. . .'.[4] To the *sanctus*, likewise, is

---

[1] Br. 310, 28; and 315, 6 etc. One notices how the address differs from the majority of the trinitarian doxologies discussed hitherto, which have: 'To thee (the *Father*) belongs honour with *thy* Son and the Holy Spirit.'

[2] Br. 320, 18; 341, 2—both cases common with the Chrysostom liturgy. In the first case, the borrowing from the Greek St James liturgy is fairly clear; see Br. 47, 16b and 49, 6, where the ending of the prayer shows only a stylistic difference: $\grave{\epsilon}\lambda\acute{\epsilon}\epsilon\iota$ instead of the $\chi\acute{a}\rho\iota\tau\iota$ more usual also in the St James liturgy.

[3] Akin to this again is a short text at the taking of the throne at the beginning of the reading, likewise common with the Chrysostom liturgy, Br. 314, 17: Give the people peace $\tau\hat{\eta}$ $\delta\upsilon\nu\acute{a}\mu\epsilon\iota$ $\tauο\hat{\upsilon}$ $\acute{a}\gamma\acute{\iota}ο\upsilon$ $\sigmaο\upsilon$ $\pi\nu\epsilon\acute{\upsilon}\mu\alpha\tauο\varsigma$ $\delta\iota\grave{a}$ $\tauο\hat{\upsilon}$ $\tau\acute{\upsilon}\piο\upsilon$ $\tauο\hat{\upsilon}$ $\tau\iota\mu\acute{\iota}ο\upsilon$ $\sigma\tau\alpha\upsilonρο\hat{\upsilon}$ $\tauο\hat{\upsilon}$ $\muο\nuο\gamma\epsilon\nuο\hat{\upsilon}\varsigma$ $\sigmaο\upsilon$ $\upsilonἱο\hat{\upsilon}$, $\mu\epsilon\theta$' $ο\tilde{\upsilon}$.

[4] Br. 322 f; the second 'through whom' ($\pi\alpha\rho$' $ο\tilde{\upsilon}$) can be referred to the Holy Spirit ($\pi\nu\epsilon\hat{\upsilon}\mu\alpha$ $\tau\grave{o}$ $\acute{a}\gamma\iotaο\nu$) as readily as to Christ; in the first case, Christ is the mediate source. Somewhat more strongly than in other oriental liturgies, a kind of Mediator position of the Holy Spirit finds expression in various passages of the Byzantine liturgy, in that God through him sanctifies and strengthens, or in that through him one becomes capable of the service of God. In this connexion, the following passages

attached, as in the Syrian anaphora, a lengthy meditation on the divine economy of salvation, in which the redeeming office of our Lord is splendidly set forth in the words of St Paul.

The *Chrysostom liturgy* of the ninth century runs, in general, parallel with the Basilian formulary, and resembles it throughout in the theological structure of the prayers, which are merely much shorter, and here and there entirely lacking. Thus there is no Οὐδεὶς ἄξιος directed to Christ at the Cherubic hymn, nor the 'antiphons' with their prayer to Christ. But instead the first prayer of all, at the prothesis, is addressed to Christ; it begins: 'Lord our God, who hast offered thyself as a spotless Lamb for the life of the world, look down upon us.' The ending is that of the parallel prayer (addressed to God) of the Basilian liturgy: 'For hallowed and praised is thy revered and glorious name, of the Father and of the Son and of the Holy Ghost.'[1] Moreover, the χάριτι ending appears, not only in places parallel with the Basilian liturgy, but also where the sister liturgy has a pure trinitarian ending, viz. in a prayer derived from the Greek liturgy of St James.[2]

In *either* liturgy, therefore, only one passage shows a christological ending with neither the ending nor its prayer being of evidently foreign origin. The passage is the same in both liturgies, viz. that at the end of the prayer of Blessing before the Communion: χάριτι καὶ οἰκτιρμοῖς καὶ φιλανθρωπίᾳ τοῦ μονογενοῦς σου υἱοῦ, μεθ᾽οὗ εὐλογητὸς εἶ σὺν τῷ παναγίῳ ... πνεύματι.[3] Is this passage also to

from the Basil liturgy, apart from the epiklesis, Br. 329, 29, are relevant: Br. 317, 17; 336, 20; 337, 12; 341, 20. Further passages occur with the prayers in question also in other liturgies: Br. 316, 18; 319, 13. 30.

[1] Br. 309 f. Since this prayer makes it known only from the content that it is addressed to Christ, while the address itself runs, as elsewhere, κύριε ὁ θεὸς ἡμῶν, one could say, strictly speaking, as also for the majority of the other prayers of both liturgies, that they are simply addressed indifferently to the 'Lord', without making it clear whether Christ or the triune God is meant. In fact, Christ and his work, outside the restricted area around the institution account, is mentioned relatively seldom.

[2] Br. 312, 26 (at the Little Entrance), and 32, 31 (enarxis of the St James liturgy; see above, p. 66, n.4), where is a somewhat different, but also christological ending. The χάριτι formula may also in this case have been taken, with the prayer concerned, from there.

[3] Br. 341, 2.

4

be ascribed to a foreign source? This does not seem to be the case. The prayer of Blessing before the Communion is an ancient institution in the East, appearing even in the *Euchologium* of Serapion, and in Byzantium belonging to fifth-century or older material.[1]

From this state in the ninth century, the Byzantine liturgy in both its formularies underwent a further vigorous development, especially up to the fourteenth century. This consisted mainly in the elaboration of the preparatory rites.[2] Together with this went a multiplication of the prayers and accompanying texts.[3]

With this growth in liturgical texts, is there also a change, *pari passu*, in the way the prayers are addressed? On the whole, the ancient heritage is faithfully preserved. The one place in the Chrysostom liturgy in which it surpasses its sister liturgy by having a prayer with the christological ending (χάριτι) has disappeared,[4] the parallel prayer in the Basilian being used for both formularies. This ends in the usual way: ὅτι πρέπει σοι πᾶσα δόξα ... τῷ πατρὶ καὶ τῷ υἱῷ καὶ τῷ ἁγίῳ πνεύματι. Hence each formulary retains two prayers with the χάριτι ending: the one of older stock before the Communion, and the Offertory prayer, which is probably from Syria;[5] and in these there is reference merely to the compassion of his Only-begotten, for the sake of which God will hear us. Nowhere is the appeal simply through Christ, for even in this case the attached doxology takes only the μεθ' οὗ form.

The trinitarian theme of adoration before the majesty of the

---

[1] *Χρυσοστομικά* 358–9. It would also be conceivable that only the χάριτι ending here belongs to the oldest kernel and formerly closed the Canon portion. The Communion blessing prayer could have grown out of the petition for the fruits of the Communion and have taken with it the old doxology, whereupon the remaining section of the Canon now ending with the intercessory prayer would have gained the present doxology: καὶ δὸς ἡμῖν ἐν ἑνὶ στόματι ... ἀνυμνεῖν τὸ ... ὄνομά σου τοῦ πατρὸς καὶ τοῦ υἱοῦ καὶ τοῦ ἁγίου πνεύματος. Br. 337, 20. Cf. on duplication of doxologies in this part of the Mass, F. Probst, *Liturgie des vierten Jahrhunderts* 198, 264 f.

[2] In this development, the symbolical representation of the passion of Christ in the preparation of the sacrificial gifts plays a large part: Br. 356 f. (slaughter of the lamb), 379 (burial, after the Great Entrance with the sacrificial gifts), 393 (division of the lamb).

[3] A summary of the gradual growth is given in the table in *Χρυσοστομικά* 358/9.

[4] Br. 368, 6; cf. 312, 15.      [5] Br. 382, 13 and 392, 25.

triune God, which directly terminates most of the prayers—except for the two above—is therefore preserved in the older prayers as a fundamental chord. It comes out, indeed, rather stronger than before. Thus the response to the invitation to offer thanks before the Preface is no longer ἄξιον καὶ δίκαιον, but has been enlarged to the expository ἄξιον καὶ δίκαιόν ἐστιν προσκυνεῖν πατέρα, υἱὸν καὶ ἅγιον πνεῦμα, τριάδα ὁμοούσιον καὶ ἀχώριστον.[1] On the other hand, the new growth of prayers and prayer-texts shows a preference for addressing 'Christ our God', the Son of God: 'Incense we offer thee, Christ our God, for a pleasing, spiritual odour of sweetness. Receive it on thy heavenly altar above, and send down on us in return the grace of thy all-holy Spirit.'[2] Other prayers leave it undecided whether they are addressed to Christ or to the triune God.[3] But in this later form of the Byzantine liturgy it is quite clear that, in general, little stress is laid on differences of address, and the occasional prayer addressed to Christ is not felt to interrupt the flow of prayers in any way. In praying to Christ one meets above all 'our God'. The change to another prayer, perhaps with the old address 'Lord our God' and the ending 'to thee we send praise on high, to the Father and to the Son and to the Holy Ghost', is not switching the address, but merely broadening it from the Second Person to the three Persons of the Godhead.[4]

If, then, Christ as Mediator is hardly considered, there appears all the more in the corresponding passages in older as in newer prayers,

---

[1] Br. 384, 20 compared with 321, 26. But the enlargement is still missing even today in some editions; see A. v. Maltzew, *Liturgikon* 122 f.n. Cf. also Br. 382, 22 as against 320, 29.

[2] Br. 359, 34.—Cf. up to the beginning of the lessons Br. 354, 17; 356, 19; 360, 14; 361, 7, 22. Further, the prayer before the Gospel Br. 371, 36 (the same in older form in the Greek St James anaphora Br. 38, 6 with the address to God the Father). Two Communion prayers Br. 394, 17 and 398, 12. In addition, there are changing poetical passages, as Br. 364, 365, 368 f. Also the diaconal litanies end with the summons: τὴν ζωὴν ἡμῶν Χριστῷ τῷ θεῷ παραθώμεθα, Br. 363, 24; 365, 6; 391, 19.

[3] E.g. Br. 360, 20; 370, 30; 395, 33.

[4] In the context of prayers from an earlier period, on the contrary, the contrast between God and Christ appears again in a clear light, even outside the above-mentioned salvation history parts; thus there is mention of the 'body and blood of thy Christ', or of the 'judgment-seat of thy Christ', Br. 338 f.; 343 etc.

various other obsecratory phrases, e.g.: ἕνεκεν τοῦ ὀνόματός σου,[1] διὰ τῆς σῆς εὐσπλαγχνίας,[2] τῇ σῇ χάριτι,[3] ὅτι ἀγαθὸς καὶ φιλάνθρωπος θεὸς ὑπάρχεις,[4] κατὰ τὸ πλοῦτος τοῦ ἐλέους σου[5]— echoing the East Syrian liturgy, and also the prayers and psalms of the Old Testament, whose austere character is likewise reflected in the prayers of this liturgy.

The intercession of the saints, besides, comes more to the fore. In the liturgy of the ninth century the prayer of the trisagion runs into the trinitarian doxology: πρεσβείαις τῆς ἁγίας θεοτόκου καὶ πάντων τῶν ἁγίων τῶν ἀπ' αἰῶνός σοι εὐαρεστησάντων (ὅτι ἅγιος εἶ...).[6] In the developments since that period, this or a like-meaning phrase recurs more frequently.[7] At the beginning and at the end of the liturgy, moreover, appear prayers addressed respectively to the Mother of God and St John Chrysostom.[8]

The Byzantine *liturgy of the Presanctified* confirms the picture already gained. The ninth century[9] manuscript has all the priest's prayers directed simply to God. Furthermore, in the wording of the prayers we often find the contrast—from salvation history—between God and 'thy Christ'. Of the eight prayers ending with a trinitarian doxology, only two show a christological transition.[10] The present text[11] again shows a marked expansion of the preparatory part, in which, nevertheless, old elements appear: besides the chant Φῶς ἱλαρόν, a further prayer with the χάριτι conclusion.[12] Other enlarged prayers with trinitarian doxologies beg now, in four passages,

---

[1] Br. 353, 22.    [2] Br. 359, 9; cf. 364, 25.    [3] Br. 363, 19; cf. 398, 18.
[4] Br. 366, 25; 374, 4; cf. 361, 15.    [5] Br. 373, 8; cf. 376, 5.

[6] Br. 314, 5 (370, 9). In the Chrysostom formulary, the Communion prayer of thanks Br. 342, 25 and the εὐχὴ ὀπισθάμβωνος (Br. 344, 9), introduced in the eighth to ninth century, still had a like ending.

[7] Thus, in the beginning, at the allocation of the separate particles to the commemoration of different saints (Br. 357, 28; 358, 35), in the repeated formula of absolution (Br. 361, 12 = 398, 29), and at the blessing of the deacon (Br. 372,14). The refrain of the first antiphon runs (Br. 364): Ταῖς πρεσβείαις τῆς θεοτόκου, σῶτερ, σῶσον ἡμᾶς. Cf. also the ending of the repeated diaconal litany, Br. 363, 21 etc.

[8] Br. 354, 13. 23; 399, 18. 26. Cf. 388, 8a.    [9] Br. 345–52.

[10] Br. 348, 16: κατὰ τὴν δωρεὰν τοῦ Χριστοῦ σου, μεθ' οὗ. Br. 350, 24: χάριτι... τοῦ μονογενοῦς σου υἱοῦ, μεθ' οὗ.

[11] German in A. v. Maltzew, *Liturgikon* 163–94.    [12] P. 167.

to be heard 'through the intercession of the holy Mother of God and all thy saints'.[1]

At the same time, certain prayers or declamations, apart from choral passages,[2] are now addressed to 'Christ our God'. Others apply to the Apostles for their intercession, but above all to the all-holy Mother of God, to whom also the first greeting is dedicated.[3]

## 2. ARMENIAN LITURGY

The Armenian liturgy stands in the same relation—as daughter—to the Byzantine as the Ethiopian to the Alexandrian. The structure of the Mass and many similarly worded texts of the extra-anaphora ordo show the relationship. In addition, the Armenian Mass liturgy presents East Syrian elements, which go back to the period of the christianization of Armenia; as well as Roman elements, which have been preserved, from a period of rapprochement in the later middle ages (around the fourteenth century), also in the non-Uniate (Mono-physite) liturgy. But indigenous material also exists in plenty, and only this need be discussed in detail. To it belongs above all the normal anaphora, named after St Athanasius. As the oldest manuscripts go back only to the fourteenth century, when the evolution was almost complete, from this angle an earlier stage is beyond our reach.[4] However, there exists in accessible form a commentary by *Chosroë the Great* (about 950) on the prayers of the Mass, in which the prayers in use at the time from the Gospel onwards are for the most part quoted verbatim.[5]

If we examine the Armenian Mass, in the first place to the extent it is treated by Chosroë, on the order of address in its prayers, we find: from the Great Entrance onwards right through the anaphora to the Communion inclusive, the prayers are addressed to God, though the address itself takes many different forms. Also, the

---

[1] Pp. 167, 171; cf. 168, 176 f.
[2] Pp. 165, 175, 177, 189, 194.    [3] Pp. 177, 164.
[4] Br. 412–57 gives in English translation the text of the non-Uniate Armenians according to printed editions of the nineteenth century.
[5] P. Vetter, *Chosroae Magni episcopi monophysitici explicatio precum missae* (Freiburg, 1880). Br. 428–55, 15 corresponds to the text cited by Chosroë.

Father's name occurs several times. Christ is occasionally mentioned in his role as Saviour and Mediator, even apart from the attractive mediations on salvation history in the Eucharistic prayer before and after the *sanctus*. Yet there is scarce a passage to be seen in which he is thought of as Mediator of the prayer.

The first prayer to be considered, a kind of Offertory prayer, closes with χάριτι formula and trinitarian doxology.[1] A like ending is given to the prayer of blessing before the Communion, i.e. at the point where the Byzantine liturgy has probably its sole indigenous χάριτι ending. It runs: 'Qui fons es vitae et caput misericordiae, miserere conventui isti, qui inclinatus adorat divinitatem tuam . . . imprime animis eorum figuram formae corporis ad hereditatem et sortitionem futurorum bonorum per Christum Jesum Dominum nostrum, cum quo te Spiritum Sanctum et Patrem omnipotentem decent gloria . . .'; the 'per' may refer to Christ as Mediator of the benefits.[2]

In the intercessory prayer after the epiklesis the sacrifice is thrice quoted as title for a hearing: '*Per hoc* (sc. sacrificium) concede caritatem, firmitatem, exoptatam pacem ecclesiae tuae sanctae . . .; *per hoc* concede aeris temperiem . . .; *per hoc* dona requiem omnibus iam in Christo defunctis'.[3]

On the periphery of the Mass liturgy discussed by Chosroë there also occur, however, prayers addressed to Christ, viz. two at the

---

[1] Manducantibus nobis medicinam remissionis peccatorum dona panem hunc et vinum, *per gratiam* et caritatem Domini nostri et Redemptoris Jesu Christi, quocum te Patrem omnipotentem una cum vivificante et liberante Spiritu Sancto, decent gloria . . . (Vetter 16 f., Br. 432 f.).

[2] Vetter 50 f. *Chosroë* understands the *per* in the sense of 'gratia eius adiuvante'. In the doxology, the Holy Spirit (with the Father) appears here to be addressed. Probably the address 'fountain of life' (cf. *vivificans* in the Credo) first occasioned this. The modern text of Br. 446, 32 has even kept in the address: '*Holy Ghost*, which art the fountain of life.'

[3] Vetter 37 f. = Br. 439, 30, 36; 440, 1—intercessory prayer after the epiklesis. In like manner, the deacon then prays with the people (Vetter 47; Br. 43). Cf. also the manner of expression of *St Cyril of Jerusalem*, which he employs precisely for intercessory prayer after the epiklesis: Εἶτα . . . ἐπὶ τῆς θυσίας ἐκείνης τοῦ ἱλασμοῦ παρακαλοῦμεν τὸν θεὸν ὑπὲρ κοινῆς τῶν ἐκκλησιῶν εἰρήνης, ὑπὲρ τῆς τοῦ κόσμου εὐσταθείας; thereupon also the commemoration of the dead is mentioned. The close relationship of the two-sided intercessory prayer leaps to the eye. *Cat. myst.* 5, 8 (Br. 466, 4).

beginning before the Great Entrance.[1] The wording of the second shows that there the address to Christ cannot be original: 'Pace tua, Christe, redemptor noster, quae cogitationes omnes exsuperant et verba, firma nos . . . conjunge nos cum vere te adorantibus *qui in spiritu et veritate te adorant*, quoniam sanctissimam Trinitatem decet gloria. . .'.[2] Also a prayer of thanks after the Communion is directed to Christ,[3] who is invoked as the Good Shepherd.

If with this picture we compare the *present* Armenian liturgy, we find in the latter a great increase in the number of prayers to Christ, and that indeed already within the anaphora, or the Mass discussed by Chosroë. Two prayers have entered here from Byzantium.[4] Others are inserted before the epiklesis, before the Communion and at the end.[5] In addition, there are choral insertions. Christ is addressed in his prayer especially by the deacon. While the priest quietly recites the Preface addressed to the almighty Father, in many places on feast-days the deacon recites another Preface out loud, which carries over its Christ-address to the *sanctus*: 'We thank thee, Christ, for the true redemption always and everywhere, through which the hosts praise thy marvellous (Resurrection), the seraphim tremble . . . and they cry with sweet voices and say. . .'. In words of like meaning, already at the Great Entrance, deacon and choir had welcomed the sacrificial gifts with a kind of Preface and the *sanctus*.[6] Here therefore the prayer of the old type has, superimposed on it, a later layer of the prayer addressed to Christ. At the prayer of the faithful in Chosroë the invitation had run: . . . 'Rogemus Deum Patrem et Dominum omnipotentem.' Here also

---

[1] Vetter 4–7; Br. 428 ff.

[2] Cf. Phil. 4: 7 (pax *Dei* quae); John 4: 23 (*Patrem*). Chosroë observes the difference of the address here no more than elsewhere, but in this passage he appears to presuppose a later alteration of the text. Vetter 7.

[3] Vetter 56: Christe redemptor noster; Br. 454, 22 the address in the same prayer runs as in Byzantium: 'O Christ, our God.'

[4] Br. 430 f.: Οὐδεὶς ἄξιος at the Great Entrance; 448, 6 at the elevation of the Host. See above p. 74 f.

[5] Br. 438, 35; 449–52; 457.

[6] Br. 435, 23; 430, 20. In the quoted deacon's Preface, a Roman prototype seems to betray itself in a few phrases: 'Semper et ubique'; 'per quem majestatem tuam laudant angeli'; 'tremunt potestates'. This would give an origin after the thirteenth century.

Christ at least has been inserted.[1] Thus the tendency is revealed to bring out the Godhead in Christ, to honour in him God *pure and simple*.

This development of the liturgy goes a step further when in two passages of the anaphora in connexion with the new Christ-addressed prayers passages of praise and thanks to the individual Persons of the Trinity are inserted.[2] Since the old prayers seem to be directed to the Person of the Father (the name 'Father' is now understood of the First Person), the Son and the Holy Ghost also should not be passed over. The address to the Holy Spirit, which Chosroë as yet does not know or does not consider, is in this way now provided for in addition in special prayers, inside and outside the anaphora.[3]

Other prayers are addressed simply to the 'Lord'. This applies in particular also to prayers of Byzantine origin in the extra-anaphora ordo of the Mass, viz. those in which frequently the criterion of the mode of address, the end-doxology, is omitted. Others avoid at all costs the choice of a definite address, as they also avoid mentioning Christ in any way as Mediator. Precisely for that reason, these outer areas of the Mass liturgy are rather rich in mediator and obsecratory phrases of another kind, such as could be used even for Christ-addressed prayers:[4] '*Through the holy Church* let us beg the Lord to

---

[1] Vetter 1; Br. 428, 7: 'Let us . . . request of the Lord God and of our Saviour Jesus Christ.' The end of the prayer Br. 429, 19 presupposes only the address to Christ.

[2] Br. 447: 'Blessed be the holy Father, true God. Blessed be the holy Son, true God. Blessed be the Holy Ghost, true God.' Similarly, Br. 454, where the third sentence goes: 'We thank thee, O true Spirit, who hast renewed the Holy church. Keep her spotless by faith in the Trinity henceforth and ever.'

[3] Br. 439, 23; 446, 32 (see above p. 82, n. 2). Br. 417 f., the bishop prepares himself for the sacrifice by two long prayers to the Holy Spirit, 'who is the dispenser of the work'. Gregory of Narek (tenth century) is named as the author.

[4] Only the Roman vesting-prayers, which in the middle ages in some places, e.g. in the later Mozarabic Mass (PL 85, 523 ff; cf. on the contrary MEL V, 230 f.n.), ended with the 'per Christum Dominum nostrum', have here the—weakening, however—χάριτι ending, e.g. 'Lord put upon me the helmet of salvation to fight against the power of the enemy: by the grace of our Lord Jesus Christ unto whom is fitting glory . . .'. A variation of the Roman *Indulgentiam* after the similarly derived *Confiteor* ends: 'through the grace of the Holy Ghost, the potentate and merciful, unto whom be glory for ever' (Br. 413–6). A short prayer after the words of consecration over the chalice runs (Br. 437, 23): 'Heavenly Father, who didst give thy Son unto death . . ., we beseech thee *through the shedding of this blood*, have mercy. . .'.

free us through it from sins and to aid us *through the grace of his mercy*.'[1] '*Through the intercession of thy Virgin-Mother* hear the prayers of thy servants.'[2] '*Through the intercession of thy heavenly hosts* preserve the throne of Armenia.'[3] 'Let us beg the Lord to free us *through his holy cross* from sin and preserve us in life *through the grace of his mercy*.'[4] Even the Lord's flesh and blood are termed, in relation to him himself, 'intercessors'.[5] Thus the Armenian liturgy, too, appears clearly as an edifice on to which the centuries have built, each in its own style and spirit.

---

[1] Br. 416, 15. The idea of the Church as a holy community comes out vividly in this liturgy in many passages.

[2] Br. 419, 16a; cf. 415, 12. 20; 424, 12b.        [3] Br. 420, 16.

[4] Br. 456, 32.        [5] Br. 451, 4; cf. 452, 23b; 439 f; 443.

# VII
# LITURGIES OF THE GALLIC TYPE

BRIDGING the gap between the oriental liturgies and that of Rome are the liturgies of the Gallic type.[1] Except for sparse remains in Milan and in Toledo, these liturgies have been out of use for a millennium, but in the past their domain stretched over the whole of extra-Italian Western Europe, including Upper Italy.[2] With regard to the Mass, in the various countries there early began a period of active new creation of liturgical prayer-texts within the common pattern.[3] The ruling principle was that everywhere a majority of formularies was to be available either for particular feasts or for free choice. In these, apart from the fore-Mass with its chants and intercessions, at least in the earlier period, only a diminutive part was accepted as *ordo Missae*: greeting formulas, *sanctus*, words of institution, Pater noster and the like. The rest of the formulary, consisting of a series—not everywhere the same—of differently

[1] I follow here the terminology of A. Baumstark in his article 'Liturgien' in the *Kirchliches Handlexikon* I (1912) 681 f. According to this, the common so-called Gallican liturgy (of Gaul), together with others, is one of the liturgies of the Gallic type, which we may refer to briefly as 'Gallic' liturgies.

[2] The origins are not clear.

[3] The theory, evolved by L. Duchesne, of Milan as starting-point of the *Gallic liturgies* is no longer tenable after the studies of E. Griffe, 'Aux sources de la liturgie gallicane': *Bulletin de Littérature eccl.* 52 (1951) 17–43.

named prayers, which for the most part began just after the readings, was subject to variation. The most important are the *orationes* after the litany of the Faithful, after the diptychs and after the Kiss of Peace, the Preface, the postsanctus and the postpridie (after the Consecration), the prayers before and after the Pater noster and after the Communion, as well as a last, usually threefold, prayer of blessing.

In Upper Italy and in the British Isles, however, this indigenous liturgy after the seventh century gave way gradually to the Roman usage. All that remains to us from these countries are hybrid-forms of native and Roman liturgy,[1] which we need not examine in detail. On the other hand, certain documents of more or less purely indigenous rite are still extant for Gaul and Spain.

## 1. GALLICAN LITURGY

For Gaul, two collections deserve to be discussed as representative of the rest. The first consists of the *Mone Masses*,[2] named after their first editor, who discovered them as the under-writing on a Reichenau palimpsest. According to A. Wilmart, who corrected Mone's arrangement of the sheets, they consist of six Sunday Masses, of which the first is in metrical form, and one is in honour of St Germanus of Auxerre (d. 448).[3] The discussion over their age

---

[1] For Ireland: Bobbio Missal, seventh century; Stowe Missal, eighth to ninth century. Milanese (Ambrosian) sacramentary and missals since the ninth century. The latter, in the style, and frequently also in the wording, of the prayers, are particularly close to the Roman liturgy.

[2] F. J. Mone, *Lateinische und griechische Messen aus dem 2–6 Jahrhundert* (Frankfurt, 1850). Also printed PL 138, 863–82. The Mone Masses have been newly edited and introduced in the appendix to the edition of the *Missale gallicanum vetus* by Mohlberg-Eizenhöfer-Siffrin (Rome, 1958), 61–91. The manuscript of the Mone Masses is assigned to the period 630/40. The derivation from *Verantius Fortunatus* can be considered probable only for the first of these Masses; L. Eizenhöfer, *Revue Bénédictine* 63 (1953) 329.

[3] *Revue Bénédictine* 28 (1911) 377–90. According to A. Wilmart's ordering, only the first three formularies are incomplete, in these cases isolated leaves being missing. Often, for one prayer, especially for the Preface (which is here called *contestatio*), there are duplicates—for choice. Mone had distinguished eleven (fragmentary) Masses.

produced the mid-seventh century as the period of the under-
writing, while the fifth to the seventh century was given for the
origin of the text.[1]

The prayers vary widely in length. One of the shortest may
serve us to begin with as an example: 'Ad pacem. Exaudi
nos, Deus salutaris noster, et in consortio nos divinorum
sacrificiorum dignanter admitte ac pacem tuam benignus largire
P.D.'[2]

The address to God and the end-formula 'Per Dominum', as in
this prayer, are the rule. The address has no fixed form.[3] Often, God
is addressed expressly as Trinity: 'Dignum et iustum est te laudare,
Trinitas Deus, qui hominem . . . effeceras.'[4] The address to Christ is
used expressly only in the further course of a fourth Preface of W6
(M9): 'Dignum et iustum est . . ., tibi semper gratias agere, Domine
sancte Pater omnipotens aeterne Deus; tu . . .; tu agnus immacu-
latus, tu Pater (sic) sempiternus es Filius.' The same address is
presupposed in two further prayers.[5]

The end of the *orationes*[6] is in every case a 'through Christ' phrase,
generally abbreviated: 'p.d.'; 'p.d.nm'; 'p.d.J.Xm', *inter alia*. The few
passages in which the ending is written out in full show no uniformity
of wording. Thus a Collect in W3 (M7) runs: 'Exaudi nos, Deus
pater omnipotens, et praesta quae petimus per unigenitum et
primogenitum Jesum Christum Filium tuum Dominum et Deum
nostrum, viventem manentemque tecum cum Spiritu Sancto in

---

[1] I cite the different Masses with their numeration after Wilmart (and the new
editors) and add that after Mone in brackets, e.g. 'W1 (M8)' = 1st Mass after
Wilmart, 8th after Mone. Here and in the whole section on the Gallic liturgies I
give the text, in general, with tacit correction of the mostly rather poor orthography,
as it is printed from the manuscripts.

[2] W4 (M2). For *ac* there is *hac*, which Mone wrongly corrected to *hanc*.

[3] Usually the name of God, *Domine* or *Deus*, with or without attribute, is used.
Especially in the Preface, 'sancte Pater omnipotens' is often added. Also 'Pater
Domini nostri Jesu Christi' occurs.

[4] W2 (M6); cf. the Preface and the first prayer of W5 (M3).

[5] Embolism of W3 (M1) and in the prayer *Post prophetiam* of W7 (M10).

[6] Post prophetiam, post nomina, ad pacem, post secreta (Consecration),
embolism, postcommunio, sometimes also postsanctus.

aeterna saecula saeculorum.' The same prayer recurs at the end of
W3 (M1) with the ending: 'Praesta quae petimus per Dominum
Jesum Christum Filium tuum qui vivit regnat Deus in saecula
saeculorum.'[1] But the letters 'p.d.' are added in a few places where
they hardly derive from the author: thus in the postsanctus of the
metrical Mass W1 (M8):

> Vere terribilis sanctus . . .
> Qui proprium genitum, per quem virtute paterna
> Tunc adolescentis formasti exordia mundi,
> Mittere sede poli demum dignatus es orbi
> qui reparator adest nostrarum animarum.
>
> p.d.n. qui pridie.

Neither could God send his Son 'p.d.n.', nor Christ act as restorer
of our souls 'p.d.n.'.[2] Consequently, a suspicion remains that in other
cases, too, the attached end-formulas belong to a framework for
which the text was not designed throughout. Does this framework
derive, perhaps, only from the spreading Roman usage? That
possibility is hardly to be accepted. Also, the theme of praying
through Christ appears in certain passages to be firmly tied to the
text, at least if one includes the short *orationes* mentioned, of which
the greater half consists of the end-formula written out in full.
Outside the *oratio* endings, however, only two passages can be cited:
the beginning of the Preface of W4 (M2): 'Dignum et iustum est,
nos tibi gratias agere, Domine Deus, per Christum Jesum Filium
tuum, qui, cum Deus esset aeternus, homo fieri pro nostra salute

---

[1] Similarly, but with mention of Father and Holy Spirit, in the last sentence of
an epiklesis prayer (post secreta) of W3 (M5): 'ut . . . sit eucharistia . . . legitima,
per Jesum Christum Filium tuum Dominum ac Deum nostrum qui vivit et regnat
tecum cum Spiritu Sancto in aeterna saecula saeculorum.' Somewhat different is
the epiklesis prayer of W4 (M2), where the last words run: 'legitima sit eucharistia
per Jesum Christum . . . cui est apud te, Domine, cum Spiritu Sancto regnum
sempiternum, perpetua divinitas in saecula saeculorum.' On the other hand, the
postcommunio of W3 (M1) approximates to the former end-formula.

[2] Similarly, *inter alia*, in the postsanctus of W3 (M5); cf. post prophetiam of W7
(M10), where the prayer obviously addressed to Christ would end 'p. dmn. nm
Jhm'.

dignatus est'—and the ending of the Preface of the metrical Mass W1 (M7), following on the praise of the saving passion of Christ:

> Per quem cuncta tibi, quae sunt coelestia, semper
> . . . resonant his vocibus hymnum.[1]

Here and perhaps again in the above-quoted collects of W3 (M1) and W3 (M7), it is clear that really the intention is to offer the *prayer* through Christ, while the formula given at length in other cases suggests rather that God is besought to bestow on us his *gifts* through Christ—unless one prefers in all cases to take the words elliptically: '(For this we beg thee) through Christ.' Nevertheless, it will be perfectly apt to take the formula equally as a formula about whose meaning one worried little, although the doxological ending was still varied.

Little as Christ's title of Mediator is defined, yet his work of redemption is commonly the main theme of the praise offered to God in the Preface. In eleven out of fifteen Prefaces, God's plan of salvation is praised, i.e. the restoration of mankind through Christ or through Baptism.[2] It is striking that the *Sanctus* chant is introduced in about half the cases in such a way that it seems to be offered to Christ.[3] Agreeing with this in W3 (M5) and W4 (M2) is the continuation in the postsanctus, which in the latter Mass goes briefly: 'Vere sanctus, vere benedictus Dominus noster Jesus Christus, Filius tuus. Qui pridie.' On the contrary, W5 (M3) with its opening 'Benedictus Deus . . ., etiam Unigenitus pro parte qua caro factus est' vividly recalls *Ap. Const.* VIII, 12: ''Αγιος γὰρ εἶ . . . ἅγιος δὲ

---

[1] Here in the manuscript follow two verses which are superfluous, just as the first word of the attached 'cui ss ss ss' cannot have been intended by the author. Ancient liturgical prayers of pure Gallican origin, in which without exception the address to God and the ending 'Per Dominum nostrum' is used, are shown also by, *inter alia*, a palimpsest fragment published by A. Mai, printed PL 138, 883. Cf. L. Duchesne, *Origines*[4] 155.

[2] Of the four others, one is addressed directly to Christ, two praise the greatness of God in his saints (Germanus, Prophet Elias).

[3] This is very clearly the case, moreover, in the last Preface of W6 (M9), also in the second, at least, of W2 (M6): 'Ipsum igitur omnes angeli . . . conlaudant dicentes.' In the other cases, the formula-type 'cui merito', usually not further written out, could at a pinch be referred to God (the Father, the Triune), who was addressed at the beginning.

καὶ ὁ μονογενής σου υἱός, ὅς ... εὐδόκησεν ... ἄνθρωπος γενέσθαι.

The *Missale Gothicum*[1] is also a relatively reliable witness of pure Gallican liturgy. It shows the usage of a church in the Frankish Empire (Autun?) about 700 and contains Masses *de tempore* from the Vigil of Christmas to Pentecost, six Sunday Masses and a number of Masses in honour of saints; only the latter are strongly influenced by Roman liturgy.[2] The Sunday Masses, especially, agree with the Mone Masses in the order of address of the prayers. These prayers are addressed to God and end with the expression 'Per.', without, however, this being a strict rule. The same may be said of the Masses on the feasts of saints. In the other Masses, on the other hand, one cannot speak of a rule at all. A great part of the prayers do indeed keep to the same style. The end-formula is often written fully, again in varying form: 'Per (ipsum coaeternum tibi) Dominum nostrum Jesum Christum Filium tuum, qui (semper) tecum (beatus) vivit (dominatur) et regnat (Deus) in unitate Spiritus Sancti in saecula saeculorum';[3] or, if the form of the summons to prayer is chosen: 'Per Dominum nostrum Jesum Christum Filium suum secum viventem semperque regnantem';[4] or at Easter: 'Per resurgentem a mortuis Dominum nostrum';[5] or simply: 'Per eum qui tecum vivit'.[6] As is evident, these and similar variations of the wording do not aim to bring home more clearly the prayer-mediation of our Lord; they do not go beyond what is said with the word 'per'. However, the 'per Christum' occurs occasionally also outside the end-formula: 'Immaculatas sacris altaribus hostias offerentes, omnipotentem Deum per unigenitum Filium suum ... deprecemur';[7] also sometimes in the course of the Preface. There is at least a related theme in the introduction to the Pater noster on Maundy Thursday: 'Vivi panis alimenta et sacri sanguinis dona sumpturi dominica prece mentes et corda firmemus. Agnoscat

[1] Muratori II, 517–658. New edition by L. C. Mohleberg, *Missale Gothicum*, (Rome 1961).

[2] DACL 6, 532 f.

[3] Mur. II, 537, 517, 540, 544; also: 'Qui tecum et cum Spiritu Sancto vivit', Mur. II, 544.

[4] E.g. Mur. II, 533, 538, 543.    [5] Mur. II, 581 ff.

[6] E.g. Mur. II, 544.    [7] Mur. II, 578.

Altissimus Filii sui vocem, et verba Christi ad aures paternas concordis populi clamor adtollat et dicat: Pater.'[1]

Many other prayers, however, choose the *address to Christ*, though again no universal rule emerges. Christ-addressed prayers occur at every part of the Mass: in the *orationes* 'post prophetiam, post precem, post nomina, ad pacem, ante' and 'post orationem dominicam, post communionem', also at the blessing over the people before the Communion. Yet the address is nowhere retained in a whole formulary, except possibly on Palm Sunday, an authentic Gallican feast of later date, whose Mass, however, bears the old name: 'in symboli traditione.'[2] Only the postsanctus, retained in optative-form, ends with the request, 'ut (Deus) quicquid praefiguravit in mysteriis, reddat in praemiis. Per Christum Dominum nostrum. Qui pridie.' On this day, by way of exception, even the Preface is addressed to Christ the Lord: 'Vere dignum et iustum est, tibi Domine . . . dicere laudem in hac die ieiunii et laudis tuae triumphali praeconio, quo ab Hierosolymis et Bethania occurrerunt tibi plurimae populorum catervae una voce perstrepentes: Osianna fili David. . . .' And the introduction to the Pater noster makes even this a prayer to Christ: 'Venerabilibus informator praeceptis, incitati munere pietatis, qui Mariae flentis lacrimas non spernis, Lazaro dignanter cognomentum fratris imponis, ecclesiae soboles appellas ore gratiae coheredes: tibi supplices clamamus et dicimus: Pater.' And the following embolism runs: 'Exerce liberator in nobis iuris proprii facultatem, qui Lazarum virtute . . . remuneras, favorem plebis excitas, et Patris voce concina gloriaris omnipotens Deus. Qui in T(rinitate perfecta vivis et regnas in saecula saeculorum).' Here it may well be said that the character of the feast, of which the theme is above all homage to Christ, was a determining factor in the address. Something similar is the case with Christmas and the Epiphany, where likewise the prayer to Christ is very prominent, as well as with the Mass 'in inventione sanctae crucis', occasioned by Heraclius' recovery of the Cross in 629, whence again a later

---

[1] Mur. II, 579. The Pater noster is therefore here a Communion prayer recited by the people.

[2] Mur. II, 575–7. Cf. A. Baumstark, *Vom gesch. Werden* 86.

formulary.[1] On the other hand, on other feasts of our Lord, at Easter and the Ascension, a Christ-addressed prayer does not occur at all and in the intervening period only seldom, probably because in these cases the theme of redemption is in the foreground, to which the prayer *through* Christ is more suited, but also because the formularies are older.

Many prayers addressed to Christ are recognizable as such only in their endings. The address at the beginning goes frequently, as elsewhere: 'Domine' or 'Deus', with or without an attribute. In the ending, chiefly two formulas appear: 'quod ipse praestare digneris, qui cum Patre et Spiritu Sancto vivis et regnas'[2] and: 'Salvator mundi, qui cum (coaeterno) Patre et Spiritu Sancto vivis (dominaris) et regnas,'[3] both with many variations, for the most part, however, given in abbreviated form. As example, we may give the beginning and end of the *collectio ad pacem* of the Mass *in adsumptione s. Mariae*: 'Deus universalis machinae propagator, qui in sanctis spiritaliter, in matre vero virgine etiam corporaliter habitasti . . . precamur supplices, ut pacem qua(m) in adsumptione matris tunc praebuisti discipulis, solemni nuper largiaris in cunctis, Salvator mundi, qui cum Patre et Spiritu Sancto vivis.'[4] Here it is obvious that Christ is considered above all according to his divinity, and this aspect comes out still more palpably in various hybrid-forms in which the two prayer-types, to God and to Christ, flow into one another, or in which the mediator phrase is no longer used meaningfully. Thus, in the *collectio post communionem* on the feast of the Circumcision: 'Refecti spiritali cibo et caelesti poculo reparati omnipotentem Deum, fratres carissimi, deprecemur, ut qui nos corporis *sui* participatione et sanguinis effusione redemit, in requiem aeternam iubeat conlocare. Per Dominum nostrum Jesum Christum Filium suum.'[5]

A valuable and comprehensive document of the old Gallican

[1] Cf. H. Kellner, *Heortologie*[3] 251 f.

[2] Mur. II, 519, 521, etc.

[3] Mur. II, 519 ff. For the formula 'Salvator mundi', cf. H. Linssen, Θεὸς σωτήρ: JL 8 (1928) 1–75, esp. 32 ff.

[4] Mur. II, 546 f. Mostly for this ending there is only the expression *Sal*.

[5] Mur. II, 535.—Cf. the prayer 'post secreta' in probably the latest formulary of the collection, on the feast of St Leodegar (d. 680). Also the *Salvator mundi* is found employed in an unusual manner, e.g. Mur. II, 607 ('in inventione s. crucis'). Certain prayers leave the question open as to which is the order of address,

liturgy has only very recently been deciphered and made accessible: the Irish palimpsest sacramentary of Munich, which has proved to be really a Gallican sacramentary copied in Ireland about the middle of the seventh century.[1] The character of its collects shows it to be closely related to the Mone Masses. Here, too, in the 158 more or less intact formulae, the invitatories are included with them and the order of addressing God consequently preserved; the conclusion 'Per Dominum nostrum Jesum Christum' is as a rule retained. That the formula of Christ as Mediator is not a mere formula is shown by places where it fits into the texture of the collects (Nos. 11, 23, 70). In many places the mystery of redemption is unfolded with great love. But even here there are exceptions to the rule, and the impres-sion is given that these were not unintentional. Among the few instances where the *sanctus* appears to be addressed to Christ (Nos. 30, 48, 103, 151) the most noteworthy is that for the feast of St Martin, in which the thanksgiving is passed on to God the Father: 'et gratias agimus tibi Jesu Christe qui talem ecclesiae tuae praefecisti pontificem,' and then continues: 'merito tibi (probably referring to both names), Domine virtutum, coeli coelorum ... non cessant clamare dicentes: sanctus' (No. 151). Several collects addressed to Christ also appear, but these are already marked as such by the address at the beginning. The most notable, apparently a post-mysterium formula, is the one in which there recurs simply the veni-epiclesis from the apocryphal *Acts of St. Thomas* (3rd century) about which more will be said later.

Of the remaining Gallican sacramentaries, the *Missale Francorum,* with its already strong Roman imprint, is of no interest to us. But a short analysis of the *Missale gallicanum vetus*[2] may be added. Since the

opposing to the indifferent address *Domine* some such ending as: 'Praesta, omni-potens Deus, qui (in Trinitate perfecta) vivis et regnas in saecula.' Mur. II, 548; cf. II, 553, 555. The oft-occurring abbreviation 'quod ipse praest.' may mean: '. . . Praestare digneris qui (in Trinitate perfecta) vivis', or: '. . . Qui cum Patre et Spiritu Sancto vivis.' The former solution occurs in prayers to God the Father; cf. Mur. II, 522 (post or. dom.). 534 (post secr.), as in those to Christ, Mur. II, 577 (post or. dom.).

[1] A. Dold and L. Eizenhöfer, 'Das irische Palimpset-sacramentar' in Clm 14429 (Beuron 1964).
[2] Muratori II, 698–759; new edition by L. C. Mohlberg, *Missale Gothicum Vetus*, (Rome 1958). I cite the numbers of this edition.

sacramentary stems only from the eighth century, it is not surprising that even here a considerable part of the prayer-material is of Roman origin and shows Roman order of address. But the same order of address is followed also in the greater part of the texts which are proper to the sacramentary, in part with the explicit note *per*, thus in nineteen of the twenty-six prayer-formulas of the Easter Vigil (Nos. 137–62), that is, here not only in the orationes but also in the prayer summonses. However, one also perceives that the *per* is often tacked on to the text without any thought, thus in No. 145: 'Virginis filium deprecemur . . . Per Dom.'; similarly, No. 198. In a smaller part of the formulas the prayer is directed to Christ, and this not always in a purely accidental and irregular fashion; for the Christ-addressed orationes are found chiefly on the great feasts of our Lord: in the vigil service of Christmas (No. 57) and in the Easter *biduana* (115–8; 120, 122, 125). In the latter, the prayer on Good Friday at the ninth hour shows a fervour and warmth of feeling which A. Baumstark (*Vom geschichtlichen Werden der Liturgie* 91) has not without reason compared with the experiences of later mystics: the crucified is, as today, held up to the gaze and from the Cross is besought the kiss of the beloved bridegroom; yet it is not forgotten that he is no longer the Crucified; for to this petition is added: 'licet post crucis trophaeum' (No. 118). The address to Christ is presupposed also by the formulas of the Last Blessing, especially those of the solemn Pontifical Blessing, when they end: 'Quod ipse praestare (dignetur qui cum Patre . . .)' (No. 36 and elsewhere). The address to Christ, it must then be said, is also often chosen without apparent reason; it comes in the middle of a prayer which has the address to God (No. 5; cf. No. 47); occasionally also the Preface has a phrase according to which the sanctus appears to be addressed to Christ: 'Quem laudant . . .' (Nos. 250, 255; cf. 233), so that Christ is therefore considered simply as the manifestation of God. A singular case, which in its way betrays a logical train of thought, is that of a Communion prayer of thanks addressed to Christ which ends: 'Per Spiritum Sanctum qui in unitate Patris et Filii coaeternus vivit et regnat in s.s.' (No. 12).

## 2. MOZARABIC LITURGY

As various accounts bear witness, for Spain the sixth and seventh centuries were the period of the great liturgical compositions.[1] When in 711 the west Gothic Empire collapsed before the Moorish assault, Toledo was the ecclesiastical centre of the territory occupied by the Moors. From here, also, from now on the liturgical life of the Church in that area was regulated. Thus the old native liturgy of the Gallic type carried on in Spain when elsewhere it had already disappeared. Only after the recapture of Toledo did the indigenous liturgy, now called Mozarabic,[2] have to give way, here too, to the Roman. It was long dead when Cardinal Ximenes revived it, not without admixture of Roman material, and established its usage in the first place for a chapel in Toledo. It is, however, especially its rich stock of Mass formularies, with which it surpasses every other liturgy—also preserved—in manuscripts, mainly ninth- to eleventh-century, whose content has been made accessible latterly through good editions, filling two volumes of folios.[3]

The Mozarabic Mass shows a further stage of development of the prayer-type of the Gallic liturgy. The primary order of address, just as in the *Missale Gothicum*, texts from which also recur in part here and there,[4] is in most formularies more or less penetrated with prayers to Christ. *Christ-addressed prayers* are found again in every

---

[1] F. Probst, *Die abendländische Messe* 379 ff, 391 ff.

[2] *Mozarabes*—the arabicized.

[3] M. Férotin, *Le liber ordinum* (Paris, 1904) (MEL V) gives the Rituale together with over sixty Mass formularies for different requests and occasions, principally after a manuscript of 1052. Here, pp. 229–43, an *ordo Missae omnimodae*, which also contains the invariable parts of the Mass, not elsewhere preserved for the older Gallic liturgies. A second volume, M. Férotin, *Le liber mozarabicus sacramentorum*, (Paris, 1912) (MEL VI), mainly after a manuscript of the ninth century, contains 165 Mass formularies for the whole Church year. I cite both the volumes simply with their numeration in the MEL (V and VI) in addition to columns. The *Missale Mixtum* of Cardinal Ximenes, which appeared in 1500, is printed with the notes of A. Lesley in PL 85. It offers a selection from the formularies preserved in the manuscripts. Apart from the additions in the ordo Missae, there is little to distinguish the texts of the different Masses compared to the earlier texts.

[4] Cf. the Masses on the feast of St Saturninus, VI, 29 ff.; on the Finding of the Cross, VI, 318 ff, and on the Assumption of our Lady, VI, 592 ff.

part of the Mass, most of all on feasts of our Lord and at their fore- and after-celebration, without, however, one specially favoured class being capable of distinction here. Of feasts of saints, there are the feasts of the Apostles and that of Holy Virgins[1] which show a greater preference for the prayer to Christ. Yet hardly a formulary could be found in which the address to Christ is kept right through without exception, even prescinding from the facts that not only the first texts of each formulary, the so-called *missa*, but on occasion also other passages choose the form of an address to the people, and that particularly postsanctus and benedictio of Christ the Lord frequently speak in the third person: 'May he be praised, may he bless.' Prefaces to Christ are rather rare. But they are found, e.g., at the Epiphany and in Paschaltide.[2] On the other hand, expressly Christ-addressed prayers appear only occasionally and at times are even missing entirely in the *Missae quotidianae* and *dominicales*, as also in most votive Masses for particular requests.

Only the *sanctus* in such Masses is generally so introduced as to be offered to Christ, on the assumption that his name is already mentioned in the Preface. Thus it may go: 'Praesta per Jesum Christum Filium tuum, Dominum nostrum—quem conlaudant angeli . . . dicentes: Sanctus',[3] or as in the Mone Masses: 'Cui merito omnes angeli atque archangeli non cessant clamare ita dicentes.'[4] But often Christ's name is lacking and with it this attribution of the *sanctus*.

On the other hand, the cases are rare in which the postsanctus does not continue the preceding chant as praise to Christ, e.g. 'Vere sanctus, vere benedictus Dominus noster Jesus Christus Filius tuus; qui suorum martyrum N. passiones ponit ad cultum.'[5] Evidently in the *sanctus* a particular stress was laid on the attached joyful greeting of Palm Sunday: 'Osanna, fili David, benedictus qui venit in nomine Domini, osanna in excelsis.'[6] As this greeting is directed to the Redeemer making his entry, probably also it was preferred to give the preceding and following parts the same direction. In addition, this postsanctus has to end with a mention of Christ in

---

[1] Bridal theme; cf. espec. VI, 489–97.
[2] VI, 88 ff., 246, 290 ff., 303 f.      [3] V, 311, 11.      [4] VI, 528, 4.
[5] VI, 483.                              [6] V, 237, 19.

order to lead into the institution account. Thus this prayer sometimes begins indeterminately: 'Vere sanctus es Domine', but ends
perhaps with the acclamation: 'Deus Dominus et Redemptor
aeternus.'[1]

Especially in longer Prefaces, the case also occurs of the address
changing; for example, when it runs in the beginning:
'Domine sancte, Pater aeterne . . . per Jesum Christum', and somewhat later: 'Ob hoc, Jesu bone, per te . . . introire ad Patrem
quaerimus.'[2] In an Advent Preface[3] we have in the beginning:
'Dignum et iustum . . . est, Domine Jesu Christe, Deus noster . . .',
then: 'clementissime Deus. . .', and towards the end: 'Praesta, unita
aequalis et indivisa Trinitas, Deus noster.' On the other hand, the
unity of the address is not really touched by another, rather frequent
conjunction: 'Dignum et iustum est . . . tibi gratias agere, Domine
sancte, omnipotens Pater, et Jesu Christo, Filio tuo.'[4]

Thus a mixture of prayers to God and to Christ occurring with
little regularity proves, from what has already been said, to be
characteristic of the Mozarabic liturgy. In a large part of the
prayers, however, the address cannot be determined at all. The
address *Domine* or *Deus* (*omnipotens*) obviously leaves the matter undecided. Indeed even the term *pater* is found here and there referring
to Christ.[5]

But the other criterion in particular is almost entirely destroyed;
the *end formulas*, which show a degenerate condition. Férotin has
attached to the *Liber ordinum* a table, 'Doxologies diverses', in which
he lists 134 different endings[6]—doxologies in the wider sense. The

---

[1] VI, 520.    [2] VI, 210; cf. 237 f, 391 ff.    [3] VI, 17.
[4] VI, 66; cf. 99, 147, 241, 256, 260, 280 etc.
[5] Thus, the Preface on Wednesday of the third week in Lent begins: 'Dignum et
iustum est, nos tibi gratias agere, Domine sancte, *Pater* aeterne omnipotens Deus,
qui paras adinventiones tuas sapienter et disponis omnia suaviter. Qui adscendisti
super occasum, Dominus nomen est tibi. Tu es panis vivus et verus, *qui descendisti*
de coelo, ut dares escam esurientibus, immo ut ipse esses esca viventium . . . (VI,
186 f.).' In another Lenten Mass, the Pater noster is indisputably addressed to
Christ: 'Miserere nostri, *fili David*, ne . . . sine fructu perveniamus ad patriam, ut
parsimoniae nostrae propitiatus ex victimis, exaudias vocem nostrae confessionis,
cum *ad te* proclamaverimus e terris: *Pater* (VI, 177 f.).' Here Christ is presumed to
be receiver of the sacrifice. Similar cases V, 248, 20; VI, 232, 24; 492, 23; 540, 15.
[6] V, 534–41.

greater part are, rather, obsecratory formulas. Most of the endings put the Amen in front and are so ordered that they can be used without considering the style of address of the prayer: 'Per ineffabilem bonitatem tuam, Deus noster, qui cuncta regis'; 'Concedente misericordia tua'; 'Te praestante, Deus noster, qui vivis'; 'Quia Deus es'; occasionally also: 'Per te Deus' and 'Per te Christe'. The acclamation 'Salvator mundi (qui cum Patre . . .)', on the other hand, is not usual as an ending to Christ-addressed prayers.[1] It is clear that many of these formulas go back to former christological phrases of the prayer directed to God: 'Through Christ', 'through the grace and mercies of Christ'—in which the idea of personal mediation through Christ was suppressed.

Frequently the prayers end with Amen without one of these end-formulas being remarked. But from the *Missa omnimoda* it appears that these endings,[2] in the absence of any other instructions, were provided for, more or less invariably, within the narrow frame of the ordo Missae, and were to be drawn from there. Here also, the endings show the same indifferent quality: they were to be applicable to all prayers. They only vary the above-quoted examples. The postpridie and the (invariable) thanksgiving prayer after the Communion close in the same manner: 'Te praestante, summe Deus, qui in Trinitate unus Deus gloriaris in saecula saeculorum.'

Only the prayer at the Kiss of Peace, *ad pacem*, is provided with a christological ending: 'Praesta per auctorem pacis et caritatis, Dominum nostrum Jesum Christum Filium tuum, cum quo tibi est una et coaequalis essentia in unitate Spiritus Sancti regnantis, Deus, in saecula saeculorum.' This ending may be observed, however, also in cases where the prayer for peace is addressed to the Son,[3] whereas others addressed to Christ alter the formula to make sense: 'Quia tu es vera pax nostra vivens,'[4] or: 'Per te qui es vera pax.'[5] Also the (invariable) embolism after the Pater noster, which is expanded into

---

[1] Férotin specifies a prayer in the *Rituale* which is directed to God and ends: 'Salvator mundi, qui in Trinitate (V, 94).' Thus, e.g., in the *Missa de die s. crucis* (VI, 318 ff.), which offers a detailed form of the corresponding Mass of the *Missale Gothicum* (Mur. II, 607 f.,), the ending *Sal.*, here four times, though not always appropriately, occurring, is substituted by other formulas.

[2] V, 229–43.                          [3] Cf. VI, 269, 295: 'Per auctorem,'
[4] VI, 381; V, 254 A. 1; 281.          [5] V, 283, 342, 362.

a long intercessory prayer, ends its request: 'Per Christum Dominum nostrum, qui tecum, Deus Pater, et cum Spiritu Sancto vivit et regnat gloriosus, pius et misericors, unus in Trinitate Dominus, per infinita saecula saeculorum.'[1] Similarly, in the postsanctus, which according to the *Missa omnimoda* would end 'Christe Domine ac Redemptor aeterne', in places where this acclamation would not seem in place, the connexion to the institution account is made with the words: 'Per Christum (Dominum et Redemptorem).'[2] Probably also elsewhere, it again sometimes occurs that a prayer ends: 'Auxiliante Domino nostro Jesu Christo,'[3] or 'Per gratiam Christi,'[4] *inter alia*; but these are exceptions, and not seldom such phrases are then used in an absurd manner.

Only the *Preface* still shows in about half of all cases, once in its course, the phrase 'per Christum Dominum nostrum', and then usually in the beginning: 'It is meet and just that we thank thee through Christ our Lord.' Thereon follows in praise the description of one of his works. When the 'per Christum' comes towards the end with little definite meaning, there follows usually the transition to the *sanctus*: 'Cui merito.' In certain cases, when no festal theme, no commemoration of a saint, no particular request is urgent, it even happens that the mediatory office of our Lord is here represented in greater detail. Thus the wording is specially clear in the *Missa omnimoda*:

> Dignum et iustum est nos tibi semper gratias agere, omnipotens Deus noster, per Jesum Christum Filium tuum Dominum nostrum, verum pontificem et solum sine peccati macula sacerdotem. Per quem te, aeterne Pater et Domine, omnimoda intentione deposco, ut oblationem hanc famulorum tuorum benigne suscipias ... ut ... te incessabiliter cum angelis conlaudemus ita dicentes: Sanctus.[5]

[1] V, 241. This ending may represent the old doxology at the end of the Canon.
[2] E.g. V, 299, 343; VI, 379.    [3] V, 248.    [4] VI, 328.
[5] V, 237. The theme is more prominent still in the short Preface of a Sunday Mass, the Spanish origin of which is, however, not certain: 'Dignum et iustum est, omnipotens Pater, nos tibi gratias agere per Jesum Christum Filium tuum, verum aeternum pontificem et solum sine peccati macula sacerdotem. Cuius sanguine omnium corda mundante, placationis tibi hostiam non solum pro delictis populi sed etiam pro nostris offensionibus immolamus, ut omne peccatum, quod carnis fragilitate contrahitur, summo interpellante pro nobis antistite absolvatur. Cui

It is a different structure of religious ideas and therefore another origin, even though it only belongs further back in time, which is revealed in these few formularies, which so decisively stress the priesthood of Christ, as compared with the great mass of the others which obviously suppress the idea.

There is also mention elsewhere of the priesthood of Christ now and again;[1] more often, it is true, of him as sacrificial victim. But the word *sacerdos* or *pontifex* does not necessarily always refer to the mediatory office: it can also on occasion indicate his activity in the performance of the eucharistic sacrifice. For only thus can one understand the mention even of God *tout simple* as *sacerdos*.[2] In general, the economy of salvation according to its great themes and therefore the place of Christ in the history of salvation is in only a fraction of the formularies the subject-matter of the Eucharistic Prayer. It is such most often in formularies for Lent, Easter and ordinary Sundays. In the attempt to ring the changes as much as possible, elsewhere a strictly limited feature of the mystery celebrated in the feast, an event from the Gospel, e.g., the conversation with the Samaritan woman, the raising of Lazarus, is often made the theme of the Preface, frequently in broad homiletic style. In the same way, on feasts of saints, the thanks offered to God in the Preface often becomes a long panegyric, a poetic biography of the saint, that frequently takes more than a folio page. Particularly in votive and requiem Masses, the praise of divine providence suddenly changes to a prayer of petition.

merito' (VI, 632). The Preface is found in the recension of the Gelasianum by M. Gerbert (*Monumenta vet. liturg. Allem.*), p. 148, and in the Gregorianum Mur. II, 325 f. But cf. also *Fulgentius*, Ep. 14, 36 (PL 65, 424): 'Nam bene nosti nonnunquam dici: Per sacerdotem aeternum Filium tuum Dominum nostrum Jesum Christum.' Another Preface has towards the end (VI. 649, 7): 'Per ipsum Dominum nostrum Jesum Christum Filium tuum mediatoremque nostrum.' Cf. V, 299, 10. To this pertains also the postsanctus of a Lenten Mass (VI, 222): 'Per eum te igitur flagitamus, omnipotens Pater, ut *eo intercedente* sanctificans ieiunia nostra dones nobis vitam aeternam, quem pro nobis oblatum suscepisti hostiam vivam.'

[1] VI, 517, 22; 528, 15; 419, 29; 237, 24; 239, 31; 243, 14 (the last three cases belong to Maundy Thursday).

[2] VI, 527: 'Per quem (sc. Filium tuum) te quaesumus . . ., ut in conspectu tuo offerentium vota custodias et ut verus sacerdos veram hostiam meritis coelestibus benedicas.'

On other occasions, the majesty of God, the unfathomable mystery of the *Trinity* provides the subject-matter. Among the *Missae quotidianae* the trinitarian Preface of the Roman liturgy[1] occurs in twofold, somewhat different wording. The Holy Spirit, except for such cases in which the trinitarian theme is directly touched on, is mentioned relatively seldom, apart from the post-pridie, which often recalls an oriental epiklesis. The Preface on Palm Sunday, the Mass for which is quite dominated by the *Traditio symboli*, reads for the most part like a short excerpt from the *Athanasianum* in poetically elevated speech.[2] And it is characteristic of the Mozarabic liturgy that the *Gratias agamus* before the Preface, as in Byzantium, has acquired the form: 'Deo et Domino nostro, Patri et Filio et Spiritui Sancto, dignas laudes et gratias referamus.'[3] Here, probably, we must seek the key to the theological character of this liturgy. The authors were in fact engaged in the struggle against the Arianism of the Visigoths and against their falsification of the doctrine of the Trinity. The triune God is the receiver of our prayer and of our sacrifice,[4] the Son no less than the Father, which is also expressed by the address being directed now to the Father, now to the Son, or remaining indifferent.[5] As the mediatorship of our Lord is almost entirely suppressed, the intercession of the saints, particularly on feasts of saints, automatically becomes all the more

---

[1] VI, 519 f., 619 from two manuscripts of the ninth and tenth century respectively.

[2] VI, 224 f. Cf. G. Morin, *JThSt* 12 (1911) 161–90; 337–61.

[3] V, 236, 38. This wording is omitted again in the *Missale Mixtum*. PL 85, 547. For the Roman *trinitarian Preface*, cf. A. Chavasse, *Le sacramentaire gélasien* (Tournai, 1958), 254–60, who shows that that preserved in the Roman Mass served as a model for both the Mozarabic wordings, and that in it phrases recur in striking manner from the sermons of Leo the Great. For the suggestion that its author could not have been Leo himself but a cleric outside Rome of the sixth to seventh century, cf. J. A. Jungmann, 'Um die Herkunft der Dreifaltigkeitspräfation': *ZkTh* 81 (1959) 461–5. But Prof. Chavasse informs me (Letter of 30.12.1959) that my conjecture of a Spanish author is practically excluded by the fact that the sermons of Leo the Great were still unknown in the early middle ages in Spain.

[4] 'Trinitas Deus' thus is an address often used, e.g. VI, 154, 6; 172, 15; 368, 32; 393, 17; 443, 30. Cf. the same expression in *Fulgentius*, e.g. *c. Fabianum* fragm. 34 (Mi 65, 822).

[5] Christ seldom appears expressly as the receiver of the sacrifice. Cf. perhaps the Postpridie VI, 56 f., 63, 352, or the prayer Post nomina VI, 498. In the old 'Missa de initio anni' (VI, 83 f.) it goes: 'Christe, qui es Alpha et $\Omega$, initium et finis, tu benedicito his sacrificiis ob principium praesentis anni tibi oblatis.'

prominent. Exceptionally, prayers also occur which are addressed directly to saints.[1]

The picture thus obtained is not altered if we look at the oldest existing manuscript, which is from Verona and is attributed to the seventh to eighth century.[2] The part preserved here of the Mass of Wednesday in Holy Week shows the same text as later manuscripts. The prayer *ad pacem*, e.g., unites precisely the characteristic traits of the Mozarabic prayer-type:

> Praepara nos tibi, *Salvator* noster ac Domine, per pacis bonum *in hostiam* vivam, ut qui crastinum sumpturi sumus dominicam coenam, nulla ab invicem convellamur discordia, sed fructu pleni tuae dulcedinis sumamus in crastinum flumina caritatis, quae profluentia decurrunt e visceribus tuis. Amen. Praesta, *Pater*, quia tu es pax.[3]

Likewise, the Masses in the *Missale mixtum* of 1500 show, as far as they recur there, only small deviations. These lie principally in the use of the end-formulas, which are laid down in the *ordo Missae* as identical for all formularies. The development of the Mozarabic liturgy was in essentials complete by about 700. While the other end-formulas here also are selected so that they can be used without reference to the style of address of the prayer concerned, that for the prayer *ad pacem* goes somewhat unusually: 'Quia tu es vera pax nostra et caritas indisrupta vivis tecum et regnas cum Spiritu Sancto unus Deus in saecula saeculorum.'[4]

Further elaboration is found in the *Missale mixtum* only in the invariable *ordo Missae*.[5] Anything that might have been said about

---

[1] VI, 406, 497 (Postpridie): to Mary; VI, 378 (Post nomina): to St Christina.

[2] Cf. VI, 947.

[3] VI, 232. The address to Christ, evident even here, is clearer in the preceding *orationes*: 'Jesu bone'; 'Christe filius Dei Patris.'

[4] PL 85, 115, 546. Here the address to Christ seems to be presupposed for the prayer for peace but, as in the first formulary PL 85, 115, it is not used. More correctly, two formulas are here mechanically joined, viz. that already mentioned above at the end of the prayer for peace directed to Christ: 'Quia tu es vera pax nostra (vivens)', and that at the end of the prayer for peace directed to God the Father: '(Per auctorem pacis ... qui est vera pax nostra) et caritas indisrupta vivens tecum et regnans cum Spiritu Sancto' (V, 320); in addition, the reminiscence of the form 'qui vivis', which was suggested by the Spanish pronunciation of the *vivens*.

[5] PL 85, 522 ff.

the *ordo Missae* for the earlier period has already been noted in discussing the end-formulas, which comprise a large part of the ordo. It remains to mention a prayer of preparation, the author of which is *Julian of Toledo* (d. 690). It confirms the type established above:

> Accedam ad te Domine, in humilitate spiritus mei, loquar de te, quia multam fiduciam et spem dedisti mihi. Tu ergo fili David . . . Mitte ad me unum de Seraphin . . . ut lingua mea, quae proximorum utilitati deservit, non erroris redoleat occasu, sed vitae aeternae sine fine praeconio resonet. Per te Deus meus, qui vivis et regnas in saecula saeculorum. Amen.[1]

In the *Missale mixtum* there is in addition a series of prayers at the vesting, at the confession of sins, and at the preparation and offering of the sacrificial gifts, the latter of which, here as in the East, in great part precedes the readings. Of these prayers, of which several recur in the Roman liturgy and are obviously taken from it, most are addressed to God and in that case often end 'per Christum Dominum nostrum'. In some, Christ is addressed. To these belong the request, inserted before the Consecration, to him for the performance of the latter: 'Adesto, adesto, Jesu bone pontifex, in medio nostri, sicut fuisti in medio discipulorum tuorum, et sanctifica hanc oblationem, ut sanctificata sumamus per manus sancti angeli tui, sancte Domine et Redemptor aeterne.'[2] Also the *Gratias agamus* has here gained the form: 'Deo ac Domino nostro Jesu Christo Filio Dei, qui est in coelis, dignas laudes dignasque gratias agamus.'[3] Here, then, the naming of the three divine Persons has given ground in favour of the Christ-address, although elsewhere the preference is not abandoned for directing the prayer at times expressly to the Trinity.[4] At the start of the Mass Mary also is invoked in three passages, in the *Ave* or the *Salve Regina*—as the rubric says in the first passage, 'ut ipsam in hoc sacrificio mediatricem et adiutricem habeat'.[5]

---

[1] V, 230; with unimportant variants PL 85, 538 f.

[2] PL 85, 550. A. Lesley has already perceived that this prayer must have been inserted later.

[3] PL 85, 547.

[4] Cf. the prayer immediately after the Communion, PL 85, 567: 'Domine Deus meus, Pater et Filius et Spiritus Sanctus, fac me te semper quaerere et diligere et a te per hanc sanctam communionem, quam sumpsi[t], nunquam recedere, quia tu es Deus et praeter te non erit alius in saecula saeculorum. Amen.'

[5] PL 85, 523, 525, 529.

# VIII
# THE ROMAN LITURGY

THE oldest existing monument of the Mass liturgy of Rome is in *Hippolytus'* church order already discussed. When after the mid-third century the change was made from Greek to Latin as the language of worship, most probably it was joined with a far-reaching reform of liturgical prayer.[1] The principle of part of the Mass varying according to the feast-days of the Church's year afforded from now on the opportunity for the composing of ever new formularies, the sacerdotal prayers for which were assembled in the sacramentaries.

The surviving manuscripts of the latter, however, date from only about the start of the seventh century. They fall into three groups: the *Sacramentarium Leonianum*, a lone manuscript, originating probably about 600 as a private, barely-arranged collection of Mass formularies, which, however, passes on pure Roman practice from the fifth to sixth century;[2] the *Sacramentarium Gelasianum*, of which there exist only two redactions, only the older one (Cod. Reg. 316,

---

[1] Cf. A. Baumstark, *Vom geschichtlichen Werden* 80. Jungmann, *Missarum So emnia*[5] I, 63–77.

[2] L. A. Muratori I, 293–484. New editions by C. L. Feltoe (Cambridge, 1896) and Mohlberg-Eizenhöfer-Siffrin (Rome, 1965).

eighth century) to be discussed here;[1] finally, the *Sacramentarium Gregorianum*, a revision ascribed to *Gregory the Great*, which with later accretions was sent by Pope Hadrian I about 790 to the Emperor Charlemagne. This last sacramentary is preserved in many manuscripts of which the best, according to H. Lietzmann, goes back to that copy of Hadrian.[2] It shows here, however, an appendix, deriving from *Alcuin*, taken from the Gallican-Gelasian formulary up to then in use in the Frankish Empire; in later manuscripts this appendix is already worked into the sacramentary itself. Hybridforms of this sacramentary, as it developed now on Frankish and German soil, are also extant intermittently from a later period. The acceptance of such elements, as they now streamed back from the liturgical practice of French and German Churches to Italy, into the later liturgical books of Rome, makes the chief difference which characterizes the last stage of development—for the most part fixed by *Pius V*—of the Roman liturgy—apart from the increase in new formularies for the later feasts.

In order to begin again with the oldest part, the kernel, we should take in order, first the Canon, then the Preface, the *orationes* and the

---

[1] Mur. II, 493–764; new critical editions by H. A. Wilson (Oxford, 1894) and Mohlberg-Eizenhöfer-Siffrin (Rome 1960).

If in this chapter editions of the later Gelasianum remain unconsidered, this is justifiable in that fundamentally they adhere to the Roman manner and only here and there show the influence of Gallic-Frankish tradition, and thus hold out for us no independent source of information. However, there should be mentioned the *fragments* and separate texts pertaining to the older Roman liturgy which are now provided in a manner suitable for inspection in the appendix, to the just mentioned edition of the Leonianum by Mohlberg-Eizenhöfer-Siffrin, *Sacramentarium Veronense* (Rome, 1956). There are *orationes* and Prefaces, numbered as formulas 1332–546. They all end with *per*. In particular, this is the case also with the thirty-nine Advent *orationes* of the *Rotulus of Ravenna* (Nos. 1332–70), which is assigned to the sixth century; only in the end section, which appeared subsequently, the second formula (1546), prescribed for Christmas Eve, has the irregular ending: 'Qui vivit et regnas.' Admittedly, in the Rotulus of Ravenna, certain formulas which in reality are directed to Christ (e.g. No. 1344: 'incarnationis tuae') show that the *per* is sometimes only added mechanically.

[2] H. Lietzmann, *Das Sacramentarium Gregorianum nach dem Aachener Urexemplar* (LQ) 3), (Münster, 1921). From the edition in Mur. II, 1–507, the following belong to the pure Gregorianum: II, 1–138; 241–72; 357–61. The edition by H. A. Wilson, *The Gregorian Sacramentary under Charles the Great* (London, 1915), which gives the same text in the right order, shows no deviations of significance for our enquiry.

remaining changeable prayers, finally the *ordo Missae* outside the Canon.

We meet the *Canon* first in the *Gelasianum*. Its wording differs only in inessentials from that familiar to us.

The prayer shows here the simplest conceivable characteristics. It approaches God the Father[1] through Christ our Lord. Indeed, the mediator formula 'per Christum Dominum nostrum' appears not only twice before and three times after the Consecration, at the end of each independent section,[2] but also right at the outset of the whole prayer: 'Te igitur, clementissime Pater, per Jesum Christum Filium tuum Dominum nostrum supplices rogamus'—an indication that the phrase had not become for the author of the Canon a mere formula. In addition, there is the solemn doxology at the end of the Canon: 'Per ipsum et cum ipso . . .'; this will have to be touched on later.[3]

The Canon is basically only the continuation of the Eucharistic Prayer begun in the *Preface*, and as such reaches its climax with the accomplishment of the sacrifice.[4] Whereas now the prayers at the offering of the sacrifice, together with the added intercessory prayers (*Memento*), in Rome belong to the invariable content of the Mass and form the 'Canon', the true thanksgiving, as the variable portion, has been separated from it.[5] The thanksgiving for the great

[1] 'Clementissime Pater'; 'ad te Deum Patrem suum omnipotentem'; 'Domine'; '(omnipotens) Deus'.

[2] It is a question here of prayers of later insertion; cf. Jungmann, *Missarum Solemnia*[5] I, 70 ff.

[3] See Part Two, Ch. XII. In Gelasianum, the *Memento* for the dead, and with it in one case the end-formula 'per Christum Dominum nostrum', is missing. The Stowe Missal adds the end-formula, in spite of agreement of the remainder of the text, only to the last of the three passages after the Consecration: 'largitor admitte. Per.'. On the other hand, it is found in all five passages in the Canon of the Ambrosian Mass, which with a few variants is accepted as an older form of the Roman Canon. DACL 1, 1407–14.

[4] Cf. the name εὐχαριστία for the Mass. In the church order of Hippolytus, the text of the Mass is introduced with the phrase: '(Episcopus) dicat gratias agens', and at the end of the whole formulary there is a note to the effect that the bishop need not use these exact words for 'giving thanks'; he may do it in his own way with other words. Cf. R. H. Connolly, *The so-called Eng. Church Order* 64–6, 176, 179 f.

[5] In the Gelasianum, the *Prefatio communis* is still expressly within the Canon under the heading 'Incipit canon actionis'—as representative of the others, whose texts, being more proper to the occasion, in part had to be inserted in this universally observed framework.

benefits of God certainly had to receive a changing hue according to festal seasons and occasions, just like the other prayers and the lessons. In fact, the *Sacramentarium Leonianum* contains a special Preface for every Mass, sometimes several from which selection could be made, exactly as in the Gallic liturgies. Of the fifteen Prefaces of the present-day Missal, four are of recent date: de S. Joseph; defunctorum; those of the Sacred Heart (1929) and of Christ the King (1925), through the happy paraphrasing of the work of the redemption, return to the original theme of the Eucharistic prayer. The *Prefatio de B. Maria Virgine* is attributed to Urban II (1095). The *Prefatio de Cruce* may be of like age.[1] The other nine are already found among the Prefaces of the *Gelasianum*, as they also recur in the *Gregorianum*. But for only seven of these is there evidence of ancient Roman origin, as the Prefaces *de Quadragesima* and *de Trinitate* appear only in the alcuinic appendix of the latter sacramentary.[2] Of these seven, three are in the *Leonianum*, viz. the Prefaces for the Ascension, Pentecost and feasts of the Apostles; today's Christmas Preface is only with difficulty recognizable among the nine Christmas Prefaces.[3] The remaining three of the seven cannot be compared, because in the *Leonianum*, besides the Canon with the *Prefatio communis*, the formularies for the period January to April, which includes the Prefaces for Epiphany and Easter, are missing.

Beside the *Prefatio communis*, the texts of all these seven old Roman Prefaces have in the course of time undergone greater or lesser changes or, as in the Easter or Pentecost Prefaces, have been accepted only in shortened form in our Missal. But for us only the changes in the Preface of the Apostles are of great interest.

As it stands in our Missal, this Preface, in contrast to all others, passes immediately to a petition: 'Vere dignum et iustum est

[1] It is named with the others in the spurious brief of Pelagius II, which is incorporated in the *Decretum Gratiani*. That appearing in the Sacramentarium Gregorianum (Mur. II, 318) on the feast of the Finding of the Cross is not identical with the present Preface.

[2] Mur. II, 288 (and 300), and II, 285 f. (and 321 f. 381 f.) respectively.

[3] Cf., for example, Feltoe 163, 29; also, in the present-day Preface of the Ascension, there are strictly speaking two Prefaces of the Leonianum combined in one: Feltoe 20 f.

aequum et salutare, te Domine suppliciter exorare, ut gregem tuum, pastor aeterne, non deseras.' And this petition, according to most liturgiologists, would be directed to Christ, in contrast to all other Prefaces of the Roman Missal and—we may add—of the Roman sacramentaries in general. Yet the text, as we have it today, strictly speaking leaves undecided whether the address is to God the Father or to Christ. The ancient wording, however, shows that the Preface, like all others, was directed simply to God the almighty Father and therefore today, too, is not to be claimed as an exception; further, that it also began as a prayer of thanks. It runs in the *Leonianum*:[1]

> Vere dign(um et iustum est, aequum et salutare, nos tibi semper et ubique gratias agere, Domine sancte, Pater omnipotens, aeterne Deus) suppliciter exor*antes*, ut, gregem tuum, pastor aeterne, non deseras et per beatos apostolos continua protectione custodias, ut iisdem rectoribus dirigatur, quos operis tui vicarios eidem contulisti praeesse pastores *per* (Christum Dominum nostrum; per quem. . .).[2]

The words in brackets, which are not given in the manuscript, were obtainable from the *Praefatio communis* or known from customary usage. It was elsewhere, also, the arrangement in the Roman Mass-books of the Middle Ages: the unchanging introductions were mostly indicated only by the two artistically executed letters VD. On the other hand, in the old manuscripts of the Gallic liturgies, one was accustomed to find the introductory phrases of the Preface written out in full. These were also, especially in the Mozarabic liturgy, far more subject to change, and sometimes led at once to a petition.[3] On the Roman Mass-books migrating north, not always accompanied by their living use, the above abbreviation could easily

---

[1] Feltoe 50, in the last Mass of June; In ( ) the complement of the opening and closing words presumed as self-evident by the text.

[2] Cf. with this as a parallel the *oratio*: 'Gregem tuum, pastor bone, placatus intende et per beatos apostolos perpetua protectione custodi, quos totius ecclesiae praestitisti Filii tui vicarios esse pastores per (Feltoe p. 42; cf. p. xx).' Even today in the *Oratio pro papa*, God the Father is called 'fidelium pastor et rector'. The human shepherds are therefore not only 'vicarii Filii Dei' but also 'vicarii Dei'.

[3] The Preface of one Mozarabic Sunday Mass begins, e.g.: 'Dignum et iustum est te, Domine, orare semper et invocare, qui servorum tuorum precibus . . . annuis (MEL VI, 627; cf. MEL V, 301, 420).' Similar examples are to be found in the Rogation Masses in the *Missale Gothicum* (Mur. II, 610 ff,); in the first of these the Preface begins: 'Vere dignum et iustum est, te in observatione ieiunii quaerere . . ., te itaque rogamus.'

be misunderstood. While the oldest manuscript of the *Gelasianum*
(Vat.), already indigenous to Gaul, still reads 'VD Suppliciter
exorantes',[1] Wilson's apparatus notes the reading of a later manuscript printed by H. Ménard, which clearly marks the transition to
the later wording, for in the first place it removes the isolated
*exorantes* and at the same time probably already presupposes a
shortened introduction: '(... Gratias agere) *et te* suppliciter
exor*are*', while the remaining manuscripts, with the omission of the
'(... gratias agere et)' already show the text as it stands in the
*Gregorianum* and as the Roman Mass-books since then have given it:
'Vere dignum et iustum est, aequum et salutare, te Domine suppliciter exorare.' In the meantime, together with the other minor
changes, the *per Christum* at the end became lost and made room for
the continuation *et ideo*. Thus disappeared from the Preface of the
Apostles, under the influence of the Gallican liturgy, with the
Eucharistic character, the christological Mediator theme also.

Also, the latter characteristic is held by the Preface of the Apostles
in common with—out of other Prefaces of the present-day Missal—
only the *Praefatio de Trinitate*, which apparently arose entirely within
the territory of the Gallic liturgies: 'Vere dignum ... aeterne Deus,
qui cum unigenito Filio tuo ... unus es Deus ... ut ... adoretur
aequalitas; quam laudant angeli. ...' The *gratias agere* is here
retained in the introduction; but the continuation is more a confession of faith and adoration in respect to the mystery of the
Trinity than a thanksgiving. The Preface is lacking in the *Leonianum*
and in the authentic *Gregorianum*, but is found in the Alcuinic
appendix to the latter as in the *Gelasianum*, and, as already mentioned
above, in twofold form in the Mozarabic liturgy. From here it may
have come first to Ireland. For it is in part worked into the Preface
which precedes the Canon in the Stowe Missal.[2]

All eleven other Prefaces of the present-day Missal are true

---

[1] Wilson 186. For the original form of the Roman Preface of the Apostles, see
Jungmann, *Missarum Sollemnia*[5] II, 156, which gives more details.

[2] See the text e.g. in *ZkTh* 10 (1886) 3 f. On the Trinity Preface cf. p. 102, n.3,
above, and Part Two, Ch. XII. below. In the Alcuinic appendix it is still only
the third, along with eight other Sunday Prefaces, obviously chiefly for free choice
on days without a Preface. In addition, here as also in the Gelasianum (Wilson
129), it is assigned to the first Sunday after Pentecost, which later became Trinity

prayers of praise and thanks, in the centre of which stands Christ our Lord, either as subject-matter, as the great gift for which God the almighty Father is offered thanks: thus on the three great feasts of our Lord, Christmas, Epiphany and Easter; or expressly as the High Priest through whom the acknowledgement is offered to God: in the *Praefatio communis*; or both together: in the seven other Prefaces.

These are all constructed on the plan of the *Praefatio communis*. Either, after the address to God the Father the special reason for thanks is introduced, e.g.: 'Vere dignum ... aeterne Deus, qui salutem humani generis in ligno crucis constituisti', and every time so that at the end the Saviour of the world appears as final reason for thanks, e.g.: Satan must be overcome 'per Christum Dominum nostrum'. Then from here onwards the praise of God soars upwards, out of the mouths of angels and men, through him back to the throne of the divine majesty: 'Per quem maiestatem tuam laudant angeli.'[1] Or, the theme of Christ the Lord as Mediator of the Eucharistic prayer is taken up immediately at the outset, yet another phrase of the standard Preface, the *Praefatio communis*, being brought into the opening part: 'Vere dignum ... *gratias agere* ... aeterne Deus *per Christum* Dominum nostrum'; and in the continuation the redemptive work of our Lord is depicted in the light of the feast of the day: how he ascended into heaven in order to give us a share in his godhead, how he pours out the Holy Spirit on his own and how in him the promise of a blissful resurrection shines upon us (Ascension, Whitsun, *defunctorum*); and therefore we praise God with the angelic hosts in the *sanctus*. The *per Christum* is not repeated in these passages.

Among these types thus abstracted from the eleven Prefaces mentioned may be distributed, with few exceptions, all 267 Prefaces of the Leonianum. On the chief feasts of our Lord, joy over the

Sunday, while the *communis* seems to be provided for ordinary Sundays (Mur. II, 285, 321, 382). Cf. H. Kellner, *Heortologie*[3] 90. In Gerbert's text (*Monumenta vet. lit. Alem.* I, 130 f.) the attempt is made to assimilate it to the Roman Prefaces: '. . . Adoretur aequalitas, per Xrum. quam laudant angeli'. See the text of the Mozarabic Liturgy MEL VI, 519 f., 619.

[1] Praefatio communis, de cruce, de b. Maria Virgine, de S. Joseph; to some extent, also, the Preface of Lent: God gives the salutary effect of the fast, as every other grace, through Christ our Lord.

coming, or over the work, of the Redeemer fills the whole Preface. His mediatorship is object rather than constitutive element of the Eucharistic prayer. Hence the *per Christum* at the end often gives place to an *unde profusis gaudiis* (et sim.) ; here, too, it may be hardly contained in the (shortened) opening words.[1] The others are constructed on the plan of the *Praefatio communis*. Almost always, at the end, the invariable ending, is signified by the word *per*. Once, in a fourth Ascension Preface, it is written out in part: 'Vere dign. teque suppliciter exorare, ut . . . concedas, quo Redemptor noster conscendit, attolli ut . . . capiamus quod nunc audemus sperare promissum per hunc eundem Ihm Xrm Dnum nostrum per quem te laudant angeli' etc.[2] The *per* set down on its own indicates, then, according to the context, either 'per quem' or 'per Christum Dominum nostrum per quem'. E.g.: 'Vere dign. quoniam tu sanctis tuis et patientiam tolerantiae et in beati fine certaminis das triumphum per (Christum Dominum nostrum per quem)';[3] 'Vere dign. qui se ipsum tibi pro nobis offerens immolandum idem sacerdos et sacer agnus exhibuit per (quem)'.[4] Whether the *per Christum* is to be inserted also in the opening part represented by *Vere dign.* remains in many cases uncertain; in some, however, as in the last quoted example, the context demands it. It may be omitted in cases where the proper text is joined to the address to God the Father by a relative pronoun: 'Vere dign. (. . . aeterne Deus) qui nos per mundi caligines tamquam luminaribus coeli sanctorum tuorum exemplis instituis et intercessione prosequeris per.'[5]

Some Prefaces occur which indicate another ending, e.g., *et ideo*, and in which the *per Christum* is not demanded at the beginning either. These would be the sole, very rare cases in which there is no evidence for the christological theme in the old Roman Preface.[6] In so far, however, as in later manuscripts of the other sacramentaries

---

[1] Feltoe 21, 6, 14; 160, 16; 161, 24; 163, 8; 164, 12; cf. 33, 20; 35, 4.
[2] Feltoe 21.  [3] Feltoe 7.  [4] Feltoe 11.  [5] Feltoe 8.
[6] It may be that 'per Christum' is to be added to the opening part when a new clause follows: 'Vere dign. (. . . per Christum Dominum nostrum) quia tu es gloriosus in sanctis tuis, quibus et in confessione virtutem et in passione victoriam contulisti; propterea cum angelis etc.' (Feltoe 3). On the other hand, it is not inserted in a Preface in honour of the archangel Michael: 'Vere dign. (. . . Deus) teque profusis gaudiis praedicare in die festivitatis hodiernae quo . . .'. The ending is 'et ideo' (Feltoe 106).

the shortened formulas are written out, such cases come sporadically to light. But then, as long as the Roman origin of the Preface itself is assured, the question remains whether the christological phrase has not been dropped only in consequence of a similar change to that indicated above for the Preface of the Apostles.[1]

Here another not unimportant phenomenon must be mentioned. Among the fifty-four Prefaces of the earlier Gelasianum occur some cases in which, clean contrary to the rest of the Roman tradition, there is given as terminal phrase: 'Quem laudant' (instead of some such ending as 'Per quem'), so that the passage of praise that follows on together with the *sanctus* (in the numbers I, 48, 50, 58, 63, 65, 78) is directed to Christ, or (no. I, 80) to the Holy Spirit (in no. I, 84, our trinitarian Preface, simply God is intended). For the first three cases, the investigation of the formularies concerned by Chavasse[2] expressly shows that we have to deal with later layers of the sacramentary, which were inserted only after the sixth century. In one case, (No. 78), for the same Roman Preface the original form of the text with 'Per quem' is kept in the *Missale Gothicum*.[3]

In the *Leonianum*, every Mass formulary has on the average just as much its own Preface as its own *orationes*. Whence the beginnings of a like phenomenon to that presented by the Mozarabic liturgy: through the effort to vary the Eucharistic prayer each time, its content often became removed from the central facts of the history of salvation to a point on the periphery, to the consideration of a particular feature in the divine dispensation, to the triumph of a

---

[1] In the Gregorianum proper, only one belongs here with certainty, viz. the first of two Prefaces in honour of St Anastasia (Mur. II, 7), in which the 'per Christum' is missing. Cf. with it that quite parallel, only further elaborated, in honour of St Cecilia (Mur. I, 457 f. = Feltoe 150 f.), which ends with *per*. In the text of the Gelasianum reproduced by M. Gerbert the last words of the opening are always written out; for the most part in the form: 'V.D. aeterne Deus.' In the cases where in this passage the 'per Christum' is accordingly missing, it stands regularly at the end. Sometimes, however, there is a choice: 'Per Xrm vel et ideo' (*Monumenta vet. liturg. Alem.* I, 183, 196) or: 'per quem vel et ideo' (I, 10).

[2] See above, p. 102.

[3] Ed. Mohlberg 1961, No. 357; cf. Chavasse 604. Even in the other cases, there is no question of a fixed tradition; cf. the Prefaces which recur in the later Gelasianum of the Cod. S. Gall. 348 (ed. Mohlberg, no. 873 et passim). The phrase 'Quem laudant' is not Roman, but native to the Gallic liturgical area.

martyr which God grants, or even to a petition, which follows on the introductory words. In consequence the description in longer Prefaces at times becomes somewhat prolix,[1] not to speak of the contemporary pictures of morals into which other Prefaces develop, which, however, can hardly belong to public worship, for that reason.[2] This defect and the wish to secure for the Eucharistic prayer its full impact, as is entirely suited to a great part of these Prefaces, may have led subsequently to the making of a selection from them. The *Gelasianum* numbers in H. A. Wilson's edition only fifty-four, of which a part are already again of Gallic origin; the *Gregorianum* in the edition of H. Lietzmann only fifteen, of which however only eleven are for Masses said by an ordinary priest. In the Gallican appendix of the latter, on the other hand, there are over a hundred Prefaces. Principally, the Prefaces for feasts of saints came to be curtailed. Then the *Praefatio communis* comes to the fore, which earlier was quite unknown as an independent Preface, being superfluous. Although here the essential features of the Eucharistic Prayer come out strongly, no attempt is made to express the actual object of gratitude. This is reserved to the Prefaces of feasts.[3]

For the prayer of praise and thanks of the Preface there thus results, as a rule still maintained today: it is directed to God the Father almighty and usually, in earlier times probably without exception, in such a manner that Christ is expressly named in it as Mediator of the prayer. Much the same may be said, also, of the supplicatory prayer of the *orationes*. The *orationes* (collect, secret, postcommunion) are addressed to God 'through our Lord Jesus Christ'.[4] This rule is not once broken in the *Leonianum*. Hundreds of *orationes* show the same end-note *per*. The formula itself is nowhere written out in full.[5] The rule is adhered to equally strictly in the

[1] Cf. the Prefaces in honour of St Stephen or of St Cecilia.

[2] But cf. now J. Pomares, *Gélase I. dix-huit messes du sacramentaire Leonien* (Paris 1959).

[3] The Leonianum provided also Prefaces of this type which were probably prescribed for Sundays, e.g. Feltoe, p. 145: 'Vere dign. in cuius resurrectione mirabili mors occidit redemptorum et orta est vita credentium et ideo cum angelis etc.'

[4] Since the end-formula 'per Dominum nostrum' demands a more detailed historical enquiry, it will not be treated until Part Two, ch. IV.

[5] In a Postcommunion for the Ascension it is given in part: 'Exaudi nos Ds salutaris noster, ut per haec sacrosancta mysteria in totius ecclesiae confidimus

*Gelasianum*, as far as the Mass-prayer is concerned. Only, here, in *orationes* in which towards the end Christ is already named, to avoid an accumulation of words, it simply carries on 'qui tecum vivit'.[1] In the rest, the ending here also is always given in the same manner with *Per.* or *Per Dominum.*, occasionally also *Per eundem Dominum nostrum.*[2]

The uncertainty begins only in the *Gregorianum*. Lietzmann makes here, too, all *orationes* of the original Aachen copy end with *per*, but acknowledges[3] that a sure 'reconstruction of the original' in this matter 'seems excluded'. Although the *per* is still supported with witnesses in all cases, in other manuscripts there emerge at the Advent Masses some Collects, mostly already in use at an earlier date, that now have the ending *Qui vivis*, because here they were thought of as directed to Christ. With the old rule once broken, the number of Christ-addressed *orationes* in some Churches grew ever greater, albeit slowly and without a strict uniformity being observed as between different places. Beside those which arose only through alteration of the ending, soon others also were composed which were

corpore faciendum, quod eius praecessit in capite per eundem Ihm Xrm Dnm nostrum' (Feltoe 20. Ibid. p. 49, 14 and 86, 7 the *per* is also omitted, as self-evident). At the end, the manuscript contains a supplement by another, but hardly much later, hand. There are two *orationes*, which both end 'per Xrm Dnm nostrum'; then follows an invocation to the martyrs: 'Suscipite venerabiles martyres . . .' and a prayer at the 'Benedictio fontis', which ends: '. . . Renatum in Xro Ihu cum quo vivis et regnas in unitate Sps Sancti in saecula saeculorum.' Cf. the similar end-formula in the Gelasianum: Wilson 87, 117, 158 ('cum quo vivis').

[1] Wilson 4 f. In texts which belong to the *Rituale*, the address to God is also in general retained. Exceptions, however, are two prayers for the dead, of which the second has the authentic Gallican ending: 'Salvator mundi, qui cum Patre vivis dominator et regnas Deus in unitate Spiritus Sancti in saecula'; the first: 'Qui cum Patre et Spiritu Sancto vivis et regnas in saecula saeculorum.' Here belong also two passages from the baptismal rite (p. 59, explanation of the Our Father); the second runs: 'Potens est Dominus Deus noster (to whom the Our Father was directed) ut . . . ad coelestia regna faciat pervenire. Qui vivit et regnat cum Deo Patre in unitate Spiritus Sancti . . . .' P. 295, for a prayer which is addressed to God the Father, the ending is given: 'Qui vivis et regnas in unitate'. Cf. the Gallic parallels above, p. 93 f., 98 f., 103 f.

[2] The formula appears to be written out in full in an *oratio* p. 81, which, however, scarcely belongs to the sacramentary; that is, it shows the same wording as we have today; only the word *Deus* is here, just as in the Embolism of the Gregorianum (Mur. II, 6), inserted in a different place: '. . . Regnat Deus in unitate Spiritus Sancti per omnia.'

[3] P. xxv.

addressed more or less clearly to Christ from the beginning. The following table gives a summary of the Christ-addressed *orationes* in the Roman Missal of 1924.[1]

| | COLLECTS | SECRETS | POSTCOM. | MASS | TOTAL |
|---|---|---|---|---|---|
| Proprium de tempore: Sundays & Ferias | 7(7) | – | 2(2) | 1 | 10(9) |
| Proprium de tempore: inserted feasts[2] | 2 | – | 2 | - | 4 |
| Proprium de sanctis | 21(4) | 7 | 12 | 2 | 42(4) |
| Missae votivae | 1 | – | 3 | – | 4 |
| Missae defunct. | 1(1) | – | 2(2) | 1(1) | 4(4) |
| | 32(12) | 7 | 21(4) | 4(1) | 64(17) |

[1] After the *Editio decima iuxta typicam Vaticanam* of the Missal restored by Pius X (Ratisbon, 1924). The blessings added at the end and the 'Missae propriae quae in aliquibus locis celebrari possunt' are not taken into account here, nor are the prayers at the beginning for the 'Praeparatio ad missam' and for the 'Gratiarum actio'. Alongside the figure for the present-day Christ-addressed *orationes* is given in brackets the number which existed in an earlier period with essentially the same wording but with the ending *per*, found solely with the aid of the Leonianum and the Gelasianum, the latter in the editions of both Wilson and Gerbert. Only in two cases are the Gregorianum (Collect for the Vigil of the Assumption) and the present Pontifical (Absolutio ad tumbam), respectively, involved. By 1962 the situation had somewhat changed. To the seven Roman secrets directed to Christ one more was added in 1932, that for the feast of St Gabriel Possenti, the Passionist; the Mass formulary to which it belongs is at the same time the third in the history of the Roman Mass in which all three *orationes* are addressed to Christ, the other two being remarked on p. 120, n. 3; the feast of the Seven Dolours (prescribed for the whole Church in 1727) and the feast of the founder of the Passionists, Paul of the Cross (canonized in 1867). The figures for the Christ-addressed *orationes* for the period up to 1924 otherwise need not be enlarged only in the Proprium Sanctorum: one collect (1925, feast of St Teresa of the Child Jesus), two postcommunions (1936, feast of St John Bosco; 1940, feast of St John Leonardi, whose formulary, however, had already been prescribed 'pro aliquibus locis'). In the other thirteen Mass formularies inserted in the Proprium Sanctorum since 1924, the old Roman order of address with 'Per Dominum' is followed again. Since 1937, there have been no more exceptions to the rule. Thus the figures show clearly the late influence of baroque piety and, on the other side, that of the liturgical renewal on the Missale Romanum.

[2] Feast of the Holy Family and Corpus Christi.

Hence more than a quarter of the *orationes* which now express or presuppose the address to Christ and end with *qui vivis* were formerly considered simply as prayers to God which were offered through Christ. In the majority of cases, the reason for the switching of the address is clear. The seven collects in the first row all belong to Advent. In four cases the cry for help now took the form: 'Excita, quaesumus Domine, potentiam tuam et *veni*,' or: '*Adventus* tui consolationibus adiuventur.'[1] In some cases these four *orationes* show even in old manuscripts of the *Gregorianum* the ending *qui vivis*. One would now rather understand the Coming of the *Parousia Christi*. In the three others, God's gracious visitation is prayed for (tua *visitatio*).[2] For at least two of them, the oldest copies of the *Gregorianum* give the corresponding ending with *per*.[3] The same is found in the two *orationes* of the All Souls Mass. In the collect, God is named: 'Fidelium, Deus, omnium conditor et *redemptor*'; the postcommunion has: 'Tuae *redemptionis* facias esse participes.' The custom now was to speak of Redeemer and redemption only in respect to Christ.[4] The *Absolutio ad tumbam* after the Mass of the Dead, which begs the divine judge to show mercy: 'Ne intres in iudicium cum servo tuo,' and which in the Missal seems to presuppose the address to Christ ('qui vivis et regnas'), today still retains in the *Pontificale Romanum* the ending 'per Christum Dominum nostrum'.

In the *Proprium de sanctis*, of the four Collects that have changed their endings, two concern the Apostle Peter: 'Deus, qui b. Petro . . . pontificium tradidisti,' and: 'Deus, cuius dextera b. Petrum . . . erexit et coapostolum eius Paulum . . . liberavit.' Here the aim is to derive the evidence for Peter's prerogatives concretely from the hand of his master. The third *oratio*, 29, VIII, in comparison with its

[1] First and fourth Sundays of Advent, Ember Wednesday and Friday. With *per*: Wilson 218, 214; Gerbert I, 202, 205. Cf. John 14: 23, 'et Pater diliget eum et ad eum veniemus' (the Coming is here also referred to the Father).

[2] Third Sunday of Advent, Ember Saturday. With *per*: Wilson 217, 222; Gerbert I, 205, 206.

[3] E.g. Mur. I, 135, 177, whereas the four mentioned above already end here with 'qui vivis'.

[4] On the other hand, with *per* Feltoe 146; Wilson 308 f.; cf. the name for God σωτήρ in Paul. In the *Rituale Romanum* tit. VIII, c. 29 ad 6 an *oratio*, 'Deus, qui totius orbis conditor et humani generis redemptor . . .' even today ends with 'per Christum Dominum nostrum'.

form in the *Gelasianum*, shows an insertion: 'Sancti Ioannis Baptistae [praecursoris et] martyris tui', and in consequence has the *qui vivis*.[1] The fourth pertains to the Vigil of the Assumption and first appears in the *Gregorianum*: 'Deus, qui virginalem aulam beatae Mariae, in qua habitares, eligere dignatus es, da quaesumus, ut sua nos defensione munitos iucundos faciat (sc. 'Christus'; *Miss. Rom.*: 'facias') suae interesse festivitati, qui tecum vivit.'[2] It was natural to relate the dwelling of God in the Virgin, which earlier was understood in the sense of the *Dominus tecum*,[3] to the incarnate Son.

Both the postcommunions in the first row are missing in some manuscripts of the *Gelasianum*, but both appear with *per* already in the *Leonianum*.[4]

Though the first Christ-addressed *orationes* of our Missal arose on Frankish soil simply through the Roman ending being displaced by a Gallican here in customary use,[5] yet the type thus produced

---

[1] With *per*: Wilson 181, 186, 196.

[2] Thus Muratori II, 113; Lietzmann: 'festivitati', 'per'.

[3] Cf. 'Spiritus Sancti habitaculum' in the Collect of 21 Nov., Presentation of Our Lady.

[4] Feltoe 5, 76. The one from Easter Wednesday runs: 'Ab omni nos Domine quaesumus vetustate purgatos sacramenti (*Miss. Rom*: + tui) veneranda perceptio in novam transferat creaturam per'; the other: 'Sumpsimus Domine sacri dona mysterii humiliter deprecantes, ut quae in tui commemorationem nos facere praecepisti, in nostrae proficiant infirmitatis auxilium per.' This *oratio* may be the only case in which the *per* actually seems somewhat forced; but 'commemoratio' can be understood in the sense of 'laus'. The *oratio* recurs with 'qui vivis' in the present Missal also on the twenty-second Sunday after Pentecost and in No. 12 of the *orationes diversae* (above counted only once). In Gerbert I, 129 it ends: 'Per te Ihu Xre', a pure Gallic, and particularly Mozarabic, ending. Cf. with this C. Mohlberg, *Das fränkische Sakramentarium Gelasianum* (Münster i. W., 1918), oratio No. 835 the correction.

[5] The Gallican 'qui vivis' had different forms, according as a prayer to Christ or to God the Father was to be indicated, or again as this distinction was to be entirely ignored; see above, p. 93 f. Out of these varieties, only the end-formula 'qui vivis . . . cum Deo Patre' has entered the Roman liturgy, and this in such a way that the expression 'Qui vivis' in the *orationes* of the Mass always stands for this formula, thus presupposing the address to Christ. Other end-formulas from the liturgies of the Gallic type appear only sporadically: 'Per te, Christe Jesu, Salvator mundi, qui in Trinitate perfecta vivis' (at the blessing of the candles at Candlemas), and the ending of the second *oratio* in Prime: 'Salvator mundi, qui vivis.' In a prayer in optative form: 'Adiuvante Domino nostro Jesu Christo qui . . . cum Patre et Spiritu Sancto' (blessing at the 'Missa pro sponso et sponsa'). In a prayer

seems to have formed the pattern for the Christ-addressed *orationes* that in the succeeding period were composed directly as such. For they begin strikingly, in much the greatest part, with an address such as *Deus qui* or *Domine*[1] and make it evident only in their further course that by this vague title Christ the Lord is to be understood.[2] Even *orationes* from recent times are composed on this model.[3] This external assimilation of the Christ-addressed *oratio* to the *oratio* hitherto usually directed through Christ to God the Lord made easier the rise of the somewhat levelling rule by which a number of *orationes*, as they came to be inserted side by side since the later Middle Ages, are to be strung together without regard to the address used. Only the first and the last have the end-formula appropriate to them.[4] Only later does there appear with this practice, but then in ever increasing number, *orationes* which begin immediately in a definite address: '*Domine Jesu (Christe)*.' Within the variable part of the Mass, the oldest example of this would be, perhaps, the Collect of Sixtus V prescribed for the whole Church on the feast of the

---

to God the Father: 'Qui vivis et regnas cum eodem Unigenito tuo et Spiritu Sancto Deus' (Blessing of the fire on Holy Saturday). Also in both the thanksgiving texts of the *Benedictio mensae*: 'Agimus tibi gratias' and 'Benedictus Deus', the closing 'qui vivis (vivit)'—corresponding to the Gallican provenance—may not have to be referred necessarily to Christ, which elsewhere in the Roman rite always proves to be the case.

[1] The Father's name is used often for *orationes* in general only in the Leonianum: 'sancte Pater', 'Pater gloriae', et sim., e.g. Feltoe 124 f., 127 f.

[2] There is a parallel to this when in Egypt and elsewhere the old address Κύριε ὁ θεὸς ἡμῶν is adopted in the Christ-addressed prayers; see above p. 32, 53 f., 77. The oldest Christ-addressed *orationes* composed as such in our Roman Missal may be in the Corpus Christi Mass deriving from St Thomas (A. J. Binterim, *Denkwürdigkeiten der christkatholischen Kirche* (Mainz, 1829 ff,), V. I, pp. 280 ff.), with its collect (Deus qui) and its Postcommunion (Fac nos, quaesumus Domine). For the relevant *orationes* in the Masses of the Finding of the Cross and Mary Madgalen are most probably later. For the chronology of the Roman calendar of feasts, there is a good survey in DACL 5, 1439–52.

[3] Cf. the feast of the Archangel Gabriel. The new collect prescribed since 1909 for the feast of St Paulinus begins: 'Deus, qui omnia pro te in hoc saeculo relinquentibus . . . vitam aeternam promisisti,' and ends: 'qui vivis'.

[4] Thus in the Mass for the Dead, with three *orationes* coming together, there is added to the second collect (directed to God) a third, the Christ-addressed *oratio Fidelium*, with the ending suited to itself only: 'qui vivis et regnas cum Deo Patre.'

Stigmata of St Francis (17 Sept.): 'Domine Jesu Christe, qui frigescente mundo . . . passionis tuae sacra stigmata renovasti.'[1]

In the table above, the eye is caught further by the relatively small number of the *secrets* addressed to Christ. This is evidently connected with the secret being the oldest Offertory prayer. This finds expression in the secret's older name, *oratio super oblata*, which only after the eleventh century was universally displaced by the present name and is today still retained in the Ambrosian rite. If anywhere, here above all it is fitting to keep the old order of address in the praying and offering, through Christ to God, as it exists unaltered in the prayers of offering of the Canon and is conformable to the nature of the act. Indeed, here quite late, beside the formula, on occasion the *per Christum* receives pregnant expression; thus on the feast of the Visitation of Our Lady (celebrated since the thirteenth century): 'Unigeniti tui, Domine, nobis succurrat humanitas, ut . . . oblationem nostram tibi faciat acceptam Jesus Christus Dominus noster, qui tecum vivit.' The oldest of the seven secrets addressed to Christ is that of 13 June.[2] Here the theme of the sacrifice to God the Father still hovers over the prayer: 'Praesens oblatio fiat, Domine, populo tuo salutaris, pro quo dignatus es Patri tuo te viventem hostiam immolare, qui cum eodem Deo Patre.' The other six, of which four make Christ the Lord appear as receiver of the sacrifice, all belong to formularies which only after the eighteenth century were prescribed for the whole Church.[3] But not only the Christ-addressed secrets but also the collects and postcommunions of this class, among the well over a thousand *orationes* of the Roman

---

[1] In the *ordo Missae*, in the three prayers immediately before the Communion, the transition to this address is already completed earlier. In the Masses 'pro aliquibus locis', mainly deriving from a later period, in which the Christ-addressed prayer is already much more frequent without, however, being definitely predominant, the address goes already in about half these cases: 'Domine Jesu (Christe).'

[2] Antony of Padua; the feast universally prescribed by Sixtus V.

[3] On the feast of the Sacred Heart (before 1928): 'Tuere nos Domine, tua tibi holocausta offerentes.' Similarly on the feasts of the Seven Dolours of Our Lady (cf. here also the postcommunion), Paul of the Cross (d. 1775), Alphonsus Liguori (d. 1787). The secrets of the Solemnity of St Joseph and of St Francis Caracciolo (d. 1608) do not contain the idea of sacrifice. The formularies for the Seven Dolours and Paul of the Cross were, until 1932, the only ones in the missal in which all three *orationes* are directed to Christ.

Missal, even today are relatively rare exceptions. Thus they are lacking entirely in the *Commune sanctorum* and in the Masses of Lent. Among the 105 *Orationes diversae* only one occurs. The *orationes* of most Mass formularies show throughout the same order of address as Preface and Canon: through Christ to God the Lord.

The other variable texts of the Mass, which are used for the individual formularies, are, apart from the readings, mainly intended for the chant (*introitus, graduale, offertorium, communio*). They thence exhibit in all cases a greater freedom, corresponding to their poetic character, even when in content they are prayers. Therefore here occasionally not only Christ the Lord is greeted or besought in direct address but also Mary and the saints, whereas the latter are certainly mentioned in the *orationes* of their feasts, but, as compared with the true Mediator between God and man, remain in the background.

Just as the Canon comprises the fixed core round which lie the varying Prefaces and *orationes*, so the *ordo Missae* comprises an outer ring which encloses both and also partly penetrates between their separate constituents. Its evolution[1] is characterized, in the same way as the corresponding parts of the liturgy in the East, by gradual growth to become an ever more pronounced stratum. In this process, the structure of the prayer becomes noticeably removed from the older type, so that the *ordo Missae* as a whole chiefly represents an extra-Roman elaboration of the Roman rite.[2]

The Prayers at the foot of the altar, in their first half, consist of a complete form of introit, in the second, of a confession of sins, and must not occupy us further.[3] The two prayers at the mounting of the altar are both addressed to God the Lord, but bear clear traces of their different origins. Whereas one might expect the ordinary conclusion 'per Christum nostrum' rather in the second passage, only the first, *Aufer a nobis*, shows it. This prayer appears also as a collect

---

[1] Cf. Jungmann, *Missarum Sollemnia*[5] I, 341 ff.; II, 3 ff., 341 ff.

[2] Cf. E. Bishop, *Liturgica historica* 1 ff. ('The Genius of the Roman Rite'); L. Eisenhofer, *Katholische Liturgik* (Freiburg i, B., 1924), pp. 183 ff.; V. Thalhofer-L. Eisenhofer II, 36 ff.

[3] Yet it may be remarked that at the absolution the reason for the forgiveness hoped for is indicated simply with a sign of the Cross.

already in the *Leonianum*. The second begs forgiveness for sins 'per merita sanctorum'.

Between the readings we meet a pair of prayers, again of the same age, of which likewise the first only, *Munda cor meum*, ends with *per Christum*, while the second in the Solemn Mass, as a blessing over the deacon, ends with the naming of the three divine Persons. Also the various Offertory prayers appear only from the ninth century together with the single offering prayer of old, the secret, now separate, now united in changing order, and thus accompany the preparation of the gifts. They all retain the address to God the Lord, but in different ways. The first begins: 'Suscipe sancte Pater,' the last: 'Suscipe sancta Trinitas.'[1] Even the invocation 'Veni sanctificator, omnipotens aeterne Deus,' with the request for the sanctification of the sacrificial gifts, as only God can grant it, must not necessarily be understood of the Holy Spirit.[2] Of all these prayers, only the last—together, in the solemn Mass, with the blessing of the incense—use the customary end-formula 'per Christum Dominum nostrum'. On the other hand, the place of our Lord in the history of salvation, uniting divinity and humanity, is magnificently expressed in the venerable oratio 'Deus qui humanae substantiae',[3] which accompanies the symbolic mixing of the water and wine. Since Christ is named at the end of the text of this prayer, it closes with *qui tecum* and no longer uses the full end-formula.

In the second half of the Mass, outside the Canon, there comes first the ancient middle-member between Canon and communion, the Pater noster with its continuation, the embolism. The embolism, in its address and ending, still keeps entirely to the style of the ancient orationes: 'Libera nos, quaesumus Domine . . . Per eundem Dominum.' Formerly, it was immediately followed by the Breaking and the Communion. But in the course of time there grew up around these latter a narrow circle of prayer, whose individual prayers

---

[1] The address to the Trinity occurs in prayers of Gallican origin; cf. above pp. 88, 102, n. 4; DACL 1, 2598 f.

[2] Though in Missals of the middle ages it sometimes shows the addition 'Sancte Spiritus', in other cases it again has, instead, the ending 'per Christum Dominum nostrum'; see *Micrologus* c. 23.

[3] Leonianum (Feltoe 159).

also here, but more uniformly than is the case in other liturgies, choose the address to Christ, whose body and blood are to be received. They begin with the *Agnus Dei* chant, which is discussed below.[1]

The prayers which now begin are all later than the *Agnus Dei*. Separately or in various groupings before or after the communion, they appear about the ninth century, but in their present arrangement only from the fourteenth century. The first three, a prayer at the Kiss of Peace and two for the private preparation of the celebrant at the communion, have the definite address 'Domine Jesu Christe' with corresponding end-formula, which here in its slight variation reflects something of the multiformity of the Gallican *oratio* endings of this type. The 'Domine non sum dignus' of the centurion of Capharnaum ends the preparation.

Of the short prayer-texts which then accompany the reception itself, or follow it, again the last is clearly directed to Christ: 'Corpus tuum, Domine, quod sumpsi . . . qui vivis et regnas in saecula saeculorum.' The intervening matter does not clash, at least, with this address. 'Quod ore sumpsimus' is indeed an old postcommunion which already occurs in the *Leonianum*[2] and is still used on Thursday in Passion Week, both times ending with *per*, which here, however, is omitted.

Outside this circle of communion prayers, there only remains the last of the true Mass prayers: 'Placeat tibi, sancta Trinitas.' It appears for the first time in the eleventh century. With its ending 'per Christum Dominum nostrum', it fits harmoniously into the order of address as resumed, in most cases, in the *postcommunio*.

---

[1] Part Two, ch. XIV.        [2] Feltoe 69.

# PART TWO

# HISTORY OF THE CHRISTOLOGICAL THEME IN LITURGICAL PRAYER

*We now proceed to consider what can be the explanation of the striking difference which we were able to observe in the various liturgies in regard to the manner in which the Christ idea is built into the prayer.*

*Ecclesiastical and dogmatic history must be our guide in this enquiry. While we thus seek to follow the historical line of development more light should be shed on the meaning and point of individual forms. The natural starting-point, however, and the necessary background for the understanding of all the later changes is provided by the data in the books of the New Testament itself.*

# IX

# INSTRUCTIONS AND BEGINNINGS IN THE NEW TESTAMENT

Dɪᴅ the Lord Christ himself give guiding principles as to the place he wished to occupy in the prayer of his disciples, the worship of his Church? On prayer, the Lord often gave instructions; they have their climax in the Our Father, which he taught his disciples at their express request. As they were bound to expect, he there directs them to the Father, to whom they are to offer praise and petition. Thus at other times he always spoke of the 'Father', of 'your Father', probably also simply of God (Luke 18:7; John 4:24), when he spoke of prayer. Consequently his teaching signified no break in this respect with what they had been used to from of old; only a new spirit was to enter into their prayer; it was to become simpler, more heartfelt, more trustful.

Thus he also teaches the woman at Jacob's Well, who raises the question of Garizim versus Sion (it is therefore of liturgical prayer that she is speaking): '. . . The hour is coming, and now is, when the true worshippers will worship the Father in spirit and truth, for such the Father seeks to worship him. God is spirit, and those who worship him must worship in spirit and truth' (John 4:23 f.). But what does 'spirit and truth' mean here? In fact, probably the same as that which recurs several times, only put more concretely and definitely, in the parting words of the last evening, when he teaches the disciples to request the Father *in his name*. The whole parting discourse is an instruction on the attitude of mind which they are to maintain as his disciples and Apostles and in which the Holy Spirit will confirm them. This outlook is the natural fruit of their interior union with him, their Master, which he teaches them to grasp in the parable of the vine and the branches. This attitude and state of soul is also henceforth to rule their prayer. It is only another way of putting it when, immediately following that parable, we find (John 15:7): 'If you abide *in me*, and my words abide in you, ask whatever you will, and it shall be done for you,' and when other passages[1] say that whatever they ask in his name, that will be given to them.[2]

Thus the Lord Christ in any case wishes to be not only an outward teacher of prayer, but beyond this a determining factor, indeed *the* determining factor, in the state of soul of those who pray as Christians. Whether and how this new impetus then makes itself felt in words as well, whether in so doing the name of Jesus is mentioned, will depend on the forms and ceremonies in which prayer is offered.

May the disciples of Jesus also pray *to* him? The Lord himself appears in the same farewell discourse to give a reply to such a question. For after saying that he goes to the Father, but that they will work wonders; that they have only to ask in his name, and he will grant it, so that the Father will be glorified in the Son, he adds: 'If you ask *me* anything in my name, I will do it' (John 14:14). This sounds like a comforting condescension to his disciples, who indeed were wont to come to him in all their concerns, and who could not

---

[1] John 14:13; 15:16; 16:23, 24, 26; cf. Matt. 18:19 f.

[2] 'That praying in the name of Jesus means nothing else but praying in the unity of faith with the Saviour is clear from 15:7, where the same promise of unconditional hearing of the disciples is given on the condition that they abide in him and his words abide in them; here the explanation is given of ἐν ὀνόματί μου ... It is a praying and doing in vital communion with Jesus and in the power of this organic union. Mostly, there is added the further note that the content and tendency of this working and praying is ordered to the revelation of salvation and its purpose.' P. W. von Keppler, *Unseres Herrn Trost, Erklärung der Abschiedsreden und des hohepriesterlichen Gebetes Jesu*[2] (Freiburg, 1914), pp. 99 f.

think of themselves in this hour when they were to perform wonders, without his helpful proximity.[1] Even the prayer to Jesus is, accordingly, permitted and authorized; he had indeed revealed himself even as true God. But the Lord himself lays no special weight on its being used.[2] He also says nothing about its being necessary to offer worship to him, although he demands the recognition of his divine-human dignity.[3]

At different encounters with the Lord after his Resurrection, however, as a natural consequence of all that had occurred, the disciples in fact rendered him worship.[4]

How is this reserve of the Lord with regard to the worship owing to himself to be understood? In the light of his whole position in the history of salvation it is understandable. '. . . The Son of Man came not to be served but to serve' (Mt. 20:28). He is the Mediator between God and men (1 Tim. 2:5). Though he stands in regard to his dignity always at the side of God, whose nature as much as the nature of man he possesses undiminished, yet in regard to his work,

---

[1] Cf. A. Klawek, *Das Gebet zu Jesus* 23–9. On p. 26, he says: 'Thus v. 14 contains a certain concession to the disciples; it was not on his own initiative that Jesus mentioned the prayer to himself, or else he would probably have done it earlier and would not have clothed this new idea in a conditional clause; rather, he was led to it by the circumstances.'

[2] Cf. Keppler 101 f.

[3] At John 5:22 f. he says: 'The Father has given all judgment to the Son, that all may honour the Son, even as they honour the Father. He who does not honour the Son does not honour the Father.' The honour here demanded most probably implies that one recognize the rightness of the worship given to the Son, but lays no stress on it. We are concerned here, rather, in the great dispute with the Jews, chiefly with faith. The honour intended here is in the first place a recapitulation of all those demands which Jesus has made at other times and which were already constantly met by the Apostles, in essentials, by virtue of their discipleship: belief in him, as they believe in God (John 14:1); commitment without reserve, not only to his teaching, but also to his person (Matt. 10:32); a love which is equivalent to the love with the whole heart and with the whole soul as it is demanded for God (Luke 14:26). A. Klawek would go further, and by the honour here demanded would 'understand an external veneration, similar to the worship of God hitherto, made manifest especially by public worship, and in which prayer plays a leading part' (*Das Gebet zu Jesus* 22). Even then, the claim is not yet made that prayer must also be addressed to the Son.

[4] Matt. 28:17; John 20:28. In the other passages in the Gospels in which is mentioned an *adoratio* (προσκύνησις) of Jesus in the course of his earthly life, the meaning of a reverential greeting is more probable. A. Klawek 12 ff.

his object and his life-task, he is quite as fully on the side of men. Not as a king's son had he come into the world, to receive the homage owed to God by men; he had been born the poorest of men, so that as the first of men at the head of mankind, he might give God the honour due to him, dying and rising again to open the way to God for mankind. Therefore he renounces in his life all homage, as much as he renounces the good things of the life of paradise which were due to him as one not touched by the hereditary guilt and as he renounces all privileges, which would rather hinder him in his work as Redeemer. That was his attitude above all for the period of his public activity. But also for the period of his glorification he allowed himself no other homage than that which his disciples, taught by the Holy Spirit, were to render him. Even where in his last discourse he speaks of the future, even where John from later recollection recalls just those themes and passages of Jesus in which the Godhead of his master shines out at its brightest, even here the instructions of the Lord hardly overstep that line.[1]

How then did the primitive apostolic community solve this problem? A. Klawek has examined the pertinent evidence from the writings of the New Testament and comes to the decision: 'Since Jesus was accepted as Lord and indeed as Lord of all . . . , the Christians regarded themselves as his servants, as they had hitherto been . . . servants of Jahweh; the same act of faith which they had earlier awakened in their hearts only towards the God of Israel, they now directed to Jesus as well. Out of this faith arose the worship of Jesus. This much is certain, that the Saviour did not receive after his death at any time purely human honour, such as is customary towards distinguished persons whom men recall with gratitude and to whom they devote commemorative speeches.'[2]

We also find subsequently sporadic examples and traces of the prayer directed to Christ. The last words of St Stephen are: 'Lord Jesus, receive my spirit; Lord, do not hold this sin against them' (Acts 7:59). What was, indeed, more natural than that the first martyr should call on him for whose teaching he is about to give his

---

[1] John 14:1, 13, 14. Cf. John 4:21, 23.
[2] *Das Gebet zu Jesus* 36 f. From this work most of the exegetical data which follow are also drawn.

life? Also Paul mentions that he turns at times to Christ in prayer.[1] But this is private prayer, to which he devotes himself on matters touching his vocation as an Apostle, which had indeed been allotted him by the Lord Christ before Damascus. In addition, the Apostle often weaves into his speech short prayers—or uses them at the end of the letter—in which he begs of our Lord grace for his faithful, or he attaches to his statement about Christ a short passage in praise of him, just as occurs also outside the pauline epistles.[2] From all this the conviction shines out clearly enough that Jesus is worthy of adoration, which the very title, *Kyrios*, itself manifests. This is expressed with great emphasis in Phil. 2:10 f: '. . . At the name of Jesus every knee should bow.'[3] Nevertheless, the actual use of the prayer addressed solely to Christ was rather an exception than otherwise, as appears even in the private prayer-life of the Christians, at any rate in that of St Paul.[4]

The communal prayer of the Christians, however, Christian public worship, is addressed to the Lord *God*. For the community in Jerusalem, it was connected above all with attendance at the temple. '. . . Day by day, attending the temple together and . . . praising God.'[5] While Peter lay in prison, 'earnest prayer for him was made to God by the church' (Acts 12:5). James deplores the incongruity in the use of the tongue: 'With it we bless the Lord and Father, and with it we curse men, who are made in the likeness of God.'[6]

---

[1] I Tim. 1:12: 'I thank him who has given me strength for this, Christ Jesus our Lord, because he judged me faithful by appointing me to his service'. Since the 'Lord' in Paul, outside quotations from the Septuagint, is always Christ, 2 Cor. 12:8 is also pertinent: 'Three times I besought the Lord about this, that it (the messenger of Satan) should leave me'; probable also Acts 22:16, where the newly-converted is urged by Ananias 'to call on his name'.

[2] 2 Tim. 4:18: ᾧ ἡ δόξα εἰς τοὺς αἰῶνας τῶν αἰώνων. Likewise Rom. 9:5; Heb. 13:21; I Peter 4:11; 2 Peter 3:18; Apoc. 1:6. With the same passage of praise to Christ end, later, many homilies of the Greek fathers.

[3] Cf. also Hebrews 1:6.

[4] As compared with the two above-mentioned examples of the prayer to Christ, forty-five prayers directed to God have been identified in Paul. In the doxologies, the ratio is two to eleven (without Hebrews). Cf. Klawek 74, 80.

[5] Acts 2:46 f.; cf. 4:21, 24.

[6] James 3:9. There is also mention of a more incidental praise of God in Acts 10:46; 11:18; 16:25; 21:20.

But also the Christians are sometimes called ἐπικαλούμενοι τὸ ὄνομα τοῦ Ἰησοῦ.[1] The expression has been frequently studied and variously explained. Most likely, it labels the Christians as those 'who call upon the name of Jesus'. This appears to contradict the fact just established, but does not. The invocation of the name of Jesus constitutes, according to A. Steinmann (re Acts 9:14), precisely the 'confessional' trade-mark distinguishing the Christians from the Jews: the naming of one rejected by the Jews is a very important element in their prayer and public worship. In what way the name of Christ was now mentioned, that perhaps the Christians' prayer was directly addressed to him, is however not yet stated. The expression itself derives from the saying of the prophet Joel (2:32): '. . . All who call upon the name of the Lord shall be delivered,' where the invocation was in the first place to be understood of sharing in the communal worship of the temple. This saying was familiar to the Christians and was soon applied by them to Christ.[2] Thus it acquired the meaning: he who takes part in the worship of Christians, who here with the whole community prays as a Christian in the name of Jesus, will be saved.[3]

But in what form did the theme of Christ now appear in the public worship of the early Church? Leaving aside the confession of Christ, which could not be separated from Baptism, and the memorial of the Lord, which constitutes the centre of the eucharistic celebration, thanks for the salvation promised to the Fathers and now bestowed in Christ appears the self-evident subject matter of the community's prayer, as it also indeed appears as subject matter of the prayer at the beginning of many Epistles. To give expression to these thanks, chants were immediately at hand, such as the Magnificat and Benedictus. New compositions tended to change to a distinct emphasis on the name and work of the Redeemer, and also early on to be directly addressed to him in praise.[4]

---

[1] Cf. Acts 9:14, 21; I Cor. 1:2; II Tim. 2:22; Romans 10:12.

[2] Cf. Romans 10:13 f. as against Acts 2:21.

[3] Cf. E. von der Goltz, *Das Gebet in der ältesten Christenheit* 129. Klawek 39–45.

[4] The Apostle speaks of hymns and canticles which the faithful should sing, at one time to the 'Lord', at another to 'God' (Eph. 5:19; Col. 3:16), and he himself quotes texts (Eph. 5:14; I Tim. 3:16) which obviously belong to such hymns in praise of the Redeemer, just as they were used in the common assemblies. Also, the

But what interests us above all is the ordinary *prose prayer*, which offers up adoration, thanks and petition. In Acts 4:24–30 one such is handed down to us as, according to A. Steinmann's conjecture, Peter himself probably recited it in the assembled community after his return from the judicial interrogation on account of the healing of the man born lame. It begins: 'Sovereign Lord, who didst make the heaven and the earth and the sea and everything in them', then indicates what the great ones of the earth have perpetrated against Jesus and what they now threaten to repeat against his own, and ends with the request for frankness in speaking, and attestation of their words by God's mighty hand, 'while thou stretchest out thy hand to heal, and signs and wonders are performed through the name of thy holy servant Jesus'. As Peter has just been enabled to heal the man born lame in the name of Jesus, in confidently looking up to him, so may God grant it also at other times to the young Church. The one who prays is engrossed with the idea of Jesus, in whose name the prayer ends, although in what relation the Lord stands to the act of praying itself is not expressed.

Here, various passages in the Epistles come to our aid. In Paul, the expression recurs, 'praying in the name of Jesus', viz., in connexion with the prayer of thanks: the faithful are at all times to give thanks to God the Father for everything in the name of our Lord Jesus Christ (Eph. 5:20), just as (Col. 3:17) they are admonished: 'And whatever you do, in word or deed, do everything in the name of the Lord Jesus, giving thanks to God the Father through him.' The prayer is to be performed, as is one's whole life, in union with Christ, in his name.[1] More precisely, they should thank God

chants of the Apocalypse in which God and the Lamb are praised may have had their parallels in public worship here below. God and the Lamb are praised side by side in the hymns at 5:13; 7:10; 11:15; 12:10 ff. To the Lamb alone are the chants in 5:9 f. and 5:12 sung, the former in the second person: 'Worthy art thou.' In several others God alone is named. Also, the 'Maranatha' (I Cor. 16:22; Didache 10:6) appears to be an invocation to Christ (Our Lord, come!), not a statement (Our Lord has come). F. J. Dölger, *Sol salutis*[2] (1925) pp. 198–219; especially p. 209.

[1] Cf. M. Meinertz for both passages. It is remarkable that Paul does not use the expression 'in Christ' for the life of prayer—elsewhere he uses it more than a hundred times in order to express the life-giving element in which the whole behaviour

'through him'. Rejected by the world, they go out to him from the camp and 'through him . . . continually offer up a sacrifice of praise to God, that is, the fruit of lips that acknowledge his name' (Hebr. 13:13 ff.). Similarly, Peter urges the faithful to employ the gifts of God in the spirit of God, 'in order that in everything God may be glorified through Jesus Christ.'[1] This 'through him' is now at times introduced also into the actual prayer. At the beginning of the Epistle to the Romans (1:8), Paul says: 'First, I thank my God through Jesus Christ for all of you', and at the end of the same Epistle: 'To the only wise God be glory for evermore through Jesus Christ!'[2] Jude also ends his Epistle with such a passage of praise: 'To the only God, our Saviour through Jesus Christ our Lord, be glory. . . .' It is thus retained above all in communal public worship, in liturgical prayer. 2 Cor. 1:20 seems to show this particularly well: 'For all the promises of God find their Yes in him. That is why we utter the Amen through him ($\delta\iota\grave{o}$ $\kappa\alpha\grave{\iota}$ $\delta\iota'$ $\alpha\grave{\upsilon}\tau o\hat{\upsilon}$ $\tau\grave{o}$ $'A\mu\acute{\eta}\nu$), to the glory of God.' Here there is clearly an allusion to a liturgical custom, but there is a possible doubt over the meaning. Does the liturgical practice serve only as an image, and do the faithful therefore give their Amen to the divine promises, and through Christ only in so far as through him they have recognized them as true, because in him they are fulfilled (R. Cornely), or because Jesus through his grace causes in them this operation of faith (J. Sickenberger)? On the basis of the examples just quoted, the practice of prayer represented especially by Paul suggests the interpretation: the faithful, in public worship, by the Amen declare their agreement with the *prayer*

---

of the faithful should move, the organism as members of which they should live and act. Passages such as Phil. 3:3 and Romans 15:17 are already somewhat remote. This is still more the case with others which E. von der Goltz cites, p. 94, f.n. 1. In Eph. 3:21 the $\grave{\epsilon}\nu$ is not a more precise determination of the *activity* of praying ($\alpha\grave{\upsilon}\tau\hat{\wp}$ $\acute{\eta}$ $\delta\acute{o}\xi\alpha$ $\grave{\epsilon}\nu$ $\tau\hat{\eta}$ $\grave{\epsilon}\kappa\kappa\lambda\eta\sigma\acute{\iota}\alpha$ $\kappa\alpha\grave{\iota}$ $\grave{\epsilon}\nu$ $X\rho\iota\sigma\tau\hat{\wp}$ $'I\eta\sigma o\hat{\upsilon}$). In such cases Paul uses rather $\grave{\epsilon}\nu$ $\grave{o}\nu\acute{o}\mu\alpha\tau\iota$ $'I\eta\sigma o\hat{\upsilon}$ $X\rho\iota\sigma\tau o\hat{\upsilon}$. This expression, in the language of John, with its more pronounced hebraizing tendency, means scarcely more than the simple $\grave{\epsilon}\nu$ $X\rho\iota\sigma\tau\hat{\wp}$, but in Paul it seems to have a nuance of its own: it seems, just as I Cor. 6:11; 5:4; Acts 16:18; 19:13, to indicate that his name is at the same time mentioned, and therefore shows an $\grave{\epsilon}\pi\iota\kappa\alpha\lambda\epsilon\hat{\iota}\sigma\theta\alpha\iota$ $\tau\grave{o}$ $\acute{o}\nu o\mu\alpha$ $'I\eta\sigma o\hat{\upsilon}$ $X\rho\iota\sigma\tau o\hat{\upsilon}$ or else declares that he is present in a special way to the soul of the one who is praying.

[1] I Peter 4:11; cf. 2:5.      [2] 16:27; cf. 7:25, also Eph. 3:21.

*offered through Christ,* for indeed it is he whom God has given us as Saviour and Mediator.[1]

This raises the question: What is the precise meaning of the expressions: to pray through Christ; honour is due to God through Christ? There can be no doubt that this manner of speaking is based on the idea of the Mediator position of our Lord: '. . . There is one God, and there is one Mediator between God and men, the man Christ Jesus' (1 Tim. 2:5); that is, Christ is our Mediator not only in that he once reconciled us to God and gained for us grace and salvation, but in the sense that he evermore lives on with God, as head of the Church, as our advocate. To him the faithful belong but, as they proudly confess, he is now elevated to the right hand of God. This interpretation of his mediatory office comes out plainly in several passages of the New Testament: 'But if anyone does sin, we have an advocate with the Father, Jesus Christ the righteous' (1 John 2:1). John makes use of a concept from the law: παράκλητος, advocate, legal representative, which was so familiar to the readers that one spoke precisely in this connexion of taking proceedings *through* such a representative, διά τινος. Similarly, Rom. 8:34: 'Who is to condemn? Is it Christ Jesus, who died, yes, who was raised from the dead, who is at the right hand of God, who indeed intercedes (ἐντυγχάνει) for us?' In the Epistle to the Hebrews, we meet the same idea, enriched with the conception of the eternal priesthood of Christ, which is here the real theme. While the Levitical priests passed on and had to be relieved by others, Christ remains for

---

[1] Thus also A. Klawek 77. Cf. his conclusion, p. 78: 'The Apostle evidently commends to his communities the prayer διὰ Χριστοῦ and thus effects its general diffusion.' Likewise E. von der Goltz 160. The above interpretation of the passage is also represented by P. Bachmann in T. Zahn's *Kommentar zum N.T.*, VIII³ (Leipzig, 1918) 75. He determines more closely the meaning of the phrase as follows: 'As in this explanation there is obviously a play on the words, it is very probable that Paul did not intend the δι' αὐτοῦ merely as an expression of the awareness of the community accompanying and fulfilling the Amen, but as an indication of the actual custom of joining the Amen to an explicit mention of the name of Christ (= through Jesus Christ. Amen!), although it probably happened that the διὰ Ἰησοῦ Χριστοῦ appeared in some form in the doxology spoken separately by the reader or one praying, and the congregation then, with its simple Amen, assented not only to the praise in general but also to the inner dependence on Christ thus declaring itself.'

ever. 'Consequently he is able for all time to save those who draw near to God through him, since he always lives to make intercession for them' (7:25). Through Christ's mediation man draws near to God: not only for the first time through faith (11:6) but continually we must 'draw near to the throne of grace, that we may receive mercy and find grace to help in time of need', therefore doubtless in prayer. And this we can do because we have there a great high priest who has passed through the heavens, and who yet sympathizes with our weaknesses (4:14–16; cf. 10:22)—just as we also should continually offer up a sacrifice of praise through him (13:15).

Christ therefore in his glorified humanity makes intercession for us, even as, while still on earth, he promised the Apostles he would pray for them to the Father.[1]

But how is this intercession, the mediatorship, intended in relation to the prayers which his own constantly offer up through him? The Mediator idea was nothing new to the converts from Judaism, nor to those from paganism, neither was the idea of the mediation of prayers.[2] But they were accustomed to think of angels, heavenly beings, who carried the prayer from the hearts of men to God's throne. Paul built on this Mediator idea, but at the same time purified it, when he represented Christ as Mediator of prayer (1 Tim. 2:5): 'There is *one* mediator.' There is no mention here of

---

[1] John 14:16. This should probably be seen as an express intercession, a real activity of the Lord (Suarez, Petavius, J. B. Franzelin), although it is not supplication as men offer it on earth, in feeble helplessness, but a pointing to his perfect work of atonement as God-man, a 'self-confident pleading of his deserts in the interest of the Redemption' (J. Pohle); he has kept his scars even in his glorified body. Cf. J. Margreth, *Das Gebetsleben Jesu* 76–106, 111–3, 256–76. On p. 268 he shows how in Christ all prayer has a priestly character and therefore is of itself related intimately to his sacrifice: 'It is in him a liturgical act in the strict sense of the word, a true activity of his high priesthood. The deepest reason for this is that the God-man through his personal character is high priest; to be man means for him the same as to be God-man and, because the hypostatic union is in its origin his priestly consecration and in its permanence his priestly character, it means the same as to be high priest.'

[2] Cf. J. Lebreton, *Les origines du dogme de la Trinité* 40, 172 ff., and the discussion in A. Klawek 75–7, where he develops four corrections which Paul makes to the pre-Christian idea of prayer-mediation.

the transmission of prayer. Christ exercises his office of Mediator in
that he supports ($\epsilon\nu\tau\upsilon\gamma\chi\acute{\alpha}\nu\epsilon\iota$) the prayer.[1]

We must not now, however, ourselves think of this support as an
intercession of the Lord each time someone prays. In this sense
John 16:26 f. is probably to be understood, which, to be sure, was
said chiefly for the consolation of the downcast disciples: 'In that
day you will ask in my name; and I do not say to you that I shall
pray the Father for you; for the Father himself loves you.' But the
prayer of the individual who belongs to Christ, to his Church, gains
only in him its full resonance before God. Jesus' holy soul vibrates
with the prayers of his Church, i.e. he is aware of the prayers of his
own and concurs with them, as long as they are good. He has indeed
fellow-feeling with us. Likewise, the Church's prayers of praise to
God gain meaning and value only because Christ as high priest
stands at her head and joins in them. Through him, God is constantly paid the highest honour, even without our help, since his
divine glorified humanity is the finest flower of creation, the supreme
revelation of God. 'Through him', 'in his name' we too, however,
may make our prayers, sanctified and elevated, arrive before God's
throne. He does not stand in the way, preventing a direct prayer-
relationship between the creature and his creator, as a short-sighted
criticism of the Mediator idea would suppose. But the prayer of
the creature attains power and effectiveness when it is a prayer 'in
the name of Jesus', *in Christ*, and when it therefore arrives before
God *through Christ*.

Both formulas, 'in Christ' and 'through Christ', of which the first especially
is peculiar to St Paul, have been the subject of special research. The former
characterises, according to A. Deissmann,[2] 'the relationship of the
Christian to Jesus Christ as a locally conceived existence in the pneumatic
Christ'. F. Prat[3] accepts the explanation as a common meaning of the
formula which is applicable to most, but not to all, cases, and refers to the
doctrine of the Mystical Body of Christ. Just as, instead of this latter

---

[1] Also the angels, strictly speaking, cannot 'carry to God' the prayers of the
servants of God other than by uniting their prayers to those prayed on earth. Thus
in this generic idea of prayer-mediation there is no difference between the angels
and Christ. Cf. J. Margeth 263.

[2] *Die neutestamentliche Formel 'In Christo Jesu'* (Marburg, 1892), p. 97.

[3] *La théologie de s. Paul* II[e] 478.

expression, 'Christ' alone is used, in order to indicate the personal Christ together with his Church, so also the faithful live and act as members of that organism, of that body, i.e. 'in Christ', as they are also 'in the Holy Ghost' which animates that body; thus their prayer, too, is performed 'in Christ'.

A. Schettler has sought to produce a uniform meaning for the formula 'through Christ' also:[1] 'The formula is the specific expression for the entire dependence of the Christian on his heavenly head. Where it is used, it is done to guarantee the share of Christ in every expression of the life of the faithful' (p. 62). Comparing it with the formula 'in Christo', he makes the distinction 'that ἐν Χριστῷ marks off, as it were, the area in which the salvific plans of God operate, while διὰ Χριστοῦ always postulates an action of Christ' (p. 76). The latter formula would therefore be more definite, since in it there is always a reference to an act of the personal Christ ascended to heaven. Here, however, Schettler carries his idea too far, for the formula, at least in Paul (apart from the Epistle to the Hebrews), in its application to prayer must signify only 'an action proceeding from Christ', and never a high-priestly mediation of prayer in such a way that Christ would, as it were, be set in motion by an act of man.[2] As A. Klawek[3] shows, this exegesis already falls down at Romans 1:8: Πρῶτον μὲν εὐχαριστῶ τῷ θεῷ μου διὰ Ἰησοῦ Χριστοῦ περὶ πάντων ὑμῶν. The passage would, according to Schettler, state, 'that Paul knows himself to be authorized through Christ to feel grateful joy over the faith of the Romans'. The treatment of this pauline text is, moreover, characteristic of the attempts of all those who wish to weaken the idea of the mediation of prayer in Paul; cf. R. Cornely on the passage.

The meaning of the two formulas 'in Christ' and 'through Christ' and their relation to each other probably receives its finest and fullest expression in the words of I Peter 2:4 f.: 'Come to him, to that living stone, rejected by men but in God's sight chosen and precious; and like living stones be yourselves built *into a spiritual house*, to be a holy priesthood, to offer spiritual sacrifices acceptable to God *through Jesus Christ*.'

From the aforesaid, the pedagogical significance of a way of prayer in which Christ the High Priest stands before the eyes now becomes clear also. When prayer is performed, so to speak, through the prayer of Jesus, it goes forth purified. He who so prays declares himself agreed from the outset that everything that is not in accordance with the mind of Christ be struck away from his prayer. The

---

[1] A. Schettler, *Die paulinische Formel 'durch Christus'* (Tübingen, 1907).
[2] Pp. 61 f.; cf. pp. 41 f.    [3] Pp. 75 f.

high-priestly mediation of Christ admittedly does not require that in the wording of the prayer Christ be expressly besought: 'only from within the relation (ἐν Χριστῷ) in which he stands to the individual believer and to the Church, does he mediate every prayer, and in reverse every Christian prayer reaches God not otherwise than through Christ'.[1] But there is a favourable reaction on the one who prays and his prayer when he is reminded also by the spoken word of the holy fellowship with Christ into which he was received through Baptism and through which his prayer arrives before God. This word need not then simply run: 'through Christ', 'in the name of Jesus', or the like. We find in the apostolic writings texts of praise, prayers and prayer directions which employ none of these phrases, and where they are used their purpose is not always a reference to the Mediator of the prayer.[2] One did not need so much to tie oneself to such an expression in a period of which the thinking and praying were in any case filled with the memory of the risen and glorified Master, and in which the majority of prayers, which perhaps find an echo in the letters of the Apostles, contain gratitude for the salvation graciously bestowed in Christ.

Nevertheless, a factor deserves to be underlined that must again have served in a special fashion to keep alive in the consciousness at prayer the mediatory position of Christ, viz. the particular form of address. Christ not only himself prayed to his Father, he also taught his people to name God in prayer *Father*. Through him, indeed, the relationship of men to God has been altered. Now there is atonement and peace, confidence (παρρησία) and free access to God. Through him, all have won the power to become God's children.[3] Thus from now on we frequently meet the name of Father for God in the mouth of the Apostles, especially, too, in connexion with prayer. God has sent the Spirit of his Son into our hearts, who there cries: 'Abba', 'Father', and we also cry in him: 'Abba', 'Father.'[4] In other passages, however, the name 'Father'

---

[1] Klawek 77.

[2] E.g. Acts 4:30. Doxologies in which Christ is not named: Romans 11:33 ff.; 2 Cor. 11:31; Gal. 1:5; Phil. 4:20; I Tim. 1:17; 6:16; I Peter 5:11. Cf. von der Goltz 135.

[3] Cf. Romans 5:1 ff.; Eph. 3:12; John 1:12.     [4] Romans 8:15; Gal. 4:6.

appears, but not applied directly, as if indeed it had been thought too daring to use this intimate name repeatedly. Instead, there is added to the name 'God' the Father's name with reference to him who is truly God's only-begotten Son, and who in his humanity is again one with us, as our brother and head and Lord: 'Blessed be the God and Father of our Lord Jesus Christ';[1] '. . . That together you may with one voice glorify the God and Father of our Lord Jesus Christ' (Romans 15:6).[2] The expression 'our Lord' refers to the fact that we belong to Christ; but he is 'in the bosom of the Father' (John 1:18), with him to whom we cry when praying. This is obviously also a fitting way to adopt the mental attitude of the prayer offered in the name of Jesus.

Both ways, however, of introducing our Lord into spoken prayer, viz. the use of the formulas that refer to the Mediator and the addresses mentioned certainly point to a happy solution to the problem in ordinary prayer of giving due honour to the divine-human Redeemer, without abandoning the natural, primary direction of all prayer to God, the Lord and Creator.

*Postscript 1962.*

In the picture of the directions and beginnings in the New Testament, inasmuch as it is meant to be a necessarily concise sketch of the facts, no material change is needed. Yet there are a few

---

[1] Εὐλογητός ὁ θεὸς καὶ πατὴρ τοῦ κυρίου ἡμῶν 'Ιησοῦ Χριστοῦ. 2 Cor. 1:3; Eph. 1:3; Col. 1:3; I Peter 1:3.

[2] The theological sense of the expression seems to be correctly rendered by *Hervaeus*: 'Benedictus Deus, qui Christum secundum humanitatem creavit et secundum divinitatem genuit atque ita est Deus et pater eius', an exposition which most exegetes follow. For other paraphrases, see J. Knabenbauer on Eph. 1:3, R. Cornely on 2 Cor. 1:3. Perhaps the idea could also be theologically reproduced as: 'God, whom Jesus has made known and who in the first Person is the Father of Jesus Christ.' It is most probably not necessary to understand the whole praise of the first Person, so as then to suppose an appropriation, since in any case the salvific designs and mercies of God *tout simple*, of the triune God, are praised. The emphasis in the address is on 'God', at whom elsewhere also the prayers are directed. But the word gains from the addition 'Father of our Lord Jesus Christ' a milder, specifically Christian overtone. Cf. the same idea, only in more detail, Hebrews 13:20: 'Now may the God of peace who brought again from the dead our Lord Jesus, the great shepherd of the sheep, by the blood of the eternal covenant, equip you with everything good.'

INSTRUCTIONS IN THE NEW TESTAMENT

works to be listed that have appeared in the meantime, which touch on our subject-matter at various points and clarify certain details.

The answer to the question (p. 131 f.), to what extent prayer to Christ occurs in Paul ultimately depends on what one understands by prayer. E. Orphal, *Das Paulusgebet* (Gotha, 1933), has produced figures in which he finds 131 passages containing the prayer to God and eighty-three the prayer to Christ (5, 147 f.). He takes 'prayer' in the widest sense. Cf. Klawek, above p. 131, note 4, for a contrary opinion. That also in the public worship of the community not only were invocations (Maranatha) and hymns directed to Christ but also formal prayer to Christ in use, may neither be proved nor entirely excluded.

Attention is given to the liturgical prayer in J. Nielen, *Gebet und Gottesdienst im Neuen Testament* (Freiburg, 1937), in which in particular the chapter 'Das gemeinschaftliche Gebet' (145–77) concerns us. Referring to W. Heitmüller, *Im Namen Jesu* (Göttingen, 1903) (especially pp. 257–65: 'Das Gebet im Namen Jesu'), he accepts the view that at least in the fourth Gospel the repeatedly mentioned 'praying in the name of Jesus' derives from an already existing custom of mentioning in communal prayer the name of Jesus in some way, perhaps (Col. 3:17, cf. with Col. 2:4 ff.) in opposition to a Jewish custom of invoking angels (159 f.). Paul himself prefers in the same sense the phrase 'through Christ', which expresses more clearly a 'true Mediator activity of Jesus'. One could put the equation: 'One who "lives in Christ" does everything, works and prays "through" or "in the name of" Christ' (161). Some contributions to the question of prayer 'through Christ' are to be found also in J. Wobbe, *Der Charisgedanke bei Paulus* (Neutestamentliche Abhandlungen 13, 3) (Münster, 1932). The idea of 'thanking through Christ' (Romans 1:8 in particular), in the sense that Jesus is to be understood as Mediator of the thanks, is further secured by him against various objections, as they have been evolved by Schettler, *inter alia* (misunderstanding of Romans 7:25; omission of the expression in the pauline prayer of petition). The johannine praying in the name of Jesus is treated comprehensively by Baldassare da Valdiporro, 'La preghiera nel nome di Gesù in San Giovanni': *Studia Patavina* 8 (1961) 177–212. Referring to the theological side, he rightly stresses that there is no question of a magical use of the name—from which Heitmüller (*loc. cit.* 258 f., 265) is not far removed—but of prayer ascending 'from the communion, in love and life, with him' (209).

With regard to the direction of prayer, Nielen establishes that 'as a rule, the community prayer is addressed to God in the name of Jesus Christ, seldom directly to Jesus' (169).

Nielen also discusses the labelling of Christians as the ἐπικαλούμενοι τὸ ὄνομα τοῦ Χριστοῦ, which has nothing to say about a custom of community prayer directed to Christ; it was probably invented not by the Christians themselves but by jealous Jews (163 f.). The same expression is elucidated in further detail in A. Hamman, *La prière I. Le Nouveau Testament* (Tournai, 1959), 270–9. Hamman establishes that the expression does not imply a prayer 'to Christ', but 'the confession of his sovereign rights, the invocation of his mediatorship in the sacraments, in exorcisms and in prayer' (271). As far as Paul in particular is concerned, the prayer to Christ is in his (Paul's) eyes legitimate, but is avoided by him 'because it does not seem to him sufficiently to take account of the absolute "primauté" of God, the initiative in the work of redemption, which is reserved to the Father, the historical course of the mystery of salvation, the rhythm of which he wills to maintain' (279). Hamman also treats in detail the invocation 'Abba' (267–9). This Paul must have found already in the original Aramaic community; it will have been taken from Jesus's own mouth (Mark 14:36) and could be used in the liturgical gathering, as a kind of summary of the Our Father, since it means 'our Father' as much as 'my Father'.

The treatment I give of the material in the New Testament, with respect to the more precise theological meaning of the mediatorship of Christ, was challenged; the latter was considered too much under the one aspect, viz. that Christian prayer is purified and elevated in virtue of its flowing through Christ, as it were. Here in particular begins the criticism that Odo Casel has made of the book (see above). Casel finds that the mediatorship of Christ is conceived 'too much from the purely moral angle' (177); the *per Christum* must 'be understood physically: the God-Man is essentially Mediator of every prayer that takes place ἐν Χριστῷ ἐν πνεύματι; he acts always as head of the Mystical Body' (178). As a completion of the explanation put forward by me, this criticism is fully acceptable. Christian prayer is depicted in this sense also by P. Ketter, 'Vom Gebetsleben des Apostels Paulus': *Theol.-prakt. Quartalschrift* 91 (1938) 23–40, when he declares: 'Paul prays, since he is a Christian, "in the Spirit" . . . Such a prayer in the name of Christ and out of the fullness of the indwelling Holy Spirit, who is the Spirit of Christ, will of its nature be directed to God "through Jesus Christ our Lord" ' (26 f.).

# X

# THE DEVELOPMENT UP TO THE
# FOURTH CENTURY

To judge from all the accounts and records that have been preserved, the theological character of the liturgical prayer that we have already noted in the apostolic writings was retained until well into the fourth century throughout the Catholic Church. However, the lines drawn by the apostolic writers were made more firm. Prayer was addressed to the Lord God 'through Jesus Christ'. We see this from the memorials of the period,[1] the christological mediatory formula bearing this sense having been adopted occasionally, or even regularly, at least in the concluding words, as in Hippolytus and Serapion. Again and again the Lord

[1] The sparse liturgical notes from pre-Nicean writings have been collected together by F. Gabrol and H. Leclerq in their *Reliquiae liturgicae vetustissimae*, 2 parts (MEL 1), Paris, 1902, 1913. The reproduction of the texts is not always accurate. For the later period, valuable assistance is afforded by the much-cited works of Th. Schermann, F. Probst, F. E. Brightman (appendices), and Petavius. Postscript 1962: A comprehensive collection of *Early Christian Prayers* is provided by A. Hamman, *Prières des premiers chrétiens* (Paris, 1952) (English translation, London, 1956). Intended for a wide circle of readers, it interprets very broadly the words 'prayer' and the 'first Christians'. In the meantime the scientific publication of the same author has appeared: A. Hamman, *La prière II, 'Les trois premiers siècles'* (Paris, 1963). The chapter 'Le Christ dans la prière chrétienne' in J. Lebreton's *'Histoire du dogme de la Trinité' II, De S. Clément à S. Irénée* (Paris, 1928), 201–44, examines scientifically at least the relevant evidence as far as the third century.

Christ is brought into prominence, at least in a general way, as the Mediator between God and man. Even in a work written at the end of the fourth century, the *Apostolic Constitutions*, we still find hardly any traces of another mode of liturgical prayer.

This conclusion is fully confirmed by the scattered liturgical accounts and prayer-texts. In its main lines, the religious life of the Christians is depicted more especially by the apologists. Justin explains to Tryphon that our Lord Jesus Christ entrusted us with the bread of the Eucharist to remind us of his suffering for mankind, 'so that we may thank God for having created the world with all that it contains, for the sake of man, and at the same time for having freed us from our baseness and for completely overthrowing the powers and principalities, by means of him who submitted to suffering in accordance with his decision'.[1] Through the name of Christ the Christians have become a priestly race; 'Wherefore God has shown his goodwill betimes to all those who offer sacrifices in his name (διὰ τοῦ ὀνόματος τούτου), the celebration of which has been regulated by Christ, namely, according to the Eucharist of bread and wine, as they are celebrated by the Christians in every place on earth' (c. 117).

About the year 305 Arnobius summed up the meaning of Christianity in these concise words: 'Nihil sumus aliud Christiani nisi magistro Christo summi regis ac principis veneratores.'[2]

But in most of the texts relevant to our purpose the position given to Christ in relation to prayer is much more intimate. Christ is indeed our teacher in prayer and sacrifice, but this is secondary compared with the basic fact that he himself constantly supports our prayer. Cyprian draws attention to this at the beginning of his explanation of the Our Father: 'Agnoscat Pater Filii sui verba, cum precem facimus; qui habitat intus in pectore, ipse sit et in voce, et cum ipsum habeamus apud Patrem *advocatum* pro peccatis nostris, quando peccatores pro delictis nostris petimus, advocati nostri verba promamus. Nam cum dicat, quia quodcumque petierimus a Patre in nomine eius, dabit nobis—quanto efficacius inpetramus quod

---

[1] *Dial. c. Tryph.*, c. 41 (*Corpus Apologetarum*, II³ p. 128, Otto).

[2] *Adv. nationes* 1, 27 (CSEL 4, pp. 17, 27. Reifferscheid). Cf. similar statements in Irenaeus, *Adv. haer.*, II, 32, 5.

petimus Christi nomine, si petamus ipsius oratione?'[1] Tertullian
remarks against Marcion that the lepers who had to show themselves to
the priest and offer the sacrifice commanded by Moses indicate that
man freed from sin must offer a gift to God in the temple: 'Orationem
scilicet et actionem gratiarum apud ecclesiam per Christum Jesum
catholicum Patris *sacerdotem*'.[2] Clement of Alexandria testifies:
'. . . We glorify God by prayers . . . by honouring him through the
most just Logos ($\tau\hat{\omega}$ $\delta\iota\kappa\alpha\iota\sigma\tau\acute{\alpha}\tau\omega$ $\lambda\acute{o}\gamma\omega$ $\gamma\epsilon\rho\alpha\acute{\iota}\rho\sigma\nu\tau\epsilon\varsigma$); through whom
we receive knowledge, through whom we praise him whom we have
come to know.' But throughout his whole life the true gnostic
honours the Logos and through him the Father. Nay, souls that
follow virtue live constantly 'in the forecourts of the Father, as close
as can be to the great High Priest'.[3]

The priesthood of Christ, which governs our actions and prayers,
is mentioned quite frequently, especially in the writings of the
earlier period, with a naturalness one would hardly expect—an
indication that the idea was generally familiar. Pope Clement I
ends the first, general part of his letter to the Corinthians with the
observation: 'That is the way, beloved, by which we find our
salvation, Jesus Christ, the high priest of our sacrificial gifts ($\tau\grave{o}\nu$
$\grave{a}\rho\chi\iota\epsilon\rho\acute{\epsilon}\alpha$ $\tau\hat{\omega}\nu$ $\pi\rho\sigma\sigma\phi\rho\rho\hat{\omega}\nu$ $\grave{\eta}\mu\hat{\omega}\nu$), the advocate and helper in our
weakness.'[4] Towards the end of the whole letter (cc. 59–61), which
was intended for reading out at public worship, his admonitions turn
into a prayer, a praise of God, joined to petitions for the needs of
the Church. We may regard it as the oldest and most venerable
form of the 'universal prayer of the Church'. Clement ends his
prayer with a doxology 'as it was his custom to end in the divine

---

[1] *De dominica or.* c. 3 (CSEL 3, p. 268, 10. Hartel).
[2] *Adv. Marc.* IV 9 (CSEL 47, p. 443, 2. Kroymann).
[3] *Stromata* VII, c. 6 f. (GCS: Clem. Al. III, pp. 23, 24 ff.; 27, 9 ff; 34, 15 ff.
Stählin). Here may be added two other remarkable texts: Ignatius of Antioch,
*ad Eph.* 4, 1 f. 'Christ is sung' with the accord that binds the presbyters to the
bishop. All together are to form a single choir and 'sing to the Father with one
voice through Jesus Christ'. Novatian, *De Trinitate* c. 14 (PL 3, 909), which is
important for us: 'Si homo tantummodo Christus, quomodo adest ubique invo-
catus . . .? Si homo tantummodo Christus, cur homo in orationibus *mediator*
invocatur, cum invocatio hominis ad praestandam salutem inefficax iudicetur?'
[4] c. 36, 1 (*Patres apostolici* 1, p. 144, 3. Funk).

service in Rome':[1] 'Thou who alone art able to bring about these and even greater benefits among us, we praise thee through the high priest and advocate of our souls, Jesus Christ, through whom is to thee honour and glory now and through all generations and to all eternity.'[2]

Bishop Polycarp of Smyrna ends his admonitions to the Philippians with the prayer: 'May the God and Father of our Lord Jesus Christ and he himself, the eternal high priest, the son of God, Jesus Christ, build you up in faith. . . .'[3] Another prayer of his has been preserved in the account of his martyrdom (in the year 155 or 156) given by the community of Smyrna, the prayer he spoke at the stake before all the people: 'Lord, almighty God, father of thy beloved and blessed son (παιδός) Jesus Christ, through whom we came to know thee . . . I praise thee for having deemed me worthy of this day and hour, that I may share with thy martyrs in the chalice of thy Christ . . . For this and for everything I glorify thee through the eternal and heavenly high priest Jesus Christ, thy beloved son, through whom honour (belongs) to thee (with him and the Holy Ghost) now and throughout the ages yet to come.'[4] The first of two prayers written on a papyrus brought to light in Central

---

[1] Cf. E. von der Goltz, *Das Gebet in der ältesten Christenheit*, 192–207.

[2] c. 61, 3 (*Patres apostolici*, 1, p. 180, 6. Funk). Similarly, c. 65, 2. The doxologies in Clement's letter are treated exhaustively by A. Stuiber: 'Doxologie', in *Reallexikon für Antike und Christentum* IV (1959) 215 f.

[3] c. 12, 2 (*Patres apostolici* 1, p. 310, 13. Funk).

[4] *Martyr. Polycarpi*, c. 14 (*Patres apostolici*, 1, 331 f. Funk): σὲ δοξάζω διὰ τοῦ αἰωνίου καὶ ἐπουρανίου ἀρχιερέως Ἰησοῦ Χριστοῦ ἀγαπητοῦ σου παιδός, δι' οὗ σοὶ σὺν αὐτῷ καὶ πνεύματι ἁγίῳ ἡ δόξα . . . H. Lietzmann finds the liturgical tone of the whole prayer remarkable and as a result of his examination of it says that it is certain that in this account, which was composed as early as 156, in Smyrna, 'at least fragments of prayers have been used which had their place in the Mass prayers, round about the Consecration'. ('Ein liturgisches Bruchstück des 2. Jahrhunderts', *Zeitschrift für wissenschaftliche Theologie* 54 (1912) 56–61). Similarly, before him, J. A. Robinson: *The Expositor* 9 (1899) 63–72. The authenticity of the last part of the doxology is disputed. The attestation of the above reading selected by F. X. Funk is not entirely convincing. The words σὺν αὐτῷ καὶ πνεύματι ἁγίῳ may be a later insertion, as suggested above. The ἀρχιερέως, however, shows that not the whole doxology is spurious, since the word was later hardly used at all. Cf. the controversy on the subject in JThSt 21 (1920) 97–105; 23 (1922) 390–2; 24 (1923) 141–6. E. von der Goltz (in E. Hennecke, *Neutestam. Apokryphen*[2], 604) still held fast to the whole doxology in 1924. Hamman, *La prière* II (1963) 139 f., decides for the shorter text as above.

Egypt in 1911 has a similar ending. It was probably a Church prayer for a fast day: δὸς ... ὑπομένειν σε ἄχρι ἐσχάτης ἀνα⟨πν⟩οῆς διὰ τοῦ ἀρχιερέως τῶν ψυχῶν ἡμῶν Ἰησοῦ Χριστοῦ, δι᾽ οὗ σοὶ δόξα καὶ τιμή καὶ κράτος εἰς τοὺς αἰῶνας. Ἀμήν. According to its editor, C. Schmidt,[1] 'we can ascribe our prayer, if not to the second, then certainly to the third century'.

Besides the frequent use of the appellation, ἀρχιερεύς, sacerdos, for Christ, it is noticeable that up to the end of the second century the overseers of the Christian communities were content to be known as ἐπίσκοποι, πρεσβύτεροι, ἡγούμενοι and the like, but not priests, ἱερεῖς. S. von Dunin-Borkowski has made a study of the matter[2] and has shown an illuminating reason for it. The functions of a ἱερεύς as commonly accepted by the Jews and pagans of the time were simply not met with by the Christians in their presbyters. The Jewish priest, in virtue of his divine commission, prayed, sacrificed and expounded the Law, and was truly a mediator between God and Israel. The priest of the Hellenistic pagans, who served a particular shrine, where he had to ascertain the will of the deity and foretell the future, was likewise an independent middleman between the deity and the people. Both were regarded as mediators on account of their personal position and dignity. It was their special talent with which they tried to win God's benevolence. In Christianity, on the other hand, there was no human person exercising an independent mediation between heaven and earth. Here, only Christ could be called ἱερεύς and ἀρχιερεύς, and he was eminently worthy of the title, since he alone has a sacrifice to offer worthy of God. What the Christian presbyters do, they do only as his instruments and in his name. He is the priest, on whose behalf they perform the sacred act of the Eucharist; it is he who is ever standing at the throne of God; it is through his hands that all offerings and prayers make their way to God.[3] It is only in union with him that a priest-

---

[1] *Neutestamentliche Studien für Heinrici*, 77.

[2] 'Die Kirche als Stiftung Jesu' (*Religion, Christentum, Kirche*, ed. G. Esser and J. Mausbach, II (Kempten, 1913) Part III, 55–70.

[3] Thus the priesthood of Christ has two functions; he not only speaks for us in heaven, as we are told in the Epistle to the Hebrews, but is also the principal priest in the eucharistic celebration on earth, a celebration that was always known to be a sacrifice, albeit the Jewish and pagan term θυσία was used at first with a certain

hood exists on earth. And this union with Christ is manifest first and foremost in the Christians as a whole, in his Church, which is his bride, and his very body. That is why, in the Apocalypse,[1] in the splendour of the Lamb, all Christians appear as priests of God. That is why Peter[2] calls the body of the faithful a holy priesthood.

Only a closer look at that organism of the body of Christ distinguishes those organs that have a special share in the priesthood and the mediation of Christ, in virtue of their particular services and powers. From the second half of the second century, the expressions ἱερεύς and *sacerdos*, with this particular meaning, acquired domiciliary rights in the vocabulary of Christian theology. 'The Christian conceptions had become so much a part of the faithful that the use of a Jewish or pagan expression did not, as before, immediately call to mind pagan and Jewish conceptions. . . . Originally the Christian celebrants were undoubtedly called ἱερεῖς, to emphasize a certain analogy with the Jewish priesthood. This intention is still clearly discernible in Irenaeus and the Syrian *Didascalia*.'[3]

Though this emphasis laid by the early Fathers on the priesthood of our Lord in their liturgical prayer shows only their devotion to the heritage of the New Testament, in another direction it was not long before a further development took place. Certainly, as we have just seen, the liturgical prayer of this period was in its external character as well as inwardly a prayer 'in the name of Jesus', a praying 'in Christ' in the fullest sense. Nevertheless, as in apostolic times, it was not these particular phrases which were most used to express the christological motive in the wording of the liturgical prayer. These phrases implied only the atmosphere of the Christian community, its association with Christ. For this reason, at least where Greek was spoken, the phrase 'through Christ' was preferred; in a much more definite way it brought immediately to the minds of the faithful the eternal high priest of their prayers and sacrificial gifts: we praise thee through Jesus Christ our Lord. On the other

timidity (Dunin-Borkowski, 65 f.). This second function is stressed by Cyprian, *Ep.* 63, 4 (CSEL 3, p. 703, 11, Hartel), 'Nam qui magis sacerdos Dei summi quam Dominus noster Jesus Christus, qui sacrificium Deo Patri obtulit et obtulit hoc idem quod Melchisedech obtulerat, id est panem et vinum, suum scilicet corpus et sanguinem'.

[1] Apoc. 1:6; 5:10; 20:6.    [2] Peter 2:5, 9.    [3] See Dunin-Borkowski 64.

hand, it was only natural, especially in prayers of praise and gratitude, to want to express in a fixed and ever-recurrent form the soul-pervading joy of possessing a new world of peace and grace, whence issued a joyful hymn of praise to God, and prayer became a prayer in Christ: in Christ, that is, as members of the body of Christ and as children of his kingdom, as his holy people. In many cases in St Paul the equally simple '*in the Holy Spirit*' proves to be exactly synonymous with 'in Christ'. St Paul liked best to epitomize the new life received in Baptism and governing the Church as the possessing of the Holy Spirit: the Christian lived and moved in the Spirit. Just as the Holy Spirit prays and sighs in us (Romans 8:26) and cries 'Father' (Gal. 4:6), so in him we cry 'Father' (Romans 8:15) and the faithful pray 'in the Spirit' (Eph. 6:18) and sing 'spiritual' songs (Col. 3:16; Eph. 5:19). What is done in Christ is done also in the Holy Spirit, since it is he who pervades and animates the body of Christ.[1]

From this it was only a short step to beginning or ending the prayer: 'We praise thee through our Lord Jesus Christ in the Holy Spirit', or (by taking the prayer of the Holy Spirit to ourselves in a more personal way and by ranging it alongside the service of the high priest) 'We praise thee through our Lord Jesus Christ and through the Holy Spirit'. It seems that this latter form is recognizable first, viz. in the liturgical descriptions given by Justin the Martyr. In places where he makes only a passing reference to divine service he mentions merely praying through Christ,[2] but in his detailed account of the Eucharistic celebration he reports thus: 'After that, bread and a beaker, with water and wine, is brought to the leader of the brethren; he takes it and sends up praise and glory to the Father of all in the name of the Son and the Holy Spirit and says a long thanksgiving for our having been deemed by him to be worthy of these gifts.'[3] Almost the same phrasing recurs in a later passage

---

[1] Cf. W. Reinhard, *Das Wirken des Hl. Geistes im Menschen nach den Briefen des Apostels Paulus*, Freiburg i. B, 1918, pp. 49 ff., 77 ff.; F. Prat, *La Théologie de s. Paul*, II⁶, 345 ff, 479 f.

[2] Δοξάσωμεν τὸν θεὸν διὰ τοῦ βασιλέως τῆς δόξης, διὰ τοῦ κυρίου τῶν δυνάμεων (Dial. c. Tryph. c. 29).—Τὸν θεὸν ἀεὶ διὰ Ἰησοῦ Χριστοῦ συντηρηθῆναι παρακαλοῦμεν (ib. c. 30).—Cf. above p. 145.

[3] Apol. I, 65 (Corpus Apologetarum I³, p. 178. Otto): δόξαν τῷ πατρὶ τῶν ὅλων διὰ τοῦ ὀνόματος τοῦ υἱοῦ καὶ τοῦ πνεύματος τοῦ ἁγίου ἀναπέμπει.

whose chief concern apparently is with the agapes.[1] Certainly there is a doxology of this kind in Clement of Alexandria: he who prays steadfastly 'will be given true cleansing and immutable life by the good father in heaven, to whom be glory and honour through his son Jesus Christ, the lord of the living and the dead, and through the Holy Spirit. . .'.[2]

Origen, on the other hand, expressly recommends that a prayer be ended 'by praising the Father of all through Jesus Christ *in* the Holy Spirit'.[3] And this is the one form that recurs regularly in the prayer-endings in Serapion and the *Ap. Const.* VIII,[4] and which spread over all the East in the fourth century. Serapion gives us the best commentary on it when at the blessing of the baptismal water he prescribes prayer for the baptizands, that they may become spiritual and capable of worshipping God through Christ in the Holy Spirit.[5] The idea is already, after all, foreshadowed in a passage in St Paul, except that he was not confining himself to prayer but was comprehending the whole scheme of salvation: 'Through him we both (Jews and Gentiles) have access in one spirit to the Father' (Eph. 2:18).

But not only by naming of the Holy Spirit was the formula 'through Christ' extended and, alongside the high priest who offers the prayer to God, an indication given of the hallowed source of all Christian prayer and thought. In Hippolytus we find a prayer ending: 'Laudantes te per puerum tuum Christum Jesum, per quem tibi gloria et virtus, Patri et Filio cum Spiritu Sancto, *in sancta Ecclesia* et nunc et in saecula saeculorum.'[6] Thus the holy Church on earth is ranged alongside the Mediator in heaven; and there are

---

[1] c. 67, 1 (Corpus Apologetarum I, p. 184. Otto): '*Ἐπὶ πᾶσί τε, οἷς προσφερόμεθα, εὐλογοῦμεν τὸν ποιητὴν τῶν πάντων διὰ τοῦ υἱοῦ αὐτοῦ Ἰησοῦ Χριστοῦ καὶ διὰ πνεύματος τοῦ ἁγίου.*

[2] Quis dives salvetur c. 42, 20 (GCS: Clem. Al. III, p. 191, 10. Stählin): *ᾧ διὰ τοῦ παιδὸς Ἰησοῦ Χριστοῦ τοῦ κυρίου ζώντων καὶ νεκρῶν καὶ διὰ τοῦ ἁγίου πνεύματος εἴη δόξα.*

[3] *De oratione* c. 33 (GCS: *Orig.* II, p. 401, 15, 25; p. 402, 34. Koetschau).

[4] See above, pp. 23, 13.

[5] See above, p. 13. The suggestion may be found here, too, that catechumens may well be able to pray through Christ, but not yet in the Holy Spirit.

[6] Hauler 109; cf. 107; see above p. 7 f.

other cases in which it is mentioned on its own: 'Tibi gloria, Patri et Filio cum Sancto Spiritu, in sancta ecclesia.'[1]

Except in Hippolytus, the phrase 'in the holy Church' seldom occurs as an element of doxologies. P. Cagin[2] cites two other passages: the end of the first pseudo-Cyprianic prayer[3] and the ending in the Latin martyrium of St Ignatius.[4] Another example is the doxology following the epiklesis in the East Syrian anaphora of the Apostles.[5] Traces of a similar reinforcement of a prayer by the mention of the holy Church have survived in the Ethiopian liturgy,[6] more clearly in the Syrian-Jacobite[7] and most of all in the Armenian liturgy.[8] They may point to an earlier custom prevalent throughout

---

[1] Hauler 108; cf. 111. In this way the doxology is mentioned too: c. Noet. c. 18 (PG 10, 289): Αὐτῷ ἡ δόξα καὶ τὸ κράτος ἅμα πατρὶ καὶ ἁγίῳ πνεύματι ἐν τῇ ἁγίᾳ ἐκκλησίᾳ καὶ νῦν ... Hippolytus seems to have used this form when the doxology was to stand on its own, in the sense of an objective statement: 'To thee belongs all honour in the holy Church'. The Church, which strictly speaking embraces the whole body of the faithful together with their Head, is the objective cause, the work wherein God is glorified. The sense is the same as in Eph. 3:21, where Christ is a deliberate addition: αὐτῷ ἡ δόξα ἐν τῇ ἐκκλησίᾳ καὶ ἐν Χριστῷ Ἰησοῦ. Cf. Hippolytus, Εἰς τὸ ᾆσμα c. 17 (GCS: Hippol. I, pp. 356, 21–359, 6. Bonwetsch): 'For clearly Solomon's couch prefigures none other than Christ ... The righteous of the nations, come together, rest thereon, praising the Father and the Son and the Holy Spirit, to whom be honour for ever.' This is only a new form of the same thought. On Solomon's couch = in Christo = in sancta Ecclesia. Cf. also J. A. Jungmann, 'Die Doxologien der Kirchenordnung Hippolyts: ZkTh 86 (1964) 325 f.

[2] Eucharistia, Paris, 1912, pp. 303 f.

[3] In Cyprian (CSEL 3 Appendix, p. 146, 1, Hartel): 'Unus in uno, Pater in Filio, Filius in Patre, Spiritus Sanctus, per quem et cum quo est tibi in sancta ecclesia honor ...' The confused theological structure of the prayer revealed here relates it in this form to a later period. The Greek original text (ed. by T. Schermann: Oriens christ. 3 [1903] 303–23) seems to have been given its present shape about the year 400.

[4] n. 4255 of the Bibliotheca hagiographica latina of the Bollandists; Ruinart p. 14.

[5] Br. 288, 1: 'We will give thee thanks and praise thee without ceasing in thy Church redeemed by the precious blood of thy Christ ...' (see above, p. 71).

[6] Br. 198, 31; 200, 1: 'Thine own holy body, which we have presented on thine holy altar in this holy apostolic church.' The expression probably has the meaning chiefly of a church-building in its present context.

[7] Br. 81, 26; 34.

[8] 'Through the holy Church let us beseech the Lord, that through her he will deliver us from sins' (Br. 416, 15; cf. 416, 20; 417, 6). 'We thank thee, O Father almighty, who didst prepare for us the holy Church for a haven of rest and a temple of holiness, where the holy Trinity is glorified' (Br. 454, 4). Cf. the strong emphasis on the Church in other passages too, e.g. 435, 33; 452 f.

Syria, which would provide a parallel with Hippolytus's form of doxology. The same idea of the Church in a similar context is to be seen in a prayer in Serapion: 'Lord . . . who revealest thyself in heaven and art known by the pure spirits, who art praised on earth and dwellest in the Catholic Church . . . grant that this Church be a living and true Church, grant that it may have divine powers and pure angels as servants ($\lambda\epsilon\iota\tau o\nu\rho\gamma o\acute{\nu}s$), that it may praise thee purely.'[1] That the two phrases 'in the Holy Spirit' and 'in the holy Church' are based on one and the same idea is clear from the meaning given to the former by Basil,[2] when he asks 'In what other place should we sacrifice than in the Holy Spirit? . . . The spirit is truly the place of the saints, and the saint in his turn is a dwelling-place of the spirit—and is called his temple'. For Basil, 'in the spirit and in the truth' is tantamount to 'in the Holy Spirit and in Christ'.

The history of the kerygmatic summaries of the faith, which is bound up with the history of the creed, throws a remarkable light on this manner of developing the prayer-scheme by naming the Holy Spirit, or the Church, along with Christ the Mediator. Here only a brief comment will be made. In their missionary sermons the Apostles regularly gave prominence to the two pillars of the faith, the one God, the God of the Fathers, and Jesus Christ, the Messiah who had been promised and now sent by God and attested by the Resurrection. This was as the case demanded, and as the Lord himself had summed up the true life: 'That they know thee the only true God, and Jesus Christ whom thou hast sent' (John 17:3). Also in Paul's epistles,[3] God's salvific decree in Christ is his constant theme when he praises the grandeur of the Gospel. Earth's response to this joyful news from heaven is prayer, which returns to God through the same Christ. What lay outside this basic theme, i.e. the exposition of the blessings brought by Christianity, shows from the beginning no such definite formulation. The blessings are manifold indeed: the kingdom of God, sonship, Resurrection, and the rest. Tertullian, for example, was wont to set out the substance of the

---

[1] n. 10 (24). Cf. similar observations of Eusebius of Caesarea on the praise of God 'in the Church', in F. Probst, *Liturgie des 4. Jahrhunderts* 39 f. Similarly also even in the Old Testament, e.g. Ps. 149:1: 'Laus eius in ecclesia sanctorum.'
[2] *De Spiritu Sancto* c. 26 (PG 32, 184 f.).      [3] Cf. especially Eph. 1:3.

faith under three heads: God, Christ, Resurrection. 'Non enim ex hoc alius Deus quam creator et alius Christus quam ex Maria et alia spes quam resurrectio annuntiabatur.'[1]

Other writers, however, give greater prominence to summaries of the blessings made accessible by God through Christ 'in the holy Church'.[2] These include, of course, those early creeds and baptismal questions that bring about the cleansing from sin and the resurrection of the flesh 'in the holy Church' or through it.[3] But the predominant account was that in which the Holy Spirit, the uncreated gift, himself took the highest place as the source of all other blessings. This mode of description occurs in catechetical writings and sketches from the end of the second century.[4] Here the content of the faith is so set out that the mystery of the Trinity appears at the same time; with Christ the Lord, who is truly son of God, there appears in the one who sent him the person of the Father. But the Holy Spirit is their gift. What had always formed part of the Church's teaching and, especially in Baptism, was brought vividly before all eyes[5]—the confession of the three divine persons—was thus combined with the exposition of the divine work of salvation; the $\theta\epsilon o\lambda o\gamma\iota a$ and the $o i\kappa o\nu o\mu\iota a$ have been fused together. The trinitarian frame has been filled with the content of the apostolic preaching and thus, in the course of time, elaborated into the creed-forms familiar to us.[6] It is

---

[1] De praescr. haer. c. 23 (Öhler II, p. 22); cf. c. 36; De virg. veland. c. 1.

[2] Clemens Alex., Strom. VII, c. 17; Ignatius, Ad Ephes. c. 5; Clemens Rom., I. Cor. c. 59:4.

[3] Cf. my notes on the creed in the papyrus of Dêr-Balyzeh: ZkTh 48 (1924) 465–8.

[4] Irenaeus, Epideixis c. 6, 99, 100; Novatian, De Trinitate, c. 29 (cf. A. d'Alès: Gregorianum 3 [1922] 420 ff., 505 ff.; Origen, Περὶ ἀρχῶν, praefatio c. 4; cf. Hippolytus, c. Noet., c. 14.

[5] Matt. 28:19; Didache c. 7, 1.

[6] The result of the process is first met with in the Epideixis of St Irenaeus. A. Nussbaumer, O. Cap., has shown in Das Ursymbolum nach der Epideixis des hl. Irenäus und dem Dialog Justins (Paderborn, 1921) that after the trinitarian pattern has been removed, the same sequence of themes remains as governs in the main the sequence of thought in Justin's dialogue with Tryphon the Jew—the original subject-matter of the creed. A. Harnack previously attempted to reconstruct the creed itself by another approach: A. Hahn, Bibliothek der Symbole[3] 390. Cf. also J. Haussleiter, Trinitarischer Glaube und Christusbekenntnis in der alten Kirche (Gütersloh, 1920).

certainly not by chance that the development of this three-membered outline of the faith was contemporary with an analogous expansion of the prayer-scheme. God's word to man is echoed by man's response to God: 'We praise thee through Christ in the Holy Spirit'[1] or 'We praise thee through Christ in thy holy Church'. What, however, is surprising, is as follows. Liberal Protestants have contended—at least, in the past—that the idea of the Trinity sprang from that form of belief in God, Christ and the (impersonally conceived) Holy Spirit that by chance acquired preponderance over other attempts at triadic formulations. Yet now we meet, at least at the beginning of the third century, in Hippolytus, not indeed a creed, but what is very near to it, a doxology that joins together both the Trinity and such a triad, while making the clearest possible distinction between them. On the one hand, 'per *quem tibi* gloria in *sancta ecclesia*'; on the other, the 'tibi' unfolding into the three divine Persons: 'Patri et Filio cum Spiritu Sancto.' As a prayer, this form of doxology may be rather cumbersome; theologically it is of the utmost clarity. It shows that the word 'God' as a form of address, even when it was joined with 'Father of our Lord Jesus Christ', as it usually was in Hippolytus, meant that the prayer was directed not towards the divine Person of the Father, but simply to God, the triune God.

Since the Son, the Lord Christ in his godhead, appears here as the recipient of the glory together with the Father and the Holy Spirit, it is clear that in the preceding phrase 'per puerum tuum . . . per quem' he is regarded in another respect, namely in his humanity; it is only in his humanity, as 'the man Christ Jesus' (1 Tim. 2:5), that he can be the Mediator, Redeemer, and high priest.[2] His

---

[1] How closely creed formula and prayer pattern interlock may be seen from two examples: on the one hand, the creed-like prayer interpolated by Irenaeus (*Adv. haer.* III, 6, 4 [Mg 7, 862 f.]): 'Lord, God of Abraham . . . let the holy spirit reign in us through our Lord Jesus Christ . . .'; on the other, the words, hinting at the prayer, from the *Ap. Const.* VI, 14, 2, which form the opening of a confession of faith: one God must be 'worshipped through our Lord Jesus Christ in the holy Spirit'.

[2] Admittedly, his human activity derives its world-redeeming power from its belonging to a man who is joined to the Logos in the oneness of the Person, i.e. who is God.

humanity is also indicated by the messianic title 'per puerum tuum'
= διὰ παιδός σου.[1]

It is indeed surprising to find in Hippolytus, of all people, a
doxology so dogmatically correct, seeing that he was charged with
ditheism, for not having given sufficient consideration to the oneness of the divine nature in his theory of the relationship between
Father and Son.[2] But this need not necessarily have prevented him
from adhering to the clear distinction between the divinity and
humanity of Christ, simultaneously with the trinity of God, as indeed
it is expressed in our doxology. Although the introductory and concluding formulas of liturgical prayers were the first to be given a
fixed wording, in contrast to the freedom otherwise prevailing, there
is reason to suppose that the trinitarian shaping of this doxology was
the work of the theologian Hippolytus. Whether he was also the
first to insert the term 'in sancta ecclesia' is open to doubt. The
lofty conception of the Church apparent in the doxology is certainly
typical of Hippolytus.[3] But it is by no means peculiar to him; it was
the common property of the period.[4]

The picture of the early Church's manner of praying which we
have so far gained mosaic-wise is confirmed by the monograph *On
Prayer* compiled by Origen after the year 232.[5] In it we find the same

[1] The appellation παῖς θεοῦ can mean 'son of God', but also 'servant of God'.
The latter's significance is clear: Is. 42:1; Matt. 12:18. It is also used in the
Acts: 3:13, 26; 4:27, 30. J. Lebreton (*Les origines du dogme de la Trinité* 264)
comments on the passage: 'Il est donc plus sûr de laisser au mot sa signification
ambiguë, qu'il avait probablement pour l'auteur des Actes et que pour nous du
moins il a toujours, lorsque le contexte n'en détermine pas la valeur.' In our context at least, the title may well refer to Christ's messianic role, to his mediatory
position, which, as already noted, presupposes divinity. In other contexts it is less
self-evident: *Did.* c. 9, 10; 1 Clem. c. 59: *Martyr. Polyc.* c. 14.

The expression παῖς θεοῦ has been comprehensively illustrated by J. Jeremias
(*Theol. Wörterbuch zum NT*, V, 653–713), the starting-point being the 'God's
servant' passage in Is. 42. Cf. the expression διὰ τοῦ Χριστοῦ σου in the *Ap. Const.*,
but also in the later Greek liturgies. Here there is present the same contrast as that
which governs the whole doctrine of redemption: that between the triune God and
Christ the Mediator between God and man.

[2] Cf. A. d'Alès, *La théologie de saint Hippolyte* (Paris, 1906), 33; K. Graf Preysing,
ZkTh 41 (1917), 596 f.; H. Dieckmann, ZkTh 48 (1924) 314–22.

[3] Cf. A. d'Alès 36–9.

[4] Cf. S. von Dunin-Barkowski, *Die Kirche als Stiftung Jesu* 104.

[5] GCS: Orig. II, pp. 295–403. Koetschau. Cf. E. von der Goltz, *Das Gebet in der
ältesten Christenheit* 266–78.

basic ideas, though strongly modified by the bold eccentricity of his thought. In this work we are offered, besides an explanation of the Lord's Prayer, essays on the meaning of prayer in general, its value, efficacy, preliminary conditions, arrangement, and composition. He begins with the proposition: what is impossible for us mortals because of its sublimity 'according to God's will becomes possible through the boundless grace of God, which is poured out by God over mankind through the servant of infinite grace towards us—Jesus Christ and the co-operating Spirit . . . Who would dare say that it is possible to know the thoughts of the Lord? But this, too, is vouchsafed by God through Christ. . . .' For we have received the Holy Spirit, who plumbs the depths of the Godhead (c. 1). Only thus is it possible to speak of prayer, just as only with the help of the Spirit is it possible to pray well. 'For the soul cannot pray unless the Spirit prays first and she hearkens to it, as it were. Nor can it sing psalms and praise the Father in Christ, rhythmically and melodiously, in measured and harmonious tones, unless the Spirit . . . extols and praises him beforehand' (c. 2, 4). These ideas recur repeatedly. Finally, when he is speaking of the construction of a good prayer, in three passages he stipulates that a prayer should begin, and in some cases also end, with 'Praise and glory to the Father of all through Jesus Christ in the Holy Spirit'; we must begin with the 'glorification of God through Christ, who is co-equally glorified, in the Holy Spirit, who is co-equally praised' (c. 33, 1, 6). But his special concern is that Christ should be acknowledged as high priest. He who has recourse to prayer with a pure heart receives a share in the divine Logos who, to be sure, is in the midst even of those who know him not and gives his support to every prayer. He is indeed the high priest of our sacrificial gifts. But as a real advocate ($\pi\alpha\rho\acute{\alpha}\kappa\lambda\eta\tau os$) he prays only for those who obey his injunction to pray constantly and steadfastly through him (c. 10, 2). Moreover, it is not only the high priest who prays with those who pray aright, but also the angels in heaven and the souls of the saints who have left this life (c. 11, 1).

The expression $\epsilon\mathring{v}\chi\mathring{\eta}$ $\tau o\hat{v}$ $\lambda\acute{o}\gamma ov$ $\theta\epsilon o\hat{v}$ itself looks out of place, not so much because it sounds discordant continually to be speaking of the transfigured Saviour 'praying', without any softening phrase and with all the humble, beseeching attitude implicit in the word; but rather because we prefer to allude to him as praying in his humanity, in which he fulfils his office of high priest on our behalf. Christ's high priestly mediation is mentioned frequently in other writings by Origen, in particular in the work against Celsus. In the opinion of J. Lebreton,[1] it here appears that Origen in fact ascribes the mediatory office of the Son of God not to the Incarnation, but to the Logos as such—a view once held by Philo the Jew, whose philosophic ideas Origen blended in a fatal manner with the Christian. In the two seraphim who in Isaias chant 'Holy, holy, holy', Origen sees the Logos and the Holy Spirit praising the Father.[2] This is hardly the same as the Logos *in his human nature* glorifying the Father, or the Holy Spirit *in mankind* sighing and praying, i.e. teaching it to pray.[3] Origen's discourses on Christ the high priest appear to be infected by his subordinationist conception of the Trinity. Also, the words we have heard him use about God acting through Christ in the Holy Spirit,[4] taken together with his theories, appear in a similar, rather uncertain light. Not only in the work of redemption itself and within the framework of the order of salvation does the activity of God seem to him to be so determined, but even now the divine illumination and providence take this path.

[1] *Revue d'Histoire ecclésiastique* 25 (1924) 20, 24.

[2] Περὶ ἀρχῶν I, 3, 4; in Is. I, 2. 'Origen's Conversation with Heraklides', an Egyptian papyrus discovered in 1941 and edited by J. Scherer (*Sources chrétiennes* 67; Paris 1960, p. 62), is further evidence of the way in which Origen connected the high priesthood of Christ with his divinity. Heraklides, unable to reconcile the unity of the divine nature with the divinity of Christ, is referred by Origen to the liturgical order: 'The sacrifice is always offered to almighty God through Jesus Christ as the offerer to the Father according to his divinity (διὰ 'I. Χρ. ὡς προσφόρου τῷ πατρὶ τὴν θεότητα αὐτοῦ; on the difficult word προσφόρου the editor has a note on p. 65). There is not to be a double offering; rather, the offering must be made to God through God.'

[3] It is true that a similarly sounding expression is to be found also in Irenaeus, *Epideixis* c. 10 (BKV² 4, p. 9. Weber): 'Now this God is glorified by his Word, which is his eternal Son, and by the Holy Spirit, which is the wisdom of the Father of all. And their powers, those of the Word and of wisdom, which are called cherubim and seraphim, praise God. . . .' The thought here is less definite and expressly distinguishes the Logos and the Holy Spirit from the cherubim and seraphim. For the liturgical character of this passage, see J. A. Robinson, *The Demonstration of the Apostolic Preaching* (London 1920), p. 41.

[4] c. 1, 1; cf. c. 18, 1.

Origen imagines that the divine action is so graduated that the action of the Father alone extends to all creatures; he uses the Word to influence those endowed with reason and the Holy Spirit, in addition, to sanctify them.[1] Still, his explanation of divine action is less dangerous in that in fact he considers a divine action both through the Logos and through Christ in his humanity.[2]

Thus forewarned, we are less surprised by what we read further on in the work on prayer, so far as it concerns our theme. In c. 14 Origen distinguishes four kinds of prayer on the lines of I Tim. 2:1: προσευχή, δέησις, ἔντευξις, εὐχαριστία. Whereas the last three kinds—petition, intercession, thanksgiving—may be addressed also to men, though above all to Christ, he will have prayer in the strict sense (the προσευχή), which is aimed at higher blessings and is joined with praise, directed only to God, not Christ. Here it has been remarked[3] that Origen is advocating only what in any case was and is the practice of the Church in liturgical prayer. J. Lebreton[4] rejects this view, but his 'decisive' reason—that in c. 16, 1 Origen urges that all four kinds of prayer be addressed to God—is hardly valid since Origen makes this latter demand without excluding other recipients of the prayer. In a neighbouring passage, however, (c. 15, 16) Origen adduces reasons that go further: 'If one is to pray aright, one must not pray to him who prays himself', 'whom the Father has made the high priest and advocate', who calls us his brethren. He interprets the sentence 'Let all God's angels worship him' (Heb. 1:6; Deut. 32:43 [Septuagint only]) as a mere greeting of Christ. 'Let us then pray to God through him, and let us all speak in the same way, without division in the manner of prayer. Or are we not divided when some pray to the Father, others to the Son? They commit a sin of ignorance (ἰδιωτῶν ἁμαρτίαν) who in excessive simplicity, without scrutiny and reflection, pray to the Son, whether with the Father or without the Father' (c. 16, 1).

---

[1] Cf. Περὶ ἀρχῶν I, 3; II, 7.

[2] Cf. also A. Palmieri (Dictionnaire de théologie catholique, V, 710, s.v. Esprit-Saint), who joins T. de Régnon in defending Origen against the charge of subordination-ism. Cf. also Hamman, La prière II (1963) 305 f.

[3] By P. Maran among others: PG 17, 792–5.        [4] Loc. cit. 22–4.

Clearly, at this point, Origen has arrived at a theory with which he has remained alone in the Church. Even in the earliest Fathers there is evidence of private prayers to Jesus and of hymns of praise to him.[1] Besides, Origen contradicts his own doctrine in other passages where he defends the worship of Jesus against the charge of polytheism, or inserts praises of and prayers to Jesus into his homilies.[2] At the same time it should be noted that in his monograph Origen was speaking of *ceremonial* prayer, and that he had in mind communal prayer ('are we not divided?'); also, in other passages (c. 20, 1; c. 31) he strongly recommends communal prayer in the Church. He may well have been thinking of the communal prayer of the people which, according to Justin, preceded the eucharistic prayer recited by the προεστώς (*Apol.* I, 65); and which we meet in later oriental liturgies as an elaborate prayer recited alternately by the deacon and the congregation; it was addressed for preference to Christ, or simply to the 'Lord'. At that time this prayer was certainly not yet subject to any strict regulation,[3] though at an early period deacons in particular may have been empowered to conduct it. This view is also suggested by the fact that the person to whom he was writing, Ambrosius, was himself a deacon[4] and hence must have had a special interest in an instruction on prayer. Possibly Origen wanted to be sure that in this sphere, too, the type of the liturgical prayer through Christ to God be retained, but his arguments in support of it were not very happy.

Although, therefore, Origen is a good witness of the prayer addressed to God through Christ in the Holy Spirit,[5] it is clear that the interpretation he gave it was harmful. Paul had emphatically demanded the role of Mediator for the *man* Christ Jesus; and in the Epistle to the Hebrews is shown with equal clarity on the one hand that Christ is truly the Son of God, who reflects the glory of the

---

[1] Cf. A. Klawek, 102 ff; J. Lebreton, 'La prière dans l'Église primitive' in *Recherches de science religieuse* 14 (1924), 5 ff., 97 ff.

[2] Evidence in F. J. Dölger, *Sol salutis*², p. 115, n. 2.

[3] Cf. 1 Cor. 14:16; *Did.* 10:7.    [4] O. Bardenhewer, II²‚ 197.

[5] Formal prayers of this kind have not been handed down to us by Origen, but his homilies often end with the prayer that God may grant us the favour in question 'through Christ', 'in Christ', and also 'through Christ and through the holy Spirit'. (In Gen. II, 6 [PG 12, 175]).

Father and is worshipped by the angels, and on the other that it is only in his humanity that he stands by our side, ready to serve as high priest like Melchisedech.[1] In Origen, however, qualities of a creature and of a serving subject, befitting humanity, are transferred to his divine nature, which is thus put in doubt. Another circumstance increased the danger to which liturgical prayer was exposed by these speculations. Since the theological prayer pattern had been given a trinitarian form by the insertion of the Holy Spirit, not only had the addressing of the prayer to the Father been given more clearly than ever the sense of an address to the first divine person[2] but Christ too comes into prominence pre-eminently as the Son of God. Moreover, he now seems to have been named in the doxology preferably in virtue of his divinity, if only to make the three divine Persons more clearly known as such. Praise and glory are sent up to the Father 'through the Son and the Holy Spirit'. This language was, according to the rules of the *Communicatio idiomatum*, completely justified; it merely shows belief in the unity of the person in Christ. Our high priest is also Son of God. There was also little room for misunderstanding, at least if at the same time an allusion was made to his humanity, such as 'through Jesus Christ, thine only-begotten Son'. This, however, was not always done.[3]

Though the text of the prayer itself left it open, whether the Son as such, the Logos, was regarded as the Mediator with the Father, this interpretation was definitely suggested when such ideas were advocated at the leading school of theology. Elsewhere, it is true, they were regarded as new-fangled and Pope Dionysius I (259–68)

---

[1] Heb 1:2 ff.; 2:9 ff.

[2] Cf. the analogous phenomenon in the field of the creeds. Since the fourth century, expositors of the creed have usually understood the confession of 'God the Father almighty' in this sense. Cf. on the other hand, for the earlier period, J. Tixeront, *Histoire des dogmes* I (Paris, 1905), 160, where he comments on the opening words Πιστεύω εἰς θεὸν πατέρα: 'Πατέρα est probablement primitif . . . et ne designe pas la personne du Père, mais affirme simplement l'universelle paternité de Dieu comme créateur.'

[3] Cf. above (p. 151) the doxology and the form of expression used already by Clement of Alexandria. Serapion also speaks several times of the Logos or the only-begotten Son: 14 (2): ὅτι διὰ τοῦ μονογενοῦς σοὶ ἡ δόξα καὶ τὸ κράτος ἐν ἁγίῳ πνεύματι. Cf. 8 (30); 16 (4); 20 (8).

condemned some of their excessive forms, inculcating the traditional
doctrine of the unity of the divine nature.[1]

Apparently, however, the mode of prayer used hitherto remained
in force without arousing misgivings. It was still in use when, a
hundred years after Origen, there had long taken root the complete
heresy on the same point—*Arianism*. The Son was declared bluntly
to be a creature, different in nature from the Father. It was taught,
moreover, that in becoming man the Son had taken to himself
merely a human body, the place of the soul being taken by the
Logos; the latter was, indeed, only a created, changeable spirit like
the human soul. Only the Logos as such, according to the Arians,
could therefore be the subject of thinking and willing, of mediation
and the priesthood.[2] To an Arian it was the same in the end whether
one said: 'We praise God through Christ', or 'we praise the Father
through the Son'. In either case it could only be the Son, the Logos
as such, who was here subordinated to the Father. There being no
other evidence from the past, the old liturgical formula provided
the Arian with a welcome argument for his heresy.

However, the two liturgies of the fourth century which are extant
still show the old features, though they do not simply present the old
tradition but are rather re-editions of it. In Serapion's *Euchologium*
the old prayer pattern appears in all its purity of style, only still with
the marked tendency of the terms always to show the trinitarian
relationship, which is also the first theme of the preface. The prayers
are not simply addressed to God through Christ in the Holy Spirit,
but almost always 'through thy only-begotten Jesus Christ in the
Holy Spirit' or just simply 'through the only-begotten'. The
address in the very first prayer[3] is: 'We pray thee, father of the only-
begotten', and obviously also in the other prayers it is to be understood of the first divine Person. In this case it did not require much
ill-will to conceive the 'only-begotten' as being the Logos subordinate to the Father, and this in spite of Serapion being the highly-
esteemed friend of St Athanasius, the foremost opponent of Arianism.
And even Athanasius occasionally made use of a doxology of this

[1] H. Denzinger-C. Bannwarth, *Enchiridion*[14] n. 48–51.
[2] J. Tixeront, *Histoire des dogmes II* (Paris, 1909), 27.          [3] 1 (30).

kind at about this time.[1] There was an unwillingness to relinquish the right to pray as one always had prayed, despite the danger of heretical misinterpretation.

Whereas Serapion's *Euchologium* dates from the middle of the fourth century, the liturgy of the *Apostolic Constitutions* is thought to have been compiled about fifty years later. In the *Constitutions* the prayers have far less of a trinitarian stamp than in Serapion. Whereas in the didactic portions Christ is often called ὁ μονογενὴς θεός and in the context of the prayers is occasionally mentioned as 'thy only-begotten Son',[2] even the mediatory formulas have only 'through Christ', 'through thy Christ', 'through Jesus Christ our hope' and the like, thus refraining from stressing the divinity of Christ at this point, like our shorter Roman ending, 'per Christum Dominum nostrum'. Rather often, Christ is described as high priest, sometimes also as παῖς θεοῦ. The extension 'in the Holy Spirit' is added normally,—but not invariably[3]—only in the concluding doxology.[4] Also, the prayer's address to God is clearly not to be taken as addressed to the first of the divine Persons, although in one instance at least the phrasing is similar to that used by St Paul: everlasting God, Father of our Lord Jesus Christ.[5] The compiler of this liturgy kept to the forms that had been handed down to him and designated Christ principally as Mediator. The misuse of these forms by the Arians has thrown a suspicion on him that he himself was an Arian. And it is difficult to defend him perfectly.[6] Nevertheless the comment made by F. X. Funk on all eight books of the *Apostolic Constitutions* applies with even greater force to the liturgy:

[1] See the end of the 'Letter to the Bishops of Egypt and Libya against the Arians' (c. 356–7; PG 25, 593): τοῦ κυρίου καὶ σωτῆρος καὶ θεοῦ καὶ παμβασιλέως ἡμῶν Ἰησοῦ Χριστοῦ, δι' οὗ τῷ πατρὶ ἡ δόξα καὶ τὸ κράτος ἐν πνεύματι ἁγίῳ.

[2] In VIII, 5, 2, the address is ὁ θεὸς καὶ πατὴρ τοῦ μονογενοῦς υἱοῦ σου τοῦ θεοῦ καὶ σωτῆρος ἡμῶν.

[3] Cf. VII, 47, 3; 49.

[4] A certain restraint regarding the trinitarian extension of the complex 'God and Christ' is betrayed in requiring that the testimony in favour of the chosen bishop be given 'before the judgment seat of God and Christ, in the presence also, of course, of the holy Spirit' (VIII, 4, 5: Παρόντος δηλαδὴ καὶ τοῦ ἁγίου πνεύματος).

[5] Cf. VIII, 20, 1.

[6] This is upheld at least for his redaction of the 'Gloria in Excelsis' (VII, 47) by B. Capelle, 'Le texte du "Gloria in Excelsis"' in *Revue de l'hist. eccl.* 44 (1949) 439–457.

almost all the questionable phrases are to be found also in the Catholic Fathers.[1] J. Lebreton sought to demonstrate the influence of Origenistic theology in the *Apostolic Constitutions*, and in so doing adduced some motives worth considering.[2] Yet even the evidence on which he lays most weight and which seems to him to show subordinationist and Origenistic-Arian tendencies,—viz. the prominence of the high priest and the lack of prayers addressed to Christ —need not be decisive. So long, therefore, as neither the assertion and argument of the Arians, nor even of Origen, is also attested one cannot, at least as far as the liturgy is concerned, speak of Arianism and subordinationism but only of a tenacious adherence to the traditional form of prayer, which the compiler had in common with Serapion and with the Roman liturgy.

Looking back over the first centuries of the Christian era we may come to this conclusion: to judge from all that survives in documents and accounts of the Church's life in this period, liturgical prayer, in regard to its form of address, keeps with considerable unanimity to the rule of turning to God (described repeatedly as the father of Jesus Christ)[3] through Christ the high priest, but in such a way that the scheme that came down from the Apostles was organically developed. It was not until the end of the fourth century that we meet, by way of exception, prayers to Christ the Lord, and these are not within the Eucharistic celebration proper but in the fore-Mass and in Baptism. On the other hand we know that in private prayers,

---

[1] F. X. Funk, I, p. xix. Cf. also O. Bardenhewer, IV, 271: the *Apostolic Constitutions* provide 'no definite information about the dogmatic standpoint of the compiler'. It is more feasible to rank him alongside Eusebius of Caesarea, as is done by E. Schwartz (*Über die pseudo-apostolischen Kirchenordnungen*, Strasbourg, 1910, pp. 16 f.). Eusebius is also in agreement with him, when it comes to liturgical prayer, in presenting Christ preferably as High Priest of all, through whom we offer our sacrifice to God the Father, and who also himself prays in his believers. For a series of passages from his works, see F. Probst, *Liturgie des 4. Jahrhunderts* 52, 67, 71 f.

[2] *Revue d'histoire ecclésiastique* 24 (1923), 29–33, and *Recherches de science religieuse* 13 (1923), 322–9 ('La forme primitive du *Gloria* prière au Christ ou prière à Dieu le Père?').

[3] The designation of God as Father, especially also as 'Father of our Lord Jesus Christ', is rarer in original liturgical works of the later period. But the development, which cannot be gone into in detail at this point, runs only partly parallel with the history of the christological conception of the Mediator. Cf. the observations already made above in Part I.

both in apostolic times and later, the prayer to Christ was well-known and customary.[1]

Another school, however, has made several attempts to defend the probability of an earlier and extensive use of the prayer to Christ, even in the liturgy, by reference to the apocryphal *Acts of the Apostles*, in particular the *Acts of St Thomas* and *Acts of St John*.[2] These writings of the second and third centuries include (beside prayers for miraculous help, intercessions for the newly converted and the like) a series of prayers that must be classed as liturgical: prayers for the exorcism of evil spirits, prayers of praise and thanksgiving and finally formal prayers for Baptism and Communion; and these prayers are in fact regularly addressed to Christ. How is this remarkable phenomenon to be explained and evaluated? Any answer will depend on one's view of the origin of these writings. The usual view—so E. Hennecke and his collaborators[3]—is that they derive for the most part, not from Catholic but from heretical, especially Gnostic and Docetic, circles. Hence great caution is required in drawing conclusions from them about contemporary religious life within the Church.

[1] My ascertainment—overlooked in many recensions—that personal prayers to Christ were 'well-known and customary' even before the fourth century, merited further exposition and confirmation. Cf. K. Baus, 'Das Gebet der Märtyrer' in *Trierer Theol. Zeitschr.* 62 (1953) 19–32. According to him, prayer to Christ is definitely predominant in the prayers of the martyrs used by succeeding generations. Cf. also the accounts given on p. 144 f.—For the subsequent period, see also K. Baus, 'Das Gebet zu Christus beim hl. Hieronymus' in *Trierer Theol. Zeitschr.* 60 (1951), 178–88.

[2] For these Acts, cf. O. Bardenhewer I[2], 574–84; and E. Hennecke, *Die neutestamentlichen Apokryphen*[2] 171–5, 256–8. The prayers are discussed by E. von der Goltz, *Das Gebet in der ältesten Christenheit* 290–311.

The attempts made by W. Bousset (*Kyrios Christos*, Göttingen, 1913) and G. P. Wetter (*Altchristliche Liturgien*, I, *Das christliche Mysterium*, Göttingen, 1921) to present Christ as the cult-hero of the earliest (Greek) Christians, to whom naturally they would also pray, are mere speculation. A. Harnack has come to practically the opposite conclusion, that Jesus has no place in the Gospel and consequently no place in the prayers of the first Christians. According to J. Michl, 'Apostelgeschichten (apokryphe)', *Lexikon f. Theologie u. Kirche* I (1957) 751 f., the *Acts of St John* are a story dating from the middle of the second century, full of Gnostic, Encratistic and Docetic views, while the *Acts of St Thomas* were probably written in the first half of the third century and had a wide circulation, especially in Gnostic circles.

[3] Op. cit., pp. 168, 173, 257.

Another group, represented especially by C. Schmidt, discerns in this literary jungle memorials of the faith of the common people, of the popular Christianity of the pre-Nicean Church as a whole.[1] But here we must heed the voice of the official Church, of the bishops and the ecclesiastical writers (especially those of the fourth and fifth centuries) which decisively rejected these writings.[2] The religious ideas they reveal,[3] deriving, like the stories themselves, from various sources, are in any case anything but clear theologically. This is especially true of the conceptual content of the prayers that are scattered about these writings. The prayers of a liturgical character in particular—if in fact they reflect an actual liturgical practice—seem to derive from such circles infected with heresy. This is also highly probable in the case of the liturgical address to Christ, which is regularly used.

A. Klawek, who is in no doubt about the Gnostic origin of these prayers, is however of the opinion that in the address to Christ we have a custom taken over by the Gnostics for their liturgy from the Catholic Church. He says that 'since, as far as is known, it was not part of the Gnostic system to introduce such prayers as that to Jesus, the only explanation is that they inherited the prayer to Jesus from the Church'.[4] We will therefore see briefly whether in fact there is no evidence for such an innovation by the Gnostics. We must first describe the most important prayers.

The prayers of praise and thanksgiving consist for the most part of a series of laudatory salutations addressed to Christ: 'O how mighty thou art, Lord Jesus Christ, I do not know ... Father, full of compassion and pity for mankind, who did not esteem (thyself), we glorify and extol and praise

---

[1] See his arguments occasioned by the edition of the so-called *Epistola Apostolorum* (TU 43, Leipzig 1919), also the discussion by F. Haase, *Oriens christ.*[2] 10/11 (for 1920–21; Leipzig, 1923) 170–3. A. Hamman, *La Prière* II (1963), giving remarkable reasons, presents the hypothesis that these writings originate from an early untheological Judeo-Christian monasticism of Syria (pp. 176, 184, 188, 211, 219 ff.).

[2] Cf. F. Piontek, 'Die katholische Kirche und die häretischen Apostelgeschichten, bis zum Ausgang des 6. Jahrhunderts' (*Kirchengeschichtliche Abhandlungen* ed. by M. Sdralek 6, pp. 1–71, Breslau, 1908), pp. 53 ff.

[3] In the *Acts of St John*, for instance, F. J. Dölger, *IXΘΥΣ*, II. 'Der heilige Fisch in den antiken Religionen und im Christentum' (Münster i. W.) 1922, 559, n. 4, draws our attention to a number of ideas which are of Hellenic origin.

[4] *Das Gebet zu Jesus* 111.

thee . . . holy Jesus; since thou alone art God and no other, thou against whose might all onslaughts are of no avail, now and for ever. Amen.'[1] One such prayer ends: 'We glorify and praise thee and thy invisible Father and thy Holy Spirit and the mother of the whole of creation.'[2] In the *Acts of St Thomas* the baptismal ceremony opens with a ninefold acclamation: 'Come, holy name of Christ . . . come, power of the most high . . . come, highest gift, come, mother of mercy, come, community of the male', etc.;[3] likewise, the Eucharistic ceremony.[4] Other Eucharistic prayers beg Christ to come down on earth: 'Jesus . . . come and commune with us!'[5] or a fruitful reception of the Eucharist is prayed for;[6] or Christ is praised under various titles and with regard to all the saving gifts he has brought or announced.

Some of these prayers to Christ are, as they stand, theologically unexceptionable,[7] but others, as is shown in the examples cited, reveal a strong admixture of foreign elements, and it is those that make comprehensible the transition to the address to Christ in the ceremonial prayer. Among them is the visible appearance, the christophany, which frequently crystallizes Christ's descent into the liturgical assemblies, and which apart from this plays an important part in the Docetic tendency in many parts of the acts, both of St John and St Thomas. Then the confusion of other personified heavenly powers with the persons of the trinity, sometimes even within the prayers, betrays the spirit of the Gnostic doctrine of the aeons: in the Gnostic systems the first being, the unknown God, and the $\mu\acute{\eta}\tau\eta\rho$, are joined by a growing host of aeons, which includes Christ among the better-known forms. With the ever increasing growth of Christianity in the Gnosis—originally heathen but ordered to the idea of salvation from the beginning—Christ the Saviour, in any case the only figure that was anchored to history, naturally soon assumed an outstanding position. Especially in the stories of the Apostles, the Christian element inevitably came to the fore. But the doctrinal structure of Christianity has been broken, the various parts have been made independent and they have been incorporated only in so far as they fit into the system.

[1] *Acta Joh.* c. 77 (AAA II, 1, p. 189, 16. Bonnet); cf. *Acta Thomae* c. 59, 60 f., and the long exorcism, c. 47 f.
[2] *Acta Thomae* c. 39 (AAA II, 2, p. 157, 16. Bonnet). According to Hennecke, the last 'and' should be deleted: the Spirit is the mother.
[3] c. 27 (AAA II, 2, p. 142, 13. Bonnet).        [4] *Ibid.* c. 50.
[5] *Acta Thomae* c. 49, 50 (AAA II, 2, p. 166, 5, 15. Bonnet). In several instances he appears in visible shape among the assembly as a handsome youth.
[6] *Acta Thomae* c. 158.
[7] *Acta Joh.* c. 85, 109; cf. *Acta Thomae* c. 47 f. In several of the texts it is not clear which heavenly power is being addressed, e.g. *Acta Thomae* c. 15.

It is not surprising, therefore, that God himself is mentioned only incidentally. He remains the unknown God, as everywhere else in the Gnosis, a murky figure, hardly inviting to a serious prayer-relationship. In his stead, Christ attracts all the more interest for he is the rescuer of the souls of light from the thrall of matter. So it follows naturally from the Gnostic system that prayers are addressed to him, particularly in liturgical celebrations,[1] and that he finally becomes the cult-hero. A. Klawek[2] mistakenly relies on W. Bousset in stating that in Gnosticism 'the cult of Jesus came to yield first place to the veneration of the "mother" '. Quite the opposite occurred. With the christianization of the Gnosis, the former exclusive cult of the mother was gradually overtaken by the Christ cult, while still keeping an important place, as is shown by the prayers already mentioned, with their invocations to the mother.[3] Clearly, for the compiler of the *Acts of St Thomas* the saint's words addressed to the risen Christ, 'My Lord and my God!' (John 20:28) serve as a model for his prayers. Those in c. 10. 144. 167[4] open with these words and must obviously be addressed to Christ.

Another feature of these apostolic legends has been remarkable from the first: the persistent equating and identification of Christ with God the Father. This was done, whether knowingly or not, to adapt Christian concepts to an alien system, in harmony with the heretical Modalism of the time. T. Zahn,[5] with particular reference to the *Acts of St John*, has coined the word 'panchristism' for this 'formal suppression of the distinction between Jesus, God, and Spirit'. Thus the compiler of these legends is reproved by the Patriarch Photius (d. 891): 'He asserts that the wicked God of the Jews, who has as an assistant Simon the Magician, is someone other than Christ, whom he calls good; he confuses everything and calls him father and son.'[6] This comes out especially in the prayers, where Christ is addressed as 'Father', as has already been shown in our first example.[7]

---

[1] To judge from these narrations, there can hardly be question of the actual celebration of Mass. In the *Acts of St Thomas* there is no mention of bread and wine, only at the most bread and water (Encratites). And it is the same with baptism. Cf. F. Piontek, *Die katholische Kirche und die häretischen Apostelgeschichten* 5.

[2] P. 111, n. 5.

[3] Cf. the articles 'Gnosis' and 'Gnostiker' by W. Bousset in Pauly-Wissowa, *Realenzyklopädie* VII, especially cols. 1513 ff., 1525 ff., 1544 ff.

[4] In c. 10 and 167 corresponding exactly with John 20:28: Ὁ κύριός μου καὶ ὁ θεός μου (AAA II, 2, pp. 114, 5; 281, 6. Bonnet).

[5] *Geschichte des neutestam. Kanons* II (Leipzig, 1890–2), p. 839.

[6] In Hennecke 170.

[7] Cf. *Acta Joh.* c.112 (AAA II, 1, p. 212, 1. Bonnet): θεὲ Ἰησοῦ ὁ τῶν ὑπερουρανίων πατήρ. Similarly c. 77, 109. In *Acta Thomae* c. 144, the address 'My Lord and my God' forms the bridge enabling the Our Father to continue as a prayer to Christ.

This should be sufficient proof that the address to Christ in the liturgical prayer of these writings need not be explained as a heritage from Catholic liturgy.

And this throws light on another fact. In the year 393 a Council was held at Hippo, at which St Augustine, then still a priest, was one of the participants. The much-quoted can. 21 of this synod, confirmed by the third Council of Carthage in 397, ran as follows: 'Ut nemo in precibus vel Patrem pro Filio vel Filium pro Patre nominet. Et cum altari assistitur, semper ad Patrem dirigatur oratio. Et quicumque sibi preces aliunde describit, non eis utatur, nisi prius eas cum instructioribus fratribus contulerit.'[1] A. Klawek remarks on the popular writings presupposed here: 'Perhaps we may regard them as apocrypha with a Gnostic-Sabellian flavour, in which God the Father was thrust too far into the background.'[2] The instruction has rightly been understood to mean that, in spite of the Arian heresy, the synod would not permit prayers in divine services to be addressed to Christ. But this only explains the *Filium pro Patre*. The synod also forbids the naming of the Father in place of the Son. This seems to presuppose a contrary usage; the Patrem pro Filio appears superfluous. H. Goussen[3] explains it as a later insertion made in confusion. It is only when we follow Klawek's suggestion that this difficulty also disappears. The instruction was evidently aimed against writings in which the ideas, or at least the names, of Christ and God, Father and Son, were wantonly confused. Otherwise the Father could not have been put in place of the Son at the same time.

This, then, is certain of writings of the type of apocryphal stories of the Apostles: they speak principally of Christ, but he seems to be identified simultaneously and repeatedly with the Father, and is even called 'Father'. In the *Acts of St Peter (Actus Petri cum Simone)*, however, which we have not yet touched on, we find not only prayers of this kind[4] but also nearly the opposite. Peter begins the

---

[1] Mansi, *Collectio concil.* III, 884. 922; C. J. Hefele, *Konziliengeschichte* II² (Freiburg 1875), 53 ff., 65 ff.: English translation, *A History of Christian Councils* (Edinburgh, 1871–96) II, 398 ff., 408 ff. Cf. can. 9 of the eleventh Synod of Carthage (407), where it is again stressed that use may be made only of those prayer-formularies that have been examined by the Council and assembled by judicious persons.

[2] P. 113, n. 1.      [3] *Theol. Revue* 23 (1947) 17.      [4] Cf. especially c. 39.

entreaty for the raising of a dead man: 'Pater sancte Filii tui Jesu Christi, qui nobis virtutem tuam praebuisti, ut *per te* petamus et impetremus.'[1] Along with the address, which was fixed, as was customary in Church services, the author has retained a recollection of the Church's praying 'through Christ' but, unbeknown to him, it has changed (quite logically in fact) into a prayer—through the Father ('per te')—'Patrem pro Filio nominat'. For these *Acts of St Peter* belong to the same group of apocrypha, and here too Gnostic features have been identified, especially in the prayers.[2] Along with the *Acts of St John* and *Acts of St Thomas*, a legend about St Peter belongs to the collection which, as we have seen, was judged adversely by Photius. Writings of this kind were in fact circulating in Africa at the time of St Augustine. F. Piontek produces evidence[3] that the great doctor of the Church was certainly acquainted with the Acts of St Thomas and St John, and probably also those of St Peter. They were highly esteemed by the Manicheans, to whom he had adhered for a while. As a Catholic and a bishop he condemned these 'fables' with the utmost severity.[4]

It is clear, therefore, that the canon was directed against the adoption of prayers from such writings as included these semi-Gnostic, apocryphal stories of the Apostles. Liturgical prayer as found here, the Council laid down, was definitely not to be addressed to Christ instead of the Father; and equally, in the mediatory formula, the Father was not to be put in the place of Christ. The prayer to Christ in these writings is therefore no heritage from the Catholic Church, at any rate not from its official liturgical practice. On the contrary, it may be that some injudicious priests of that time thought of taking over these fabrications as a heritage for the Catholic Church, no doubt with good intentions and possibly also as a deliberate counter to Arianism, which had diminished the honour due to the Son.

In general, we come to this conclusion: Up to the fourth century, the prayer directed to Christ was widely used, both privately and in the form of hymns and acclamations. It is not among the official

---

[1] c. 27 (AAA I, p. 74, 4. Lipsius).        [2] G. Ficker in Hennecke 230.
[3] *Die katholische Kirche und die häretischen Apostelgeschichten.*        [4] Piontek 26 ff., 53 ff.

prayers said by the leader of the liturgical assembly. For the latter, the rule was the prayer offered to God 'through Christ'. We may say, going beyond this, that the Christians of this early period were conscious of praying to Christ, the head of the Church, as the normal way of praying because it was the normal way of believing—and so much so that, even in private prayer, a prayer addressed to Christ was regarded as being addressed through Christ to God.[1]

---

[1] To quote a few passages in support: in the *Praedicatio Petri* (first third of the second century) the worship of Christians is contrasted generally with that of the Greeks and of the Jews. The Christians are the third race: wherefore 'take notice of what we hand over to you, so that you may worship God through Christ in a new manner'; in Clement of Alexandria, *Strom.* VI, 5, 41; cf. Hennecke² 146. Tertullian, *Apologeticum* 21, 28 (CSEL 69, 59): 'Dicimus et palam dicimus et vobis torquentibus lacerati et cruenti vociferamur: Deum colimus per Christum . . . Per eum et in eo se cognosci et coli Deus vult.' Optatus, 1, III c. 11 (CSEL 26, 98 f.) asks his Donatist opponent: 'Eum qui Deum Patrem per Filium eius ante aram rogaverit, paganum vocas!' See also the passage from Novatian already cited (p. 146, n. 3). Finally we may cite the words with which Augustine asked for prayers for a sinner: 'Orate pro illo per Christum.' (*Enarr. in ps.* 61, 23; PL 36, 747; CC 39, 793.)

# XI

# REACTION OF THE ARIAN STRUGGLES ON LITURGICAL PRAYER. THE DISPUTE OVER THE DOXOLOGY

In order to support their heresy, the Arians zealously collected all texts in which a 'humbling' (ταπεινά; cf. Phil. 2:8) was attributed to Christ, especially a subordination to the Father. They particularly favoured the texts of Scripture in which there was a mention of the praying of Jesus. On the tacit assumption that the Logos took the place of the human soul, they concluded triumphantly: therefore the Son himself is subordinate to the Father; consequently, he is only a creature.

They found the same theme expressed even more clearly, if that were possible, in the Church's liturgy, ready formulated in the formulas of the traditional prayer schema: the Catholic Church herself daily recognizes the subordination of the Son to the Father when she offers her prayer to the Father through the Son.

Among the fragments of Arian writings[1] brought to light by A. Mai occurs one that takes this theme as its subject:[2] She herself

[1] PL 13, 593 ff.

[2] PL 13, 611 ff. This liturgical fragment has been published, with notes, by G. Mercati, 'Antiche reliquie liturgiche', in *Studi e Testi* 7, (Rome, 1902) 47 ff.: 'Frammenti liturgici latini tratti da un anonimo ariano del sec. IV/V'; he supposes a single author for all fragments and is inclined to look for him in the circles of the declining earlier Arianism of North Italy, which Ambrose withstood. New edition by Mohlberg-Eizenhöfer-Siffrin, *Sacramentarium Veronense* (Rome, 1956) 201 ff.

constantly puts the Father before the Son—so argues the Arian author—and then condemns all who do the same. He finds this preference (of the Father to the Son) in the laying-on of hands and blessings when the words run: 'Deus et Pater Domin nostri Jesu Christi.' He finds it in the creed, when there is asked, at first: 'Credis in Deum Patrem omnipotentem?' and only afterwards: 'Credis et in Christo Jesu Filio eius?' Above all, however, in the Mass: 'Omnes, qui praeponunt Patrem Filio, condemnant et tamen ipsi praeponunt Patrem Filio, in oblationibus suis dicentes: Dignum et justum est nos tibi hic et ubique gratias agere, Domine sancte, omnipotens Deus: Neque est alius *per quem* ad te aditum habere, precem facere, sacrificationem tibi offerre possimus, nisi per quem tu nobis misisti.' With this, he quotes at length from a further Preface in which, in the first instance, there is only mention of the fact that the one spoken to (Domine sancte Pater omnipotens aeterne Deus) has sent us Christ as Redeemer and restorer: 'Cuius benignitatis agere gratias tuae tantae magnanimitati quibusque laudibus nec sufficere possumus, petentes de tua magna et flexibili pietate accepto ferre sacrificium istud, quod tibi offerimus stantes ante conspectum tuae divinae pietatis, *per Jesum Christum* Dominum et Deum nostrum, per quem petimus et rogamus.'[1] Also elsewhere in these fragments the praying of Christ and the prayer through Christ are especially emphasized and used in an Arian sense.[2]

The echo of what we meet here directly in examples from the West[3]—viz. the Arian misinterpretation of the priestly and media-

[1] As Mercati notes, the second fragment gives the impression of a eucharistic prayer in which the *sanctus* is lacking, as in Hippolytus.

[2] PL 13, 605, 619. An Arian confession of faith (ibid. 624 f.), with the citation of various Scripture passages, gives special prominence to 'et summum sacerdotem esse Filium Deo Patri et mediatorem esse inter Deum Patrem omnipotentem et omnem creaturam'. Cf. ibid. 613: 'Exaudi⟨t⟩ nos Pater et miseretur per Filium, quia genua et cervicem flectimus Patri per Filium.'

[3] The sermons of the Arian Maximinus (PL 57, 781–832), who in the year 427 opposed St Augustine in a debate, exhibit in their closing sentences a great number of doxologies which for the most part are well in the line of tradition, and contain the 'per Christum', sporadically also the 'in Spiritu Sancto'. Apart from this, the Arianism is betrayed only in some favourite epithets applied to the divine Persons; thus in *serm.* VII: '(Exultemus et laetemur . . . in Domino Deo nostro et) ipsi solo ingenito per Unigenitum gratias agamus adorantes in Spiritu Sancto inluminatore et sanctificatore nostro per omnia s.s.'; B. Capelle, 'Un homiliaire de l'évêque arien Maximin': *Revue Bénéd.* 34 (1922) 81–108; for the doxologies: pp. 90–2.

tory position of Christ—we see everywhere in the East in the
refutations by the Fathers. From Athanasius onwards, they are
already giving the correct reply. They distinguish between
οἰκονομία and θεολογία. Chrysostom makes a brief and pointed
contrast: They say, prayer pertains to the divinity (θεότητος) but
we, to the order of salvation (οἰκονομίας). And he then shows, from
the words of the prayer in the garden itself, that prayer 'is to be
attributed to the order of salvation and to the weakness of the flesh'.
As man, Christ exercises his priesthood in heaven, and only as man[1]
and in his place in the economy of salvation[2] does he pray: 'secundum
hominem rogat'.[3] 'In that he is Son and God',—thus, somewhat
later, Cyril of Alexandria explains the text John 16:23[4]—'along with
the Father, he bestows good things on the saints . . ., but in that he is
named Mediator and high priest and advocate he offers the prayer
to the Father for us. For he is the source of confidence (παρρησία)
of us all before the Father'.[5] But the Arians did not allow themselves
to be put off by such distinctions in using the formulas of the
traditional prayer-schema as catchwords for their new teaching.
This was particularly the case in the Greek countries. Thus the old
manner of praying fell, here and there, into bad odour. This
applies especially to the three-membered doxology, in which one
sent up to God the Father honour and glory through the Son in the
Holy Ghost. For although the custom of praying through Christ had
the same significance in the prayer of petition as in the prayer of
praise, it found especially solemn expression in the latter and above
all in the doxology which ended the liturgical prayer.

Doxologies, especially at the end of a prayer, were already in use in the
Old Testament,[6] and appear to have been cultivated in particular by the
hellenistic synagogues. The doxology was a passage of praise which was
always dedicated to God alone. Therefore even a text in praise of Christ in
the form αὐτῷ ἡ δόξα εἰς τοὺς αἰῶνας was already fundamentally a recogni-

---

[1] ὡς ἄνθρωπος, ἀνθρωπίνως: Theodoret.
[2] οἰκονομικῶς ὡς ἄνθρωπος: Ammonius d. J.
[3] Ambrosius.                    [4] PG 74, 460 f.
[5] More detailed evidence in J. Margreth 24 f. Cf. Petavius, De Incarnatione l.
12, 11, 6.
[6] Cf., e.g., the endings of the books of the psalter.

tion of his divinity.[1] For the various elements of the doxology, for its different types and for their use in the primitive Church, especially in connexion with Our Father, see F. H. Chase, *The Lord's Prayer in the Early Church* (Texts and Studies, I,3; Cambridge 1891) 168–76. For doxologies and forms of titles among the Stoics and in the earlier Hellenism, see E. Norden, *Agnostos Theos* (Leipzig 1913). Among the Greek Fathers we find the doxology used much more frequently than in the West. They use it to end not only the prayer but frequently also homilies and letters. This occurrence of the doxology, in combination with the dating given in O. Bardenhewer (III[2]), will be of service to us in what follows. Admittedly, some caution is necessary here as end-doxologies are particularly exposed to correction by copyists.

In two cities of the East, viz. in Antioch and in Caesarea (Cappadocia), the religious dispute subsequently was centred on these doxologies.

In Antioch, where, after the banishment of the Catholic Bishop Eustathius in the year 330, the Arians had the upper hand, the two laymen, Diodorus of Tarsus and Flavian, were the focus for the minority of convinced Catholics in this city. The latter felt themselves challenged by the doxology $\Delta \delta \xi a \ \pi a \tau \rho i \ \delta \iota' \ v i o \hat{v} \ \dot{\epsilon} v \ \dot{a} \gamma i \omega \ \pi v \epsilon \dot{v} \mu a \tau \iota$— most probably recited by the Arians with the necessary emphasis— and about this time they began to use, instead, in their own liturgical assemblies, in the psalm-chant at the sanctuaries of the martyrs and then also in the common Church, the form: $\Delta \delta \xi a \ \pi a \tau \rho i \ \kappa a i \ v i \hat{\omega} \ \kappa a i \ \dot{a} \gamma i \omega \ \pi v \epsilon \dot{v} \mu a \tau \iota.$[2] The two doxologies thus became passwords of the two parties. Bishop Leontius (344–58), who himself was favourably disposed towards the Arians but also did not want to be entirely out of favour with the Catholics, was put in a dilemma by

---

[1] Cf. J. Lebreton, *Les Origines* 268. For the history of the doxology, there are now also available the summary accounts by A. Stuiber, 'Doxologie': *Reallexikon f. Antike u. Christentum* IV (1959) 210–26; J. M. Nielen and J. A. Jungmann, 'Doxologie': LThK III (1959) 534–6. A comprehensive picture of the early Christian doxologies, admittedly from a particular point of view, is provided by J. M. Hanssens, *La liturgie d'Hippolyte* (v.s. p. 10) 343–70. In particular, reference should be made to the survey of the end-doxologies of the homilies and writings, respectively, of John Chrysostom (pp. 362 f.) and of Cyril of Alexandria (pp. 363 f.). The conclusion confirms the picture given above.

[2] An inscription preserved from this period from the hinterland of Antioch, from Central Syria, is characteristic. Dated the year 368–9, it runs: $E \dot{v} \sigma \epsilon \beta i \omega$ $\chi \rho \iota \sigma \tau \iota a v \hat{\omega}. \ \Delta \delta \xi a \ \pi a \tau \rho i \ \kappa a i \ v i \hat{\omega} \ \kappa a i \ \dot{a} \gamma i \omega \ \pi v \epsilon \dot{v} (\mu a) \tau \iota.$ DACL 4, 1526 s.v. Doxologie; ibid., two undated inscriptions of the same type.

this Catholic counter-attack; as Theodoret relates of him he resorted to a quiet recitation of the doxology in public worship. Even those standing next to him could never catch more than the final words: εἰς τοὺς αἰῶνας τῶν αἰώνων,[1] and, referring to his white hair, he once remarked: When this snow has melted there will be a lot of slush, meaning when after his death this dispute over the doxology was decided, it would lead to grave conflicts.

A similarly critical situation resulted in Caesarea, where likewise there was a strongly Arian-minded party; only here, St Basil the Great was on guard as bishop. He began one day, when praying with the people, to use in protest against the Arian interpretation of the old doxology the formula, 'to the God and Father *with* the Son *together* with the Holy Spirit' (τῷ θεῷ καὶ πατρὶ . . . μετὰ τοῦ υἱοῦ σὺν τῷ πνεύματι τῷ ἁγίῳ) alongside the other, '*through* the Son *in the* Holy Spirit' (διὰ—ἐν).[2] This raised a storm. Basil was reproached for using texts which were not only alien and novel, but also opposed to each other. This last complaint clearly indicates in what sense the old doxology was generally understood.

The uproar gave Basil an opportunity to give in detail the reasons for his action, a thorough discussion of the two formulas of praise which he put forward in the year 375 in his work *De Spiritu Sancto*, dedicated to Bishop Amphilochius of Iconium[3]—although he

---

[1] Theodoret, *Hist. eccl.* II, 24, 3 (GCS: Theod. p. 153, 10. Parmentier). Cf. the fragment of Theodore of Mopsuestia PG 139, 1390. It was therefore already a custom of the time for the liturgist in some prayers to pronounce out loud only the last words, as an ἐκφώνησις (cf. Br. 35, 17 et passim), but the doxology belonged even then to the loud-spoken text. The introduction by Flavian of the doxology mentioned is also recorded by Philostorgius (*Hist. eccl.* III, 13), who belonged to the Arian party of the Eunomians and wrote about 430. According to him, there would have been in use, besides the old doxology with διά and ἐν mentioned by Theodoret, yet another, which hitherto had been quoted in the form: δόξα πατρὶ ἐν υἱῷ καὶ ἁγίῳ πνεύματι (PG 65, 501); it would therefore come nearest to the prayer-schema recorded by Justin (διὰ υἱοῦ καὶ ἁγίου πνεύματος). Also, Sozomenus, *Hist. eccl.* III, 20 (PG 67, 1101) records in this sense: οἱ μὲν πατέρα καὶ υἱὸν ὡς ὁμότιμον ἐδόξαζον· οἱ δὲ πατέρα ἐν υἱῷ. J. Bidez's Berlin edition of Philostorgiuss however, reads: δόξα πατρὶ καὶ υἱῷ ἐν ἁγίῳ πνεύματι (GCS: Philost. p. 43, 31). It i, then not really apparent why this formula did not satisfy Flavian. Cf. the com, prehensive F. Cavallera, *Le schisme d'Antioche* (Paris, 1905), 52, 328; DACL 1-2284 (s.v. 'Antienne').

[2] *De Spir. S.* c. 1.        [3] PG 32, 67-218.

doubted whether he could gain a hearing at all, so great were the passions aroused (c. 30).

His opponents wanted to take the old formula with διά—ἐν, which they used at every breath,[1] in the sense that these prepositions stand quite generally for the distinguishing properties of divine persons: as the ἐκ belongs to the Father: from him all things proceed, so also the διά pertains to the Son, the ἐν to the Spirit: the Father produces everything through the Son in the Holy Spirit. But from the difference of terms they deduced a difference in essence of the divine Persons—thus, the Arians concluded, the Son is unlike the Father (c. 2).

Resolutely as Basil opposed this interpretation, he maintained not only the rightness of that doxology, but also the lawfulness of the *formula for the activity of God* which was bound up with it. From this we may see how difficult the situation had become. The formula of activity of God 'through the Son in the Holy Spirit' had actually been used for a long time by Catholic Fathers to represent the relations between the divine Persons, above all in the act of creation. The beginnings of this, albeit with an unusual interpretation, we have already met in Origen.[2] The formula was inspired by Scripture passages, e.g. Romans 11:36, where the Apostle praises God's greatness, ὅτι ἐξ αὐτοῦ καὶ δι' αὐτοῦ καὶ εἰς αὐτὸν τὰ πάντα, Eph. 4:6: εἷς θεὸς καὶ πατὴρ πάντων ὁ ἐπὶ πάντων καὶ διὰ πάντων καὶ ἐν πᾶσιν, and 1 Cor. 8:6: ἡμῖν εἷς θεὸς ὁ πατήρ, ἐξ οὗ τὰ πάντα καὶ ἡμεῖς εἰς αὐτόν, καὶ εἷς κύριος Ἰησοῦς Χριστός, δι' οὗ τὰ πάντα καὶ ἡμεῖς δι' αὐτοῦ. One could also appeal to John 1:2; Hebrews 1:2; Col. 1:16, where, likewise to elucidate the divinity of Christ, it is said that the world is created through the Logos, through the Son. On the other side, there was the influence of St Paul, according to whom the new life of the faithful is established and determined 'through Christ'.[3] This formula, which frequently

---

[1] c. 25: Οὐδαμοῦ γὰρ εὗρον λεγόμενον τὸ · Σοὶ τῷ πατρὶ ἡ τιμὴ καὶ ἡ δόξα διὰ τοῦ μονογενοῦς σου υἱοῦ ἐν τῷ ἁγίῳ πνεύματι · ὅπερ τούτοις ἐστὶ νῦν καὶ αὐτῆς, ὡς εἰπεῖν, τῆς ἀναπνοῆς συνηθέστερον.

[2] Cf. above pp. 158 ff., and also the quotation from Irenaeus, p. 155, n. 1

[3] See above p. 137. Cf. T. de Régnon, *Études de théologie positive sur la sainte Trinité*, III (Paris, 1898), 68–70, 82–8; R. Cornely on Romans 11:36.

recurs[1] in his letter to Serapion,[2] Athanasius opposes in particular the Sabellian heresy, which recognized only the Person of the Father. He stresses that although there is only *one* divine activity, all three divine Persons share in it. At the same time, he shows that the Holy Spirit cannot be a creature, as the Father has created all things 'in him'. With the same significance, the formula also occurs with a small variation in the nineteenth of the anathemas which Pope Damasus sent after the Roman synod of 380 to Paulinus of Antioch: 'Si quis non dixerit, omnia per Filium et Spiritum Sanctum Patrem fecisse id est visibilia et invisibilia A.S.'[3]

Therefore, besides the formula developed for the praise of God, to represent the Trinity, there had been elaborated an analogous formula of the divine activity, that is, of the divine creative activity, not only the divine salvific activity, which earlier[4] was chiefly discussed. Then in the formula of the divine creative activity the δι' υἱοῦ could properly be understood only of the divinity of Christ.[5] In the formula of praise, however, the διὰ Χριστοῦ or δι' υἱοῦ was to be understood only of the humanity of the Son.

It was thus natural to contrast these two formulas with each other, and to think of one as a reply to the other, and thus to obliterate the distinction between the two meanings of the δι' υἱοῦ, substituting in the formula of creative activity a διὰ Χριστοῦ for the

---

[1] PG 26, 529–675.

[2] Ep. I, 24, 28 (ὁ γὰρ πατὴρ διὰ τοῦ λόγου ἐν πνεύματι ἁγίῳ τὰ πάντα ποιεῖ) 30, 31; ep. III, 5.

[3] H. Denzinger-C. Bannwart, *Enchiridion*[14] No. 77; A. Hahn, *Bibliothek der Symbole*[3] 271 ff. The formula of the divine activity is given a new look by C. Vagaggini, *Il senso teologico della liturgia* (Rome, 1957), 162–98. The liturgy is seen as a continuation of salvation history, which is based on the movement of God the Father through the Son in the Holy Spirit, and which is completed in the public worship of the Church as a return through Christ to the Father.

[4] See above, pp. 158 ff.

[5] Cf. the acute exposition of St Thomas, *S. Theol.* I, qu. 34, a. 3. A. Schäfer, *Erklärung des Hebräerbriefes* (Münster i. W., 1893) paraphrases it (re Hebrews 1:2) as follows: 'Since all the Father's thought, including the thought of creation, finds expression in the Son, but this latter proves effective outwardly in bringing forth out of nothing, then the Father creates, not without, but only through the Son.'

διὰ τοῦ λόγου or δι' υἱοῦ,[1] just as, in the praise-formula, it had already long been the custom to put in place of the original διὰ Χριστοῦ a δι' υἱοῦ.[2] This is shown most clearly in the prayers of Serapion. 'Through the only-begotten', on the one hand, God is to grant the gifts besought, and 'through the only-begotten' praise is offered to God. Also, the full formula is, in like manner, used in either case. The prayers always end with a διὰ μονογενοῦς σου and a ἐν ἁγίῳ πνεύματι, but at one time so that it is prayed that a gift be granted, and therefore the divine activity follows 'through thy only-begotten in the Holy Spirit', at another time so that the Holy Spirit is drawn into the doxology: 'Through whom to thee (is) glory . . . in the Holy Spirit.'[3]

For the adversaries of St Basil, the two formulas are indistinguishable. The Son is for them simply the middle-member between God and world; they are concerned only to stress that all reciprocal activity between the two takes place in the same way essentially 'through' him, just as the Holy Spirit for them is only the sphere 'in' which God and world meet. Indeed, one can even say: although they use the doxology, they have in mind, rather, the formula of activity understood in their sense, so as to reduce the Son, here also, to the Father's instrument, and to put the Spirit on a level with space and time.

As against this, Basil now declares: The holy Scriptures know nothing of a fixed assignment of the prepositions in question to the three divine Persons, nor of a corresponding order of precedence among them (c. 4 f.). If rank is in question, then the same rank is due to the Son as to the Father and therefore also the same worship with him (μετά). But in prayer we also bear in mind the good things that have fallen to us, our special leading to God (προσαγωγή), our claim to a home with him (οἰκείωσις), and we wish to acknowledge that this comes to us 'through him and in him'. Therefore, if the formula with μεθ' οὗ corresponds to adoration, that with δι' οὗ

---

[1] The world is created 'through Christ' inasmuch as he is the Son of God. Cf. especially the *Ap. Const.*; see above, p. 12; also, our Roman canon: 'Per Christum Dominum, per quem haec omnia semper bona creas.' The expression was hardly coined more after 451.

[2] Praise to the Father 'through the Son' inasmuch as he is man and High Priest.

[3] See above, p. 24 f.

corresponds to thanksgiving. Both are justified side by side. Scripture, indeed, calls Christ not only Son of God, but also pastor, king, physician etc.—because of his manifold activity, rich in grace for us. This activity of the Son, however, was entirely voluntary, not proceeding from a lower nature as Son; the Father creates through the Son, but this does not mean that the power of the Son is valued the less any more than the creative power of the Father appears as sufficing on its own; rather, the unity of the divine will ($\theta\epsilon\lambda\acute{\eta}\mu\alpha\tau\sigma$) is merely explained in this manner (cc. 6–8).

Basil now turns to the Holy Spirit, whose adorability and equality with Father and Son he proceeds to defend in detail. When we praise him with ($\sigma\acute{v}\nu$) Father and Son, we conform even more exactly to the biblical expression of Baptism into the Father and Son and Holy Spirit (c. 10, 26) than when the praise of God is 'in' the Holy Spirit.[1] But also praying in the Holy Spirit is justified. As the Holy Spirit is in us, so are we in him. 'As the parts are in the whole, so every one of us is in the Holy Spirit; we are indeed all in one body baptized into one Spirit ($\epsilon\grave{\iota}s$ $\grave{\epsilon}\nu$ $\pi\nu\epsilon\hat{\upsilon}\mu\alpha$). The Holy Spirit is also, in a sense, the place in which we should adore God, just as Paul speaks 'in the Spirit' or 'in Christ'. When we offer praise 'in' the Holy Spirit, what is given expression is grace, rather than ourselves and our own weakness, since without the Spirit we are unable to praise God worthily; when we offer it 'with' the Holy Spirit, then what is expressed is, rather, the dignity of the Spirit (c. 26). Thus Basil still defends the old prayer schema 'through Christ', but he understands the Mediator phrase no longer in the definite sense of the high-priestly mediation but rather generally as an expression for his redeeming activity, which is at the basis of our praying.[2] Also, the

---

[1] Bishop Amphilochius, to whom the word is dedicated, refers, in a synodal letter of the following year, 376, in the same sense to the baptismal formula and remarks: 'We have received the commission not only so to baptize, but also so to teach. . . . Therefore we must . . . so believe as we are baptized, and so praise ($\delta o \xi \acute{a} \zeta \epsilon \iota \nu$), as we have believed . . . We must in the doxology praise the Spirit together with Father and Son.' *Epistola synodica* (PG 39, 96 f.).

[2] Here Basil approaches the interpretation of the formula which A. Schettler would already suppose for Paul (see above, p. 138 f.). This interpretation occurs expressly somewhat after Basil in Theodore of Mopsuestia, when he would explain Romans 1:8 ('I thank my God through Jesus Christ for all of you'): the Apostle

dividing-line between the δι' υἱοῦ of the redemption and that of the creation is not drawn clearly throughout. This is an indication of just how strongly, even in him, the formulas of praise and of creative activity jostle each other, and thus lose their clearly-marked individuality; it further shows the influence of the theological speculation on the Trinity and creation, as it had continuously developed from the time of the Apologists and Origen. It is all the more comprehensible that he did indeed defend the old prayer schema but, with the misleading quality which it had, especially in its contemporary form, hardly valued it very highly.

Up to now, Basil had argued mainly from Scripture, but at the end of his work he appeals to the Church's tradition, to a series of witnesses who already, before him, had practised worship of the Son and the Holy Ghost at the same time as the Father, or had taught it more or less clearly (c. 29). He finds the trinitarian praise, in all shapes, in Dionysius of Alexandria (d. 265),[1] in Julius Africanus,[2] finally in an ancient evening hymn, the author of which is unknown to him.[3] He then refers to the use of the same doxology in the Church of Neo-Caesarea, which had been transmitted to him by its bishop, Gregory Thaumaturgus (d. ca. 270).[4] 'In the East'—obviously Antioch is meant—this cry has become precisely

does not wish to use the Lord to give thanks to God, but he says: I thank God for you, Christ giving us reason for our thanksgiving (PG 66, 788). See R. Cornely on this passage.

[1] The ending of a letter: Τῷ δὲ θεῷ πατρὶ καὶ υἱῷ τῷ κυρίῳ ἡμῶν Ἰησοῦ Χριστῷ σὺν τῷ ἁγίῳ πνεύματι δόξα καὶ κράτος εἰς τοὺς αἰῶνας τῶν αἰώνων.

[2] In his world history written about 220: . . . εὐχαριστοῦμεν τῷ παρασχομένῳ τοῖς ἰδίοις ἡμῖν πατρὶ τὸν τῶν ὅλων σωτῆρα καὶ κύριον ἡμῶν Ἰησοῦν Χριστόν, ᾧ ἡ δόξα μεγαλοσύνη σὺν ἁγίῳ πνεύματι εἰς τοὺς αἰῶνας.

[3] Αἰνοῦμεν πατέρα καὶ υἱὸν καὶ ἅγιον πνεῦμα θεοῦ. This is the hymn Φῶς ἱλαρόν, which greets Christ as the glad light, and which is still customary today in vespers of the Byzantine liturgy. Cf. T. Schermann, Die allgemeine Kirchenordnung etc. p. 470. See the text in J. B. Pitra, Analecta sacra I (Paris, 1876), p. lxxiii. A fragment allied to this hymn, dated to the third century, has very recently come to light in a papyrus from Oxyrhynchus; it contains the following: ὑμνούντων δ'ἡμῶν ⟨π⟩ατέρα χ' υἱὸν χ' ἅγιον πνεῦμα . . . C. Wessely, Les plus anciens monuments du christianisme écrits sur papyrus 282 f. (= Patrologia Orientalis 18 [Paris, 1924], 506 f.).

[4] The treatment of the mystery of the Trinity in his famous creed well confirms this. Cf. A. Hahn³ 253–5. On the other hand, homilies bearing his name which end with trinitarian doxologies are spurious.

the recognition mark of the true faithful. From Mesopotamia, he has learnt that in the language there (Syriac) no link other than 'and' is known in the doxology at all, nor indeed is even possible—an assertion that at first sounds rather surprising. Also, he is aware that he is at one with the West in the use of the prayer form in question.

The praise defended by Basil, directed in parallel fashion to the three divine Persons, was in fact nothing unprecedented. It may be in place here to note the most important passages elsewhere in which it is preserved to us from more ancient times. We have already met it above in Hippolytus,[1] there not isolated but chiefly harmoniously united with the mediatory schema which, indeed, Basil also did not wish to suppress. It was there only the development of the prayer-address to God, whom they knew as three Persons. This address passed into the *Canons of Hippolytus*, which cannot be precisely dated: 'Gloria tibi, Patri et Filio et Spiritui Sancto, in saecula saeculorum.'[2] Clement of Alexandria, at the end of his *Paedogogus*,[3] invites us to join in a prayer to the Logos. The address includes the Father: υἱὲ καὶ πατήρ, ἐν ἄμφω, κύριε; then comes the request for a peaceful journey to the city of God, in order to praise him: αἰνοῦντας εὐχάριστον αἶνον τῷ μόνῳ πατρὶ καὶ υἱῷ, υἱῷ καὶ πατρί, παιδαγωγῷ καὶ διδασκάλῳ υἱῷ, σὺν καὶ τῷ ἁγίῳ πνεύματι. From Origen, the ending of *Hom.* 37 *in Luc.* can be reckoned here:[4] 'Loquamur et laudemus Deum in Patre et Filio et Spiritu Sancto, cui est gloria et imperium in saecula saeculorum.'[5] Certain of the catecheses of St Cyril of Jerusalem delivered in the year 348 show a trinitarian end-doxology: ἐν τῇ βασιλείᾳ τοῦ πατρὸς ἡμῶν, ᾧ ἡ δόξα σὺν τῷ μονογενεῖ καὶ σωτῆρι Ἰησοῦ Χριστῷ σὺν τῷ ἁγίῳ καὶ ζωοποιῷ πνεύματι.[6] A work of St Athanasius ends: ὅτι τῷ θεῷ καὶ πατρὶ πρέπει δόξα . . . σὺν τῷ συνανάρχῳ αὐτοῦ υἱῷ καὶ λόγῳ ἅμα τῷ παναγίῳ καὶ ζωοποιῷ πνεύματι. . . .[7] The work *De virginitate*, written ca. 370, probably by Athanasius, teaches a grace after meals which is closely related to our grace *post coenam* and which likewise ends with the

---

[1] *Church order*; c. Noet. c. 18; εἰς τὸ ᾆσμα c. 17; see above, pp. 7, 152, n. 1.

[2] See above, p. 10.     [3] III, c. 12 (CGS: Clem. Al. I, p. 291, 1–12. Stählin).

[4] In the translation of Jerome; PG 13, 1896.

[5] Cf. *In Num. hom.* 22, 4; also *De or.* c. 33, 1 (GCS: Orig. II, p. 401, 14. Koetschau) κατὰ δύναμιν δοξολογίας . . . λεκτέον τοῦ θεοῦ διὰ Χριστοῦ συνδοξολογουμένου ἐν τῷ ἁγίῳ πνεύματι συννυμνουμένῳ.

[6] Cat. 7 (I, p. 226. Reischl); cf. Cat. 13; Cat. myst. 1, 5. The majority end, like the homilies of Origen and others, with a short text in praise of Christ: ᾧ ἡ δόξα εἰς τοὺς αἰῶνας.

[7] *De decretis Nicaenae synodi* (PG 25, 476).

trinitarian doxology: 'Misericors et miserator Dominus escam dedit timentibus se'; δόξα πατρὶ καὶ υἱῷ καὶ ἁγίῳ πνεύματι καὶ νῦν καὶ ἀεὶ καὶ εἰς τοὺς αἰῶνας.[1]

The further history of the Gloria Patri, especially in the West, has often been described.[2]

The texts adduced show all three persons put in the usual order: Father, Son, Holy Ghost, only with the aid of different particles: σύν, ἅμα, καί. This order was obvious and self-evident when the praise-text appeared as an independent element as, in particular, in the psalm-chant and at the end of letters. Basil speaks now of the joining with μετὰ (τοῦ υἱοῦ), and by that he means without doubt the form of the doxology which in the liturgical prayer starts out from a mention of the Son, and which similarly we later find frequently in the Greek liturgies: μεθ' οὗ (σοὶ ἡ δόξα) σὺν ἁγίῳ πνεύματι. This form marks the decisive recasting of the prayer-

---

[1] c. 14 (TU 29, 2a, p. 49, 6, von der Goltz). This form with καί—καί can already be traced to the Antiochene model. Athanasius was familiar with the situation there. Also, Gregory of Nazianzus shows some examples of this type: Or. 19 (PL 36, 1064): λειτουργῶμεν θεῷ τὴν αἴνεσιν τὴν μίαν πατρὸς καὶ υἱοῦ καὶ ἁγίου πνεύματος. . . . The speech was made 374–5. The still later Or. 45 (PG 36, 664) ends with the address: 'Then will we offer thee sacrifice, ὦ πάτερ καὶ λόγε καὶ πνεῦμα τὸ ἅγιον, ὅτι σοὶ πρέπει πᾶσα δόξα. . . . Here, however, likewise the influence of Antioch may already have been felt. The interest which Basil shows in the goings-on there will have been shared by his friend. A hymn in a papyrus fragment from Fajjum closes with the words: δόξατο (i.e., τῷ) πατρὶ ἀληλούηα, δόξατο (i.e., τῷ) υἱῷ καὶ το (i.e., τῷ) ἁγίῳ πνε(ύ)ματι ἀληλούηα, ἀληλούηα, ἀληλούηα. The fragment was earlier put at the beginning of the fourth century (G. Bickell; see A. Harnack, *Geschichte der altchristlichen Literatur bis Eusebius* I [Leipzig, 1893] 467). C. Wessely disagrees: 'Écriture cursive du IV–V siècle' (*Patrologia Orientalis* 18 [Paris, 1924] 438 = *Les plus anciens monuments du christianisme écrits sur papyrus* 214).

[2] Cf., e.g., H. Leclercq: DACL 5, 1525–8. The 'little doxology' appears in the form familiar to us with the addition 'Sicut erat' in the year 529 at the Council of Vaison; but cf. also the ending of the εὐχὴ προσφόρου in the *Euchologium* of Serapion, 13 (1) 19: . . . ἐν ἁγίῳ πνεύματι, ὥσπερ ἦν καὶ ἐστὶν καὶ ἔσται εἰς γενεὰς γενεῶν καὶ εἰς τοὺς σύμπαντας αἰῶνας τῶν αἰώνων. Ἀμήν. The same ending, word for word, is found in the Coptic St Mark (Cyril) anaphora. Br. 180, 11. It also occurs in the same passage in the Greek St Mark liturgy, Br. 134, 31, and in the Arabic *Testament of our Lord (Oriens christ.* 1 [1901] 25, 15); in the latter, the priest recites the doxology: 'Filio tuo dilecto et Spiritui Sancto'; then follows the rubric: 'Populus et clerus dicunt Ὥσπερ ἦν.' Outside Egypt, a similar added clause occurs in Gregory of Nazianzus, in his Or. 17 (PG 35, 981), delivered 373: ἐν Χριστῷ Ἰησοῦ τῷ κυρίῳ ἡμῶν, ᾧ ἡ δόξα . . . σὺν τῷ πατρὶ καὶ τῷ ἁγίῳ πνεύματι, ὥσπερ ἦν καὶ προῆν καὶ ἔσται καὶ νῦν καὶ εἰς τοὺς αἰῶνας τῶν αἰώνων. Ἀμήν.

schema, the evolution of which we have followed up to now to the stage of the praying to the Father through (διά) the Son in (ἐν) the Holy Spirit.

An intermediate form, which at first sight appears somewhat strange, occurs sometimes, so it seems, in the transition period. Basil himself quotes (*De Spir. S.* c. 29) of his own accord the expression of Eusebius (d. 340): Τὸν τῶν προφητῶν ἅγιον θεὸν φωταγωγὸν διὰ τοῦ σωτῆρος ἡμῶν Ἰησοῦ Χριστοῦ σὺν ἁγίῳ πνεύματι καλέσαντες. This joining by διά—σύν recurs in the eighteenth catechesis of Cyril of Jerusalem, where he closes his discourses with a praise of God: ᾧ ἡ δόξα, τιμὴ καὶ κράτος διὰ τοῦ κυρίου ἡμῶν Ἰησοῦ Χριστοῦ σὺν τῷ ἁγίῳ πνεύματι.[1] It seems that Father and Holy Spirit are intended as receivers of the glory, which is offered through the Son. But in reality the Holy Spirit is joined rather with Christ (σύν instead of καί), or, perhaps, more correctly: Cyril is concerned primarily to confess the oneness of God, somewhat in the sense of his remark (Cat. 16, c. 4): we confess not three gods, ἀλλὰ σὺν ἁγίῳ πνεύματι δι' ἑνὸς υἱοῦ ἕνα θεὸν καταγγέλλομεν, and (c. 24): Ὁ πατὴρ δι' υἱοῦ σὺν ἁγίῳ πνεύματι τὰ πάντα χαρίζεται.[2] Also, in the following, seventeenth, catechesis (c. 21, 31), he gives the formula of activity in a free manner. Probably it was from Eusebius, whom he translated, that Rufinus derived this same doxology, which he uses in his explanation of the creed[3] and which he also brings into his translation of Origen.[4] A related doxology closes also the second of the ancient Christian prayers published by C. Schmidt:[5] ἵνα ... δοξάσηται τὸ[ν] ... παντοδύνα⟨μ⟩όν σου κράτος ἐν Χριστῷ Ἰησοῦ τῷ ἠγαπημέ⟨νῳ⟩ σου σὺν ἁγίῳ πνεύματι. The coincidence with Cyril of Jerusalem and Eusebius may also confirm and determine more precisely the dating of this prayer to the fourth century proposed by the editor.

In many later texts, it is true, and especially in individual manuscripts, cases occur in which Father and Holy Spirit receive the homage; but here we are in a period which has lost the understanding of the doxology, or we have simply an error of copyists, who, from the formula now to be discussed containing δι' οὗ καὶ μεθ' οὗ, omitted the latter member.[6] This hybrid-form of the doxology, probably because of its twofold character, seems to enjoy

---

[1] II, p. 340 f. Rupp.                    [2] II, pp. 208, 236. Rupp.

[3] PL 21, 386: '(per Christum Dominum nostrum) per quem est Deo Patri omnipotenti cum Spiritu Sancto gloria et imperium in saecula saeculorum.'

[4] E.g. *In Lev.* 1, 3 (PG 12, 411, 434).        [5] P. 72; see above, p. 148.

[6] Cf. the *Testament of our Lord*, above p. 16, or the case mentioned above, p. 7, n. 5, from late Ethiopic manuscripts of Hippolytus (R. H. Connolly's version), as well as above, pp. 47 and 51 f., the endings of Ethiopic anaphoras.

a certain favour with later editors. It was used, *inter alia*, probably without much reflexion, in the papyrus of Dêr-Balyzeh;[1] it is taken over in the *Ap. Const.*, and even proposed as an improvement for the Hippolytan church order.[2] Texts in which only Father and Son appear as receivers of praise, on the other hand, occur more often in all periods. There is nothing surprising about them, as in them the thought of God and Christ predominates over that of the divine Persons as such.

Is Basil in the year 375 the first to have accomplished the change to the doxology with μετά—σύν? Athanasius already used it before him; indeed, if dating and translation are to be relied on, as early as 335.[3] The festal letter of 335 ends:[4] 'Patrem semper adorabimus per Christum, per quem et cum quo sit ei gloria et imperium per Spiritum Sanctum. . . .' This combined form ( = δι' οὗ καὶ μεθ' οὗ) presupposes the simple.[5] In Greek, the simple ending is preserved in the letter written before 356 to a monk:[6] ἐν Χριστῷ Ἰησοῦ τῷ κυρίῳ ἡμῶν, οὗ τῷ πατρὶ δόξα καὶ τὸ κράτος σὺν ἁγίῳ πνεύματι;[7] at least, soon after Basil, Gregory of Nazianzus also used the same form. It appears in a eulogy to the Holy Ghost[8] delivered about 380.

Basil by his *démarche* had intended only to oppose the Arian misinterpretation of the traditional prayer schema with διά—ἐν, not

---

[1] See above, p. 25, n.3.

[2] By T. Schermann, *Ein Weiherituale der römischen Kirche am Schluss des ersten Jahrhunderts* (Munich, 1913), 21, and by E. Hennecke, *Neutestam. Apokryphen*[2] 575 ff. ('through whom to thee is honour, power and glory, together with the Holy Spirit'). The same reconstruction in J. M. Hanssens, *La liturgie d'Hippolyte* (Rome, 1959) 343–370 (esp. 368) and in the new edition by B. Botte 11, 17, 23. (cf. above p. 8, n. 1).

[3] Earlier festal letters are extant with the ending: 'J. Chr., per quem gloria . . . Patri per Spiritum Sanctum', similarly also even in later writings occasionally; see above, p. 163, n. 1.

[4] PG 26, 1396 f.

[5] The authenticity is supported by the form 'per (for διά or ἐν) Spiritum Sanctum', which later, with the encroachment of the dogmatic struggle, was abandoned for the acknowledgement of the Holy Spirit, in order clearly to characterize him also as co-receiver of the praise (σύν). Cf. the festal briefs of 342 and 347. The latter already has: 'Per quem et cum quo gloria sit et imperium Patri eius *et* eiusdem Spiritui Sancto' (PG 26, 1430).

[6] PG 26, 1176.    [7] Cf. the last letter to Serapion of the year 362 (PG 26, 676).

[8] Or. 41 (PG 36, 452): ἐν αὐτῷ τῷ λόγῳ καὶ θεῷ καὶ κυρίῳ ἡμῶν Ἰησοῦ Χριστῷ . . ., μεθ' οὗ ἡ δόξα καὶ τὸ σέβας τῷ πατρὶ σὺν τῷ ἁγίῳ πνεύματι. Even earlier, ca. 373 (Or. 8 and 17; PG 35, 818. 982) he uses the related forms: ᾧ ἡ δόξα—καὶ— σὺν and ᾧ ἡ δόξα—σὺν—καὶ.

to abolish the schema itself. He had therefore used the new and old forms of praise side by side. The attitude of other Fathers was similar. But alongside this practice there also came into use a combined form, uniting the important elements of both. Thus in Athanasius perhaps already by 335;[1] also, in Cyril of Jerusalem, this ending is unanimously attested for the fifteenth catechesis. It became the norm in the numerous letters of St Cyril of Alexandria (Patriarch 412–44). The chief variations are shown in the following general formula: δι' οὗ καὶ μεθ' οὗ (or δι' αὐτοῦ καὶ μετ' αὐτοῦ) τῷ (θεῷ καὶ) πατρὶ (εἴη) ἡ δόξα (καὶ τὸ κράτος . . .) εἰς τοὺς αἰῶνας τῶν αἰώνων. He was anxious not to discard the element of mediation (δι' οὗ). This concern of his also throws light on some passages in his writings in which he just as much praises Christ as Mediator and high priest as he defends his divinity and the unity of the Person in him.[2]

The attitude of St John Chrysostom, on the other hand, is remarkable. His homilies also have, as a rule, a trinitarian end-doxology, following a mention of Christ, through whose favour (χάριτι) the grace concerned is implored. If now these homilies are arranged, as far as possible, in chronological order, the following results: the oldest homilies given in Antioch, up to about 390, mostly alternate between the simple (μεθ' οὗ) and the combined (δι' οὗ καὶ μεθ' οὗ) trinitarian doxology; indeed, some series of sermons prefer the latter. By contrast, the later homilies and those of Constantinople have only the simple μεθ' οὗ formula, with which occur other pure trinitarian praise-texts.[3]

This clearly implies a falling-off of interest on the part of the preacher in the idea of prayer-mediation, or, of course, a changed liturgical practice in Antioch, which Chrysostom simply carried on in Constantinople.

[1] See above, p. 185.
[2] Cf., e.g. *De adoratione et cultu in spiritu et veritate* 1.5 (PG 68, 385); 1.10 (ibid. 672.701). *Glaphyra in Gen.* 1.1 (PG 69, 41).
[3] For most of the homily-series, the dates in O. Bardenhewer III[2], 337 ff. allow this division. The discourses on statues, which were given in 387 and belong to the earliest, show in fifteen out of twenty-one cases the combined formula; the homilies of 389 on St John's Gospel have it in about a third of the cases. In those on Matthew of 390 it is already entirely lacking. Likewise in the 55 homilies on the Acts of the Apostles, which were delivered in 400 or 401 in Constantinople.

Here we may briefly discuss a point which is somewhat obscured by the very change we have been describing, and which is of value for the understanding of the doxologies. In the Greek and also in the Latin doxology, the verb is generally lacking, and it is often in doubt whether one should translate: 'To him *be* the glory', or, 'to him *is* (belongs) the glory'. F. H. Chase[1] thinks that everywhere it should be taken as indicative. The indicative verb is often added expressly in the doxology of the Our Father: ὅτι σοῦ ἐστιν ἡ βασιλεία καὶ ἡ δύναμις καὶ ἡ δόξα. By the side of the ὅτι, which introduces a reason, this is also self-evident. One can prove only by means of facts, not by wishes. Chrysostom lays stress on this ὅτι, relating it to the last request: 'Deliver us from evil.' If the kingdom belongs to God, then there is no need to fear evil.[2] Where this ὅτι precedes, as, for example, sometimes in Serapion, one must always presume the indicative: a fact is stated. Other signs, also, are to be found of an affirmative, *indicative* doxology. One such is when God is only awarded, by way of recognition, what he anyhow possesses: 'Thine is the power.' But also, when the external glory—which we can always wish greater—is in question, the Christian praying can find joy simply in naming the source from which flows constant honour and glory to God. Thus the doxology of Hippolytus can be paraphrased: 'We praise thee through Christ, i.e. through him through whom alone due homage can be paid thee, and is paid thee in the holy Church.' Indeed, one may always take the doxology which begins with δι' οὗ as indicative.[3] Also the article (ἡ δόξα) often characterizes the glory as something complete, that is already a matter of fact.[4]

But there also occur expressly *subjunctive*, and therefore precatory, doxologies: ᾧ ἔστω ἡ δόξα,[5] and this even with mention of the Mediator: ᾧ διὰ τοῦ παιδός . . . καὶ διὰ τοῦ ἁγίου πνεύματος εἴη δόξα.[6] Christ and the Holy Spirit are here regarded by the Alexandrian evidently only as Mediator, not as source of the praise as well.

Doxologies are *indifferent* in sense, and only in their grammatical form indicative, when the mere fact of the (oral) praise is expressed: 'To thee we send up praise'; 'to thee belongs all glory'; '(Christ) with whom thou art praised' (μεθ' οὗ εὐλογητὸς εἶ; Greek St James liturgy). The later, pure

---

[1] *The Lord's Prayer in the Early Church* 169.     [2] Chase 171.
[3] Cf. the end of the Roman canon: 'Per ipsum . . . est tibi . . . gloria'; or the postsanctus in the St Mark liturgy (see above, p. 32) and John 13:31 f.
[4] For the indicative doxology, cf. Stuiber, loc. cit. 215.
[5] Clement of Rome, I *ad Cor.* c. 32, 4 (*Patres apostolici* I, p. 140, 2. Funk).
[6] Clement of Alexandria, *Quis dives salvetur* c. 42, 20 (GCS: Clem. Al. III, p. 191, 10. Stählin).

trinitarian doxology is probably always to be taken as subjunctive, as we, in fact, are accustomed to understand it: 'Glory *be* to the Father.'

The doxology was the first to fall victim to the reinterpreting attempts of the Arians. By its side, other texts of the liturgy, with basically the same meaning, seem to have remained for a time unnoticed. Thus we saw, for example, in the *Epitome*, the remarkable fact that although the διά—ἐν of the praise-formula of the Apostolic Constitutions is everywhere replaced by the μετά—σύν, yet outside the doxology all phrases that denote Christ as Mediator have remained.[1] But this respite did not last long.[2] In particular, the further encroachment of this transforming process is to be observed in the *formula of the divine activity*, which contrasted with the praise-formula, to which it often formed the transition, especially in its christological member: 'Give (or: thou gavest) us this through Christ.'[3] The Arians, naturally, see the Son, here also, as instrument subordinated to the Father. Hence we find in the Greek liturgies of the following period, in this passage also, the phrase διά Χριστοῦ mostly replaced by the other, χάριτι τοῦ Χριστοῦ: we do not ask that the good requested be given us through Christ, but his favour with thee and loving-kindness towards men should move thee to grant it to us.[4] Thus is every appearance of subordination removed. The instrumental διά Χριστοῦ is therefore, according to its sense, twisted into a motivating διά Χριστόν and this again, to make it clear, is paraphrased.[5]

---

[1] See above, p. 14.

[2] This would suggest that the interval between the *Epitome* and its model cannot be very great.

[3] *Didache*; Serapion; *Ap. Const.* and *Epitome*; cf. Acts 4:30. For the formula itself, see above, p. 137f.

[4] The full formula of the activity of God the Father 'through the Son in the Holy Spirit' was at all times rare in liturgical prayer. Its re-casting occurs, for example, in the St James anaphora (Br. 59, 4b = 99, 35): 'Thou hast condescended to sanctify these gifts τῇ χάριτι τοῦ Χριστοῦ σου καὶ τῇ ἐπιφοιτήσει τοῦ παναγίου σου πνεύματος.

[5] Cf. Br. 120, 21b, where διά τὸν εὐαγγελιστὴν Μάρκον and χάριτι ... τοῦ μονογενοῦς σου are side by side in the same sense. But also διά Χριστόν occurs: Ren. I, 81 (διά τὸν υἱόν σου); Br. 58, 2 (δι' ὄν). One might be tempted to underrate the fundamentally different meanings of a διά with the genitive and the same with the accusative, on seeing the juxtaposition in E. Norden, *Agnostos Theos* 347 f., of, on

The change is clearly evident in the following contrast, in which the doxology also is given:

| EUCHOLOG. SERAP., e.g. 4 (28): | ST MARK LIT., e.g. BR. 115, 17: |
|---|---|
| Bless thy people . . . | Crush every foe of thy holy Church . . . |
| διὰ | χάριτι καὶ οἰκτιρμοῖς καὶ φιλανθρωπίᾳ |
| τοῦ μονογενοῦς σου Ἰησοῦ Χριστοῦ | τοῦ μονογενοῦς σου υἱοῦ |
| δι' οὗ σοὶ | δι' οὗ καὶ μεθ' οὗ σοὶ |
| ἡ δόξα καὶ τὸ κράτος | ἡ δόξα καὶ τὸ κράτος |
| ἐν ἁγίῳ πνεύματι . . . | σὺν τῷ παναγίῳ καὶ ἀγαθῷ καὶ ζωοποιῷ σου πνεύματι . . .[1] |

The expression χάρις τοῦ Χριστοῦ already occurs in the New Testament, in such a manner that we can use it in clarifying the present case. There, it is above all the favour in which Christ stands

the one hand, the New Testament manner of speaking: διὰ θεοῦ or διὰ τοῦ λόγου the world has come into being; and, on the other, the analogous language of the Stoics: δι' αὐτὸν ἄπαντα γίνεται. But we see at once the fundamental distinction, in that the first understands the origin of the world in the sense of creation, the second in the sense of pantheistic evolution.

[1] Outside Egypt, occur, beside the form with χάριτι, certain variants of it, e.g. διὰ τῶν οἰκτιρμῶν τοῦ μονογενοῦς σου υἱοῦ (West Syrian: Br. 66, 6b; cf. further variants in the Greek reconstruction of the Syrian text in A. Rücker). But in the Greek St James liturgy the change in this passage is only partly achieved. There occurs not only often the harmless, because indefinite, ἐν Χριστῷ Ἰησοῦ (Br. 31, 12; 40, 11; 68, 3b; thus also even Ap. Const. VII, 49 and often in the sermon-endings with Chrysostom), but occasionally even διὰ τοῦ μονογενοῦς σου υἱοῦ (. . . μεθ' οὗ εὐλογητός εἶ). Thus in the prayer for peace Br. 43, 16 and in the intercessory prayer Br. 57, 28; the last passage also in the Jacobite anaphoras. In the Greek St Mark liturgy, the transition ἐν Χριστῷ Ἰησοῦ τῷ κυρίῳ ἡμῶν is only in the prayer at the Kiss of Peace, but betrays here, by the doxology μεθ' οὗ εὐλογητὸς εἶ, its origin from the Greek St James liturgy (Br. 123, 29). On the other hand, this transition occurs in many passages of the Coptic sister anaphora (p. 35, n. 3 above) and may here likewise come from Syria, from the period when the Jacobites there, like the Copts themselves, still conducted their liturgy in Greek. This is corroborated by its occurrence in the Egyptian St Basil anaphora, which shows the formula not only in its Coptic but also in its Greek form (cf. above p. 36). But also early Egyptian material (cf. some letter-endings of Athanasius, e.g. PG 26, 676) could have been preserved independently, with respect to the older διά, in indeterminate Coptic form (= ἐν).

with God the Father, and for the sake of which God is gracious to us.[1] As here καὶ οἰκτιρμοῖς καὶ φιλανθρωπίᾳ is added to χάριτι the motive for hearing the request is reinforced: 'Look on thy only-begotten, to whom thy love is due and who on his side is full of mercy towards us men.'

We can also observe the gradual appearance of the χάριτι formula in the endings of the letters and homilies of the Greek Fathers. While it does not as yet occur in Athanasius, Gregory of Nyssa formulates his closing blessing, now: may (it) be granted διὰ Χριστου ἐν Χριστῷ, now, χάριτι τοῦ κυρίου ἡμῶν ᾽Ιησοῦ Χριστοῦ; on the other hand, in Chrysostom the ending χάριτι καὶ φιλανθρωπίᾳ τοῦ κυρίου ἡμῶν ᾽Ιησοῦ Χριστοῦ has already almost become stereotyped, so that often only the opening words are given.

In course of time, the precise meaning of the phrase is lost. This appears from different developments which we meet here and there. Thus, later, in prayers to Christ: 'Make me worthy (of the Communion) through thy favour';[2] or the end-formula is expanded: 'through thy favour and the goodwill of thy Father... and through the working of thy Spirit';[3] or even the original form with the following doxology is attached unaltered to Christ-addressed prayers.[4] But also in prayers to God the Father the formula occurs in developed form: 'Secundum beneplacitum tuum et per gratiam unigeniti Filii tui et per illapsum Spiritus tui Sancti.'[5] The approximation of the St Mark liturgy to that of Byzantium led finally to a blend with the doxology there: χάριτι καὶ οἰκτιρμοῖς καὶ τῇ φιλανθρωπίᾳ τοῦ πατρὸς καὶ τοῦ υἱοῦ καὶ τοῦ ἁγίου πνεύματος.[6]

---

[1] Gal. 1:6; Romans 5:15 (cf. 3:24); Acts 15:11. F. Zorell (*Novi testamenti lexicon graecum* [Paris, 1911], 618 f.) renders the expression (ἐν χάριτι, διὰ χάριτος) in the passages mentioned: 'ea gratia, qua Christus Patri carus est nobisque omnia meruit, fere id quod meritum Christi.' For the dative χάριτι in the motivating sense cf. R. Kühner, *Ausführliche Grammatik der griechischen Sprache* II[3] (Hannover, 1898), II, 438 f.

[2] τῇ χάριτί σου, Br. 63, 37; cf. Br. 118, 23.

[3] Br. 81, 10; Ren. I, 27.   [4] See above, p. 33; cf. pp. 19, 51.

[5] Ren. II, 182: Jacobite St Mark anaphora from the thirteenth century; but similarly also already in the ancient Jacobite baptismal liturgy: J. A. Assemani, *Codex liturgicus* II, 283. Cf. the more original form of the expansion above, p. 188, n. 4.

[6] Br. 543, 22.

# XII

# THE PRINCIPAL TYPES OF LITURGICAL PRAYER AFTER THE FOURTH CENTURY

WE may now go on to group the Christian liturgies according to the theological structure of their prayer, and, albeit only in the broadest terms, to characterize them. This we shall attempt primarily with reference to the texts which in the first part of this work we have ascertained, or else circumscibed, for the oldest layers of these liturgies. In this, we stand in a period which lies at a greater or lesser distance from the end of the Arian struggles of the fourth century, which portend so strong an assault on the traditional style of the liturgical prayer, in particular its doxology. The structure of the prayer is epitomized in the doxology, which presents, as it were, a cross-section through it. With the prayer swelling at the end in a powerful crescendo to a solemn praising of God, the conflicting forces in the prayer, or the way in which the one who prays sees himself vis-à-vis God, is brought out. Turning our attention first to the East, we find in the earliest layer of all liturgies the rule followed whereby at least the authentic eucharistic and sacrificial prayer, the anaphora, is addressed, not to Christ, but to God. Within this mode of address, in the East two basic types may be distinguished, which we may term briefly Greek and Syrian. Neither forget to refer to Christ the Lord. Both use basically the same common Christian thematic material which we found harmoniously arranged in the prayer-scheme of *Hippolytus*: We glorify thee, Father, Son and Holy Spirit, through Christ our Lord, united in his holy community. But, just as Hippolytus himself uses, besides the complete doxology, now the one, now the other half of this schema, so also each of the types mentioned divides the material in a fully analogous manner, the stress being laid alternately on one or other point in the same complex of ideas.[1]

The *Greek* main type, the development of which has in fact occupied us almost alone up to now, starts from the order of address: to God through Christ the high priest. The schema then becomes expanded to the form: to God through Christ in the Holy Spirit. The acknowledgement of the three divine Persons being thus brought out more clearly, there arises from this the praise of the Father through the Son in the Holy Ghost or, more precisely expressed, since immediately before the praise-text Christ is still named as Mediator of the gifts: The Son, through whom ($\delta\iota$' $o\tilde{\upsilon}$) to the Father is praise in ($\dot{\epsilon}\nu$) the Holy Spirit. These three preliminary stages subsequently almost entirely disappeared in the East, for the most part in the fourth and fifth centuries. Only a few isolated remnants of simple liturgical praying 'through Christ' have been preserved, particularly in the Apostles' anaphora of Ethiopia and on Syrian soil in the St James Liturgy.[2]

But the two following stages of the same schema mark the later and present-day branches of this Greek stem. They are characterized by the $\mu\epsilon\theta$' $o\tilde{\upsilon}$ of the doxology. The one stage retains, together with the praise passage in which, with the Son ($\mu\epsilon\theta$' $o\tilde{\upsilon}$), the Father together with the Holy Spirit is praised, at least here in the doxology the earlier mediatory $\delta\iota$' $o\tilde{\upsilon}$: $\delta\iota$' $o\tilde{\upsilon}$ $\kappa\alpha\grave{\iota}$ $\mu\epsilon\theta$' $o\tilde{\upsilon}$. This stage is predominant in the earlier layer of the prayers in the Egyptian liturgies.[3] The practice just mentioned of the Patriarch *Cyril of Alexandria*— highly honoured and much appealed to even by the Monophysites—

---

[1] See above p. 7 f. Naturally, it is not here maintained that the doxology of Hippolytus stands at the beginning of the development; it is only the themes that are being discussed.

[2] See above p. 44; 60; 63 f. (Armenian St James anaphora); p. 66, n. 4 (Br. 32, 16).

[3] Above pp. 30 ff. Cf. here also p. 32, the Preface of the St Mark liturgy.

or the usage of the Egyptian metropolis initiated by him, may here have been decisive. The same stage, albeit with some wavering, has also remained the standard for the Syrian St James anaphora as well as for the analogous new Jacobite growths. After the Churches that had become Monophysite in Syria and Egypt had changed to the exclusive use of their national tongue in the liturgy, i.e. roughly after the sixth to eighth century, this doxology and prayer-type continued in the Greek tongue only in the St Mark liturgy and, together with this, finally disappeared entirely from the Greek world.

The last stage is that of the pure μεθ' οὗ doxology. We may term it the last with regard to Chrysostom, although the combined form just mentioned can have arisen only after it. This came to predominate in the Greek St James anaphora, or, more correctly, in the Greek St James liturgy. Occasionally, it appears also in the Byzantine and Armenian liturgies, viz. in the few prayers that at the end name Christ as Mediator of the gifts. Christ the Lord is here no longer characterized as Mediator of the prayer, as high priest in the old sense. In the period when Chrysostom was active in Antioch, this doxology defended by Flavian and Diodorus had already gained acceptance[1], although the combined formula—we can call it on Antiochene soil the compromise formula—with δι' οὗ καὶ μεθ' οὗ was still used at the same time. The liturgy of the *Apostolic Constitutions*[2] about the same time and in the same area represents an attempt—probably honestly intended, although under a false apostolic mask and somewhat sharply pointed—along with other aims, to carry through a restoration of the old prayer schema, that is, going back to the earlier stages and with utilization of the Roman model of Hippolytus as well as indigenous Antiochene material. It failed; only insignificant fragments of the work or of the *Testamentum* passed into the practical usage of Syrian and Egyptian liturgies. Its prayer schema, too, has scarcely been observed more widely.

[1] The form with καὶ—καὶ used directly by them pertains in the first place to the psalm-chant. For the liturgical prayer, which in traditional manner named Christ at the end, the equivalent *form* with μετὰ—σύν in the first place corresponded to this form. This must have been the form which Leontius, as liturgist, had to recite alone.

[2] For the assessment of the prayer-type of the *Ap. Const.* cf. above at pp. 163 ff.

We cannot tell how great a danger remained of heretical mis-interpretation of the custom of praying through Christ. It was in any case a period that had learnt through bitter experience to esteem the purity of the faith above everything else. Just as the organism fighting for its life does away with less vital parts of its organs in order for the present to strengthen its central forces and in later days of well-being perhaps also to regenerate the surrendered parts, in the same way that period saw itself as obliged, for the protection of the belief in the fundamental doctrine of the divinity of Christ, in the first place in the field of the liturgical language of prayer, to give up elements which up to now had certainly rendered valuable service to the religious life. Now the matter of chief moment was to confess the true faith. As in the fourth century in the Mass liturgy there was still no Credo it was natural to give over its function to the doxology.

The gradual development of this Greek doxology and prayer type in the East excludes the majority of the prayers of the East Syrian and the Byzantine liturgies, and we can add to these, perhaps, some old elements in the extra-anaphora ordo of the West Syrian Jacobite liturgy. On the other hand, they combine well into a second, *Syrian* main type.

For the individuality and growth of this second type it is sufficient here to assemble a few facts from the liturgical texts and on the basis of these to outline a provisional hypothesis.[1] These liturgies agree in that their prayers usually end with an acclamation of praise to the three divine Persons, which are named as if on the same footing and joined with 'and'.

In the Byzantine liturgy, most *orationes* begin with the address 'Lord our God' and end: '(For thou art a good and merciful God and) to thee we send up praise, to the Father and to the Son and to the Holy Spirit, now and always and to all eternity, Amen', or: 'Thereto we praise thy honourable and glorious name, of the Father and of the Son and of the Holy Spirit. . . .'[2] In the East Syrian liturgy, the type is much more regular still, and it is generally pre-

---

[1] A more extensive enquiry would require an exact analysis of the earlier Syrian literature, probably also of the manuscripts. This would not be possible for me
[2] See above, pp. 76 ff.

ceded by a similar address. The ending, however, is in certain
sections always the same: '(That we praise thee at all times) Lord
of the universe, Father and Son and Holy Spirit for ever';[1] and
also the Jacobite fore-anaphora which, in contrast to its quite
different Greek counterpart, is attributed to native Syrian custom,
has certain examples of this kind: 'May we be worthy to offer thee
praise, Lord . . ., and all the days of our life to appear before thee
without fault, Father and Son and Holy Spirit for evermore.'[2]

It is doubtless the same doxology to which we heard Basil refer
above.[3] His actual words are: 'As I have heard from a Mesopotamian,
a man both a master of the language and of undoubted conviction,
in the language of that place it is not possible, even if one wished, to
express the doxology other than with the aid of the word "and" or,
more correctly, the equivalent expression in the native tongue.' Is
this also connected with the formula of praise with which Diodorus
and Flavian came forward in Antioch about 350? This, too, is not
to be doubted. As Theodore of Mopsuestia, himself a born Antiochene, relates in the fragment already mentioned,[4] the two monks—
later bishops—worked for the improvement of the public worship in
Antioch by turning refrains from the Syrian into the Greek, in order
to vitalize the psalm-singing, and he relates in the same breath how
they had been the first to make use of that doxology: 'Glory be to
the Father and to the Son and to the Holy Ghost.' As H. Thurston
concludes, the Gloria Patri seems to be referred to here as such a
refrain, which would be taken over from the Syrian.[5] This agrees
entirely with the abundant use made of the Gloria Patri by both the
liturgies in the Syrian tongue, both at the end of the chants and by
itself. The complementary clause generally takes something like the
form, as is usual even today in the Byzantine liturgy: ($\Delta \delta \xi a$ . . .

[1] See above, pp. 71, 73.
[2] Br. 72, 9; see above, p. 67 f.; also p. 66 and p. 65, n. 7 (Greek St James
liturgy).
[3] De Spir. S. c. 29; above p. 182.          [4] PG 139, 1390.
[5] The Month 131 (1918, I) 411 f. For the thesis that a formula fully coordinating
the trinitarian persons with 'and' had taken root in the Syrian area, J. Betz, Die
Eucharistie in der Zeit der griechischen Väter I, 1 (Freiburg, 1955) 125, f.n. 258, has
assembled a series of further witnesses: Pseudo-Clementine, Hom. 3, 72 (Lagarde
76, 17); Afrahat, Hom. 23 (TU 3/3—4, 411); Didascalia VI, 12, 1 (Funk I, 326);
Pap. Oxyrh. 1786; Hymnus vespert. graec. (Kirch, Ench. Patr. n. 108).

πνεύματι) καὶ νῦν καὶ ἀεὶ καὶ εἰς τοὺς αἰῶνας τῶν αἰώνων,[1] and as it will probably also have run in Antioch.

Therefore both forms of the trinitarian praise would be at home in the Syrian tongue, viz. that mentioned here first, mainly in the thou-style used at the end of the liturgical prayer: 'We praise thee, Lord of the universe, Father, Son and Holy Spirit for evermore'; and that in the third person for insertion on various occasions: 'Glory be to the Father and to the Son and to the Holy Spirit.' Also the former would have found its way into Antioch from the Syrian hinterland. In the *Apostolic Constitutions* VIII, 12, 50 the central part of the anaphoras, according to the majority of the manuscripts, end, in a manner unusual for the author, in the words: 'For to thee belongs ... worship, to the Father and to the Son and to the Holy Spirit, now and always. . . .'[2] Cf. also the reading of some manuscripts of the *Ap. Const.* VII, 48, 3: Σοὶ πρέπει αἶνος, σοὶ πρέπει ὕμνος, σοὶ δόξα πρέπει τῷ πατρὶ καὶ τῷ υἱῷ καὶ τῷ ἁγίῳ πνεύματι,[3] a text which still has a place today in the monastic breviary of the Latin Church.[4] If, as it seems, this is not the original reading in the *Apostolic Constitutions*, the copyist or reviser would have inserted the praise-passage as in the meantime it had become customary in Antioch at this passage, the climax of the sacrifice. Flavian, who himself was Bishop of Antioch from 381 to 404, will certainly not have refrained from the reform of the liturgy in this direction, in so far as it was still necessary.

The interconnexion between the liturgies of Byzantium and Antioch is clarified by the quotations from Chrysostom. Some of the

[1] Brightman gives it for both liturgies in the passages concerned in the form: (glory ... Ghost) from everlasting to everlasting, world without end (e.g. 76, 7; 250, 1).

[2] See above, p. 14.

[3] Funk (I, p. 456, 13) reads with the other witnesses: πατρὶ διὰ τοῦ υἱοῦ ἐν πνεύματι ἁγίῳ.

[4] Here belongs also the special doxology in the *Testament of our Lord* (likewise the threefold vocative), see above, p. 16. A further confirmation of the above hypothesis is the recent attribution of the homilies (PG 34, 449–822)—hitherto ascribed to Makarios the Egyptian (about 300–90)—to an author who 'probably was still living in the second half of the fourth century in Mesopotamia' (O. Bardenhewer III², 669; cf., on the other hand, J. Stiglmayr: ZkTh 49/1925/244–60). The doxological ending there frequently belongs to this type, e.g. hom. 3: Δοξάζωμεν πατέρα καὶ υἱὸν καὶ ἅγιον πνεῦμα εἰς τοὺς αἰῶνας, or hom. 7: Δόξαν οὖν ἀναπέμψωμεν πατρὶ καὶ υἱῷ καὶ ἁγίῳ πνεύματι εἰς τοὺς αἰῶνας τῶν αἰώνων.

liturgy will have found entrance only through him himself, the native of Antioch and former presbyter of Flavian. The liturgical practice of the new imperial city, which took a prominent part in the religious struggle of this century, and in which in 381 the Fourth General Council had proclaimed the divinity of the Holy Spirit against the last assaults of Eastern Arianism, must have been especially inclined to take over forms which in Antioch celebrated the triumph of orthodoxy as a symbol of the latter, indeed even to surpass in this, where possible, the city on the Orontes.[1]

How was this type of praise, with the direct address to the three divine Persons, arrived at in the Syrian language-area itself? In the first instance, it could appear everywhere throughout the Catholic Church, as we see it appear in Rome with Hippolytus. It was not, indeed, so very far removed from the doxologies quoted above with Basil, using the third person, which preceded the $\mu\epsilon\theta$' $o\tilde{v}$ formula. But the peculiar nature of the Syrian tongue was specially favourable for it. That is, it was unfavourable for a formula of praying 'through Christ'; for the most obvious expression, with the particle '*be*', was indeterminate and indicated rather an 'in' Christ.[2] It is therefore in fact, as Basil is assured, 'impossible' to put in sequence the divine Persons with, say, $\delta\iota\acute{a}$—$\acute{\epsilon}\nu$. Thus in the New Testament, in so far as texts are rendered from the Aramaic sister tongue of the Syrian, references are primarily to praying *in* the name of Jesus, and it has already been noticed by exegetes that praying through Christ was probably first cultivated in the Greek communities, especially by Paul.[3] While in this more refined Greek form the evolution led to

---

[1] The contacts involved here between Syrian and Byzantine liturgy would therefore be in great part attributable not to Byzantine influences in Syria, but to Syrian in Byzantium. Cf. also above p. 65, n. 7. Here, too, should be noted the interconnections, going beyond Antioch, between East Syrian and Byzantine fashions in the liturgical reading; see A. Baumstark, *Nichtevangelische syrische Perikopenordnungen des ersten Jahrtausends* (LF 3) (Münster i. W., 1921), 69 f., 174.

[2] The $\delta\iota\acute{a}$ in the $\delta\iota$' $o\tilde{v}$ $\kappa a\grave{\iota}$ $\mu\epsilon\theta$' $o\tilde{v}$ is rendered in later Syrian anaphoras by the paraphrase 'at the hands of'.

[3] A. Klawek 74 f. That Christ is high priest and Mediator also of our prayer was of course known also to the Syrians, if only from the Epistle to the Hebrews. But the language was less an encouragement to make this into a custom. With this may be connected the fact, already pointed out, that the term 'priest' for the ordained servants of the Church and their description as mediators between God and men appeared relatively early in Syria (Didascalia II, c. 25 f; Funk I, 94 ff.).

the acceptance of the more indeterminate: in Christ = in the Holy Spirit = in the holy Church, and then from the three-membered to the trinitarian prayer schema, the opportunity for this was lacking in the Syrian. On the other hand, obviously also the Syrian, like the Greek, Christians directed their prayer from the start not to the divine Person of the Father, but simply to (the triune) God. If here also, with theological reflexion, interest grew stronger in the mystery of the Trinity, it had to find a different outlet. Now the Syrian tongue, which lacks declensions, invited all the more readily the simple insertion of the words of the baptismal formula into the prayer when this could be done without altering them beyond the omission of the opening words: in Christ our Lord we praise thee, 'Father and Son and Holy Ghost', or: (we praise) thy 'name of the Father and of the Son and of the Holy Ghost'.

But what then has become of the element 'in Christ'? There was already occasion above[1] to remark that traces exist precisely on Syrian soil of the roughly equivalent phrase 'in the holy Church'. With remarkable frequency the doxological ending is preceded by the related idea: That we now and then, 'with all who are pleasing to thee', praise thee.[2] But also Christ himself is sometimes named in a similar connexion and in the same sense. He it is who enables us to praise God worthily, especially in that he has imparted to us the Holy Spirit.[3] Likewise we meet also a kind of χάριτι formula, but not, as in the Greek fashion, continued with δι' οὗ or μεθ' οὗ rather, it remains in the more primitive texts an independent member before the unaltered acclamation of the divine Persons.[4] It might here, after the

---

[1] P. 152-3. Cf. in the Byzantine liturgy passages such as Br. 315, 26b; 337, 20.

[2] See above, p. 71; cf. the Byzantine parallels—on the whole, later—above, p. 79.

[3] Cf. above, pp. 71, 76.

[4] See above, pp. 71, 73. Cf. the fragment, unfortunately decayed also at the end, from the sixth century (Br. 517, 39): '⟨...⟩ Filii tui sancti ⟨...⟩ unum simus ⟨...⟩ in bonis ⟨...⟩ adoremus et glorificemus naturam divinam potentem et sanctam in omnibus, Patrem et Filium et Spiritum Sanctum in saecula. Amen.' The independent character of the christological member, the clearer contrast between Christ and triune God, may have been expressed formerly also by the expression 'thy Christ' (or 'thy anointed'), which is familiar to the older layers of the Byzantine, as of the East Syrian, liturgy (Br. 266, 8; 274, 32; 288, 27). Cf. above p. 79, n. 4 and also pp. 12, 14, 163 (Ap. Const.).

era of religious disputes, have replaced the Syrian 'in Christ' in the same way as, on Greek soil, it replaced the διὰ Χριστοῦ, in so far as the former has not simply fallen out, which indeed, with the independent nature of this member, could easily occur.[1]

The Byzantine liturgy possesses from ancient times, however, together with the forms of the Syrian type which predominate, the χάριτι ending with the address to God the Father (μεθ' οὗ σοί), perhaps an indication that the former prayer type at the time of the foundation of the Byzantine liturgy was not, indeed, used as an unwavering rule. In reverse, then, Greek elements of this sort reached the Syrians, the East Syrians possibly with the Nestorius and Theodore anaphoras.[2] Among the West Syrian Jacobites, who took their oldest anaphora formularies from the Greeks, they became frequent also in the extra-anaphora prayers. Thus the later Jacobite insertions in the intercessory prayers of the St James liturgy do not end with the acclamation to the three divine Persons, but use the address to the Father: to thee we send up the praise and to thy Son. . . .[3]

The result is a far-reaching interchange in the typical forms of the liturgical prayer between the Greek and the Syrian East, to the extent that in the branches of the Greek liturgy persisting today, even by the early middle ages the Syrian basic type and at least in the West Syrian liturgy, the Greek basic type predominate. However, suppression, weakening or abandonment of those text elements which make Christ appear as Mediator, especially as Mediator of the prayer, is common to the whole East. Instead, the majesty of the triune God, of the Father and the Son and the Holy

[1] Prayers and forms of this type passed later from the Monophysites of Syria to those of Egypt, in the first place to the Copts, especially the praise to the three divine Persons as ending of the prayer without christological transition (see above p. 42, n. 3 ['Severus']; p. 35, n. 4 [John of Bosra']; p. 38, n. 1; cf. p. 37, n. 1). The Copts recite the Gloria Patri in Greek, and therefore took it at an early date into their Mass liturgy, perhaps first as Monophysites from Syria (cf. Br. 155, 9–22). It is lacking in the relevant passages in the St Mark liturgy, although elsewhere it is already known to Athanasius.

[2] Cf. above, p. 71, the prayer-endings quoted for these anaphoras.

[3] Cf. above, p. 59, n. 3.

Spirit, to whom in every prayer praise is offered, gains a new prominence as object of worship.[1] Granted that the Arian assault has not changed the faith of the ancient Church, yet it has profoundly influenced, at first throughout the East, the use made of different facets of the faith in the religious and liturgical life. Hence it also became a remote cause for the particular religious outlook that marks not only the liturgical prayer but also the ecclesiastical art and culture of the Christian East.

In comparison with the deep disturbance which the Arian disorders in the East brought even into the sanctuary of the liturgy, we are astonished at the calm with which in the meantime the West kept on its path. One might think that Rome stood entirely remote from the whole religious struggle, if church history did not show the opposite.

Certainly, the Latin liturgy of Rome was as yet by no means in a finished condition. Although the transition to Latin as the language of worship occurred in the third century, the principle of freedom, to which we heard Hippolytus bear witness,[2] still had a pronounced effect on the liturgical prayer formula. And also in the manner of beginning and ending the prayer—for which at first there came into being a fixed custom—a further development by Clement, Justin and Hippolytus[3] on the lines indicated, at intervals of half a century, would not now have been unprecedented. But the kind of liturgical praying which we found in the first centuries in the whole of Greek-speaking Christendom and therefore in Rome also, i.e. praying through Christ, now simply continued here in its essentials in the garb of the Latin tongue. Indeed, with the change of language a backward step, rather, is taken. There is no desire to engage in a theological or apologetic transformation of the prayer schema, nor even in that practice which it seems had been first set in motion in the last epoch of Greek as the liturgical language of Rome by Hippolytus, and realized in his community,

---

[1] The late middle ages produced a Greek translation of the Latin Mass. Characteristically, the 'Proprium de SS. Trinitate' is adopted (as 'Liturgia s. Gregorii Magni'; ed. A. Baumstark: *Oriens christ.* 4 [1904] 1–27).

[2] Above, p. 3; 107, n. 4.

[3] See above, pp. 146, 150, 151.

viz. the address of praise at the end of the prayer to the three divine Persons.[1]

This apparently applies at first to Gaul and Spain as much as to Italy and Africa; for what we meet later in those countries in forms of a divergent prayer schema is only understandable if for the time being, at any rate in the fourth century, the Roman manner remained even here in general use. As a consequence, we may speak of a third, a *Latin* basic type of the liturgical prayer. As this remained at first untouched by the dogmatic struggle of the fourth century, its characteristic elements should be discussed in more detail.

A first distinction consists in the much more sparing use of the doxology in the Latin Mass. While in the East every prayer, even the prayer of petition, at the end flows into a passage of praise, this is not the case in the West. In the Mass proper there is only one doxology, that at the end of the Canon.[2] Of the end-formulas of the supplicatory prayer, the shorter, 'per Christum Dominum nostrum', cannot make any claim to the name of doxology; the longer, only in the widest sense, with regard to its last words.[3]

The doxology at the end of the Canon, which in the Roman sacramentaries, in the Gregorianum, in the Gelasianum and also in the Stowe Missal, has exactly the same wording as in the present-day Mass, is preserved[4] in a somewhat different form in the Ambrosian rite,[5] of which the Canon is considered in part an older

---

[1] Cf. the fact established by A. Harnack (*Lehrbuch der Dogmengeschichte* I⁴, 771 ff.) that the Roman Popes Dionysius I, Leo I and Agatho, in exactly the same way as they had to give their opinion in disputes of faith, had nothing to do with the speculations on the different forms of address, but merely decided in the sense o. tradition, and with reference to it, on the questionable results of these speculationsf Admittedly, Harnack is not able to appreciate this quiet holding fast to the God-given deposit of faith. Cf. J. Lebreton, *Revue d'histoire eccl.* 25 (1924) 9, n. 1; H. Dieckmann, ZkTh 48 (1924) 314 ff.

[2] The 'great doxology', the Gloria in excelsis, belongs to the chant portions of the Roman Mass. Moreover, its use in the non-pontifical Mass, earlier restricted to Christmas and Easter, has become more general only since the ninth century. The 'little doxology', the Gloria Patri, pertains to the psalm-singing and enters the Mass only with the introit and later with psalms 42 and 25 (43 and 26).

[3] V. Thalhofer-L. Eisenhofer II, 553 uses for it the acceptable expression 'indirect doxology'.

[4] See juxtaposed canon texts DACL 2, 1886.

[5] See DACL 1, 1414; J. Pamelius, *Liturgica Latina* I, 303.

form of the Roman.[1] The difference is shown in the following juxtaposition. Both sides are preceded by the statement that God 'through Christ' creates, blesses and distributes all these good things.

|  |  |
|---|---|
|  | Et est tibi Deo Patri omnipotenti |
| *Per ipsum et cum ipso et in ipso* | *ex ipso et per ipsum et in ipso* |
| est tibi Deo Patri omnipotenti | omnis honor virtus, laus et gloria |
|  | imperium, perpetuitas et potestas |
| *in unitate Spiritus Sancti* | *in unitate Spiritus Sancti* |
| omnis honor et gloria |  |
| per omnia saecula saeculorum. | per infinita saecula saeculorum. |

The present Roman wording could at first give the impression that we had to do with a parallel to the Greek formula: 'Per ipsum et cum ipso . . . in unitate Spiritus Sancti' = δι' οὗ καὶ μεθ' οὗ σὺν ἁγίῳ πνεύματι. In fact, we find in the work going under the name of Ambrose, *De Sacramentis* (VI, 5, n. 24) a Latin doxology of this Greek type quoted from a North Italian Mass, in which it follows the Pater noster: 'Quid sequitur? Audi quid dicat sacerdos: Per Dominum nostrum Jesum Christum, in quo tibi est, *cum quo tibi* est honor, laus, gloria, magnificentia, potestas, *cum Spiritu Sancto* a saeculis et nunc et semper et in omnia saecula saeculorum. Amen.' The author also uses the doxology himself at the end of the fourth book of his work: 'May God enlighten you through his Son . . ., per quem sibi et cum quo sibi est laus, honor, gloria, magnificentia, potestas cum Spiritu Sancto a saeculis.'[2]

There is no doubt that here the praise is applied to the Father with the Son and with the Holy Ghost. It is otherwise in the Roman Canon. In the Ambrosian form, there is no expression which one could liken to the μεθ' οὗ. Moreover, the expression 'in unitate Spiritus Sancti' is not plainly equivalent to σὺν ἁγίῳ πνεύματι. We would even approach its meaning more nearly if we rendered it by ἐν ἁγίῳ πνεύματι. But here a more detailed examination is necessary.

The word *unitas* means unicity, or else physical or moral agreement, but is not used as a paraphrase for *cum*. 'Unitas Spiritus Sancti' accordingly means an agreement which is in relation to the

---

[1] A. Baumstark, *Vom geschichtlichen Werden* 52          [2] PL 16, 464, 480.

Holy Spirit, whether because he effects or constitutes it or because, indeed, he is the possession which is present in all who are agreeing. We evidently have here a connexion with the pauline phrase (Eph. 4:1–3): 'Obsecro itaque vos ego vinctus in Domino, ut digne ambuletis vocatione, qua vocati estis, ... supportantes invicem in caritate, solliciti servare *unitatem spiritus* (ἐνότητα πνεύματος) in vinculo pacis.' Most exegetes, it is true, take *spiritus* in this passage for the human spirit, not the Holy Spirit, thus: unitas spiritus = united conviction. But Chrysostom does not stand alone in interpreting it as the Holy Spirit: unitas spiritus = the unity established by the Holy Spirit.[1] The meaning of the word πνεῦμα is equally uncertain in many other passages.[2] Most probably, also, the thought of the Apostle himself carries over in the above passage from the unity of the mind to its spiritual basis: one body, one spirit . . ., one Lord, one God and Father; and although the phrase does not occur in Paul, the conception of the 'unitas Spiritus Sancti', of the unity of the faithful effected by the Holy Spirit, is so central to pauline theology—and equally patristic theology—that it is quite unnecessary to cite passages containing it.

We need refer only to Augustine, who often discussed these ideas in connexion with the unity of the Church. When the Donatist returns to the Church, he needs no second Baptism, but only now is he enfolded by 'the unity of the Spirit in the bond of peace'. And the reason is this: the man who had been cut off from the body of Christ, the Just One, could not have the Spirit of justice within himself.[3] Here, from the whole context, it is only adherence to the pauline phrase which prevents the expression from running: 'unitas Spiritus Sancti.' That this pauline phrase has found liturgical use

---

[1] Cf. J. Knabenbauer.        [2] Cf. F. Prat, *La théologie de s. Paul* II[6] 492.

[3] 'Ac per hoc nemo potest esse iustus, quamdiu fuerit ab unitate huius corporis separatus. Quemadmodum membrum, si praecidatur ab hominis vivi corpore, non potest tenere spiritum vitae, sic homo, qui praeciditur de Christi iusti corpore, nullo modo potest spiritum tenere iustitiae . . . Non quidem accipitis baptismum, qui vobis extra compagem corporis Christi inesse potuit, prodesse non potuit, sed accipitis *unitatem Spiritus* in vinculo pacis.' *Epist.* 185, n. 42 f. (PL 33, 811). Cf. Fulgentius, *Ad Monim.* 2, 10–12 (PL 65, 188–92): It is the 'unitas spiritualis' that makes the Church herself a sacrifice pleasing to God.

elsewhere in the same manner is shown by a parallel in the Greek St Mark liturgy, and so clearly that its meaning in the present wording is no longer hard to grasp.[1]

The 'unitas Spiritus Sancti' is accordingly the unity which the Church's principle of life, the Holy Spirit, produces in it and which belongs to its essence as a living organism, as 'corpus Christi'. In fact, the expression can, by a simple metonymy, denote the Church itself—just as we speak, not only of a communion which binds the members of the Church together, but also of a 'communion of saints', which is the Church herself—although the word 'Communio' expresses, just as much as 'unity' (unitas), in the first place an abstract relation. Augustine actually uses the word *unitas* also in this sense: the Church is a unity; it must be, because Christ is one. 'Ille enim unus est, Ecclesia unitas. Non respondet uni nisi unitas.'[2]

---

[1] To the cry Τὰ ἅγια τοῖς ἁγίοις the people reply: Εἷς πατὴρ ἅγιος, εἷς υἱὸς ἅγιος, ἐν πνεῦμα ἅγιον εἰς ἑνότητα πνεύματος ἁγίου (Br. 138, 10). In Egypt, this trinitarian form of the response must have been preceded by a christological form of the same, as it still is in the West Syrian and in the Byzantine Mass: 'Only one is holy, one the Lord to the glory of God the Father.' In the earlier Byzantine Mass, there is added to this text: εἰς πλήρωμα πνεύματος ἁγίου (Br. 341, 20). The sense is obviously much the same here as in the St Mark liturgy. The reception of body and blood of the only saint (= Christ) should serve 'for filling with the Holy Ghost', as Hippolytus puts it; more precisely, for the strengthening of that holy Communion among the faithful of which the Holy Spirit is the abiding bond. Cf. H.–J. Schulz, *Die byzantinische Liturgie* (Freiburg, 1964), 79. Cf. also the epiklesis prayer of the East Syrian Nestorius anaphora: Ren. II, 633 f. It is noteworthy that the words both here and in the Roman Mass accompany the elevation of the sacred host. Cf. A. Baumstark, *Die Messe im Morgenland* 157–9.

[2] In Psalmum 101, 8; PL 36, 1309. The expression 'in unitate Spiritus Sancti' has become the subject of a drawn-out controversy; see the account in Jungmann, *Missarum Sollemnia*[5] (1962) II, 329 f. or [4] (1958) II, 592–4. There is agreement on the rendering, 'in the unity of the Holy Spirit'. But it is maintained by B. Botte, *int. al.*, that this can mean only the unity that the Holy Ghost effects between Father and Son. Against this is the significant fact that the formula, which is joined to the certainly pre-anti-Arian 'Per ipsum', can only be of pre-anti-Arian origin and therefore must mean the unity in which the Holy Spirit unites the faithful. That the latter was also still a current theme in the Latin area in the fourth to fifth century can be seen again from Augustine, *Serm.* 71, 19, 32 (PL 38, 462); *Sermones post Maurinos* ed. Morin 185 f. Further texts from Augustine and parallels from Chrysostom and Basil are cited by T. Schnitzler, *Die Messe in der Betrachtung* I (Freiburg, 1955) 112 f. Eng. version *Mass in Meditation* (St Louis, No. 1, London 1959). I have attempted a theological exposition of the theme in the article 'In der Einheit des Heiligen Geistes': *Zeitschr. f. Aszese u. Mystik* 2 (1927) 3–16 (= *Gewordene Liturgie* [Innsbruck, 1941] 190–205). In the oratio-ending which refers to the living

'In unitate spiritus sancti Deo est gloria' therefore means: in the society (or union) of the Holy Spirit, in the holy Church, God is given glory.

The expression that precedes, referring to Christ, is, in both versions of this doxology, threefold. By this means, a special importance is given to it, rather as, in the Ambrosian form, the idea of glorification is given prominence by seven partly synonymous terms. But the three phrases are by no means simply equivalent; they betoken in both cases, more or less clearly, the same gradation of different ways in which God is honoured through Christ: he himself glorifies God, is a constant glorification of God: 'ex ipso', or 'per ipsum'.[1] However, he does not remain alone; his people are joined to him, and praise with him, and through his mediation, God the Lord: 'Cum ipso', or 'per ipsum'.[2] Indeed, they are absorbed in him and form one body with him, a holy people of God, a royal priesthood: 'In ipso.' Now the 'unitas Spiritus Sancti' follows on fittingly: they are held together through the common grace-giving possession of the Holy Spirit, who lives in all. This is truly a full accord for the glorification of God the almighty Father. At the same time, the priest holds in his hands the Blessed Sacrament,

and reigning of Christ 'in unitate Spiritus Sancti', it is indeed hard to maintain this interpretation. Instead, one must accept the remark of A. Baumstark in discussion of the first edition of the present book (*Oriens christ.*, 1930, 249) that the expression has been 'brought only subsequently into a hybrid combination' with the oratio-ending, so that, to give an acceptable meaning, the phrase here must be referred primarily to the relationship within the Trinity. In the end-doxology of the Canon, on the other hand, Baumstark, also, sees in the expression 'in unitate Spiritus Sancti' the correspondence to the Hippolytan 'in sancta Ecclesia'. O. Heiming (*Archiv f. Liturgiewissenschaft* 7 [1961] 210 f.) differs from this view in that, in the phrase 'in sancta Ecclesia', he sees only the earthly Church, while in 'in unitate Spiritus Sancti' he sees all creatures drawn into the praise.

[1] The *per* is generally, it is true, used for the *causa instrumentalis*, but just like διά and 'through', it can also be used for the *causa efficiens principalis*, e.g. 'through him (God; *per ipsum*) . . . are all things.' (Romans 11:36).

[2] The 'cum ipso', μεθ' οὗ, μετ' αὐτοῦ has hardly occurred up to now except in joining the Father to the Son, with whom he receives the same glory. But every time this results from the context only. The Greek μετά serves for the above purpose of joining the faithful to Christ when Origen, *De or.* 15, 4 (GCS: Orig. II, p. 336, 3. Koetschau), makes Christ say: μόνῳ γὰρ τῷ πατρὶ μετ' ἐμοῦ καὶ δι' ἐμοῦ ἀναπεμπτέον ἐστὶν ἡμῖν προσευχήν.

which Augustine praises as 'mysterium pacis et unitatis nostrae'.[1]
It was, however, only a slight variation on this that we found at the
start of the third century in St Hippolytus of Rome in the same part
of the Mass, at the end of the Canon. This is shown by the following
juxtaposition (with an unimportant change in the present text):

| | |
|---|---|
| per quem tibi | per ipsum et cum ipso et in ipso est tibi |
| gloria et honor | omnis honor et gloria |
| Patri et Filio cum Sancto Spiritu | Deo Patri omnipotenti |
| in sancta ecclesia tua | in unitate Spiritus Sancti |
| et nunc et in saecula saeculorum.[2] | per omnia saecula saeculorum. |

Besides the beginning of the Canon, the Preface schema[3] also
shows the same decided retention of the idea of the mediation of
prayer and praise through Christ.

But how is the oratio-ending 'per Christum Dominum nostrum',
or its more solemn sister-form, to be interpreted? Read together
with the preceding text, it would often suggest the interpretation in
the sense of the formula of efficacy: 'Et in electorum tuorum iubeas
grege numerari per Christum Dominum nostrum': may God
number the deceased through Christ in the company of the elect. In
this way, clearly, the analogous phrase was to be understood in
Serapion and usually also in the *Apostolic Constitutions*.[4]

On other occasions, however, its meaning is rendered just as well
in the sense of the mediation of prayer: 'Ipsis Domine . . . locum
refrigerii, lucis et pacis ut indulgeas deprecamur per Christum
Dominum nostrum'; we offer our petition through Christ.[5]

---

[1] Serm. 272 (PL 38, 1248). Cf. his exclamation: 'O sacramentum pietatis, O
signum unitatis, O vinculum caritatis!' *In Joh. tr.* 26, 13 (PL 35, 1613).

[2] Cf. above p. 46. For the interpretation cf. Jungmann, *Missarum Sollemnia* II[5]
(1962) 328–31, 580 ff.

[3] See above, pp. 111 ff.            [4] See above, pp. 22 ff., 12.

[5] The perusal of the homily-endings of the Latin Fathers leads to the same double
result. This is true, especially, of Hilary. He ends with a mention of Christ, on
which follows, nearly always, the same praise-text: '(Dominus noster Jesus
Christus,) qui est benedictus in saecula saeculorum.' Sometimes the mention takes
the form of a 'per Dominum nostrum Jesum Christum', in the sense, now of
mediated effect, e.g. *In Ps.* 129 (PL 9, 725), now of mediated prayer, e.g.
*In Ps.* 67 (PL 9, 469): 'Ut (plebs) . . . Deum aeternitatis suae laude benedicat per
unigenitum et primogenitum suum Deum ac Dominum nostrum Jesum Christum,
qui est benedictus in saecula saeculorum.' Much the same applies to Leo the Great.

A useful hint is given us here, in the first place, by the present manner of writing, which places a full stop after the preceding text. Our oratio-ending is a formula in itself, at least as much as, in the East, the χάριτι formula or the Syrian-Coptic 'in Christ Jesus our Lord', and, like these, it is to be thought of primarily as an ellipsis. Unlike Serapion's style of address, the preceding text does not move naturally, towards its end, to a mention of Christ.  ·

Therefore, how is the end-formula to be completed?[1] The context in which it occurs at the beginning of the Canon gives a meaning in favour of completion in the sense of prayer mediation: 'Te igitur, clementissime Pater, per Jesum Christum Filium tuum Dominum nostrum, supplices rogamus.' And, as a rule, one need not go far for the complementary word in the orationes. It often occurs in the course of the prayer: 'quaesumus', 'deprecamur'; or it is to be gathered from the introducing 'oremus'. The longer form of the oratio-ending, however, is decisive: 'Per Dominum nostrum Jesum Christum Filium tuum, qui tecum vivit et regnat in unitate Spiritus Sancti.' We have here the transfigured God-man, whom God has glorified and elevated to royal splendour, who was dead and lives again,[2] lives in order to make intercession for those who appear before God through him.[3] This part of the Epistle to the Hebrews concerns supplicatory prayer, and its wording is used here precisely for the ending of the prayer of supplication.

Augustine ends occasionally with a summons to prayer, 'Conversi ad Dominum etc.', the text of which is written out in full, *int. al.*, in Sermon 183 (PL 38, 994). The last words here are: 'Ad beatitudinem suam perducat, per Jesum Christum Filium eius. Amen.' A detailed treatment of this formula is in F. J. Dölger, *Sol salutis* 254 ff.

[1] The question could also very well be put: Is it capable of a complement at all? Has it not perhaps become a pure formula, the precise meaning of which one would not investigate? But as this type of prayer-ending, in its long and short form, is about as old as the Roman Canon, in whose transparent structure we find elsewhere nothing of a pure formula, this question probably demands no further attention. Of course, the end-phrase 'per Christum Dominum nostrum' appears later on in such a formal, not really intelligible manner, e.g. in the work *De Sacramentis* as the ending of the second book, and in various parts of Gallican Masses (see above p. 89, 95; cf. p. 99 f.).

[2] '. . . Fui mortuus et ecce sum vivens in saecula saeculorum.' Apoc. 1:18.

[3] 'Semper vivens.' Hebrews 7:25.

We have full surety for the rightness of this view, however, from the testimony of Fulgentius (d. 533), a man who, in face of the Arian Vandal kingdom of North Africa, is in no danger of emphasizing more strongly than necessary what is apt to give the appearance of a subordination of the Son to the Father, as is his priesthood. The deacon Ferrandus had asked him: 'Unum regnum Patris et Filii et Spiritus Sancti credimus et fatemur, simul eos dominari creaturis omnibus sentientes. Quare ergo in orationibus sacerdotum "per Jesum Christum Filium tuum Dominum nostrum, qui tecum vivit et regnat in unitate Spiritus Sancti" per universas pene Africae regiones catholica dicere consuevit Ecclesia, tamquam solus Filius cum Patre possideat regnum, in unitate scilicet Spiritus Sancti, ut regnantes adunare, non simul regnare Spiritus Sanctus intimetur?' Fulgentius uses the occasion to consider the end-formula —which is already to him an inheritance from earlier generations— more deeply than the questioner had first requested.[1] In this he is strongly influenced by the interests of apologetics: 'Quoties exinde cogitavi, nihil ibi aliud maiores nostros quam fidei veritatem contra multas haereses praemuniisse cognovi.' Why do we say at all 'per Jesum Christum' and not 'per Spiritum Sanctum'? Because only Christ is Mediator between God and men, and priest for ever in the manner of Melchisedech, who has entered into the sanctuary of heaven and there makes intercession for us. The Apostle was thinking of this his priestly office when he said: 'Through him then let us continually offer up a sacrifice of praise to God' (Hebrews 13:15); likewise Peter, when he urged us to make sacrifices which we should offer to God through Christ. And he adds: 'Hac igitur ratione dicimus Deo Patri: per Jesum Christum Dominum nostrum. Nam bene nosti nonnumquam dici: per sacerdotem aeternum Filium tuum Dominum nostrum Jesum Christum'.[2] As for the real point of the question put by

---

[1] Ep. 14, Nos. 35–8; PL 65, 424–7.

[2] Both the formulas here quoted by Fulgentius would be derived in the first instance from Prefaces. Cf. above p. 100, n. 5. Fulgentius treats the same matter more briefly in *Contra Fabian.* fragm. 34 (PL 65, 812), where again he derives the practice of praying through the Son from his priestly office. In this passage, he overcomes the Arian objection concerning the subordination of the Son by the clear distinction: He is, certainly, less than the Father 'secundum gratiam humanitatis assumptae', but on a par with him 'secundum veritatem divinitatis aeternae'.

the deacon Ferrandus, it is of value for us in that Ferrandus reproduces the ordinary interpretation of the expression 'in unitate Spiritus Sancti' in this context, viz. that the Son reigns with the Father in that unity which the Holy Ghost effects between them. When we realize that primarily the God-man, who lives continuously with God the Father as our advocate, and reigns with him, is being considered then it is clear that the 'unitas Spiritus Sancti' has here the same meaning in the doxology as before, only that now it is related to another subject. We are not here concerned with the communion in which the Holy Ghost unites the faithful, but with that in which he unites the God-man himself intimately with God the Father. He is indeed 'anointed with the Holy Spirit' through the hypostatic union and through the fullness of grace.[1] This latter communion is indeed the model for the former—according to the wish of the Lord himself: 'That they may be one, even as we are one' (John 17:11, 22). Fulgentius, on the other hand, following his dogmatic interests, here passes over into the trinitarian field and shows that the Holy Spirit reigns together with the Father and the Son because he is of one substance with them; indeed he can simply be called their unity (unitas): the Son reigns with the Father in that unity which is the Holy Spirit.[2]

Medieval liturgiologists explain the oratio-ending in the same way as Fulgentius; only, the high priest theme in the formula is scarcely any longer stressed. If, in the beginning of the formula, they still see the prayer offered in the name of Jesus,[3] yet, in its continuation, they see chiefly the praise of the most holy Trinity. A doxological

---

[1] Cf. Luke 4:18; I Cor. 15:45 etc.; F. Prat, *La théologie de s. Paul* II[6], 204–7.

[2] In another passage, *Ad Monim.* 1, 2, 5 (PL 65, 184) he makes use of the oratio-ending to prove, against the Arians, that the prayers of the Catholic liturgy are not intended for the Father alone, but for the whole Trinity. 'Neque enim praeiudicium Filio vel Sancto Spiritui comparatur, dum ad Patris personam precatio ab offerente dirigitur. Cuius consummatio, dum Filii et Spiritus Sancti complectitur nomen, ostendit nullum esse in Trinitate discrimen.'

[3] Cf. in the eleventh century the *Micrologus* c. 6. It understands the 'per' clearly in a somewhat wider sense than that of prayer-mediation. With it we ask the Father, 'ut nobis per merita Christi Filii sui subveniat'. It would therefore be the same idea as that of the Greek χάριτι formula. Later liturgiologists and theologians frequently liken the 'per Christum' here to 'per merita Christi', e.g. F. Suarez, *Op. omn.* XIV, 1, 1, c. 10; F. A. Zaccaria, *Bibliotheca ritualis* (Rome, 1781) II, p. 79.

note is not, in fact, to be denied the formula, inasmuch as, together with the continuing life of the God-man as our advocate, the unending duration of his kingdom is also reflected on with praise; and inasmuch as the solemn mention of the Holy Spirit also makes the sublime image of the Trinity arise before one who prays.

The trinitarian interpretation and the referring of the 'vivere et regnare' to the godhead of Christ has led again to a small change in the text, viz. the insertion of the word 'Deus', which, incidentally, does not impair the original meaning given above. Therewith is stressed only the godhead of the high priest, which follows immediately from the unity of his Person, and which the Council of Ephesus, canon 10, emphasized against Nestorius as early as 431.[1] The hesitation over the point of insertion shows that in fact it was not in the text from the beginning.[2] Also, the addition 'Filium tuum' to the name of Christ appears, at least in the case of Rome, to have got into the text later, in the same fashion. It occurs, certainly, in Fulgentius, but is lacking in the earlier Ambrosian Mass:[3] 'Per eundem Dominum nostrum Jesum Christum, qui tecum vivit et regnat Deus in unitate Spiritus Sancti per omnia saecula saeculorum.' Similarly, the addition is missing in the Sacramentarium Leonianum.[4]

With the same tendency to find the three divine Persons as such named in the end-formula is connected Fulgentius' view of the

---

[1] H. Denzinger–C. Bannwart, *Enchiridion*[14] no. 122.

[2] The embolism in the Sacramentarium Gregorianum (Mur. II, 6) still has: 'Qui tecum vivit et regnat Deus in unitate Spiritus Sancti per omnia saecula saeculorum'; likewise, some Gallic texts (see above p. 92). The *Micrologus* c. 6 finds this insertion point more correct, but says it has already become so much a habit to insert the word 'Deus' after the name of the Holy Spirit that the old way cannot unhesitatingly be resumed. The same is repeated by Radulphus de Rivo (Mohlberg II, 138). It would, after all, be possible to take the 'Deus' also as a vocative, in the sense of a doxological end-address, as in the Syrian prayer-type. A related Mozarabic end-formula in fact so uses the 'Deus'; see above p. 99. But in the Roman Mass this was hardly the reason for the insertion. On the strength of the same trinitarian interpretation, in Gallic formularies the expression 'in unitate Spiritus Sancti' is often displaced by 'cum Spiritu Sancto' (see above pp. 88 f., 100, 103; cf. 93 f.), a form which, by the way, already occurs in the homily-endings of Leo the Great, and which brings out clearly only another side of the thought: the sovereignty of the triune God instead of the sovereignty of Christ.

[3] J. Pamelius, *Liturgica Latina* I, 294.        [4] Feltoe 20; see above, p. 114, n. 5.

prayer as directed expressly to God the Father. But also the Council of Hippo (393) already speaks of the prayer address to the Father. Perhaps there was also another occasion for this, in that very often in the African liturgy the Father's name was used for God, just as in the Sacramentarium Leonianum. In the later Roman Mass, the Father's name, except for 'Pater omnipotens', became rare, and in the orationes it does not occur at all. Would this change be intended to bring into relief again the opposition between God and Christ? In prayers which have the shorter end-formula, there is now no reason for having another prayer-address than that directly to God. In the longer oratio-ending, nevertheless, the 'Filium tuum' in apposition to the name of Christ could presuppose the address to God the Father. But there is first the question whether for that reason the address may be properly extended to the whole prayer. As the Roman liturgy at the beginning of the prayer itself chooses expressions which refer simply to God, the divine majesty, one can perhaps ˚see in the words 'Filium tuum' also merely a transitory narrowing of the prayer-address from (the triune) God to the Father. Perhaps we have in general only an ellipsis such as in the term 'Filius Dei', which likewise can denote by 'Deus' ultimately only the Person of the Father, but hardly embraces the idea of him in fact. The philosopher says of this phenomenon: 'Abstrahitur.' The end-formula could then be rendered: 'For this we beseech thee, O God, through Christ our Lord, who, in thy bosom, is the Son.' The case is otherwise with the prayers of the Greek type, where the praise is sent up 'to thee and thy Son. . .'.[1]

---

[1] When O. Casel (181) denies that the Roman orationes are directed simply to God (not restricting to the Father), one can agree with him to the extent that in the case of the addition of the solemn conclusion and, in particular, after the subsequent insertion of the 'Filium tuum' (see above 210) the address is presumed to be directed to the first divine Person. Of the original text itself, this cannot be said, for the address (Deus, Domine, etc.) contains no determination of any kind. It is clear in any case that this order of address ruled in the East throughout the East Syrian and the Byzantine liturgy (see above 71 ff., 76 ff.). But even in the West it is sufficient to point to Augustine, *Enarr. in ps.* 29 II, no. i (PL 36, 216): 'Quid est mediatorem esse inter Deum et homines? Non inter Patrem et homines, sed inter Deum et homines. Quid est Deus? Pater et Filius et Spiritus.' That the simple end-formula 'Per Christum Dominum nostrum' does not presuppose the address to the Father is indeed shown in our Mass ordo by the two prayers 'Suscipe S. Trinitas' and 'Placeat tibi S. Trinitas'. At the same time, the thesis of

The Roman liturgy also, then, does not forget to express the divinity of the Mediator and high priest, but this is done only to emphasize his dignity. It has no influence on the order of address and structure of the prayer.[1] The Roman liturgy is not concerned to change elements of the prayer into formulas of faith, to provide bulwarks against those threatening the faith.[2] These may be built from other material on the periphery of the holy city. The liturgy itself remains, in its midst, the sanctuary in which, untroubled by the noise of battle without, one only enters before God—today with the same language and in the same Spirit as was customary in the Church in the third century or so.

K. Rahner that the simple name of God in the New Testament means God as the Father (*Schriften zur Theologie* I [Einsiedeln, 1954] 91–167) (Eng. trans: *Theological Writings* I [London, 1961]) remains unaffected. Yet even this view has not been unopposed; see J. H. Nicolas O.P.: *Freiburger Zeitsch. f. Philosophie u. Theologie* 7 (1960) 428 f.

[1] Prayers in the course of which both the humanity of Christ and his divinity, when occasion offers, are clearly expressed, are not unusual in the Roman liturgy. It is enough to recall the age-old 'Deus qui humanae substantiae'. The priestly office of his humanity is finely contrasted with the power of his divinity in an oratio of the Gregorianum for Low Sunday: '. . . Ut interpellans pro nobis pontifex summus nos per id, quod nostri est similis, reconciliet, per id, quod tibi est aequalis, absolvat, Jesus Christus Filius tuus Dominus noster' (Mur. II, 76).

[2] Even the Credo was accepted into the Roman Mass relatively late—in the year 1014, at the instance of the Emperor Henry II. The remark that the Roman liturgy has not been concerned to turn prayer-elements into formulas of faith should not be taken in a strict sense, as the previously (above p. 210) mentioned introduction of 'Filium tuum' and 'Deus' into the oratio-ending at once shows. There was also a not unimportant influence of Eastern thought shown in the express recognition in the West of equally permissible formulations, such as 'Unus ex Trinitate passus est'; thus, in the brief of John II of the year 534 (Denzinger no. 201); cf. A. Grillmeier, *Vorbereitung des Mittelalters*: Das Konzil von Chalkedon II, 791–839. The neo-Chalcedonian synthesis deriving from the East received full recognition at the Lateran Synod of 649 (*ibid.* 836 ff.).

# XIII

## THE PRAYER TO CHRIST. ANTI-ARIAN COMPOSITIONS OF THE POST-PATRISTIC PERIOD

ALTHOUGH the prayer to Christ was in use by the faithful from the earliest times, it was denied a home for a long time in the solemn public worship of the community. The African synods of Hippo and Carthage banned it specifically from the domain of the sacrificial celebration.[1] This attitude of the synods, and of the older churches, whereby they rejected the prayer directed to the Son, has been found somewhat one-sided, although excusable.[2] The foregoing account, however, would suggest that no such apology is necessary. It is not the business of liturgical prayer to pay a special honour to each divine Person individually. Yet the work of the Redeemer, as also the whole of the Christian faith, could hardly be better manifested than when the prayer of God's children

---

[1] See above, p. 169.

[2] Thus A. Klawek, 113: 'Conservatism induced those taking part in the Council to act against every divergence from tradition.' Cf. p. 115: 'Although Jewish scrupulosity, dogmatic exactitude and religious conservatism saw to it that the liturgical prayer was sent up by the assembled community to the one God through Jesus Christ, nevertheless the Christians in the solitude of their rooms lifted their gaze to heaven, in order to offer their whole selves in sacrifice to the King, Lord and God there enthroned, and to beg of him health and peace of soul.'

rises from a holy community through Christ to God. Nor could there be a sounder religious upbringing of the people than their growing up into this grasp of Christianity entire in vital contact with the priest at the altar in this spirit of prayer—much as particular teaching on the different departments of the faith is still needed.

In those areas where it did not have to be the norm, as in the sacrificial prayer of the Church, to aim at giving complete and harmonious expression to the total awareness of the faith, at all times appeared spontaneously, by the side of the traditional liturgical manner of prayer, the custom of praying to Christ the Lord: in the private prayer of the individual and in popular forms which grew out of it. There were also the poetical additions which accompanied the liturgical celebration.[1] Indeed, in secondary passages, outside the domain of the anaphora, we found in the *Apostolic Constitutions* individual prayers to Christ inserted systematically even into the order of liturgical prayer.

It is chiefly in popular forms that the prayer to Christ first appears within the liturgy. Only later did the anti-Arian tendency lead to compositions of this type. The straightforward, unreflective nature of this first prayer to Christ is shown at once by the fact that frequently no distinction is made between the address to God and to Christ. Popular piety is not to be expected to be much troubled by theological considerations. All the more so where forms of supplication, mainly seeking help, are concerned.

An example of such a supplicatory prayer of extreme age which here and there has passed into the liturgy from popular usage is to be found in the so-called *paradigm-prayer*. Examples are enumerated from the Old and New Testaments of God granting his aid, and each time the request is added for help in the present case. This request remains exactly the same, whether it is for aid which God or more specifically Christ the Lord has granted and is now to grant. 'Hear us, O Lord, as thou hast heard Noah . . .; hear us, O

---

[1] Also, the poetical elements of the liturgy are to a greater extent the creations of individual piety than is the liturgical prayer proper. The great freedom of address often finds expression here in personifications. Just as in the Roman liturgy addresses are often found to the holy Cross, the Ethiopic priest calls to the house of God: 'Peace be to thee, holy church, dwelling-place of the Godhead' (Br. 211, 30); and the Syrian-Jacobite bids the altar a movingly beautiful *vale* (Br. 109, 7).

Lord, as thou hast heard Jonas . . .; hear us, O Lord, as thou hast heard Jairus.'[1] Prayers of this type now occur not only in the West, but also in the whole East, even among the East Syrians, who have remained most independent. A. Baumstark hence concludes to the existence of this manner of prayer even in the oldest Christianity.[2] Within the Mass, we see later the paradigm-prayer emerge at the end of the East Syrian Nestorius anaphora,[3] in the Preface of a Mozarabic Mass[4] and in the Irish Stowe Missal.[5]

We possess another manner of prayer of a popular kind, and of similarly venerable antiquity, in the *Kyrie eleison*. 'We have in the Kyrie eleison . . . an ancient prayer-formula. The ἐλέησον was to the Greek praying as self-explanatory as his *miserere* was to the Latin.'[6] The cry ἐλέησον, with the address κύριε, in the Old Testament psalms directed to God, meets us in the New Testament on the lips of those who implore the aid of the Saviour.[7] In the pagan cult of the sun, which was in its prime in the Church's youth, it was customary to greet the rising sun with this cry, ἐλέησον ἡμᾶς. As late as the fifth century, Eusebius of Alexandria had to deny that

[1] A. Baumstark, 'Paradigmengebete ostsyrischer Kirchendichtung': *Oriens christ.*[2] 10/11 (for 1920–1; Leipzig 1923) 1–32; J. A. Jungmann, Paradigmengebet = *Lexikon für Theologie und Kirche VIII* (1963) 74. The paradigms thus quoted are to be seen again and again represented symbolically in the catacombs, probably as types of redemption at the same time, implying a request that the Lord will show his favour equally to the departed.

[2] 'Thus a common possession of East Aramaic and Graeco-Roman Christendom goes back beyond the era of the first evangelizing of the Osrhoene and Adiabene' (p. 14). But this Christian paradigm-prayer was only an extension of one already in use among the Jews.

[3] See above, p. . 72

[4] MEL V, 255 ('missa quam sacerdos pro seipso dicere debet').

[5] ZkTh 16 (1892) 471; here yet another source of passages. Numerous further examples and parallels are remarked in Baumstark. Here, for custom outside the Mass I shall refer only to our *Commendatio animae*, where, however, the change of address for the New Testament paradigms is avoided; and also to the benediction-ary of Freising from the seventh century (DACL 6, 503). The antiphonal of St Gregory uses it in the rogation procession (J. Pamelius, *Liturgica Latina* II, 125 f.): 'Qui gubernasti Noe super undas diluvii, exaudi nos; qui Jonam de abysso revocasti, libera nos; qui Petro mergenti manum porrexisti, auxiliare nobis, Christe, Fili Dei.' There is almost the same wording in the Stowe Missal.

[6] F. J. Dölger, *Sol salutis* 63; cf. pp. 50–80; also the data following those pages. Cf. V. Thalhofer–L. Eisenhofer I, 316–20; E. Bishop, *Liturgica historica* (Oxford, 1918), pp. 115–36.

[7] E.g. Ps. 6:3; Matt. 9:27; 15:22; 17:15 (κύριε, ἐλέησον . . .).

Christians still did the same.[1] Then it was all the more natural that the Kyrie eleison should be adopted increasingly as a cry to him whom the Christians were wont to think of as a sun of justice, as 'oriens ex alto'. In liturgical usage, we find the Kyrie eleison first attested in the Ap. Const. VIII—i.e. for the end of the fourth century—as a repeated response of the people to the prayer-intentions and petitions announced by the deacon litany-fashion. The calls of the deacon are here adapted to the ordinary order of address of the liturgical prayer (to God). In like manner, the ἐλέησον cry occurs also later, e.g. in the St James liturgy after the anamnesis, in both the Greek and the Syrian forms of that liturgy: 'Have mercy on us, Lord, God, almighty Father!'[2] Used in the same way as in the *Apostolic Constitutions*, i.e. as the people's response, now in Greek, now translated, the Kyrie eleison still continues more or less in all Eastern liturgies. But the diaconal litany to which it answers shows almost throughout the prayer-address to Christ, as is the case already in the fifth century in the *Testament of our Lord*.[3] Or on the other hand the term 'Lord' simply leaves open the question—which seems of small moment for this unassuming prayer of petition—of the exact sense of the address.[4]

[1] PG 86, 453; Dölger 52.

[2] Br. 53, 17; 88, 7. The address to God is presupposed in the ἐλέησον of the people by various passages which F. Probst, *Liturgie des 4. Jahrhunderts*, lists from the Fathers, e.g. pp. 51 f. (Eusebius). 170 (Chrysostom).

[3] See above, p. 17. That the address to Christ was early employed in this popular prayer is deducible from the account of St Athanasius, *Ap. ad Const.* 10 (Br. 507, 47): 'At the invitation to the prayer for the well-being of the emperor, the people cried with one voice: Χριστέ, βοήθει Κωνσταντίῳ! Other texts, however, given in Brightman at the same passage show that the practice in this respect was not yet fixed. Also, Chrysostom occasionally assumes the address to Christ where he comes to speak of the intercessory prayer and paraphrases it as it is spoken by the people: 'We remember the departed . . . and beg of the lamb that lies before us.' *In I Cor. hom.* 41, 4 (PG 61, 361). He also makes the angels direct their prayer to Christ when they hold out to the Lord, instead of an olive-branch, his body (the Host), to beg for those for whom he has given his life. *De incompreh. Dei natura* h. 3, 7 (PG 48, 726).

[4] The Acts use the word 'Lord' in an equally indeterminate manner. '. . . It seems at times almost as if Acts had chosen a name common to God and Christ only because it was unnecessary to say more precisely whether the matter under discussion were to be attributed to God or to Christ' (S. Herner in A. Klawek 86, n. 4). This is true also of a short prayer of petition, Acts 1:24 f.

By 500 there is evidence for the Kyrie in its Greek form also in
the West.[1] In Gaul it concludes the chant of the 'Aius' (*"Ἅγιος ὁ
θεός*; Trisagion), a chant regarded also in the Roman Good Friday
liturgy as a homage to Christ, and with which it has come from
Constantinople to Gaul. In accordance with its origin and principal
use, the Kyrie in the Rule of St Benedict and even later is called
simply *litania*. It was probably only to imprint on it more clearly the
reference to Christ that in Rome as early as the end of the sixth
century it was made to alternate, in any long repetition, with
the *Christe eleison*.[2]

These and similar forms of popular prayers of petition which
found their way into the Mass liturgy remained a secondary element
which now and again were added, to a greater or less degree, to the
ancient eucharistic and sacrificial prayer without further altering its
course. On the other hand, the direction taken in the struggle
against Arianism led in the course of time in different areas of the
Church to room being made, even in the inner domain of the Mass,
for the prayer-address to Christ. The common opinion that already
in the fourth century the prayer to Christ had at once been seized
upon as a weapon against the Arians of the time, so as to confront

[1] For a detailed treatment of the Kyrie eleison, see *Missarum Sollemnia*[5] I, 429–46.
The self-evident nature of private prayers, and still more of simple invocations
directed to Christ after the early Christian period (cf. above p. 164), hardly
needed a reference. However, the 'Jesus-prayer', practised after the fourth century,
particularly in the East, deserves a mention; see H. Vorgrimler, 'Jesusgebet':
*Lexikon f. Theologie und Kirche* V (1960) 964–6.

[2] The order, Kyrie, Christe, Kyrie came only later. It receives its trinitarian
interpretation first with Amalar of Metz in the ninth century; cf. Jungmann
*Missarum Sollemnia*[5] I, 439 f. The Kyrie, Christe, Kyrie also introduce our litanies,
being followed, probably because of the trinitarian interpretation, by the invocation of the three divine Persons. However, this latter also is here only of later date.
Before the enlargement to the litany of saints, the oldest litany appears to have
been simply a prayer to Christ. The different petitions were followed by the
response: 'Miserere nobis, libera nos Domine, te rogamus audi nos.' Cf. also the
related *laudes gallicanae*, e.g. at the beginning of the papal Mass in Mabillon's Ordo
Romanus XII, 2 (PL 78, 1064 f.). They begin with the threefold invocation:
'Exaudi Christe.' The fourth invocation is: '*Salvator mundi*', answered by: 'tu illum
adjuva.' This response is also retained in the following invocation of the saints. It
is ended by the Kyrie; cf. Jungmann *Missarum Sollemnia*[5] I, 498. A series of petitions
expressly addressed to Christ, and which the people answer with κύριε ἐλέησον, is
also found already in the Egyptian Gregorius anaphora. Ren. I, 106 f, 110 f.

them with a loud confession of the divinity of Christ, is, certainly, in-
correct. It would have been a blunt weapon. Even the Arians
ascribed some kind of divinity to Christ. Indeed they prayed to him.
According to the Arian fragments published by A. Mai, even the
Holy Spirit worships the Son, that is, he alone without a mediator,
just as the Son praises the Father. And also the humanity of Christ
is drawn into this worship, with express reference to the example of
St Stephen: 'In ipso corpore, in quo salvavit genus humanum, in
ipso in dextera virtutis Dei adoratur ab omnibus.'[1] Nor is this
affected by the fact that prayer to the Son appears only as a preliminary stage to the worship proper which belongs to the Father.
In the Holy Spirit all creatures take their place by the Son and then,
through the Son, glorify the Father.—It is not strictly speaking a
question of the divinity and adorability of the Son, but of the identity
and unity of substance, of the ὁμοούσιος, and therefore of the *equal*
adorability of the Son with the Father. This was well expressed
when the same doxology was offered to the Father with the Son
(μεθ' οὗ) and with the Holy Spirit; but not merely by praying in
general to Christ, when the apparent exclusion of the Son in the
single address to the Father might again serve the Arians as a
counter argument, for there the Catholics themselves allegedly
denied worship to the Son. After the dogmatic struggle was extended also to the Holy Spirit, a motto came into being that
appropriately characterized the anti-Arian attitude from then on,
and which we meet in the different liturgies of the East: τριαδικὴ
πίστις. To cherish belief in the Trinity, that is regarded as the first
and last criterion of the true faith.[2]

---

[1] PL 13, 618 f.

[2] The slogan must already have existed before the Nestorian schism. We find it
in the Egyptian St Basil anaphora: 'Εν τριαδικῇ πίστει ἕως ἐσχάτης ἡμῶν ἀναπνοῆς
ἡμᾶς τελείωσον (Ren. I, 88); also in the Ethiopic intercessory prayer: 'Perfect
unto us the faith of the Trinity unto our last breath' (Br. 229, 13); but also among
the East Syrians, in the Mass (Br. 250, 21), as in the baptismal rite: 'As our souls
agree in the one perfect faith in the blessed Trinity . .' (G. Diettrich, *Die nestorianische Taufliturgie* 29). On the same formula (fides Trinitatis) in the West cf.
J. A. Jungmann, *Liturgisches Erbe und pastorale Gegenwart* (Innsbruck 1960) 44–52.
Cf. also the cry: ἁγία τριὰς ἐλέησον ἡμᾶς (Br. 155, 22), which in the Coptic liturgy
is still in Greek; likewise the blessing: Καὶ ἔσται ἡ χάρις . . . τῆς ἁγίας . . . τριάδος
μετὰ πάντων ἡμῶν (Br. 61, 14; 101, 13), which occurs in similar fashion in the

of his godhead ('tecum, Deus Pater, et cum Spiritu Sancto'), so also new ways of ending are now formed in which the same is said simply of God: 'Deus noster, qui vivis.' Thus the Mediator theme is already obliterated and there is no longer any reason for not addressing oneself in the liturgical prayer also to Christ, to the Son, especially when, perhaps, a feast is already dedicated to him. At the same time, remains of its earlier content might still be used as empty forms, e.g., 'praesta quaesumus Domine, ut quod temporaliter gerimus, aeternis gaudiis consequamur. Amen. Per te Dominum et Redemptorem nostrum, qui vivis cum Patre et regnas cum Spiritu Sancto'.[1] Or new phrases might be composed as substitutes for it, obsecration formulas in which, instead of the Mediator, through whom we have access to God, reference is made rather to God's or the Son's goodness and mercy.[2] Such an obsecration formula, specially composed for the prayer to Christ, was that in Spain at the end of the prayer for peace: 'Quia tu es pax vera', or that developed on Frankish soil: 'Salvator mundi, qui vivis et regnas.'

The new attitude in religious life which was brought about in Spain and Gaul[3] through religious struggle found direct expression here in liturgical prayer. The same tendency, however, was at work beyond these countries and became an important factor in the further history of the religious life in general in the West. Parallel with the decay of prayer through Christ, or, where it was already firmly rooted, the decline in its esteem,[4] the theme of the glorified

---

[1] MEL V, 242, n. 1; cf. above pp. 98 f, 103 f. Our end-formula 'qui vivis et regnas cum Deo Patre in unitate Spiritus Sancti' would most probably have originated in this way here or in Gaul; 'in unitate Spiritus Sancti' was now equivalent to 'cum Spiritu Sancto'; cf. above p. 210, n. 2.

[2] See above, pp. 93 f., 98 f., 92 f.; cf. for the East, pp. 73, 79 f., 84 f.

[3] The empire of the Arian West Goths embraced in varying degree the south of France also; and the Burgundian princes were for a long time on the side of the Arians.

[4] How strong the tendency had now become to see in this practice an obscuring of the divinity of Christ is shown by a remark of so late an author as B. Gavanti (*Thesaurus sacrorum rituum* [Venice, 1630], p. 25); he gives the rule: 'Si ad ipsam Trinitatem dirigatur oratio, dicitur: qui vivis etc., *ne videatur separari Christus a Trinitate.*' It is remarkable that he should here have overlooked the unconcern in this matter of the missal of Pius V, which ends the prayers 'Suscipe, sancta Trinitas' and 'Placeat tibi, sancta Trinitas' with 'Per Christum Dominum nostrum'.

This particular cultivation of the trinitarian theme in connexion with the anti-Arian attitude automatically implies a closer attention to the divinity in Christ, while the position of Mediator, appropriate to him in his humanity, was in practice allowed to fall more and more into the background, as it was constantly misinterpreted by the Arians. The Vandal Arians in North Africa in the time of St Fulgentius[1] in the psalm-chant ostentatiously used the doxology 'Gloria Patri per Filium in Spiritu Sancto', as a confession of their heresy; while an Arian Council of Toledo of the year 580 under King Leovigild still demanded of apostate Catholics the acceptance of this doxology, whence it was rejected by the third Catholic synod of Toledo of 589, without the doxology itself being declared heretical.[2] Indeed, the traditional formula 'per Christum' was still used, both in Syria and in Spain; but alongside it we also find used for the same purpose in both countries the typical expression 'per te Deus',[3] a symptom of how much the meaning of the former formula, as a reference to Christ, the Mediator of the prayer, was obscured, even where it still appears. Just as the 'per te Deus' may correspond to a 'propter te, propter nomen tuum', so could the 'per Christum' be taken for a 'propter Christum' ($\delta\iota\grave{\alpha}$ $X\rho\iota\sigma\tau\acute{o}\nu$, no longer $\delta\iota\grave{\alpha}$ $X\rho\iota\sigma\tauο\hat{v}$). Along with the concern for the Mediator formula, there vanishes also, however, the most important reason why the prayer in the liturgy had been directed up to now not to Christ, but

innovations. Thus the celebration of a special feast in honour of the Holy Trinity was still rejected by Pope Alexander II (d. 1073), with the remark that the Trinity is in any case honoured every day. A. Klaus, *Ursprung und Verbreitung der Dreifaltigkeitsmesse* (Werl, 1938), 106–29.

[1] Ep. 14, 37 (PL 65, 425); *Contra Fab.* fragm. 34 (PL 65, 815).

[2] Mansi, IX, 986. C. J. Hefele, *A History of Christian Councils* (Edinburgh, 1871–96), IV, 405, 416 f.

[3] See above, pp. 20, 99, 104; cf. p. 169. It is the same 'per te Deus' which we met in the apocryphal *Acts of Peter* and which the African synods opposed. A parallel phenomenon in the same three areas is the occasional direction of the Our Father to Christ; we find this in the apocryphal *Acts of Thomas*, in the Monophysite and in the Gallic liturgy; see above, pp. 49, n. 1; 93; 98, n. 5; 168, n. 7. The theological background for this uniting of God and Christ is, admittedly, essentially different in all three cases. The same fruit can grow on different soils. The Modalist appearance of forms born of the anti-Arian zeal of Monophysitism has led P. Cagin to trace the liturgy of the *Testament of our Lord* to the Modalist Monarchians of the second century (*L'Eucharistia* [Paris, 1912] 328 f.).

always to God. Indeed, since the traditional liturgical prayer was frequently made to address, no longer simply God, but God the Father, it was easy to see the lack of a prayer to Christ as a gap which it was proper to fill. Thus there resulted, in places where the anti-Arian current was strongest, from this side also the custom of the address to Christ in the liturgical prayer.[1]

In the *West*, the step could hardly have been taken before the sixth century. The extant remains of the Gallican liturgy, with the greater part of those texts which obviously were composed for the Gallican schema, agree in address and end-formula with the Roman; this applies especially to the older texts.[2] Spain is the first to show the change. Here, the Mozarabic Mass formularies are so arranged from the beginning that the prayer to Christ can at almost every point take the place of a prayer with the older type of address, without the end-formula having to be changed. As is well known, however, liturgical composition begins in Spain appreciably later than in Gaul.[3] Characteristically, even here there are primarily texts which may belong to an older structure of the liturgy, more closely related to the Roman, in which the priesthood of Christ and his office of Mediator are still clearly expressed, viz. many Prefaces and the embolism after the Pater noster.[4] But just as in the end-formula of the latter the 'vivere et regnare' of our Lord is already understood

---

[1] The final consequence of this change is the introduction of the prayer to the Holy Spirit beside that to the Son. Formal orationes of this sort have, however, attained significance only in Armenia (see above, p. 84). A prayer to the Holy Ghost opens now also the Byzantine Mass (Br. 353, 13). In the present-day Roman liturgy, under this heading there is only a prayer in the pontifical for the consecration of an abbot; in the Mozarabic, the Mass for Pentecost has various prayers to the Holy Spirit (MEL VI, 322, 336, 342 f.).

[2] See above, p. 90, n. 1. Even in 470, Archbishop Claudianus Mamertus of Vienne, which at the time lay in the sphere of influence of the dominant Arian Burgundians, with reference to Hebrews 4:15, laid great stress on the idea of the mediation of prayer through Christ in his humanity: 'Pontifex ille, credo, est, qui principaliter apud divinitatem summae Trinitatis humani generis oblata sacrificat, peccata expiat, vota commendat.' *De statu animae* I, 3 (CSEL 11, p. 36, 13. Engelbrecht). And even in the Mone Masses the older prayer schema was only to a small extent replaced by the prayer to Christ; see above, p. 88 ff.

[3] Cf. F. Probst, *Die Abendländische Messe vom. 5. bis zum 8. Jahrhundert* 379; cf. 391 f.

[4] See above, p. 99 f.

Outside the doxology, also, the opportunity was taken here and there to give expression in the liturgy to the acknowledgement of the three divine Persons. Where the Sanctus had formerly been followed by 'Holy art thou . . ., holy, too, thy only-begotten Son, our Lord and God Jesus Christ'[1] and a praise of redemption, now immediately after the Son the Holy Ghost is added: 'Holy also the Holy Spirit.'[2]

An increase in this trinitarian tendency again after the fourth century stands out especially in two areas of Christendom: on Monophysite soil where, out of zeal for the confession of Christ's divinity, they let themselves be drawn for a time into error concerning his humanity;[3] and in the Gallic-Spanish area where, up to the end of the sixth century, they were in fact compelled by the struggle against the Arian Visigoths to defend the dogma of the Trinity and to define it ever more clearly. The seventeen synods of Toledo of the fifth to seventh centuries were repeatedly occupied with this, and led to the classical formulation of the dogma in a confession—perhaps of earlier date—of the renowned—though not declared authentic[4]—eleventh synod of 675.[5] As the liturgy is being strongly developed here about this time, we are not surprised to see the threatened basic dogma especially stressed in it.[6]

Greek and Syrian St James anaphora and therefore was probably present already in the fifth century. The threefold Sanctus, *int. al.*, is related already by Theodore of Mopsuestia (d. 428) to the three divine Persons. Also elsewhere the confession of the Trinity is very strongly marked in his Mass commentary; A. Rücker, *Ritus baptismi et Missae quem descripsit Theodorus ep. Mopsuestenus* (Münster, 1933) 28 f.

[1] *Ap. Const.* VIII, 12, 28 f.

[2] Br. 51, 8 and 86, 22 (St James anaphora); Br. 284, 26 (East Syrian Apostles' anaphora); Br. 324, 9 (Byz. Chrysostom liturgy). Cf. Br. 165, 11 (Coptic St Mark anaphora). For the later West Syrian anaphoras, see above, p. 61, n. 2.

[3] This trinitarian tendency is shown, *int. al.*, by the later additions especially in the Syrian *Testament of our Lord*; see above, p. 20.

[4] Cf. H. Lennerz: ZkTh 48 (1924) 322–4.

[5] H. Denzinger–C. Bannwart[14] nos. 275 ff; cf. no. 19; nos. 294 f; no. 296.

[6] See above, p. 102. After the flowering of the Spanish Church in the seventh century liturgical texts, among other literature of Spanish origin, were disseminated, primarily in Ireland and in the Frankish Empire. Such texts were also in front of Alcuin when he edited his appendix to the Gregorianum (E. Bishop: JThSt 8 [1907] 278–94 = *Liturgica historica* 166 ff.). It was from here that there gradually got into the Roman liturgy, also, texts in which, e.g., the 'Sancta Trinitas' is addressed; as also the expressive *Filioque* in the Credo, and the feast of the Holy Trinity itself.—Rome behaved with great reserve towards all these

head of the Church receded;[1] instead, our Lord was contemplated on the one hand in his bitter Passion and death, on the other in his divinity. Thus here also the further development of the liturgical prayer, so far as such was possible, had to take this direction. The predilection for contemplating the Passion of Christ found expression, from the time of Rabanus Maurus and Amalarius of Metz, in the mystical interpretation of the ceremonies of the Mass. In the liturgical prayer, it was able to influence only some later texts of the pontifical.[2] The stronger emphasis on the divinity of Christ, however, was reflected in the prayer to Christ, which was now more widely disseminated even in the realm of the Roman liturgy, primarily in Frankish, British and German dioceses.[3]

But this change did not take place without opposition. The view of the old African synods, that at least liturgical prayer should not give up its monumental lines in favour of later and narrower forms of piety, survived in some areas with clear reference to the wording of the current regulations. In a collection of canons of about the ninth century appears a direction 'De regula collectarum: Nullus in precibus nisi ad Patrem dirigat orationem, secundum illud: Si quid petieritis Patrem in nomine meo. Et ut prius eas cum instructioribus tractet'.[4] It could have

---

[1] A related fact is that the Church now also loses practical significance as a special religious entity, as 'holy Church', as 'unity in the Holy Spirit'. It is now her organizational structure which is regarded, with the different rights, powers and means of grace which she carries in her bosom for individuals. The further development of devotional practice in the West in the early middle ages, which resulted logically from the anti-Arian attitude persisting from the era of struggle, I have sought to recount in the study, 'Die Abwehr des germanischen Arianismus und der Umbruch der religiösen Kultur im frühen Mittelalter': ZkTh 69 (1947) 36–99 (with revision in the volume *Liturgisches Erbe und pastorale Gegenwart* [Innsbruck, 1960] 3–86).

[2] Cf. the consecration of the altar equipment. For the Byzantine liturgy, cf. above, p. 90, n. 1. The same is true, *int. al.*, of the East Syrian liturgy.

[3] Cf. above, p. 115 ff.

[4] Mansi, XII, Appendix II, 109, in a capitulary 'datum in synodo cui interfuit Bonifatius apostolicae sedis legatus'. In reality, these decrees are an extract from the work of a pseudonymous Benedictus Levita (PL 97, 698–912), who has been connected with Pseudo-Isidore. The above text occurs there 1, 3, n. 418 (PL 97, 850 f.) in nearly the same form, only without the quotation John 16:23. An allusion to the *regula collectarum* is found also in Remigius of Auxerre (d. 908), *Expositio* (PL 101, 1255A).

been a claim that assisted the advance of the Roman liturgy against the Gallic liturgies. The underlying ideas were, indeed, on longer so influential as to prevent a compounding process the products of which then flowed back even into the home of the Roman liturgy.

To some extent, the development is the same *in the East*. It begins here, however, even earlier. Even in the period when in the liturgy primarily the trinitarian dogma is still underlined, we find also attempts to combat heresy at the same time by giving stronger emphasis to the divine grandeur of Christ. This should not be overlooked even in the names for Christ and God, and particularly in the Preface in the *Euchologium* of Serapion; but it may not in every case be attributable to anti-heretical design. In the Greek St Mark liturgy, the old address, 'Father of our Lord Jesus Christ' is already enlarged, and regularly goes 'Father of our Lord and God and Saviour Jesus Christ' (κύριε ὁ θεὸς ἡμῶν, ὁ πατὴρ τοῦ κυρίου καὶ θεοῦ καὶ σωτῆρος ἡμῶν 'Ιησοῦ Χριστοῦ). With the Copts, we generally see 'and King of us all' (καὶ παμβασιλέως) inserted in addition after the title 'Saviour'. In fact, only the frequent use of these titles was new. We already find their use, precisely in this combination, in Irenaeus, when he says that on the last day every knee will bend before Christ Jesus, our Lord and God and Saviour and King.[1] Another way of bringing out the greatness of Christ consists in the prayer and sacrifice offered to God being likewise 'to the glory' of our Lord.[2] In the work *De virginitate* ascribed to St Athanasius, however, there already appears the endeavour to draw Christ into the prayer-address with the Father, but then the usual ending is allowed to get into a somewhat unusual position: 'Ο θεὸς ὁ παντοκράτωρ καὶ κύριος ἡμῶν 'Ιησοῦς Χριστός ... αἰνοῦμέν σε ... κύριε, ... ἁγίασον δὲ ἡμῶν τὸ πνεῦμα καὶ τὴν ψυχὴν καὶ τὸ σῶμα διὰ τοῦ ἠγαπημένου σου παιδός, τοῦ κυρίου ἡμῶν 'Ιησοῦ

---

[1] *Adv. haer.* I, 10, I (PG 7, 549): Χριστῷ 'Ιησοῦ τῷ κυρίῳ ἡμῶν καὶ θεῷ καὶ σωτῆρι καὶ βασιλεῖ.

[2] Cf. above, p. 14. The phrase is frequent in the formularies of the Gallic type; examples also in A. Ebner, *Quellen und Forschungen zur Geschichte und Kunstgeschichte des Missale Romanum im Mittelalter* (Freiburg, 1896), pp. 414, 419.

Χριστοῦ, μεθ' οὗ.[1] In this combination of the Son with the Father, the ὁμοούσιος actually to some extent makes itself felt, which cannot be said of the simple isolated prayer to Christ. It makes its presence felt finally also, when, at the cost indeed of the clarity of other fundamental ideas, the prayer-address goes a step further by moving to and fro in one and the same prayer between Father and Son, God and Christ, as is the case, particularly, in the *Testament of our Lord*.[2] Of the christological ending of the prayer, in this work, nothing is retained except formula-type remnants, as well as re-moulded forms which avoid every appearance of a subordination of Christ, of a permanent mediatorship. The Monophysite regions from which the work derives went to extremes in the defence of the divinity of Christ. As Fulgentius rightly remarks,[3] for Eutyches there is as a consequence no longer room for the priesthood of Christ. Thus it is no surprise when we find here at the end of the fifth century, in addition, the liturgical prayer to Christ alone, in every shape, and even at the heart of the Mass, in the anamnesis, and with the deliberate alteration of an existing model.[4] In the wider domain of liturgical prayer, however, prayers to Christ occur earlier; in their formation, anti-Arian feeling and popular custom could have worked together.

The *Euchologion* of the Byzantine liturgy contains a prayer for the dead[5] which is addressed to Christ and praises him for redemption in expressions which again show an obvious relationship with the eucharistic prayer of Hippolytus. W. Weissbrodt has already

---

[1] c. 14 (TU 29, 2a, p. 49. von der Goltz). For the singular σέ, cf. the parallel manner of expression of Serapion and of Clement of Alexandria, above, pp. 23, n. 2; 182 f. The twofold address to God and Christ with singular recapitulation following on it is not a completely unusual phenomenon in Christian antiquity. It is explicitly justified by Augustine, *Enarr. in ps.* 5 (PL 36, 83 f.), where he relates the address of the psalm (Psalm 5:3), *Rex meus et Deus meus*, to Christ and God, and then remarks: *recte primo: Rex meus et deinde Deus meus. Nec tamen dixit Intendite, sed Intende.* For further examples, and particularly that in the *Te Deum*, cf. J. A. Jungmann, 'Quos pretioso sanguine redemisti': ZkTh 61 (1937) 105–7.

[2] Cf. above, p. 18 f.; cf. p. 67.

[3] Ep. 14, 38 (PL 65, 426).          [4] See above, p. 18 f.

[5] J. Goar, *Euchologion sive Rituale Graecorum* (Paris, 1647), p. 526: Θεὸς τῶν πνευμάτων . . . Χριστὲ ὁ θεὸς ἡμῶν. . . .

demonstrated this prayer for the dead *int. al.* in sepulchral use in two Egyptian grave-inscriptions dated 489 and 492.[1]

Among the six prayers to Christ of the Greek St Mark liturgy, that at the prothesis is found also in part in the Coptic and the Ethiopic liturgy and would therefore likewise derive from the fifth century. That here also the trinitarian idea stood behind the address to Christ and that the latter was still in fact unusual is shown by the christological ending with the ordinary χάριτι formula, obviously still alone customary at the time.[2]

In the same place as in the Syrian *Testament of our Lord*, viz. in the anamnesis, and in the same region of the Greek-speaking Syrian Christendom of Monophysite tendency, we see the address to Christ emerge in the *St James anaphora*. Even the time of the change of address must be about the same. In the mid-fifth century, before the St James anaphora is accepted throughout the whole of Syria and its tradition is divided into three distinct branches, the old order of address is the rule in the anamnesis, as in the whole anaphora.[3] Towards the end of the seventh century, in the recension of Jacob of Edessa, on the other hand, in the anamnesis and in the last prayer of blessing the address to Christ supplanted it, and at these two

---

[1] *Ein ägyptischer christlicher Grabstein: Verzeichnis der Vorlesungen zu Braunsberg W.–S.* (1905–6), 23. Reproduction of the second with parallel text by Goar in C. M. Kaufmann, *Handbuch der altchristlichen Epigraphik* (Freiburg, 1917), 147 f. Here the trinitarian doxology, into which even in the inscription the prayer passes, though in bad orthography, shows the pure Syrian type: καὶ σοὶ τὴν δόξαν ἀναπέμπομεν τῷ πατρὶ καὶ τῷ υἱῷ καὶ τῷ ἁγίῳ πνεύματι. In Kaufmann, there occurs on p. 145 yet another prayer for the departed, dated 409, from an Alexandrian epitaph; it is directed to Christ, and has liturgical overtones throughout: Ὁ θεὸς ὁ παντοκράτωρ, ὁ ὤν, προὼν καὶ μέλλων, Ἰησοῦς ὁ Χριστὸς, ὁ υἱὸς τοῦ θεοῦ τοῦ ζῶντος, μνήσθητι τῆς κοιμήσεως καὶ ἀναπαύσεως τῆς δούλης σου. In the case of a more remote epigraphic prayer to Christ from Nubia assigned to the year 344 (Stele of Papa Sinethe, ibid. p. 146), this dating is, however, not sufficiently probable. The doubts raised against it by A. Baumstark (ibid. p. 146, n. 1) gain greater weight from the circumstance that it is again the Syrian prayer-doxology that here appears in the same wording as that just given and whose history was outlined above.

[2] Δέσποτα Ἰησοῦ Χριστὲ κύριε, ὁ συνάναρχος λόγος τοῦ ἀνάρχου πατρὸς καὶ τοῦ ἁγίου πνεύματος, ὁ μέγας ἀρχιερεύς . . . ἐπίφανον τὸ πρόσωπόν σου ἐπὶ τὸν ἄρτον τοῦτον . . . χάριτι . . . τοῦ μονογενοῦς σου υἱοῦ, δι' οὗ καὶ μεθ' οὗ (Br. 124 f.).

[3] See above, pp. 56 ff.

points and only at these it has remained a fixed norm for all later anaphoras. Out of the intervening period seem to stem certain anaphoras which, in the use of the address to Christ, go beyond this limit which was fixed later.[1] In the St James anaphora of Jacob of Edessa, a retrograde development has already begun, a counter-movement against the tendency appearing in the *Testament* towards a sort of practical pan-Christism which treats the prayer-address to Christ and that to God as simply equivalent. This retrogression is shown here in particular in the carefully harmonious ending of the prayer to Christ in the anamnesis. To the author of the *Testament* there would have been no difficulty in making even the people's cry for mercy to 'God the almighty Father'—which was perhaps already fixed—simply follow on the prayer to Christ. Here, however, a phrase is inserted which takes Christ expressly as Mediator of this invocation: 'Thy people implore thee [and *through thee and with thee thy Father*, saying]: have mercy on us, God, almighty Father.' And also this phrase, proper to the Jacobite branch, also recurs from now on in all Jacobite anaphoras.

If we now consider, of the two anaphoras likewise stemming from Syria which the Copts have added to their St Mark liturgy, the one in which the new prayer-address to Christ is used consistently throughout its length, viz. the *Gregorius anaphora*, and if we may assume for the liturgical prayer among the Syrian Monophysites a fairly continuous line of development, it follows at once that this anaphora must have originated about the sixth century, at a period when the floodtide of Monophysite thought coincided with the commencement of fresh liturgical composition among the West Syrians. When, however, the counter-movement grew strong and a revision and reform of the liturgical prayer began, this anaphora, which departed much too far from the ancient tradition, was removed from the Syrian-Jacobite liturgical stock. It had, however, in the meantime found a home among the Copts of the same belief, whom elsewhere we see intent on taking Syrian material into their liturgy.[2]

---

[1] Above, p. 57 n. 26.          [2] See above, p. 189, n. 1; p. 199, n. 1.

Certain pointers to the Syrian origin of the Gregorius anaphora which
T. Schermann has already taken into consideration have already been
noticed in passing.[1]

A liturgical fragment found in Egypt with the same order of
address is discussed by A. Baumstark in the *Jahrbuch für Liturgiewissenschaft*.[2] It is an anaphora extract of which the centre point is
the sanctus. The existence of the sanctus alone would seem to
invalidate the assignment to so early a liturgical sphere as the gnostic
and gnostic-inclined circles. Further, the way in which the sanctus
is continued points to the type of the West Syrian anaphoras:
ἀληθῶς ἅγιος . . .—Here belongs also the εὐχὴ κλάσεως, which
H. Goussen[3] has translated from the Georgian St James liturgy. It
is directed to Christ and contains institution account and anamnesis.
Goussen explains it as the Canon-prayer of St Athanasius. This
attribution and dating is indefensible. The end-doxology belongs to
the Syrian type: 'Thine is the kingdom . . ., of the Father and of the
Son and of the Holy Ghost, now . . .'; it lends weight to the view
that here we are dealing with the sister-formulary to the Gregorius
anaphora.

The same forces as in the *Syrian Testament of our Lord* will have led
to the to-and-fro movement of the prayer-address which is frequently
noticeable in *Abyssinia*; and thus also to the remoulding of the
anamnesis in Hippolytus' anaphora into a prayer to Christ.[4] The
one-sided emphasis on the divinity of Christ among the Monophysites, even where no Arian opposition made it necessary, must
automatically have weakened the understanding of the Mediator
position of Christ and consequently of prayer through Christ.

Nevertheless there is, especially on Egyptian soil, yet another
factor to take into account in the changing of the prayer-address in
the anamnesis: the marked participation of the people who, immediately after the words of consecration, anticipate the anamnesis

---

[1] Pp. 38, n. 2; 35, nn. 2, 3; 40, n. 1. Cf. also in the following chapter, p. 240. Syrian
is, in particular, the insertion of the intercessory prayer after the institution account
(instead of in the Preface), the introducing of the Preface with the text 2 Cor. 13:14,
also the form Ἄνω σχῶμεν τὰς καρδίας (Ren. I, 98 f.).
[2] 1 (1921) 133 f.                     [3] *Théol. Revue* 23 (1924) 16 f.
[4] See above, pp. 44 f.; 48; 53 f.

with, as is natural in a simple acclamation, the address to Christ. The custom must here be rather old, as the words in question are still spoken in Greek in the Coptic St Mark anaphora.[1] Also, the fragment of the anamnesis in the papyrus of Dêr-Balyzeh may represent such an acclamation of the people.[2] But the adaptation to the anamnesis-cry of the people cannot by itself explain the switching of the address in the anamnesis-prayer of the priest. Otherwise, it would have penetrated also, for example, the other branches of the St James anaphora. Besides, the anamnesis-prayer always expresses the formal offering of the sacrifice and it must have been striking if this now followed to Christ instead of simply to God.

The reference to *Monophysitism* as explaining the change in prayer-attitude of Eastern communities should not be taken as maintaining a heretical development. The matter has become the subject of more detailed discussion; a comprehensive account is available by H. Engberding, 'Das chalkedonische Christusbild und die Liturgien der monophysitischen Kirchengemeinschaften': *Das Konzil von Chalkedon* II (Würzburg, 1953), 697–733. P. 701, also, more on the question of published literature. In his view, the disregard of the humanity of Christ which reveals itself, especially in the recession of the Mediator formula, and in fact is particularly noticeable in the areas fallen to Monophysitism—is to be traced not so much to Monophysitism as a doctrine, which, it is stated, was really only a verbal Monophysitism, but essentially to a wave of radical anti-Arianism running through the whole Eastern church. At the same time, however, this radical anti-Arianism can be seen as a tendency, still quite possible within the limits of the true faith, in the direction of Monophysitism. Cf. the section 'Il problema della tendenza "monofisitica" nella cristologia orientale' in B. Schultze 'Problemi di teologia presso gli ortodossi': *Orientalia christiana Periodica* 9 (1943, 135–70) 161–6; A. Raes, 'De byzantijnse Vroomheit en het monophysisme': *Bijdragen* 13 (1952) 298–305 espec. 305. Both articles recount objections of Eastern authors which were directed in the first place against far-reaching ideas which K. Adam has developed in his

---

[1] Similarly, in Syria this acclamation exists in identical form in the Greek and Syrian St James liturgy: Br. 52, 26; 87, 26 (see above, p. 56, n. 2).

[2] There is, it is true, a petition added here to the confession: Τὸν θάνατόν σου καταγγέλλομεν, τὴν ἀνάστασίν σου ὁμολογοῦμεν καὶ δεόμεθα; but for this also the Ethiopic liturgy supplies the parallel: 'We show thy death, Lord, and thine holy Resurrection, we believe thine Ascension; we praise thee and confess thee, *we supplicate thee* and confess thee, O Lord, our God' (Br. 232, 37).

book *Christus unser Bruder* (Regensburg, 1926) referring to the present book; thus, of S. Salaville in his book *Liturgies orientales* (Paris, 1932), of M. Lot-Borodine in the *Revue des sciences phil. et théol.* 24 (1935) 668 f., and of P. Bratsiotis at the theological congress in Athens in 1936. Both authors, however, defended the more narrowly circumscribed theses of the book in question, in particular the interpretation of the concept 'high priest' in the Byzantine liturgy, on which A. Raes, *Orientalia christiana Periodica* 7 (1941) 270, has also written. This does not mean that these theses are not capable of, or do not need, a more exact theological formulation. In that anti-Arianism, it is true, certain conceptions belonging to the even older Logos-Sarx theology seem to have been at work, which in the fourth century crystallized into Apollinarianism, into the view, that is, that the Logos was united in the Incarnation not with a whole human nature but only with the 'flesh', and thus took the place of the intellectual soul; see Engberding 700, 728 ff. For more on this, see *Das Konzil von Chalkedon* (index in the third volume). For the role of neo-Chalcedonism, see below, p. 252 f. It should also be remarked here, as had to be said in answer to S. Salaville, ZkTh 65 (1941) 232 f.: In the attempted explanation which is under discussion, there is no question as to whether, in the circles concerned, the human nature in the earthly life of the Lord or the salvific significance of his human nature has been undervalued (against which, incidentally, Engberding's exposition points in the main), but only whether Christ has been seen in his glorified humanity as Mediator with the Father. Theoretically, it is held even by Severus of Antioch (as Engberding, p. 718, shows) that Christ has remained man even in his glorified state; but a lively awareness of this was certainly lost to the generality—a fact which has equally been established, especially by French authors, of the popular piety of the West.

But how did the striking liturgical *counter-movement among the Syrian Jacobites* come into being? It is connected with a decided change in dogmatic views. The crude Monophysitism, such as Eutyches had advocated and as it faced the Council Fathers at Chalcedon, did not last long. The aphtharto-docetic tendency of Julian of Halicarnassus may have continued its influence in Syria to some degree even beyond the sixth century. However, it was soon realized, both in Syria and in Egypt, that with the evaporation of the humanity of Christ the heart of the Christian faith is destroyed. Especially in the party of the Patriarch Severus of Antioch, it is soon only the saying μία φύσις, ἐκ δύο φυσέων (instead of ἐν δύο φύσεσιν) which is maintained in heretical stubbornness against the Council of Chalcedon. Recourse is had to the Church Fathers, especially to Cyril of Alexandria, whose related manner of expression, directed against Nestorius, lent to their attitude at least a semblance of justification.[1]

The period of the Monophysite crisis coincides with a flowering of Syrian literature in Greek and then in Syriac, which included the liturgical field. Besides numerous anaphora compositions and translations of the same from the Greek into the Syriac, there appear here the first liturgical commentaries that Christian literature has to show. And here we find information on the ideas that must have directed that liturgical reform. The most important of these commentaries is that of *Moses bar Kepha* (813–903).[2] Here the question of the right order of address of the liturgical prayer is fully treated, viz. in connexion with the prayer of blessing at the end of the St

[1] Cf. J. Tixeront, *Histoire des dogmes* III[2] (Paris, 1912), 117–27. He characterizes this later tendency as 'un duophysisme de fond qui ne veut pas s'avouer, avec un monophysisme de langage presque absolu'. The Church, nevertheless, had to treat them as heretics because they on their side continued to regard the dogmatic formulations of Chalcedon as false teaching. Also in Egypt the protector of Eutyches himself, the Patriarch Dioscurus, had personally advocated a very moderate Monophysitism, which nevertheless in practice turned into Monotheletism (F. Haase, 'Patriarch Dioscur I. von Alexandrien' [*Kirchengesch. Abhandlungen*, ed. M. Sdralek, 6 (Breslau, 1908), pp. 145–233], pp. 228 ff.). A creed which in the Coptic and in the Ethiopic liturgy precedes the reception of communion, and which seems to have been prescribed in order to keep away Catholics and members of alien sects which had no public worship of their own, contains only expressions which indeed could be intended heretically, but which in their wording are no more Monophysite than the 'Gloria Patri per Filium' is Arian. The Eucharist is there declared the life-giving flesh of the only-begotten Son of God, which he took from the Mother of God and made 'one' with the Godhead. The addition 'without admixture' etc. could have been meant, in alleged opposition to the Catholics, to stress above all that in this the divinity was in no wise diminished, just as in other passages the ἀφθαρσία of the body of Christ is given prominence. See the text of the creed Br. 185, 235 f.; Ren. I, 23 f., 83 (here the obviously original Greek text within the St Basil anaphora: ὅτι αὐτή ἐστιν ἡ σάρξ ζωοποιὸς τοῦ μονογενοῦς σου ... ἐποίησεν αὐτὴν μίαν σὺν τῇ θεότητι αὐτοῦ, μὴ ἐν μίξει μηδὲ ἐν φυρμῷ μηδὲ ἐν ἀλλοιώσει.) The creed is also in the Gregorius anaphora, Ren. I, 36, 123, only changed in style to the address to Christ. For the historical exposition of this confession, cf. E. Renaudot I, pp. c–ciii.

[2] R. H. Connolly–H. W. Codrington, *Two Commentaries on the Jacobite Liturgy, by George, bishop of the Arab tribes, and Moses bar Kepha* (London, 1913).

James anaphora, which is directed to Christ.[1] Moses remarks on this: 'It should also be appreciated that all prayers in the anaphora are directed to the Father, and this comes from the fact that the sacrificing priest is a type of Christ himself, who became a Mediator between God and men, wherefore he speaks of his own body and blood, since he represents the person of Christ.' For this reason, he (the priest) also passes at the end of the anamnesis-prayer, which admittedly is directed to Christ (this is accepted as a fact), back again to the address to the Father, the Father being implored through him and with him.[2] The anamnesis prayer is the only justifiable exception: in it 'the priest praises the Son because through him we have gained access to the Father and because he is the way and the door to the Father. If, however, in the anaphora (outside this case) a prayer is found which is not directed to the Father—the error may be due to a scribe or to a priest who is badly instructed or not versed in the Scriptures—then we must correct it. . .'.

Here we have a developed theory. What is special to this theory is primarily the view that the priest takes the place of our Lord in the whole anaphora and only in the anaphora; to this is then tied the practical conclusion regarding the prayer-address, again precisely within the compass of the anaphora. The former view is already expressed earlier by Moses when in the commentary on the liturgy he passes via a discussion of the sacrificial gifts to the anaphora itself: 'What rank the priest holds.—And we say that the priest is in the place of Christ, who broke his body before him that begat him and distributed to his disciples'.[3] Moses' presentation of the priestly office, which later recurs in a similar form in the liturgical commentary of Dionysius bar Salibi (d. 1171)[4] may, however, be

[1] See above, p. 56.
[2] In this 'with', Christ is taken with the Father, not with the people; see above, pp. 63; 22 f.; likewise in Dionysius bar Salibi, c. 14 (*Corpus scriptorum christ. orient.*, Scr. Syri, ser. II, 93, p. 79. Labourt).
[3] This continues: 'So he also said: This is my body, which for you etc.'; then he adds: 'Secondly: The priest is moreover the tongue, which is in the head of the body of the faithful, which makes supplication to God for the whole church. Thirdly: he is also a painter, who portrays spiritual things by the mysteries. Fourthly again he is mediator between God and men.' P. 35.
[4] c. 6 (p. 52. Labourt).

traced further back.[1] Indeed, it seems to be of older common Syrian stock, for the same ideas and phrases also recur,[2] freely arranged, in the commentary on the East Syrian liturgy which Connolly has published as a work of Narsai (d. ca. 502).[3] This is, of course, not to say that the conclusion regarding the style of prayer-address must also at all times have been tied to this presentation of the priestly office.[4]

[1] It is found already in the same connexion in the older, shorter liturgical commentary which R. H. Connolly publishes simultaneously from a manuscript of the eighth to ninth century and which he ascribes to George, bishop of the Arab tribes (d. 724), a pupil and friend of Jacob of Edessa (agreeing with A. Baumstark, *Geschichte der syrischen Literatur* 258). The commentator says (*Two commentaries* 16): 'But the priest enacts three (parts): first a likeness of our Redeemer and Lifegiver who offered himself an oblation to God his Father for us so that that he was reconciled to us.' He adds likewise: 'secondly he is the tongue which is in the ecclesiastical body; thirdly he portrays spiritual images by a mystery.' Moses has only further analysed the thought of George, as the first and fourth parts of his commentary.

[2] The priest as representative of Christ is a theme which Chrysostom strongly emphasized, and indeed even for the beginning of the Mass celebration. It is also to Chrysostom that Narsai appeals in several passages of his commentary. That the priest at the accomplishment of the sacrifice, in the moment of consecration, represents Christ the Lord is of course a universal Christian idea which existed already with the doctrine of the consecratory power of the words of institution, which indeed are spoken in the person of the Lord. But awareness of this idea was here especially vivid. This is supported by the wording of the institution account in the St James anaphora: λαβὼν τὸν ἄρτον ἐπὶ τῶν... χειρῶν... καὶ ἀναδείξας σοι τῷ θεῷ καὶ πατρί, εὐχαριστήσας, ἁγιάσας... (Br. 51, 27; 87, 2. The same text, incidentally, occurs in the Byzantine St Basil liturgy, Br. 327 f.). Here the fact was clearly brought out that Christ himself at the Last Supper had offered the same sacrifice. Thus, Eutychius (Patriarch of Constantinople 522–82) understands the words when he remarks with obvious reference to them: Μυστικῶς οὖν ἑαυτὸν ἔθυσεν, ὅτε... λαβὼν τὸν ἄρτον εὐχαριστήσας ἀνέδειξε. De paschate et de ss. eucharistia c. 2 (PG 86, 2393; Br. 529. 529, 16). The same conception is shown for the St James liturgy by Jacob of Edessa in his letter to the Presbyter Thomas: '... We hold the pᵉristo of the bread and show it to God the Father as the Son also showed it and say: when he had given thanks etc' (Br. 493, 24). It is more distinctly expressed by the Maronite revisor of Dionysius bar Salibi (c. 30; Assemani V [= 1, IV, pars II], 350): 'Illum Patri ostendit, ut sacrificium se offerre Patri... demonstret.' Just as then in many places the power of the consecration was attributed to the whole central portion of the Mass without demarking a precise passage (epiklesis question), so the priest's representation of Christ may here be extended in consequence over the whole domain of the eucharistic and sacrificial prayers, i.e. to the whole anaphora.

[3] R. H. Connolly, *The liturgical homilies of Narsai* 7, 10 ff. Against this attribution see A. Baumstark, *Geschichte der syrischen Literatur* 112, 348.

[4] Formerly the idea of the priest deputizing in the anaphora was exploited in a quite different direction, as will be shown in the following chapter.

But it must surely be supposed that this conclusion took root among the Syrian Jacobites precisely at the time when the revision of liturgical prayer began, and that therefore the revived conception of the mediatorship which Christ exercises in his humanity in the sacrifice and also exercises through the priest, had here a regenerative influence on liturgical prayer.[1] We see its continuing influence also after Jacob of Edessa in the liturgical texts: the δι' οὗ of the end-doxology, which had already almost disappeared, slowly returns and in the textus receptus of the St James anaphora it has already become the rule again just as in Egypt from Cyril of Alexandria onwards (δι' οὗ καὶ μεθ' οὗ) it has remained the rule in the ancient texts.[2]

Thus it now becomes to some extent understandable how the extra-anaphora ordo of the Jacobite Mass shows a prayer of quite different character.[3] Precisely to this area of the liturgy the theory did not apply; thus there remained here a free field for the continuing anti-Arian tendency—which made the similarity of Father and Son take effect also in the free alternation of the prayer-address. It is, however, also possible that forms of the latter-type had already become all too firmly fixed in this outer area of the Mass celebration when the anaphora theory began to take effect. The theory has in any case a certain compromise character vis-à-vis accomplished facts: thus exemption had to be conceded even to the anamnesis prayer. The extra-anaphora Mass ordo takes its character from the Sedro prayers, and with these is already connected the name of the Patriarch John I (631–48); thus it looks as if one was content to restore

---

[1] Also, the Syrian word for anaphora, 'kurobho', the 'access' (Br. 579 likens it to προσαγωγή and refers to Eph. 2:18: 'through Christ we have access to the Father'), must have suggested the order of address 'to God through Christ' for prayers within the anaphora.

[2] In a somewhat later period the δι' οὗ is already thus fixed, at least among the Maronites, and the Mediator theme in the end-doxology has secured for itself such a place in religious awareness that this christological doxology, along with tne argument adduced by Moses from the representation of Christ, provides a new proof for the necessity of the prayer-address throughout to God the Father: 'Praeterea ex eo constat (that the prayer must be directed to the Father), quod in omnium orationum fine Deo Patri supplicet sacerdos per eius Filium Dominum nostrum Jesum Christum dicens: per gratiam . . . Filii tui, per quem et cum quo.' Thus the Maronite compiler Dionysius bar Salibi (Assemani V, 395).

[3] See above, p. 67 f.

something of the spirit of the older manner of prayer to the inner core of the Mass. The general tendency to go over in the prayer to the address to Christ also betrays itself even in Moses bar Kepha himself. Certainly he frequently lays great emphasis on the Mediator position of Christ 'who has offered himself to God the Father for us'.[1] On the other hand, however, not only is the tri-sagion[2]—as of old, probably,—directed to the Son;[3] he also pleads the explanation for the sanctus at the end of the Preface[4] that the threefold 'holy' signifies the acknowledgement, in homage, to the Son that he is one of the holy Trinity, just as he it was, also, whom Isaias (6:1 f.) saw seated on the throne above.[5] Yet in this he does not break his rule. Neither trisagion nor sanctus belong to the prayers which the *priest* recites in the *anaphora*; for only here does he and he alone take the place of Christ and must therefore address himself to God the Father.

The Jacobite anaphora theory has remained limited in its influence to its country of origin. Among the Copts and Abyssinians we do indeed find a strongly conservative persistence in the tradi-tional forms, which are certainly mixed with later material but hardly transformed; but we can see no signs of the influence of that theory. Nevertheless, among the Copts also the traces of a certain reform in the liturgical texts should not be overlooked. In the Arabic version of the *Testament of our Lord* the fluctuation of the prayer-address has been eliminated.[6] Where in other places in the Coptic liturgy the prayer to Christ occurs, especially in the fore-anaphora, it is—albeit not according to a fixed plan—nevertheless used con-sciously and expressly labelled as such ('to the Son') in the preceding rubric. Finally, the use of the Gregorius anaphora precisely on feast days may recall that in the Gallican liturgy also it is especially the feasts of the Lord which give more frequent occasion for the address to Christ. In the Ethiopic liturgy, on the contrary, the freer stand-point in this matter is the rule, rather as in the Syrian *Testament of our Lord.*

---

[1] P. 37, 11; cf. 25, 1; 46, 33; 74, 31.    [2] Br. 77, 23; the Greek Ἅγιος ὁ θεός.
[3] P. 26 f.: according to one tradition, the seraphim had already sung it before the body of the Lord hanging on the Cross, and Joseph of Arimathea had added: 'Thou who wast crucified for us.'
[4] Br. 86, 12.    [5] Pp. 49, 13–51, 10; cf. 70, 25.    [6] See above, p. 20 f.

Later, in some places, there were no Arians to be opposed nor was there a freely chosen dogmatic attitude urging in the same direction. Here, the prayer to Christ appears much later and only to a small extent. Of the Mass liturgy of the East Syrian Nestorians, little indeed can be said with certainty about the point of time at which this element appears.[1] Indeed it is surprising, in view of the dogmatic standpoint of the Nestorians, that the prayer to Christ could be admitted at all. It is they who split the God man completely into two Persons, the man Christ and the Logos. Why, therefore, do they not make the traditional manner of prayer to God through Christ the man the basic rule of their liturgical style? But in the first place, as already remarked, Syrian liturgical language from time immemorial has scarcely known the definite 'through Christ'. Then also, among the Nestorian teachers, besides Nestorius, a Diodorus of Tarsus and a Theodore of Mopsuestia hold an authoritative place, two men who from their days at Antioch had become hyper-sensitive towards everything in the liturgy that could be interpreted as an expression of Arian thought.[2] Thus the dogmatic concern of the Nestorians may have extended only to the greatest possible freeing of the divinity of Christ from humanity, and thus its protection from all appearance of a degradation which—they alleged—would accrue to it from the unity of the Person. Incidentally, among the Nestorians, the harshness of the heretical standpoint had somewhat softened even by the sixth century, seemingly under the influence of a more lively intercourse with the Byzantines.[3]

A considerable reserve towards the liturgical prayer to Christ can also be demonstrated in the Greek St James liturgy and in the Byzantine liturgy.[4] Nevertheless, in the latter just as in the East Syrian liturgy itself, the Syrian prayer type shows a certain dis-

---

[1] In the baptismal liturgy, the basic material of which is older than the Ischojabh III (7th century), one of the present prayers to Christ is ascribed to Ischojabh; the others appear to have entered the liturgy in the 12th century (G. Diettrich, *Die nestorianische Taufliturgie* 7 f., 93).

[2] The biblical exegesis of the Syrian Nestorians has always remained, according to A. Baumstark (*Oriens christ.* 2 [1902] 151), at the stage of development which is characterised by the dominant influence of Theodore of Mopsuestia.

[3] J. Tixeront *Histoire des Dogmes* III² (Paris, 1912), 57–60.

[4] See above, pp. 65 f., 74 ff.

position to accept the prayer to Christ. In general, the address was to the triune God, Father, Son and Holy Ghost, and the mediatorship of Christ was in any case no longer stressed. Thus it was only a short step from this to give prominence occasionally to the Son, the Redeemer become man, and to name him alone in the address. Yet the stimulus, it appears, had first to come from outside, as in the Roman liturgy. Among others, one of the oldest prayers of the Byzantine liturgy, which is directed to Christ and which at the same time names him most clearly as the receiver of the sacrifice, the Οὐδεὶς ἄξιος, has obviously come from Egypt, i.e. the home of the Gregorius anaphora.[1] But it is precisely this prayer, with its somewhat boldly used sacrificial theme, which seems to have provoked a reaction.

In the year 1156 there was held in Constantinople a *synod* in which was discussed the question which had arisen shortly before, whether the sacrifice might be offered also to the Son and not only to God the Father, although the Son is also priest and victim of the sacrifice.[2] The bone of contention was the passage in the Οὐδεὶς ἄξιος, or its interpretation: 'Thou it is who offers and who is offered and who receives.'[3] Soterichus, hitherto deacon of Constantinople and now elected Patriarch of Antioch, thought that many connected it with a half-Nestorian viewpoint: the nature taken by the Logos has offered its blood not only to the Father, but also to the divinity of the only-begotten.[4] When the synod declared: 'As man, Christ offers the sacrifice; as God, he receives it',[5] he was not content with this either and was therefore declared to have forfeited his patriarchate. The synod appealed for its decision primarily to that prayer 'of the great Basil' which Chrysostom had incorporated in his liturgy without altering a word.[6] It appealed, however, also to a series of Eastern Fathers, among them Cyril of Alexandria, who had all decided this question simply by reference to the two natures. It could equally have appealed to Augustine or Fulgentius in the

---

[1] Cf above, p. 41, n. 3; 75, n. 2.
[2] The acts of the Council in A. Mai, *Spicilegium Romanum* X (Rome, 1844), 1–93. Cf. C. J. Hefele, *Konziliengeschichte* V[2] (Freiburg, 1886), 567 f.
[3] Mai X, 1, 12, 41, 67.         [4] Mai X, 5.         [5] Mai X, 5, 70 ff.
[6] It seems to have entered the Chrysostom liturgy soon after the 8th century.

West. Perhaps it had been primarily liturgical-stylistic doubts that Soterichus (and others) had entertained against that manner of speaking, but he had given them unfortunate expression by combining them with dogmatic objections. On the dogmatic question no other decision was possible. The liturgical-stylistic question, however, was not touched on and therefore not clarified; indeed, it was then that the prayer to Christ with conscious antithesis in the Byzantine liturgy appears to have gained that currency which it has subsequently retained.

# XIV

# THE HIGH PRIEST AND THE EUCHARIST

OTHER writers have shown that the designation of our Lord as high priest, which was so frequent in the liturgical language of the first centuries, afterwards became comparatively rare.[1] The *Apostolic Constitutions* still show a certain predilection for the term and in their *Gloria* the word is still employed in the typical combination which we met earlier, especially round about the second century: We adore thee through the great high priest (διὰ τοῦ μεγάλου ἀρχιερέως).[2] In Latin texts, in Africa, Spain, and Rome, it occurs still later, in the same manner.[3] Here the meaning of the word is as in the Epistle to the Hebrews: Christ is the high priest who with the sacrifice he has made for us once for all has taken his stand before God and lives on as our Mediator, as one, therefore, through whom we may offer our prayers to God. It is not surprising that at a later period the word is used in those liturgies in which the idea of praying *per Christum* is still alive.

But the words ἀρχιερεύς, *sacerdos*, *pontifex*, for Christ, also occur later and even today elsewhere in the liturgical prayer. It is a remarkable fact that they are mostly used in prayers addressed to

---

[1] Cf., for instance, B. H. Lietzmann, *Zeitschrift für wissenschaftliche Theologie* 54 (1912) 59.
[2] VII, 47, 2.          [3] See above, p. 100 (with n. 5), 112, 93.

Christ. We encounter it thus in the Mozarabic Mass,[1] and thus it appears in two cases in the liturgy of St Mark. In the prayer at the prothesis already mentioned[2] the 'great high priest' is asked to show his face over the gifts of bread and wine that have been made ready. The prayer itself recurs in the Coptic and Ethiopic liturgies, but without the title of high priest, which therefore seems to be a later addition in the Greek.[3] Subsequently, after the reception of the 'fearful mysteries' of the body and blood of 'our great high priest and king Jesus Christ' the people are exhorted to thank him.[4] In the Ethiopic Athanasian anaphora[5] the epiklesis begins: 'Et iterum supplices rogamus Deum misericordiae, cuius, cum sit sacerdos, sacerdotes[6] constituti sumus, cui cum sit victima, sacrificium obtulimus.' Whereas the title of high priest is not given to Christ in most of the Jacobite anaphoras, it is used in that of John of Bosra in the institution account: 'Velut pontifex . . . gratias egit', and once again, immediately afterwards, in the anamnesis prayer: 'Tabernaculum igitur non manu factum, pontifex sancte . . . te ipsum pro nobis dedisti et sacerdotale ministerium eiusdem dignitatis praedicatoribus evangelii fundandum concredidisti.'[7] The most frequent occurrence, with three instances, is probably in the Gregorius anaphora. The concurrence here again with the anaphora of John of Bosra is noteworthy.[8] The first instance, which forms part of the much-cited prayer Οὐδεὶς ἄξιος and which is also peculiar to the Byzantine and Armenian liturgies, shows exactly, as it does there, the ecclesiastical priesthood in the celebration of the eucharistic sacrifice as deriving from his priesthood.[9] It has already been observed above that here another aspect of the notion 'high priest'

---

[1] See above, p. 101 (with n. 1).    [2] Above, pp. 33, 226.

[3] Cf. Br. 124, 23 with 148, 9 and 204, 11.    [4] Br. 140, 18.

[5] Bessarione 14 (1910) 193.    [6] 'Sacerdotem' is clearly a misprint.

[7] Ren. II, 425 f. Examples of other isolated cases, though in related connexions, in Ren. II, 322 (anaphora of Severus), 514 (of John bar Mudani).

[8] Cf. above, p. 39, n. 2. A. Baumstark (*Geschichte der syrischen Literatur* 267) is inclined to think that the Syrian text of this anaphora originated in the early seventh century. It was certainly based on a Greek text, for a fragment εὐχὴ ἄλλη τῆς κλάσεως has survived in the Egyptian Basilian anaphora (Ren. I, 76), which is palpable evidence of Egyptian reception of Greco-Syrian matter. A precise comparison of John of Bosra's anaphora with Gregory's might disclose a relation between the conditions in which they originated. Cf. above, p. 226 f.

[9] See above, p. 41, n. 3.

is considered. In this connexion a comment on the Gregorius anaphora made by E. Renaudot[1] is pertinent. The prayer in the *Prooemium fractionis* that the Lord may bless now as he once blessed at the Last Supper[2] is seen by Renaudot as the expression of the belief that in fulfilment of his promise (Matt. 28:20) Christ is present at the sacrifice through his divine omnipotence, accomplishes the mystery instituted by himself, and is invisibly operative in its execution. Renaudot further remarks that this conception is discernible in other oriental liturgies.[3] Christ is here the priest, inasmuch as he is the consecrator in virtue of his godhead or, in a more general sense, inasmuch as in the sacramental act he is the 'causa physica effectus supernaturalis'.[4]

This thought can be traced particularly clearly in the Byzantine liturgy. The first prayer of the Chrysostom liturgy of the ninth century, at the prothesis, looks like an earlier form of the prothesis prayer of St Mark's liturgy, already cited:[5] 'Lord our God, who has offered himself as a spotless lamb for the life of the world, look on us and on this bread and on this draught and make it into thy spotless body and thy precious blood to be partaken of for soul and body.'[6] In the prayer at the elevation of the Host, which is the same as in the Basilian liturgy and has already occurred in the Egyptian Gregorius anaphora, Christ with his strong hand appears also as the invisible giver of Communion: Πρόσχες, κύριε Ἰησοῦ Χριστέ, ὁ θεός ἡμῶν ... ὧδε ἡμῖν ἀοράτως παρών, καὶ καταξίωσον τῇ κραταιᾷ σου χειρὶ μεταδοῦναι ἡμῖν καὶ δι᾽ ἡμῶν παντὶ τῷ λαῷ σου.[7] The old Byzantine explanation of the Mass attributed to St

---

[1] I, 310.     [2] See above, p. 39 f., 40, n. 3.

[3] With the same phrase, 'qui tunc benedixisti, benedic nunc', it appears in the Ethiopic anaphora of Jacob of Serug (Bessarione 14 [1910] 207 f.). Cf. also the passages mentioned above on pp. 51, 52 (Ethiopic), and 104 (Mozarabic).

[4] As applied to the sacrament of Penance, this conception finds expression in a preparatory prayer in the E. Syrian Mass: 'High priest of our confession (Heb. 3:1; here clearly meaning 'who receives our confession of sin') and our absolver, O Christ ... we ask of thee forgiveness.' Br. 250, 27.

[5] Br. 124, 22; see above, p. 240.     [6] Br. 309.

[7] Br. 341 (cf. Ren. I, 120). With A. von Maltzew (*Liturgikon* 143 f.) the thought has been seriously weakened: 'And makes us worthy, through thy powerful hand, to dispense thy most pure body and thy precious blood to ourselves and through us to all the people.' Here the 'through us' no longer makes good sense.

Germanus (d. 733), though it does not have this prayer, has the same thought in mind when it rediscovers the angel with the fiery coal in the priest who, standing at the altar, holds with the tongs of his hand the spiritual coal, Christ, and cleanses those who receive and partake. And it is precisely at this point that it sees Christ as the high priest in action: 'Et enim caelestia et non manu facta sancta ingressus est Christus et apparuit in gloria Dei et Patris pro nobis factus *pontifex magnus*, qui penetravit coelos, et habemus eum advocatum apud Patrem et propitiatorium pro peccatis nostris; qui *perfecit nobis proprium suum et sanctum corpus redemptionem* pro omnibus nobis, sicut ipse dicit: Pater, sanctifica eos.'[1] It is entirely in this vein that Nicolas Cabasilas (d. 1371), in his liturgical explanation, writes of Christ's mediatorship[2] in connexion with Communion: Only he to whom the unseen Christ gives Communion receives it wholly. Here Christ performs his mediatory office, not with words and prayers, but in deed, in that he grants to everyone to be one with him according to the measure of his worthiness, and in that he imparts his grace to him. For as God was appeased only by seeing his dearly-beloved Son as man, so now he is favourably disposed towards a man only when he shows the form of the only-begotten, puts on his body, and appears as one spirit with him. Thus Nicolas explicitly transfers Christ's priesthood also to his divinity: as God he offers the sacrifice—that is to say, he performs the consecration— and as God he accepts the sacrifice, whereas as man he is himself the sacrifice. For his explanation he uses the very words of the prayer Οὐδεὶς ἄξιος: . . . διὰ τοῦτο εἶναι λέγεται ὁ αὐτὸς καὶ προσφέρων καὶ προσφερόμενος καὶ προσδεχόμενος· προσφέρων μέν καὶ προσδεχόμενος ὡς θεός, προσφερόμενος δὲ ὡς ἄνθρωπος.[3]

When we compare this idea of the high priest with that which we met with in the New Testament and in the earlier patristic writings,

---

[1] c. 60. According to the translation made by Anastasius Bibliothecarius for Charles the Bald: *Revue de l'Orient chrétien* 10 (1905) 362 f., Petrides.

[2] c. 44: περὶ τῆς Χριστοῦ μεσιτείας (PG 150, 264); also in the preceding chapter. Cf. the interpretation of the mediatorship of Christ in c. 49 (PG 150, 477A).

[3] c. 49 (ibid. 477C). It is not by accident, therefore, that in c. 30 (ibid. 436) when citing I Tim. 2:5: 'There is one Mediator between God and men, the man Christ Jesus' he omits the word 'man'. Cf. also J. Kramp, *Die Opferanschauungen der römischen Messliturgie*[2] (Regensburg, 1924), 152 ff.

we notice a remarkable change—not in a doctrine of the faith but in its formulation and nomenclature and its utilization for the building-up of religious life. The priesthood of Christ is not an entirely simple notion. Hitherto its ethical aspect has always engaged our attention; by sacrificing himself, Christ in his humanity reconciles heaven and earth. The deed done once for all goes on in heaven, where in his transfigured body he is with the Father as our Mediator and intercessor; and it also goes on on earth, in the sacrifice of the Mass, and here too Christ is high priest, not only in that he was its first celebrant but also because he is its founder and the one who is acting in the celebrant for all time. But even so it is not the whispered word of the celebrant that brings about the change; this word spoken in the name of Christ only forms the legal title on which the divine omnipotence effects the substantial change, as it did at the Last Supper.

In the view that comes to the fore in the Byzantine Mass, the three factors—Christ as giver of the commission, the priest of the Church as receiver of the commission, and almighty God—have been merged into two: the priest of the Church, who utters the word, and Christ the invisible high priest, who has not only given the commission but also in his godhead performs the work.[1] And the priest of the Church is almost entirely fused into the present but unseen Son of God, 'Christ our God', who does everything. The efficacy which we theologically attribute to the sacramental sign (ex opere operato), or to the priest of the Church in action, is, in the language of this liturgy, projected back to the almighty Son of God—which, from one point of view, is a splendid unification of the idea of sacramental efficacy.

But in that the phrase 'the high priesthood of Christ' has been filled with another, however genuine, content, and in that—by a very different way than with Philo or even Origen—a priesthood and a mediatorship of the Logos have been gained at the expense of the priesthood and the mediatorship of 'the man Christ Jesus', only a faint glimmer of the humanity of Christ has remained within the

---

[1] The work of transubstantiation is thus attributed to the second divine Person, a procedure which is no less justified than our habit of attributing the work of creation to the Father.

purview of the suppliant. Nevertheless the development has been logical and straightforward. Just as formerly with the abandonment of the δι' οὗ the impressive fact was overlooked that the uniquely guiltless high priest joins in our prayers in heaven, similarly the remembrance of the divine and human founder of the everlasting sacrifice on earth was, if not stifled, at least overlaid by the thought of the presence of God who offers the sacrifice as much as he receives it: 'For it is thou who offers and is offered, who receives and distributes, Christ our God, and to thee we send up our praise.'[1]

Where, then, are we to look for the origin of this interpretation, which, it must be admitted, is discernible in all the younger and current liturgies except the Roman? A satisfactory answer to this question would necessitate an investigation on its own. Here I shall refer in detail only to Chrysostom. With other Fathers[2] he bears witness to the Church's belief that the change is wrought by the priest's utterance of the words of institution, but we find that already with him this modest statement has been expanded to the view

[1] In his booklet *Christus unser Liturge* (Liturgia 1) (Mainz, 1924), 1, C. Pan-foeder starts out with a reference to the 'liturgy' of the old Byzantine ecclesiastical painting, a picture in which Christ appears as high priest, surrounded by angels bearing sacrificial utensils. The picture is clearly to be understood in the sense of the Byzantine liturgy with its notion of Christ's priesthood and is on the same lines as the much more usual representation of Christ as Pantocrator above the altar. Cf. H. Brockhaus, *Die Kunst in den Athosklöstern*[2] (Leipzig, 1924), 62 ff., H. Glück, *Die christliche Kunst des Ostens* (Berlin, 1923), 43. Although Panfoeder is princi-pally concerned to promote appreciation of Christ's priesthood in the sense of St Paul and the Roman liturgy—of which he has many fine things to say—it is remarkable how far he mixes up with it the oriental notion, which is of an entirely different nature and significance. For objections to the interpretation put forward here of the concept 'high priest' in the Byzantine liturgy, cf. above, p. 226 ff. It is not remarkable that in the concept of the high priesthood of Christ, alongside the original, biblical significance of the mediatorship with respect to God, the power of the sacramental Consecration is given a secondary prominence. This step in the unfolding of its meaning is apparent, *int. al.*, in Paschasius Radbertus, *De Corpore et Sanguine* c. 12 (PL 120, 1310 f.). It is clear, however, that here and there the latter significance has become top-heavy, when occasionally God *tout simple* is addressed as *Sacerdos*; for the Mozarabic liturgy, see above, p. 101, n. 2. In the East, the anaphora of Johannan ed. Fuchs (LQF 9; Münster. 1926) 15, 1.4, provides an example.

[2] Justin, *Apol.* I, 66; Irenaeus, *Adv. haeres.* V, 2, 3; *De sacramentis* 4, 4 f.; cf. Ambrose, *De mysteriis* c. 9.

noticed above. In A. Naegle's monograph[1] Chrysostom's belief is stated to have been that 'At the first celebration of the eucharistic mysteries Christ consecrated by pronouncing the words of institution and he consecrates by the same means until the end of time. Through all he says runs the basic idea that at the celebration such as it has been carried out to the present day the invisible consecrator Jesus Christ is manifested externally through the visible priesthood'. In complete accordance with the prayer in the liturgy that bears his name, the saint says: 'Believe therefore that the meal of which he partook is still being celebrated, for the meal of our day is in no way different from that one. It is not that this one is prepared by a man, and that one by himself; both are his own work. So when you see the priest administering the Eucharist to you, do not think that the priest does this, but consider rather that it is Christ you see stretching out his hand.'[2]

At this point it is instructive to study a further phenomenon, to which E. Bishop has drawn attention.[3] He suggests that from all appearances the fourth century saw a great change in the religious thinking and feeling of the faithful with regard to the Eucharist.

[1] *Die Eucharistielehre des hl. Johannes Chrysostomos, des Doctor Eucharistiae* (Strassburger theologische Studien III, 4/5) (Freiburg i.B. 1900), p. 128 ff.

[2] Hom. 50 in Matt.; PG 58, 507. Chrysostom continues: 'Similarly, when you are baptized, it is not the priest who baptizes you, but *God*, who holds your head with invisible power.' This is paralleled by the expression in the Mozarabic liturgy noted above (p. 101, n. 2), in which God is directly designated as the priest— referring to the physical causation of the sacramental effect. Cf. Naegle 298. It is also interesting to read what Naegle says on p. 131 f.: 'On the other hand, although the priest appears only as Christ's deputy at the Consecration, and does not utter the creative word in virtue of his own plenary power, it is nevertheless this pre-eminent plenary power, involving a deputyship, a representation of the God-man in the highest sense, that is one of the principal qualities that raise the priesthood beyond all human measure, and even give it precedence before the angels.' Compare this with the modest position allotted to the priestly dignity by the writers of apostolic times. There is reference, rather, to the community, the 'saints', in the midst of whom the presbyter is merely a functionary with limited authority. We have here two different ways of considering the same object. In the first—physical-ontological—the grandeur and power of God are more to the fore, regarded by man with awe and amazement. The other is ethical, regarding the finished work of this miraculous power, i.e. the sanctified Church, and knowing that all Christians are in like manner near, in Christ, to the great God.

[3] In his appendix to R. H. Connolly, *The liturgical homilies of Narsai* 92–7: II. Fear and awe attaching to the Eucharistic Service.

What is primarily the sacrament of love now takes on in the liturgy the characteristics of *fear*. This is a fact which is more or less verified in all subsequent oriental liturgies. Bishop traces this change still further back in time and thinks that the first signs of this new spiritual attitude towards the sacrament of the altar are to be found in Cyril of Jerusalem, viz. in the mystagogical catecheses which were generally supposed to have been delivered along with the others in the year 348.[1] But the traces are completely absent from the three Cappadocians. This austere feeling of sacred awe towards the sacrament, however, is characteristic of St John Chrysostom. He speaks of the awful mysteries, the dreadful sacrifice, the fearful moment. In fear and trembling one should not only approach to receive the body of the Lord and his awesome blood, but also attend divine service and sing God's praises. φρικτός, φοβερός, φρικω-δέστατος were his favourite adjectives in this connexion, not that he used them all together or at every opportunity. Bishop cannot find a trace of this attitude in the earlier Fathers, nor indeed in the earlier liturgies, in Serapion, or in the *Apostolic Constitutions*, except for one instance (VIII, 12, 2), and this he judges to be a pious formula—of the kind made up in Antioch or its vicinity in the second half of the fourth century—which was intruded into the *Constitutions*. And so he hazards the suggestion that it was Chrysostom and no one else who marks the turning-point in the conception of the Eucharist.[2]

---

[1] The isolated position of the mystagogical catecheses in this respect forces one to consider T. Schermann's thesis, which O. Bardenhewer (III² 278) rejects. Schermann, moved by the first appearance of the Pater noster in the liturgical commentary of these catecheses, and following a note in several good MSS, prefers to attribute the catecheses to Bishop John of Jerusalem (bishop 386–417) (*Théol. Revue* 10 [1911] 577). Since then the matter has been discussed intensely; cf. J. Quasten, *Patrology* III (Westminster, Md 1960), 365–7.

[2] 'St Chrysostom doubtless is the great *Doctor Eucharistiae*, and he certainly is so as the teacher of the future. But it is another question (and that is the question of import here), whether or in what degree he can be viewed as a witness to the tradition or religious sense of the past' (p. 95). It should be noted that the question here is not one of dogma, of theoretic doctrines on the Eucharist, in which Chrysostom simply kept to the old traditional lines, as Naegle himself points out. It is more a question of the use made of the Eucharist, of its incorporation into the liturgical life, in other words of a resultant of what is known by divine revelation and of forms and endeavours based on temporal, human conditions.

The appearance of fear and trembling before the mystery of the Eucharist has since been a frequent subject of investigations. It has been made clear, in the first place, that the mystagogical catechesis of Cyril in question cannot be dated earlier than the period around 383; see C. Beukers, 'For our emperors, soldiers and allies': *Vigiliae christ.* 15 (1961) 177–84. Further, it is verified that the attitude referred to appears already in Basil: *Regula brevius tract.* c. 172 (PG 31, 1195), heading: 'With what dread we . . . should receive the body and blood of Christ', on which it is given as a reason that we receive the body and blood of him who is the consubstantial God. Cf. M. J. Lubatschiwskyj, 'Des hl. Basilius liturgischer Kampf gegen den Arianismus': ZkTh 66 (1942) 20–38.

Also J. Quasten, *Mysterium tremendum: Vom christlichen Mysterium* (Düsseldorf, 1951), 66–75, maintains that the opposition to Arianism has played 'no small part' in this change of attitude (72); he sees the chief cause, however, in the new concept of our relation to Christ coming to be represented especially in the Antiochene school, too much as that of the servant to the great king. The fact that, from the fourth century, names for the emperor and the court-service owing to him were often transferred to Christ also points in this direction; cf. J. Kollwitz, 'Christus II (Basileus)': *Reallexikon f. Antike u. Christentum* II, 1259 f.

In particular, with reference to Chrysostom, the question has been studied by G. Fittkau, *Der Begriff des Mysteriums bei Johannes Chrysostomus* (Bonn, 1953), 122–45. Fittkau sees the source of the feeling of awe above all in the moving-force of the great preacher's sermons: it is the inconceivable extent of the redeeming love of God that must have shaken even the secularized Christians of the half-heathen city. Fittkau has, it is true, found little support among the critics for this explanation, limited as it is to ethical considerations. He is probably right, however, in the sense that the *tremendum*, even in the mentality of Chrysostom (and of the other Eastern Fathers), must be supplemented by the *fascinosum*. Cf. H. J. Schulz, 'Der österliche Zug im Erscheinungsbild byzantinischer Liturgie': *Paschatis Sollemnia* (Freiburg, 1959), 239–46, esp. 243, where in this connexion it is stressed that 'the prominence of liturgical solemnity and the pomp of ceremonies' which is proper to the Byzantine liturgy from this period must be attributed to 'the delight in the holy, the longing for the manifold divine presence'. In like manner, O. Casel had already pointed out in his review of this book (p. 182 f.) 'that all mystery-piety comprises fear . . . and delight'.

When we view these facts in the new light in which, in the case of Chrysostom, the notion of the high priesthood of Christ also appears, clearly Bishop's supposition gains in weight, at least in the sense that Antioch, the home of the saint and for many years the scene of his activity, may have been the soil on which that change took place towards the end of the fourth century. At all events, the two phenomena are connected. Antioch we have already come to know as the area where the bold offensive against the might of Arianism did not stop short at the undismayed confession of the Catholic antithesis, of the ὁμοούσιος; it was here that the next step was taken, by reshaping public prayer into a clarion proclamation of the consubstantiality of the Son of God. Though this did not imply in any way a denial of the Saviour's humanity—it was not until a century later that Eutyches took this further step, whereas Antioch experienced far earlier the Nestorian distinction of two Persons in Christ—nevertheless, in practice, the humanity was relegated to the background along with everything that might imply the Son's subordination or position of service. On this account the Antiochians had undergone too many bitter experiences! On the contrary, they must have been inclined to emphasize everything that manifested the divine grandeur and power of Christ. That could be done, however, nowhere more fully than in connexion with the divine actions performed by the priest in Christ's name through the sacraments of the Church, above all in the central act of the whole liturgy, in which, at Christ's word, he himself is present—'slaughtered', sacrificed, as he was on the cross.

The realistic expression 'slaughtered Christ' which recurs also in the other Fathers, may have played some part in this changing of reverence for the Eucharist into dread.[1] But the most important factor was that, when this attitude was adopted, the priest, on appearing at the Great Entry with the offertory gifts to begin the celebration proper, was in a way only the visible shadow of the Son of God, of the divine high priest, who, himself invisible, was now about to perform the great, mysterious sacrifice. The impression was enhanced by the ceremony attending on this entry with the yet unconsecrated gifts. 'The procession with the gifts was regarded as

---

[1] Cf. Br. 41, 25a.

the entry of the divine majesty of Christ.'[1] In Byzantium, from the time of the Emperor Justin II (565–78), the cherubic hymn was sung during the procession to greet 'the king of the universe invisibly escorted by troops of angels bearing spears'. Their gaze being fixed on the great work of divine omnipotence which now commenced, the faithful may well have experienced what the evangelists report several times of those who witnessed the miracles of Jesus—'they were exceedingly afraid'—and they may have drawn back in fearful awe from the divine mystery, as Peter exclaimed at the miraculous draught of fishes: 'Depart from me, for I am a sinful man, O Lord.' This gap between man and mystery may have been widened by the shutting off of the sanctuary. In the East, from now on, it was gradually withdrawn from the people, at first by means of a barrier, then finally by a solid partition called the iconostasis.[2] At the Great Entry the offerings were borne through the nave of the church and then through the doors of the iconostasis.

In most of the Eastern liturgies, as the ceremony proceeds, there are frequent phrases reminiscent of St John Chrysostom: 'awful mysteries', 'terrifying table', 'fearful and unbloody sacrifice'. But this feeling is expressed predominantly in the injunctions addressed to the people by the deacon from his place raised above them, mostly at the beginning of the anaphora, sometimes at the announcement of the epiklesis, but particularly at the invitation to Communion. E. Bishop draws attention to a certain restraint in this respect which can be ascertained in the East Syrian liturgy, which was the least influenced by oriental Greece.[3] The 'Homilies of Narsai', belonging

[1] A. Baumstark, *Die Messe im Morgenland* 113. There is no need therefore to speak of the reverence due to the Eucharist being anticipated in this case. Attention is focused it seems, not so much on the gifts as on the priest, in whose person Christ is appearing. For this reason it would seem unnecessary, *pace* J. B. Thibaut (*Echos d'Orient* 20 [1917] 38–48; cf. the short report JL 2 [1922] 165), to derive the peculiar character of the Great Entry from the liturgy of the Presanctified, in which the gifts carried to the altar were already consecrated.

[2] For the history and evaluation of the iconostasis cf. now E. Lucchesi-Palli, 'Bilderwand': *Lexikon für Theologie und Kirche* II (1958) 467.

[3] His note (op. cit. 97) that in one passage (Br. 288, 26) the word 'fearful' attributed to the Eucharist has passed from the Theodorus and Nestorius anaphoras to that of the Apostles confirms A. Baumstark's thesis that these anaphoras are of Greek origin.

to this area, which rely on Chrysostom at many points, go much further in their expressions of fear. This is further evidence that a wave of fear of the eucharistic mystery spread outwards from some Greek centre such as Antioch.

That the tendency sprang, at least partly, from the dogmatic opposition to Arianism is clear from the fact that the expressions of fear and dread are stronger and more numerous in the liturgies of the Monophysites, who carried this opposition to extremes. They are stronger in the Jacobite than in the Greek liturgy of St James,[1] in the Coptic than in the Greek liturgy of St Mark,[2] and in the Armenian liturgy than in the Byzantine.[3]

[1] The designation φοβερὰ καὶ ἀναίμακτος θυσία is common to both, also the deacon's call before the *Sancta sanctis*: μετὰ φόβου πρόσχωμεν, which also belongs to all three Egyptian liturgies. Rücker 19, 3; 53, 5. But compare also 9, 8, where the Jacobite adds μετὰ φόβου to the Greek εὐχαριστήσωμεν τῷ κυρίῳ. Again it is only the Jacobite form which, during the opening part of the epiklesis, which is said in secret, has the deacon's call: 'Bless us, O Lord! How fearful is this hour and how terrible this moment, beloved, in which the holy Spirit . . . hovers over this offered Eucharist. You should be in silence and fear as you stand and pray. . . .' Rücker 67, 5. There is an earlier and simpler form of this call in the Syro-Egyptian anaphoras of Basil and Gregorius (Ren. I, 68, 105): Κλίνατε θεῷ μετὰ φόβου.

[2] Before the Gospel, the liturgy of St Mark (Br. 119, 8), like the Ethiopian, has Στάθητε· ἀκούσωμεν τοῦ ἁγίου εὐαγγελίου; the Coptic, however, says, still in Greek (Br. 156, 23): Στάθητε μετὰ φόβου θεοῦ· ἀκούσωμεν. . . . Similarly, the call to take up positions for the sacrificial procession in St Mark's liturgy (Br. 124, 7) προσφέρειν κατὰ τρόπους στάθητε has become προσφέρειν κατὰ τρόμου στάθητε (Br. 164, 8) in the Coptic liturgy. Before the epiklesis, the Greek liturgy of St Mark has no summons at this point; the Coptic, on the other hand, takes it from the two Syro-Egyptian anaphoras—the Gregorius and the Basilian (Ren. I, 68, 105)—for the St Mark anaphora (Br. 178, 21): Κλίνατε θεῷ μετὰ φόβου. In the Basilian and Gregorius anaphoras themselves, the Copts use this summons in the vernacular with marked intensification (Ren. I, 15, 31): 'Adorate Deum cum timore et tremore.' Since, in these two anaphoras, which were originally Syrian, the summons together with the epiklesis itself comes immediately before the intercessory prayer, which in the Coptic Marcan anaphora has retained its position within the Preface, the summons was taken over from there also into the intercessory prayer of this Marcan anaphora (Br. 173, 26): 'Worship God in fear and trembling.'

[3] Common to both is a summons before Communion: Μετὰ φόβου θεοῦ πιστέως καὶ ἀγάπης προσέλθετε (Br. 395, 41), or 'Draw near in fear and partake in holiness'. After the communion (Br. 452, 16) the Byzantine expression is indeed stronger: Ὀρθοὶ μεταλαβόντες τῶν θείων ἁγίων ἀχράντων ἀθανάτων ἐπουρανίων καὶ ζωοποιῶν φρικτῶν τοῦ Χριστοῦ μυστηρίων ἀξίως εὐχαριστήσωμεν τῷ κυρίῳ; here apparently (Br. 454, 25) there is no Armenian expression for φρικτῶν. Before the anaphora both liturgies have at first στῶμεν μετὰ φόβου . . . (Br. 383, 28; 434, 31); then the Byzantine has simply: Ἄνω σχῶμεν τὰς καρδίας, but the Armenian 'Lift up your

As these examples show, feelings of fear attach not only to the Eucharist and the sacrifice in the narrower sense; here and there, the hearing of the Gospel, and prayer itself seem to tremble with the same emotions—apart from the stern tone which in Byzantium, for instance, the Syrian prayer-scheme in its present form already involves. The gap between the eternal God and sinful man keeps opening wide,[1] and it is as if one dared only momentarily to remember that it is truly bridged through Christ, and that we are not aliens but citizens with full rights of the holy city and members of the household of God. Here too, for prayer in general, the explanation is clear: as the mediatorship and humanity of Christ recede into the background, the poor creature is confronted immediately with the overwhelming majesty of God.

At the same time, we must not forget that hardly anywhere is there a lack of images that inspire in us a childlike confidence and heartfelt gratitude. The descriptions of the divine plan of salvation in the eucharistic prayer, not only of most West Syrian anaphoras and of the Byzantine liturgy of St Basil, but in general the prayers from the ancient stock of all oriental liturgies, repeatedly show the heroic

minds *with divine fear*. Before the Gospel the Byzantine has simply (Br. 372, 29) Ἀκούσωμεν τοῦ ἁγίου εὐαγγελίου, but the Armenian (Br. 426, 12) 'Hearken *with fear*', as also at the end of the Mass, before the St John's Gospel which has been taken over by Rome (Br. 456, 13).

A comparison of the Greek Jacobite liturgy with the Armenian provides a particularly clear picture. According to A. Baumstark (*Oriens christ.*[2] 7/8 [1918] 1 ff.), the Armenian represents the form taken by the Greek Jacobite in the radical wing of the Monophysites, the Aphthartodocetes (see above, p. 55, n. 3). The differences are conveniently seen in Baumstark. Here too the Armenian, even against the Jacobite, is alone with its summons (Baumstark 13, 15): 'Sursum exhibete mentes vestras *cum divino timore*!' The Greek ᾧ παρεστήκασιν χίλιαι χιλιάδες ἀρχαγγέλων (Rücker 47, 9) becomes in the Armenian (Baumstark 27, 12) 'Cui *cum timore* adstant millena milia . . . archangelorum'. The Greek address Ὁ θεὸς μέγας καὶ θαυμαστός (Rücker 57) is turned by the Armenian into 'Deus qui magnus es et *terribilis*' (Baumstark 31, 12).

[1] That the element of fear is prominent in the very conception of God is shown for instance, by an expression in the Armenian liturgy (Br. 425, 19): 'For *albeit* thou art God, thou art merciful.' Cf. the explanation given by Chosroe (Vetter 11) of the summons 'Stemus ante sacrum Dei altare cum timore' at the beginning of the Mass of the Faithful: 'De somno quasi excitat exhortatio ista, qua altare illud vocatur altare Dei, quia coram Deo stat et Filium Dei supra se habet sedentem. Qua de causa cum timore ante eam stari jubet.'

figure of the Saviour emerging from the dark clouds and calling
to his fearful disciples: 'It is I. Do not be afraid.'

Still less justifiable would it be to imagine the whole religious and
moral life that lies behind the liturgies to be so dominated by fear
as to exclude the motive of love. It is not even primarily the fear of
punishment or of a sacrilegious reception of the sacrament, but only
an unusually strong predominance of that feeling of one's own
nothingness before the greatness of God, which even in the holiest
of souls must be added to confidence and love, however little it
should impair the sense of elevation. This is brought out also in the
liturgical commentaries. Thus Maximus, in speaking of the *Sancta
sanctis*, says that there are three classes of persons invited to partake
of the life-giving mysteries: slaves, hirelings, and children. Above
the 'slaves', who obey the Lord's commandments out of fear, are
the 'hirelings', who do it for the sake of the reward, but above all are
the 'children', who do it for love.[1]

Except for one or two passages in creed-type texts, the Catholic
Church, when discussing union with communities returning to the
fold, has found nothing to amend in the dogmatic content of
oriental liturgies. The only difference is one of temperament, a preference for the austere and solemn moments in one's intercourse with
God, on the whole a characteristic which has been compared in
saintly figures of the East with the spirit of Old Testament prophecy.
For the full explanation of this peculiarity, one must take into
account, beside the experiences of the Greek Church in the fourth
century, and their after-effects, the special nature of the oriental.

At this point, some further theological remarks are now (1965) in place
on the position that Christ has acquired in the liturgical prayer of the East,
in particular in that of the Byzantine liturgy. In order to understand the
peculiar pious attitude seen in the predominant Christ-address, in the
designation 'Christ our God' and not least in the conception here described
of Christ's priesthood, we should turn first to the christology which has been
placed in a clearer light by the studies of the last decades and particularly
by the monumental work, *Das Konzil von Chalkedon*. Of decisive importance
was Cyril of Alexandria's formula of the μία φύσις τοῦ θεοῦ Λόγου

---

[1] *Revue de l'Orient chrétien* 10 (1905) 306. Pétridès. PG 91, 709 f.

σεσαρκωμένη, which had been influential earlier, and became so once again in the East after the Council of Chalcedon. In this neo-Chalcedonist way of thinking, the attention is fastened on the divine nature of the Logos, who assumes the nature of man, divinizes it and thus makes it the source of salvation for humanity. The bestowal of salvation is therefore 'seen rather from the side of the Logos and in the liturgical texts is ascribed to him as subject'; H. J. Schulz, 'Die "Höllenfahrt" als "Anastasis" ': ZkTh 81 (1959, 1–66) 48. As Schulz further explains, in this manner clearly only the first phase of the mediatorship of Christ, the movement from the Father, is distinctly revealed; 'it demands as second phase and second aspect an upwards movement from man to God' (50), as expressed in the pauline formula, 'through Christ'; in the Eastern outlook it is, indeed, not excluded, but is less in evidence. Cf. also H. J. Schulz, 'Der österliche Zug im Erscheinungsbild byzantinischer Liturgie' (above, p. 247) 241 f: 'As the divine Person of the Logos was put in the foreground, there came to be seen, in place of the human intercessor and Mediator with the Father, rather the Logos sent by the Father, who as "Mediator" sanctifies men by giving them a share in his own human nature, which is filled with grace through the union with the Godhead ... Such a christology must tend to think of the Mass chiefly as an epiphany of the triune God and his gracious self-bestowal, and to order its liturgical form according to a heavenly model.'

We must therefore conclude that East and West start from two different ways of seeing the one mystery of Christ, that neither exhausts the whole mystery and that both spiritualities—the more receptive of the East, and the active and responsive of the West—each corresponding to a like christology, must be completed in the one Catholic Church.

This colouring of fear introduced into the Eastern liturgies from the end of the fourth century is reflected also in the liturgies of the Gallic type, in the Apologies. These prayers are not entirely absent in the East but, from the early seventh century onwards, come into greater prominence in the West. The priest confesses himself a sinner and openly admits his unworthiness to celebrate the sacred mysteries.[1] A humble self-examination before celebrating is nothing fundamentally new; it has already been required by the Apostle of all partakers of the Eucharist (I Cor. 11, 27), also emphatically by the Didache.[2] But here and in the early liturgies in general it appears to

[1] Cf. the article by F. Cabrol: DACL I, 2591–2601.
[2] C. 4, 12; 10, 6; 14, 1. Cf. T. Schermann, Die allgemeine Kirchenordnung etc. 426.

be assumed that each individual, and above all the priest, must take care *before* the actual celebration that his conscience is clear, so that he may celebrate the mysteries in the presence of the holy community with complete confidence. The Apologies, on the other hand, have been drawn into the celebration itself. They occasionally interrupt the course of the prayers, even of the Preface and the Canon, although here too it must be assumed that the priest came to the altar with his conscience essentially clear, i.e. in a state of grace.

The earliest example of an Apology is probably to be found among the Mone Masses.[1] The Apologies were in full flower between the ninth and eleventh centuries. Later, this overgrowth was cut out of the Western Mass, except for some small relics which were appropriately incorporated. Among these is our confiteor at the beginning of Mass.

In the East, related preparatory prayers of the priest can be found as early as the sixth century.[2] Attempts have even been made to show that they are directly related to the Western Apologies. But perhaps it is more important to consider the common root from which forms similar to those in the East could have grown in the domain of the Gallic liturgies.

In both areas the Mediator concept has dwindled. When Christ is mentioned as high priest, it is his omnipotent godhead that the writers had in mind. The characteristics of fearfulness are attached to the eucharistic mystery less noticeably in the West than in the East,

---

[1] W. 6 (M 10): 'Post profetiam. Deus sancte ecclesiae constitutor qui stans in medio discipulorum tuorum venerationis huius sacramenta docuisti . . . inlumina faciem tuam super servum tuum, ut de meis oneribus absolutus recte etiam pro populo tuo rogaturus adsistam' (followed, in spite of the address to Christ, by the formal ending: 'P. dnm nm Jhm'). The prayer that follows is similar. Cf. ZkTh 43 (1919) 696. For the Mozarabic liturgy an early and typical example is the prayer of Julian of Toledo: 'Accedam ad te Domine in humilitate' (see above, p. 104). For the following period cf. Jungmann, *Missarum Sollemnia*[5] I, 103–5.

[2] They are fairly numerous in the present Byzantine liturgy. It is only necessary to recall the oft-repeated 'Lord, be merciful to me a sinner'! Longer texts of this kind seem to have been developed frequently, especially in the earlier stages of monophysitism. They include not only the Οὐδείς ἄξιος, but also the preparatory prayer (Br. 316, 11a = Br. 144, 20 for the Coptic liturgy. Here also Br. 144, 4, the prayer 'of Severus'). E. Bishop (op. cit. p. 96) explicitly puts these confessions of guilt on the part of the priest on a line with the expressions of fear already discussed.

it is true,[1] but that could be compensated by a more forcible expression of the correlative feeling of the individual's unworthiness. And incidentally it should not be difficult to show how closely these admissions are often connected with the later concept of Christ's priesthood (*sacerdos* = consecrator).[2]

While this development has been more operative in the East, another type of eucharistic thought has penetrated more deeply in the *West*, though at a considerably later period. Whereas in the East it was the concept of the high priest which absorbed further elements, here it is the Eucharist itself in which new relations emerge, involving a somewhat altered attitude in the faithful towards the Eucharist. In liturgical prayer proper, there are, it is true, only scanty traces of this new 'way', and they belong mostly to an earlier period in which only the first beginnings occurred. On this account, the change became all the more important for private, extra-liturgical, prayer. Nevertheless, this is an appropriate place in which to survey briefly the historical development of this spiritual attitude towards the Eucharist which has become familiar to us, since against this background we may better evaluate the different style of the earlier eucharistic piety, as retained in the liturgical prayer.[3]

---

[1] Instances are not entirely wanting, e.g. in certain Mozarabic formularies: MEL VI, 266, 33; VI, 510, 18 (postsanctus: 'Quanta nobis, omnipotens, Pater, hoc sacrificium reverentia metuendum, quo adeundum tremore').

[2] A classical example of this is the *Oratio s. Ambrosii*, which, divided among the days of the week, appears among the preparatory prayers in our Missal, and which F. Cabrol ranks with the Apologies. It begins: 'Summe sacerdos et vere pontifex Jesu Christe.' There follows a reminder of his sacrifice on the Cross and in the Mass, and various petitions for purification for the celebration, 'ubi tu es sacrificium et sacerdos mirabiliter et ineffabiliter constitutus. Quis digne hoc celebrare poterit nisi *tu, Deus omnipotens*, offerentem feceris dignum?' (Monday and Tuesday). Then again: 'Ego enim, Domine, memor venerandae passionis tuae accedo ad altare tuum licet peccator, ut offeram *tibi* sacrificium' (Wednesday). After this, God the Father might be supposed to be addressed (tu Pater noster es; sancte Pater'); but the context relates the address, in the manner of the Mozarabic liturgy, to Christ: 'Qui de coelo descendisti' (Thursday and Friday). The prayer is of the eleventh century; cf. Jungmann, *Missarum Sollemnia*[5] I, 358 f.

[3] For the historical material, which is amply available, see V. Thalhofer– L. Eisenhofer II, 336–66. The historical lines of development and their underlying ideas have been worked out and evaluated in the light of modern tendencies in a

In the piety of the early Church—and probably this is still true
of the East—the place of the Eucharist was only that of a sacrificial
offering and meal.[1] As such, it was, of course, then as much as today
at the heart of the whole liturgy and religious life. It was the unifying
bond that joined the faithful to one another before God, and which
alone made them fully into the 'body of Christ', the communion of
saints, God's people—ideas of frequent occurrence in Augustine
and others.

Connected with this is the 'material character' of the Eucharist.[2]
Although the Lord himself not only speaks of his body and blood (or
of his flesh and blood) but has also said 'He who eats me will live
because of me' (John 6:58), the usual expression for his presence in
the eucharist is 'the body of Christ' or 'the body and blood of the
Lord'.[3] Direct mention of the Lord's presence, of the presence of
Christ in person, is comparatively very rare. In this case there is
generally a particular reason for it, such as a scriptural phrase to be

series of essays by J. Kramp, collected under the title *Eucharistia. Von ihrem Wesen
und ihrem Kult* (Freiburg i. B. 1924).

Since the first appearance of this book, I have myself given detailed treatment to
the change in the conception of the Eucharist in Western piety in several articles
and lectures. It may be permissible to refer to the articles 'Der Kanon unter der
Einwirkung der Eucharistielehre des frühen Mittelalters': ZkTh 62 (1938)
390–400 (= *Gewordene Liturgie*, Innsbruck, 1941, 120–36); 'Eucharistische Fröm-
migkeit und eucharistischer Kult in Wandel und Bestand': *Trierer theol. Zeitschr.*
70 (1961) 65–79; cf. also the pertinent sections in *Missarum Sollemnia* I, 155–62;
II, 255–71. The return from the dominant *worship* of the Eucharist to the community *celebration* of the Eucharist has remained the principal theme of the liturgical
renewal; it achieved an effective break-through at the Eucharistic Congress in
Munich in 1960.

[1] During this time there is not the slightest indication of any wavering in the
belief in the Real Presence. The Anglican C. E. Hammond, Brightman's precursor
as the editor of Eastern and Western liturgical texts, put at the head of his work
(*Ancient Liturgies*, Oxford, 1878) the following passage from Renaudot (II, p. xix):
'Inde elucet magnopere ea, quae antiquam de Eucharistia totius Ecclesiae doctri-
nam confirmat, orationum rituumque similitudo inter Graecos, orientales occi-
dentalesque liturgias quae ex linguarum diversitate regionumque longinquitate,
imo ab iosis haeresibus detrimentum nullum accepit'.

[2] Kramp 84 ff.

[3] A survey of the nomenclature of the Eucharist in the writings of the pre-
Nicean Fathers is given by F. Raible, *Der Tabernakel einst und jetzt* (Freiburg, 1908),
p. 16 f.

explained or a closer consideration of the implications of the eucharistic presence.[1]

It is also much more in keeping with the context of the liturgical celebration, i.e. with the primary character of the Eucharist as a sacrifice offered to God and as a sacrificial meal of the assembled community, when the circumstances of the sacrifice are expressed in its designation, or when the instruction to eat and drink is not overlaid by emphasis on the personal dignity of the Lord. This consideration sets the standard pre-eminently for the language of the liturgies themselves. In them, when a prayer is offered 'through Christ', attention is drawn to the celestially transfigured Christ, not to the Eucharist which may be present. In numerous post-communions, especially in the Roman Mass, prayers are addressed through Christ to God for the long-lasting fruit of these 'sacred mysteries', of the eating of the 'heavenly bread'. In the Eucharist there is a much more lively sense of the means of salvation for souls and of the bond unifying the great community of Christ, than of the personal Christ who is contained therein. This is borne out by the last prayer of blessing in Serapion's Euchologium:[2]

'God of truth, friend of man, may this people retain the Communion with the body and blood, may their bodies be living bodies and their souls pure souls. Let this blessing avail in preserving the Communion and in safe-

---

[1] This mode of expression is usual with Chrysostom among others: see A. Naegle, op. cit. p. 9. But he also says, penetrating more deeply into the mystery, that here, like the shepherds, we can see the Lord 'lying in the crib' and that 'he who sits on the right hand of the Father is here' (Naegle 61, 73). Ambrose, who also makes regular use of the expression 'corpus Christi', is prompted by the words of the communion psalm 'Gustate et videte quia suavis est Dominus' to comment: 'In illo sacramento Christus est, quia corpus est Christi.' De mysteriis, n. 58 (PL 16, 426). In certain passages, even St Augustine describes as present in the Eucharist not only—as was the rule with him—the body of Christ, but also (in the manner of John 6:58) 'Christ'. These passages are collected in K. Adam, 'Zur Eucharistielehre des hl. Augustinus': Theol. Quartalschr. 112 (1931, 490–536) 500 ff.

Pseudo-Dionysius, in his Ecclesiastical Hierarchy (III, 3, 2; BKV² z, p. 123. Stiglmayr), begins his explanation of the anaphora with the cry 'But thou, most divine and holy sacrament, strip thyself of the mystifying veils. . .'. So late a writer as George Pachymeres (d. 1310), in paraphrasing the passage (PG 3, 456), observes: 'He speaks to the sacrament as if to something animated (ὡς ἐμψύχῳ), and rightly, for the great Gregory spoke in similar fashion; for this sacrament is Christ himself.'

[2] 18 (6).

guarding the Eucharist just celebrated (εἰς τήρησιν τῆς κοινωνίας καὶ εἰς ἀσφάλειαν τῆς γενομένης εὐχαριστίας) and make all together blessed and elect through thine only-begotten Jesus Christ in the Holy Spirit now and for ever and ever.'

'Communion' is indeed the normal permanent condition of 'live' Christians, whose duty it is to cherish it.[1] All their lives are lived in a spirit of communion, and it bursts into flame every time the sacrifice is completed with the reception of the 'body and blood'. Naturally, therefore, the actual reception is not preceded by any special preparation, and after it the prayer is quickly ended. Attention is directed more to the whole redemptive work of divine mercy, and after seeing oneself enveloped and surrounded by divine love, one is no longer surprised that God feeds his children with children's food. But in giving thanks for the great work of salvation, the whole ceremony of the Eucharist has been of service. In St Jerome's time the Our Father was said before communion[2] and it has been included in the liturgies ever since. The augmenting of the prayers in the communion part of the Mass begins in the East in the fourth century, in the West even later.[3]

When the liturgical prayer to Christ comes into favour, we find indeed that it is often allotted a place in the group of communion prayers,[4] but here too—as, for instance, in the prayers before communion in the Roman Mass—it is not the eucharistic presence of the Lord that is addressed; otherwise there would be no such phrase as 'perceptio corporis tui, Domine Jesu Christe'. Here too the Eucharist, the body of Christ, is still a third factor between the suppliant and the Lord Christ. In a communion prayer of the Armenian Mass the Eucharist is actually personified as distinct from Christ.[5] This way of thinking was no obstacle to the worshipping of

[1] Cf. in Roman postcommunions (e.g. 22, VIII): '. . . In eius (scil. divini muneris) semper participatione vivamus.'

[2] Adv. Pelag. 1, 3, 15; cf. F. Probst, Liturgie des 4. Jahrhunderts 103.

[3] T. Schermann, Ägyptische Abendmahlsliturgien 135 ff.

[4] See above, pp. 32, 47, 51, 63 ff., 72, 76, 83, 119, 123.

[5] Br. 451, 1: 'I am this day to partake of thy divine and awful mystery of thine immaculate body and precious blood. Wherefore having these for intercessors, I beseech thee to keep me in thine holiness.'

the blessed sacrament,[1] or to its being solemnly acclaimed by direct address: 'Ave verum corpus.'

But the first indication of a more personal intercourse with Christ present in the Eucharist is a prayer, or rather a hymn, the *Agnus Dei*, which was first sung by the clergy and laity at the behest of Pope Sergius (687–701) during the breaking of the host; thus he introduced, as E. Bishop, with some reserve, remarks, an element of eucharistic adoration.[2] Sergius was one of the Greek-speaking Syrians from the district of Antioch who supplied five occupants of the papal see between 686 and 730. It was the period of the refugees from Islam, which in the East had swamped the active life of the Church, already riven with heresy. Probably we should seek here both the native place and the fuller explanation of this familiar prayer.

When speaking of the sacrifice of the Mass, the great preacher of Antioch, Chrysostom, as also probably other Greek fathers from time to time, makes frequent use of expressions in which the sacrificial setting and the person of Christ in the Eucharist appear side by side: the sacrificed, or the slaughtered, Christ; the slaughtered lamb of God; the true Pasch; a rational lamb.[3] With no intention of citing a liturgical text, he also speaks of turning in supplication to the 'lamb of God' when remembering the dead—the lamb that lies there before us and takes away the sins of the world.[4]

This line of thought recurs in the liturgies in the ambit of Antioch. In the East Syrian Theodorus anaphora,[5] after the words of consecration, we read: 'Offerimusque coram Trinitate tua . . . sacrificium hoc vivum et sanctum, quod mysterium est agni Dei, qui tollit peccata mundi.' In the Mass ordo of the Greek liturgy of St James[6] the breaking of the host is accompanied by the words 'behold the lamb of God, who takest away the sins of the world, slaughtered

---

[1] With the Copts, the people exclaim after the epiklesis : 'We worship thine holy body—and thy precious blood' (Br. 180, 30). The old fore-anaphora of the Armenian Jacobite liturgy has 'huic (*scil.* victimae divinae) gloriam offerimus et incensum imponimus ante te, Domine' (*Oriens christ.*[2] 7/8 [1918] 10, 30). Baumstark.

[2] *Liturgica historica* 145: '. . . By this new arrangement he introduced into the Roman Mass a (possible) element of what is called eucharistic adoration.' Here there is also a thorough investigation of the *Agnus Dei* in the Litany of the Saints.

[3] A. Naegle, 153 f. Similarly in Cyril's final Mystagogical Catechesis (5, 10).

[4] *In I Cor. hom.* 41, 4 (PG 61, 361).      [5] Ren. II, 619.      [6] Br. 62, 24.

(σφαγιασθείς) for the life and salvation of the world'.[1] In the
Syrian form of the St James liturgy the parallel phrase (to which, it is
true, no date can be assigned) is already ' . . . thou art the Lamb of
God that taketh away the sin of the world. Do thou pardon our
offences and forgive our sins and set us on thy right hand'.[2]

Greater detail is revealed by the Jacobite anaphoras. The Severus
anaphora, whose Greek original is assigned to the early sixth century
by Baumstark,[3] has this phrase in the prayer of blessing before
Communion: 'Dissensionem et odium auferat a nobis agnus Dei,
qui tollit peccatum mundi.' The passage, along with the whole of
the prayer to which it belongs, is preserved in Greek in the Egyptian
anaphora of St Basil: καὶ φευγέτω . . . διχοστασία καὶ μῖσος τὸν
ἀμνὸν τοῦ θεοῦ τὸν αἴροντα etc.[4] The same anaphora explains at
another point:[5] πνευματικὸν μέν ἐστιν τὸ πρόβατον, ἡ μάχαιρα δὲ
λογική τε καὶ ἀσώματος. John of Bosna's anaphora, which is almost as
old, has the expression a little earlier on: 'Agnumque occisum super
altare videmus.'[6] In the Egyptian Gregorius anaphora, for which a
close relationship with that just mentioned has been claimed, we
have a prayer of more-or-less determined date which is addressed
directly to the lamb of God : Ὁ ἀμνὸς τοῦ θεοῦ ὁ αἴρων τὴν ἀμαρτίαν
τοῦ κόσμου . . . ἑαυτὸν παρέδωκας. . . .[7]

These examples show at least that in the Mass prayers of the West
Syrian Jacobites the expression 'Lamb of God' for Christ present in
the Eucharist was current in the sixth century and that the addressing

---

[1] In the Byzantine liturgy a similar form of words to be said at the fraction seems
not to have been accepted until a later period (Br. 393, 26): Μελίζεται καὶ
διαμερίζεται ὁ ἀμνὸς τοῦ θεοῦ. It has disappeared from the ninth-century text.
Other passages in the Byzantine liturgy in which the Eucharist is called 'spotless
lamb' are also clearly of more recent origin (Br. 356, 33–6; 309, 9b).

[2] Br. 99, 12; cf. the address to the lamb of God in Br. 73, 8; similarly in the
Jacobite baptismal liturgy (J. A. Assemani, Codex liturgicus II, 271).

[3] JL 2 (1922) 92–8; Ren. II, 329.

[4] Ren. 1, 77 f. This long prayer provides a third case—two have been established
by Baumstark—in which the Severus anaphora agrees with Greek texts. It is all
the more valuable in that this Basilian anaphora can be more or less precisely
fixed in time and place, since it is probably not more recent than its Gregorius
sister anaphora. Cf. above, p. 227.

[5] Ren. I, 63.                              [6] Ren. II, 429.

[7] Ren. I, 120. This is probably the source of the deacon's summons in the Coptic
form of this anaphora: 'Adorate agnum Verbum Dei.' Cf. Ren. I, 33, 309.

of prayers to the Lamb of God began here too about this time. Although the development with the Jacobites, for obvious reasons, parallel with the phenomena already discussed, was more rapid, there was no reason why the Catholic Syrians should not have adopted such forms, much in the same way as some of the best items in the Catholic hymn-book have been taken from the Protestants. It is therefore a completely justifiable assumption that our *Agnus Dei* originated in Syria and that it is addressed to the sacrificed Saviour present in the Eucharist.[1]

Apart from this interpolation, the Eucharist has been uniformly treated as a holy *thing* in the Roman Mass as in the other liturgies.[2] There are, however, two scriptural passages addressed to Christ which have been given a eucharistic setting: the 'Domine non sum dignus' and the 'Benedictus qui venit'. The latter is already in the *Apostolic Constitutions* (VIII, 13, 13), moreover, just before the communion; and the *Didache* (c. 10, 6) has the acclamation 'Hosanna to the God of David', which was probably meant to be uttered at the same juncture.[3]

[1] The *Agnus Dei* appears in Gaul at about the same time as in Rome. It forms the beginning of a prayer in the *Missale Gothicum* (Mur. II, 579 Post secreta): 'Agnus Dei, qui tollis peccata mundi, respice in nos et miserere nobis, factus nobis ipse hostia, qui sacerdos, ... sal(vator mundi).' It is very likely that there were West Syrian influences in Gaul, whence so many went on pilgrimage to Palestine.

[2] One or two later texts from the liturgies of the Monophysite region deserve our attention as exceptions showing a parallel, independent development such as persisted in the West only outside the liturgy. But cf. some texts of the middle ages: Jungmann, *Missarum Sollemnia*⁵ II, 460 f, nn. 28, 32. Thus with the Ethiopians the 'Domine non sum dignus' has been extended into a complete prayer (Br. 239, 15; see above, p. 48, n. 3.) In this connexion also should be mentioned the end of the confession of faith before the Communion (Br. 239, 10): 'This is he, to whom belong all honour. . .'. In the anaphora of St John Chrysostom (see above, p. 48 f.) those with sins on their conscience are warned against receiving the body and blood, but 'If the heart is pure ... we will approach our saviour. Come, let us adore and confess him' (*Der Katholik* 68 [1888] I, 425; cf. 424). Cf. also the Marian anaphora (*Der Katholik* 96 [1916] I, 264, n. 55), where the 'invisible God' evidently means the eucharistic Christ.

In the West Syrian liturgy, the Mass ordo has, beside other prayers that speak of the body and blood of the Lord, the following (Br. 102, 6b): 'Vouchsafe me, O my Lord, to eat *thee* in holiness and by eating of thy body may my lusts be driven away. . . .' and (Br. 102, 30b) 'Thee I am holding, who holdest the bounds, thee I am grasping, who orderest the depths, thee, O God, do I place in my mouth'.

[3] Cf. Baumstark: JL 2 [1922] 95.

It was perhaps when scholastic theology was at its height that the single word 'Christus' appeared on an equal footing with the older expression 'Corpus Christi' as the normal name for what is present in the Blessed Sacrament. It was at this time that the cult of the Eucharist outside the Mass began to develop.[1] This had already received an impetus from the dogmatic controversies of the ninth and eleventh centuries; and the opposition to the Reformers' denial of the eucharistic presence must have strengthened the movement further. About this time, the custom of reserving the Eucharist on the high altar became more general; the first reliable evidence of the custom is ninth-century.[2] The house of God thus begins to appear as that of the eucharistic Christ, and this is the starting-point of the custom of paying frequent visits to the Blessed Sacrament[3] and of exposing it for adoration, for which purpose new liturgical forms were composed. The only effect this movement had on the liturgy of the Mass was that in the sixteenth century the habit of genuflecting before the Eucharist became a universal prescription.[4] But the practice of exposing the sacrament on the same altar as that on which Mass was being celebrated, with the object of giving prominence to the adoration of the eucharistic Christ, never received the approval of Rome. The intention of this and similar rulings was not to discourage the eucharistic cult but to ensure that in liturgical services good taste and order prevailed, not only in external forms but also in ideas.[5]

Where the worship and awe of the Eucharist came to be fostered in a one-sided manner, it had led only to a so much greater reserve in a matter of far more importance—the Eucharist as a sacrificial

---

[1] Cf. P. Browe, *Die Verehrung der Eucharistie im Mittelalter* (Munich 1933).

[2] For the history of the reservation of the sacrament, see the comprehensive account by J. Braun, *Der christliche Altar*, Munich, 1924, II, 574–649.

[3] H. Thurston, S.J., has pointed out that apparently for the whole of the first millennium there is no reliable evidence of a church being visited by anyone for the purpose of praying before the blessed sacrament, whereas after the twelfth century accounts of such visits become ever more frequent (JThSt 11 [1910] 275–9). For the texts he examined, cf. J. Braun II, 575, 580.

[4] J. Kramp, *Eucharistia* 83 and ZkTh 48 [1924] 154–60.

[5] Cf. J. Kramp, *Eucharistia* 104 ff.

meal.[1] The very idea of the divine high priest, which was brought to the forefront in the liturgies of the Gallican type, must have increased fear of the sacred mystery and inhibited the feeling of confidence in Christ. The devotion to the heart of Jesus, in the wound of which lies salvation, may be regarded as a reaction to this fear, even in the middle ages.[2] It is still more so on its revival in the seventeenth century against Jansenism with its one-sided fostering of adoration and homage before the Eucharist.[3]

[1] As opposed to this, Pius X in his decree on frequent communion (20 December 1905) expressly stated that the Eucharist is intended to sanctify the faithful, 'non autem praecipue ut Domini honori ac venerationi consulatur'. *Acta Sanctae Sedis* 38 (1905/6) 401.

[2] Cf. K. Richstätter, *Die Herz-Jesu-Verehrung des deutschen Mittelalters*[2], Regensburg 1924. English version: *Medieval Devotions to the Sacred Heart* (London, 1925).

[3] Cf. J. W. Eberl, *Jansenisten und Jesuiten im Streit über die oftmalige Kommunion*, Regensburg 1847, pp. 1–71. In his book on frequent communion (1643), to which he gave the motto 'sancta sanctis', Antoine Arnauld laid down the rule that only those were fit to approach this table who felt an ardent devotion, striving upwards unceasingly, like the eagle, in a holy enthusiasm for God. Foregoing communion, therefore, the nuns of Port-Royal practised all the more assiduously the adoration of the sacrament, in reparation also for the indignities offered to the sacrament by frequent but ill-prepared communions. Even on their death-beds they preferred to hunger for communion rather than receive it. A Jansenistic book of devotion said that it took the world 4,000 years to prepare for the Incarnation; not 4,000, not even myriads of years, would suffice it to receive him in a manner befitting his majesty; therefore we should use the short space granted to us scrupulously.

Eberl attributes this attitude to the predominance of faith and fear in contrast to love. Behind it is the doctrine of grace, which states that it is invariably efficacious but not always bestowed, and that its irresistible pull alone can bring us to a worthy reception of the Lord of lords.

# XV

# THE VENERATION OF THE SAINTS. THE
# ARRANGEMENT OF PRAYER COMPLEXES

IT was only natural that from the very beginning the Church
should honour the memory of those who had fallen asleep in Christ,
for they now more than ever belonged to the 'communion of saints'.
The next and obvious step was to assign a place of honour to the
heroes among them, those who had died for the faith—the beginning
of the veneration of the saints. The faithful were sure that the
mutual contact they enjoyed by praying for each other when alive
could not be broken even by death. Origen speaks often of the
martyrs standing by the altar of God and of their supporting our
prayers like the angels.[1] In recent years excavations by P. Styger at
San Sebastiano in Rome have brought to light *graffiti* of the third
century in which visitors to the resting-place (as it was then) of the
Princes of the Apostles sought their intercession: 'Petre et Paule in
mente nos habeatis', 'Paule et Petre petite pro nobis omnibus' etc.[2]

Liturgically, honour was paid to the martyrs, in that services were
held over their graves, Mass celebrated on their anniversaries and

---

[1] A number of passages in this sense have been listed by E. von der Goltz, *Das
Gebet in der ältesten Christenheit* 175 and T. Schermann, *Die allgemeine Kirchenordnung*
etc. 456, 459. Cf. P. Dörfler, *Die Anfänge der Heiligenverehrung nach den römischen
Inschriften und Bildwerken* (Munich 1913), p. 27 ff.

[2] ZkTh 45 (1921) 569.

the accounts of their sufferings read; also, they were mentioned in the diptychs.[1] But in this the line was by no means sharply drawn between the commemoration of Christians who had died ordinary deaths and of those who were paid the honour of a special *cultus duliae*. In both cases prayers and sacrifices were offered 'for' them, for the martyrs as for all who had gone to their eternal rest, though the intention could not have been the same. Thus Cyprian says of the several martyrs of his Church: 'Sacrificia *pro eis* semper, ut meministis, offerimus, quotiens martyrum passiones et dies anniversaria commemoratione celebramus.'[2]

The same sort of expression was quite common in the oriental liturgies. In the *Apostolic Constitutions*,[3] for instance, the priest begins the prayer of intercession: 'Whereupon we pray to thee, Lord, for (ὑπέρ) thy holy Church . . .' and adds in the same manner prayers for the clergy, the king, and even the saints.[4]

It is clear from this that the primary meaning of praying or sacrificing 'for' anyone or 'for' anything is only 'in the case of someone', 'in the matter of something', with no more precise intention given. Thus, in other liturgies, prayers are said also 'for' the Gospels before they are read.[5] This mode of expression persisted for long afterwards. We can still read in the Mozarabic Missal of 1500:

---

[1] Cf. T. Schermann, op. cit. 455 ff., and *Abendmahlsliturgien* 40 f., cf. 47 f.

[2] Ep. 39, 3 (CSEL 3, p. 538, 10. Hartel).  [3] VIII, 12, 40–9.

[4] Ἔτι προσφέρομέν σοι καὶ ὑπέρ πάντων τῶν ἀπ' αἰῶνος εὐαρεστησάντων σοι ἁγίων, πατριαρχῶν, προφητῶν, δικαίων, ἀποστόλων, μαρτύρων, ὁμολογητῶν, ἐπισκόπων (and the other ranks of the clergy and the Church). There follows in the same manner the offering for all the laity (ὑπὲρ τοῦ λαοῦ τούτου), for the city, for persecutors, for catechumens and penitents, for good weather (ὑπὲρ τῆς εὐκρασιας τοῦ ἀέρος) and a good harvest, and finally for the absent. When the priest comes to an end, the deacon begins the litany, which is composed on the same lines and consists of exhortations to the people to pray, the first of which runs: 'Let us pray for the gift (ὑπὲρ τοῦ δώρου) that has been offered to the Lord God that through the mediation of his Christ the good God will accept it. The fourth is 'Let us remember the holy martyrs, that we may be found worthy of sharing in their struggles. We pray for (ὑπέρ) those who rest in the faith.' (VIII, 13, 3, 6,).
For the prayer 'for' saints, see Baumstark's recension 249 f., and J. B. Walz, *Die Fürbitte der Heiligen* (Freiburg 1927), 83–7.

[5] Copt. Lit. (Br. 155, 34): Προσεύξασθε ὑπὲρ τοῦ ἁγίου εὐαγγελίου, to which the people replied κύριε ἐλέησον. The same acclamation is made in the Ethiopian liturgy (Br. 219, 24): 'Pray *on account of* the holy Gospel'. Such a practice conflicts with O. Casel's interpretation (JL 2, 1922, 32 ff.).

'Offerunt Deo Domino oblationem sacerdotes nostri . . . pro universa fraternitate . . . Item pro spiritibus pausantium: Ilarii, Athanasii, Martini, Ambrosii . . . et omnium pausantium.'[1]

H. Dausend produces a related instance even from the Roman liturgy.[2] This indeterminate mode of expression is still preserved, for example in the Byzantine liturgy of St Chrysostom:[3] the sacrifice is offered to God 'for those who rest in the faith, forefathers, fathers, Patriarchs, Prophets, Apostles . . . and for every just spirit that ended in the faith'. The interpretation of the passage by A. von Maltzew[4] is indeed possible: 'This must be the expression of a prayer that God should make the saints mentioned partakers in the sacrificial celebration, so that the living, the departed and also the saints who have already entered into the glory of heaven may assemble with the angels round the throne of the Lamb.' The expression to pray and sacrifice 'for' the saints could mean: that they may join with us in the sacrifice; but also, that we thank God for their victory; or that God may be merciful to us for their sake and at their *intercession*.

St Augustine was among those who advocated the last of these interpretations: 'Ad ipsam mensam non sic eos commemoramus quemadmodum alios, qui in pace requiescunt, ut etiam pro eis oremus, sed magis ut ipsi pro nobis, ut eorum vestigiis adhaereamus.'[5] Turns of phrase which occasionally brought out this sense in solemn prayers as well, or otherwise contained an invitation to invoke the intercession of the saints, appear to have been common on Syrian soil as early as the fourth century.[6] This interpretation, however,

---

[1] PL 85, 545 f.; cf. MEL V, 235, under the heading 'nomina offerentium'.

[2] *Theologische Quartalschrift* 104 (1923) 250–9. The secret for the feasts of Gregory I (12, III) and Leo II (28, VI, now 3, VII) formerly read: 'Annue nobis, quaesumus Domine, ut animae famuli Gregorii (Leonis) haec *pro*sit oblatio, quam immolando totius mundi tribuisti relaxari delicta, Per Dominum' (cf. now the secret 'pro defuncto Episcopo', n. 3). The present text is '*ut intercessione* beati Gregorii (Leonis) haec nobis prosit oblatio'.

[3] Br. 387, 30.          [4] *Liturgikon* 133n.

[5] *In Joh. tr.* 84, 1 (PL 35, 1847). Cf. *Sermo* 159, 1 (PL 38, 868): 'Iniuria est enim pro martyre orare, cuius nos debemus orationibus commendari.'

[6] The Mesopotamian author of the works formerly attributed to Makarius the Egyptian concludes his prayer: Ναὶ δέσποτα, φιλάνθρωπε, ὑπεράγαθε, μὴ βδελύξῃ με τὸν ἁμαρτωλὸν καὶ ἀχρεῖον οἰκέτην σου, πρεσβείαις τῆς παναχράντου δεσποίνης ἡμῶν θεοτόκου καὶ πάντων σου τῶν ἁγίων (PG 34, 448). Cf. the almost identical terminating formula in the Byzantine liturgy (above, p. 80 f.).

seems to have had its opponents, and once again in those parts where the conflict with Arianism had engendered an attitude of suspicion. In his *Adversus haereses*, which he finished in 377, Epiphanius cites as the 75th heresy that of his contemporary Aërius, who in his eyes was an out-and-out Arian.[1] The latter rejected, among other things, prayer for the departed. Epiphanius showed its efficacy for the departed as well as for the Church itself.[2] He observes: 'We practise the commemoration as much for the just as for sinners—for sinners, by asking God to pity them, for the just and the Fathers and Patriarchs, Prophets and Apostles and Evangelists and martyrs and confessors, bishops and anchorites and every class, so that we separate the Lord Jesus Christ from human kind by the honour due to him and pay him worship (σέβας) in the belief that the Lord cannot be put on the same level with any man, though he be of supreme righteousness. For how would that be possible? He is God and the other is man.' This negative interpretation of the commemoration of the saints must have been specially dear to the author, since the context did not require its mention. Epiphanius seems to see the other interpretation as obscuring the christological dogma: if we give prominence to the intercession of the saints in our liturgical prayers, we put them on the same level with Christ, our unique Intercessor with God. He was writing at a time when praying 'through Christ' was still very common in the Greek-speaking parts of the East. Basil had just begun the practice of praising the Father with the Son, as well as through him. Others may have clung on still longer to the old way of praying and, like Epiphanius, have sought other means of 'separating Christ from human kind' and thus preventing his appearing as a pure creature. Meanwhile there was scarcely any dogmatic discussion of the question of the veneration of the saints. It was only considerably later, in 406, that Vigilantius's opposition gave St Jerome the occasion to defend the practice.

In any case, this was a time of crisis for the way in which the veneration of the saints was to secure a position in liturgical prayer.

[1] H. Hemmer (*Dictionnaire de théologie catholique* I, 515 f.) thought he was probably a semi-Arian.

[2] *Adv. haer.* 75, 8; PG 42, 513 f.

In the 5th Mystagogical Catechesis of Cyril (or John) it was brought out clearly that the saints were remembered so that they might pray for us, whereas prayers 'for' anyone referred only to the other departed souls.[1]

In another direction, however, some thinkers seem to have carried to extremes the ideas put forward by Epiphanius. Certain Greek and Syro-Jacobite theologians resolutely defended the doctrine that the saints must be prayed for because they had not yet attained complete happiness.[2] In later manuscripts of Chosroë's description of the Mass an interpolation has the following comment on the memento for the saints as well as for departed Christians[3] inserted into the prayer of intercession of the Armenian Mass: should anyone ask why he mentions also the just, whom we look to for intercession, you should know that though they are glorified and have entered into rest, they have not yet reached perfection, but still hunger day after day and strive still further . . . so he prays first for them, that Christ may pity them, and then mentions the others.

Apart from this, the problem was solved for the East by Christ's mediatorship in prayer being pushed well into the background everywhere, and he was made to appear principally as sharing in the worship paid to the Father. So there was no longer any scandal when God was appealed to through the intercession of the saints. Consequently most of the traditional formulas in which prayers were said 'for' the saints and in which they were remembered had the explanatory addition: that they may pray for us, that God may be gracious to us at their intercession.[4] In the later form of the Byzantine liturgy we observed also a noticeable increase in the number of

---

[1] Br. 466, 9 (= II, p. 386. Rupp): εἶτα μνημονεύομεν καὶ τῶν προκεκοι-μημένων, πρῶτον πατριαρχῶν, προφητῶν, ἀποστόλων, μαρτύρων, ὅπως ὁ θεὸς ταῖς εὐχαῖς αὐτῶν καὶ πρεσβείαις προσδέξηται ἡμῶν τὴν δέησιν · εἶτα καὶ ὑπὲρ . . . πάντων ἁπλῶς τῶν ἐν ἡμῖν προκεκοιμημένων.

[2] See the comments made by E. Renaudot (II, 332) on the prayer in the Severus anaphora: 'Fundatores ecclesiae sanctae . . . laetifica per visionem vultus tui.' Yet in other cases (II, 98 f.) he is inclined to ascribe expressions of this kind to slips of the pen.

[3] 'Dei genetricis Virginis Mariae, Joannis Baptistae, sancti Stephani com-memoratio fiat . . . Fiat commemoratio virorum ac feminarum fideliter in Christo defunctorum.' Vetter 41; there also the above-mentioned interpolation.

[4] E.g. Br. 48, 12; 94, 32; 169, 21; 264, 16; 388, 19.

cases where the appeal to the intercession of the saints, as in 'Makarius the Egyptian', forms part of the end of a solemn prayer; elsewhere the phrase would be 'through Christ' or 'through the favour of Christ'. This kind of insertion or reshaping was particularly easy in the Syrian type of prayer.[1] Even in prayers to Christ, recourse is now had to the mediation of the saints with the Lord Christ, especially where, to the religious mind, his essential mediatorship and nearness to humanity is outshone by the resplendence of his divinity.

The phases preceding the liturgical prayer in which, in Byzantium, one 'mindful of the saints' addressed Christ may be discerned in the various forms of an old Antiochene summons to prayer—

1. In the *Apostolic Constitutions* it runs: Ἑαυτοὺς τῷ μόνῳ ἀγεννήτῳ θεῷ διὰ τοῦ Χριστοῦ αὐτοῦ παράθεσθε.[2]

2. In Chrysostom the phrase has already taken the form of ἑαυτοὺς τῷ ζῶντι θεῷ καὶ τῷ Χριστῷ αὐτοῦ παράθεσθε.[3] Christ is no longer conceived as Mediator but as co-recipient of the abandonment to God.

3. The next step is indicated by the text of the Armenian liturgy: 'Let us

---

[1] Research based on the earliest Syrian literature would show perhaps the possibility of a line of development here with the following stages: we beseech God (the Father and the Son and the Holy Spirit) in Christ—in the holy Church—in Communion with all the saints—through the intercession of the Mother of God and of all the saints.—Cf. above, pp. 153, 197 f. and 266, n. 6.

[2] VIII, 6, 8; and several other similar passages. It is impossible to establish with certainty that this form was in actual use in Antioch in the fourth century and that it is not merely the compiler's proposal. F. E. Brightman is in favour of the latter explanation (JthSt 12 [1912] 313); he agrees, however, that earlier liturgical texts were used as models. Thus Justin, *Apol.* I, 49 (Corpus Apologetarum I³ p. 134. Otto) says of the newly baptized: τῷ ἀγεννήτῳ θεῷ διὰ τοῦ Χριστοῦ ἑαυτοὺς ἀνέθηκαν; and, rather differently, *ibid* I, 61 (*ibid* I³, p. 162 f. Otto): Ὃν τρόπον δὲ καὶ ἀνεθήκαμεν ἑαυτοὺς θεῷ καινοποιηθέντες διὰ τοῦ Χριστοῦ. . . . But it is certainly very probable that the form was in use in Antioch before the time of Flavian. It is not more remarkable than the almost equivalent expression which survived into a later period in the above-mentioned (p. 66, n. 4) εὐχὴ τῆς ἐνάρξεως of the Greek liturgy of St James, Br. 32, 17: . . . πρόσδεξαι προσιοῦσάν σοι διὰ τοῦ Χριστοῦ σου τὴν ἐκκλησίαν σου. For another very similar phrase, *Ap. Const.* VIII, 9, 6: Ἀναστάντες τῷ θεῷ διὰ Χριστοῦ αὐτοῦ κλίνατε καὶ εὐλογεῖσθε. There is a parallel in Serapion 4 (28) I: σοὶ γάρ, ἀγένητε πάτερ, διὰ τοῦ μονογενοῦς κεκλίκασιν τὰς κεφαλάς.

[3] *In II. Cor. hom.* 2, n. 8 (Br. 471, 32). Following the same development, the phrase appears in most of the MSS. for *Ap. Const.* viii, 14, 3 (cf. Funk I, p. 518)—entirely parallel with the treatment of the doxology; cf. above, p. 13.

commit ourselves and one another unto the Lord the almighty God.'[1] As the divinity of Christ was already in the foreground it could justifiably be thought redundant to mention him along with 'the almighty God'.[2]

4. The East Syrian form takes another step on the same path with its abandonment to 'Father and Son and Holy Spirit'.[3]

5. Finally, instead of 'the almighty God', of 'the Father and the Son and the holy Spirit', the Byzantine liturgy simply names Christ in his divinity, as elsewhere he is designated 'Christ our God'. In a kind of mediatory position vis-à-vis Christ, Mary and the saints appear: Τῆς παναγίας ἀχράντου ὑπερευλογημένης ἐνδόξου δεσποίνης ἡμῶν θεοτόκου καὶ ἀειπαρθένου Μαρίας μετὰ πάντων τῶν ἁγίων μνημονεύσαντες ἑαυτοὺς καὶ ἀλλήλους καὶ πᾶσαν τὴν ζωὴν ἡμῶν Χριστῷ τῷ θεῷ παραθώμεθα.[4]

Thereby, here and there, forms occurred which are lacking in theological clarity. For instance, blended with the prayer to Christ, the Trinity is invoked again, and the prayer continues: Grant this, good God, through the prayers of thy mother.[5] In Abyssinia,

---

[1] Br. 425, 5; 429, 5; 445, 26. The exactly corresponding appeal runs in *Ap. Const.* VIII, 10, 22: δεηθέντες ἐκτενῶς ἑαυτοὺς καὶ ἀλλήλους τῷ ζῶντι θεῷ διὰ τοῦ Χριστοῦ αὐτοῦ παραθώμεθα.

[2] We may insert here the Latin form, as it appears in the so-called *Deprecatio Gelasii*; W. Bousset, 'Zur sogenannten *Deprecatio Gelasii*' (Nachrichten der königl. Gesellschaft der Wissenschaften in Göttingen, phil.-hist. Klasse, 1916, pp. 135–62; now also in Jungmann, *Missarum Sollemnia*[5] I, 434 f.) 138 f.: 'Nosmetipsos et omnia nostra, quae orta, quae aucta per Dominum ipso auctore suscipimus . . . ipsius misericordiae et arbitrio providentiae commendamus.' It is barely possible that the 'per Dominum' is an echo of the διὰ τοῦ Χριστοῦ αὐτοῦ of the *Apostolic Constitutions*.

[3] Br. 266, 24: 'Let us commit our souls and one another's souls to the Father and the Son and the Holy Ghost.'

[4] Br. 363, 21.Similarly already in the Greek St James liturgy of the fourth century (Br. 40, 1). Cf. also Br. 495, 18; 499, 8; 391, 16. It is apposite here to suggest that the appearance of secondary mediators, which was almost inevitable with the dwindling or disappearance of the 'Per Christum', nevertheless corresponds to some extent with the early Christian formula 'in the holy Church'. Significantly, we find the equivalent of such an expression ('in union with all who have pleased thee' and the like) especially in that liturgy which from the first has not cultivated the 'Per Christum', namely the East Syrian (see above. p. 75 f.). The prominence given to the saints who support our prayers, together with the christological mediatory formula, as in the Roman *intercedentibus omnibus Sanctis*, is found also in Athanasius, *Ep. heort.* 4, 5 (PG 26, 1379 B): in the world to come we shall 'praise the God of all through Christ Jesus and through him, together with the saints, say "Amen" '. Similarly *Ep. heort.* 1, 10 (PL 26, 1366B). Cf. also the passage from Origen's *De oratione* c. 11, 1, touched on on page 157.

[5] See above, p. 68; cf. the Ethiopic anaphora of Mary (above, p. 50).

veneration of the mother of God assumed such forms that even the most reverential judgment cannot acquit of exaggeration.[1] Here, following Monophysite currents of thought, it was more than elsewhere the custom, even in liturgical prayer, to make no distinction between the address to God and that to Christ, and here there was no counter-current to keep the custom within bounds.

Subsequently, Christ as a Mediator of prayer in the strict sense or of the petition has hardly a place anywhere outside the *Roman* liturgy. It is again indicative of the calm confidence with which this liturgy was constructed that the veneration of saints takes its place within it without altering any of the existing components. Only some forms of later, extra-Roman, origin show a certain reluctance to allow Christ to appear in relation to God in a mediatory position in company with the saints; and a certain predilection to consider Christ as being included in the idea of God, and thus to speak only of God and the saints—an attitude which, it must be admitted, has become the norm in popular piety.[2]

Over against these few exceptions stands the great mass of prayers in which, it is true, there is more frequent allusion to the intercession of the saints than in other liturgies, in accord with the greater influence of the Church's year, but in a form in which Christ always

---

[1] Cf., for example, B. S. Euringer, 'Ein interessantes Kapitel aus der Mariologie der abessinischen Kirche': *Bericht über den V. Marianischen Weltkongress*, Salzburg 1911, pp. 348–54.

[2] This includes the *Confiteor*, in which the priest acknowledges his guilt 'Deo omnipotenti, beatae Mariae semper Virgini, beato Michaeli archangelo ... omnibus sanctis'. Compare this with the still unembarrassed way of speaking used by the Apostle, who exhorts Timothy (I, 6:13) to be loyal 'in the presence of God who gives life to all things, *and* of Christ Jesus' and implores him, in the presence of God *and* of Christ *and* of the elect angels' (I, 5:21); or that of a Roman inscription of the fourth century which begins: 'Deo Patri omnipotenti *et* Christo eius *et* sanctis martyribus' (C. M. Kauffmann, *Handbuch der altchristlichen Epigraphik*, Freiburg 1917, p. 166, n. 2). Similarly, in the second part of the *Confiteor*, it is only the aforesaid saints whose intercession is sought 'ad Dominum Deum nostrum', with no mention of Christ too as Mediator. Compare the language of St Augustine: 'Dominus enim noster Jesus Christus adhuc interpellat pro nobis; omnes martyres, qui cum illo sunt, interpellant pro nobis.' In Ps. 85, c. 24 (PL 37, 1099). Cf. *Serm* 285, 5 (PL 38, 1295 f.).

Of the same type as the *Confiteor* is the second of the prayers said when mounting the steps of the altar—'Oramus te Domine'—and the giving of absolution—'Precibus et meritis'—in the pontifical.

remains the sole Mediator between God and man. He stands in the midst of the saints like the sun among the stars, and their intercession is only to strengthen the prayer that we offer with them through Christ: 'Beatorum martyrum tuorum intercessio gloriosa nos protegat. Per Dominum.—Quem Doctorem vitae habuimus in terris, intercessorem habere mereamur in coelis. Per Dominum.'[1] So we surround ourselves with the protection of the saints and thus pray anew 'in the holy Church' through Christ to God, as we saw it in St Hippolytus. This finds expression especially in the intercessory prayer of the Roman Mass, which forms the largest portion of the Canon before the consecration. The offering for the Church on earth and its leaders, together with the *memento* for the faithful, may here too have been continued at an earlier period by an indetermin- ate prayer 'for' the saints, as is testified by Cyprian and is the practice, for example, in the Mozarabic Mass. In the present Canon, however, the first mention of them is of Communion with them (*communicantes*): we know that with the saints we are one people of God when we appear before God through Christ our head.

The invocation of the saints directly addressed to them, as can be shown to have been practised privately since the third century, has seldom been included among the prose prayers of the Mass liturgy. The Ethiopian anaphora of Mary with its logical arrangement is an isolated exception. In the Greek liturgies of St James and St Mark there is a greeting to the Mother of God inserted into the prayer of intercession at the point where she is mentioned.[2] Some examples show that greater liberty is enjoyed in the Mozarabic liturgy.[3]

In the Roman liturgy the invocation of the saints on Holy Saturday has won a place as a preliminary to the Mass in the

---

[1] In the East, the Coptic liturgy has a benedictory prayer of a similarly harmoni- ous structure for the end of Mass (Br. 187 f.). It mentions the intercession of the saints ('by the intercession of') and ends 'in Christ Jesus our Lord, through whom. . .'.

[2] See above, p. 33. In this case the *Ave* is said by the priest. At the same juncture in the Byzantine liturgy a hymn is sung by the choir. Br. 388. Cf. also, however, the invocation of the saints in the Byzantine Mass discussed above, p. 80 f.

[3] See above, p. 103 f. The invocation of the saints in the Stowe Missal is inserted at the beginning of the Mass, not after the Consecration. F. Cabrol, DACL 1, 2593.

setting of the *Litany of the Saints*.[1] This is a perfect example of how popular forms of prayer may be not merely received but fitted into the structure of the liturgy. The invocations of the saints, which were inserted into the original prayer to Christ, now form the main substance of this prayer. It is followed by more petitions to Christ, ending in the *Agnus Dei* and the *Kyrie eleison, Christe eleison*. The earliest pre-liturgical litany texts either break off here or add only a few versicles and psalm verses. On Holy Saturday, on the other hand, the litany is rounded off by the collects of the Mass: the invocation of the saints merges into the petition to Christ, and after the *Gloria* ends in a solemn prayer which, as always, is addressed to the Lord God through Christ. The Litany of the Saints undergoes a similar extension when, as on Rogation Days, it is recited as a prayer by itself. On these occasions it culminates in the *orationes* of the Church with their solemn ending, *Per Dominum nostrum*, with which our prayer takes the place allotted to it by God himself, as it were, in the plan of divine salvation. The manner of its recital enhances the harmonious impression of its composition. Whereas the litany itself is sung by the choir and congregation, the *orationes* are recited by the officiating priest, who for this purpose goes up to the altar.

The same stylistic rule can be found at work on other occasions, and not only in the Roman liturgy. In the ordinary Mass the congregational prayer of the Kyrie is followed in like fashion by the solemn prayer of the Church, the collect;[2] it is only on feast days that the *Gloria* intervenes. In a similar manner, the congregational offertory procession, its impressiveness increased by the singing of

---

[1] For the Litany of the Saints, see E. Bishop, *Liturgica historia* 137–64; A. Fortescue, *The Mass, a study of the Roman Liturgy*[2] (London, 1914), p. 233 ff.

[2] The Jerusalem usage should be noted; we have an account of it from the Aquitanian pilgrim Aetheria (c. 394). The litany recited by the deacon, each petition being responded to by a group of children with κύριε ἐλέησον, was concluded by the bishop delivering the *oratio*: 'Ubi diaconus perdixerit omnia, quae dicere habet, dicet orationem primum episcopus. . . .' *Peregrinatio* c. 24, 6 (CSEL 39, p. 72, 19. Geyer).

We may mention here a parallel case from Egypt. In the liturgy of St Mark, at the beginning of the Mass, each of the three lengthy prayers said by the priest is introduced by a three-fold κύριε ἐλέησον assigned to the congregation (Br. 114, 20 ff.). H. Leclercq (DACL 1, 1189) also draws attention to this latter case of concurrence with the Roman liturgy.

the *offertorium*, is concluded by the secret or *oratio super oblata*); and the distribution of communion, during which the *communio* was sung, by the postcommunion. On penitential days, with the words 'flectamus genua', the people were invited to pray silently, which they did on their knees. At the 'levate' the priest closed this prayer with the oratio.[1] In similar fashion, the oratio said by the priest in the divine office concludes the singing of the psalms. The harsher tones of the Old Testament's divine praise and earthly lamentation are succeeded at last by a prayer sealed with the fulfilment of every longing—Christ. In Lauds, Vespers, and Compline, one of the canticles from the New Testament, first heard at the start of the Christian era, always forms the transition. Similarly in Jerusalem, as early as the fourth century, every reading of the Scriptures ended with a solemn prayer.[2] Sometimes the Pater noster was, and still is, said instead of a collect.[3] And it ends each group of psalms in Matins.

Conversely, the Kyrie is also put in front of the Lord's Prayer. This arrangement occurs not only in the Roman liturgy from the time of St Benedict but also in the Jacobite fore-anaphora and in the Byzantine liturgy.[4]

It may be asked here whether perhaps the Kyrie is a way of asking Christ the Lord for his intercession, and his mediatorship for the solemn prayer which has thus been introduced. In principle, there is no objection to such a way of praying. The great theologians find it entirely admissible to approach Christ in his humanity to obtain

---

[1] Cf. L. Duchesne, *Les Origines*[4] 107-9.

[2] See the account of the Aquitanian pilgrim: *Peregrinatio* c. 24 (CSEL 39, p. 71, 16 ff.; p. 73, 15 ff. Geyer). Cf. A. Baumstark, *Die Messe im Morgenland* 80.

[3] Cf. V. Thalhofer–L. Eisenhofer II, 564.

[4] Br. 72, 7; 353, 23. S. Bäumer (*Geschichte des Breviers*, Freiburg; B. 1895, p. 127 f,) gives the following account of the prayer-order of an Abbot Nilus of Sinai, taken from a sixth-century fragment published by J. B. Pitra, *Juris eccl. Graecorum historia et monumenta* I (Rome, 1868) 220 f.: After a number of psalms he ends the prayer with Our Father and Kyrie eleison, the latter sometimes repeated at length. He seems to be paraphrasing the Kyrie when he adds: 'Son and word of God, Jesus Christ our God, have pity on us, give us the support of thy grace and save our souls!' We have here the same descending order as in *Ap. Const.* VIII, 43 (see above, p. 11) or in the last blessing of the Jacobite anaphoras (see above, pp. 56 f., 62, 231 f.)—God first, then Christ.

his intercession.[1] The preliminary Kyrie would then be a counter-part to the end-formula *per Dominum*.[2] The idea is not excluded, but neither is it given prominence. Its underlying purpose is more likely to have been that of St Ignatius's instruction in his *Spiritual Exercises*: in praying one should turn, at the end of the meditation, either first to Christ and then to our heavenly Father, or, if the occasion requires it, first to Mary, then to Christ, and then to God the Father. The suppliant should approach the throne of the divine majesty step by step, as it were, and thus close the prayer with so much the more reverence and care.[3] It is only another side of Christ's position as Mediator which thus comes out.

This meeting—especially in the Roman liturgy—with Christ the Lord, the Mediator between God and man, at all cross-roads, so to speak, is plainly characteristic of liturgical prayer in contrast to the free-growing, less restricted forms of popular piety. But what are the *purpose and importance* of this remarkable relationship?

Frequent reference to the Mediator is not necessary, either for the effectiveness of prayer or for its value as divine praise, but it is purposeful and educationally valuable. To have an educational effect on the community, to edify it,[4] to put it into a religious frame of mind, not just for the moment but to enrich its knowledge of religion and ennoble it—all this is one of the functions of liturgical prayer inherent in its very nature. Liturgical prayer must always remain prayer directed to God: it must be divine service and not community service,[5] but it is intended equally to guide the community to God and fill it with the thoughts which can kindle in all hearts the same flame of true Christian prayer. A clear proof of this

[1] Cf. J. Margreth, *Das Gebetsleben Jesu* 107 f. He cites in support Thomas Aquinas, Suarez, Petavius, and Scheeben.

[2] As the Our Father is in any case the Lord's Prayer, it is not usual to add any christological end-formula. Only the embolism, the extension of the last request, has been given the christological ending in the Roman and also in the Mozarabic (cf. above, p. 99 f.) and Coptic Masses (Br. 182, 24).

[3] Cf. the East Syrian introduction to the Pater noster (above, p. 72). For the laws governing the forms of liturgical prayer which are touched on here, see my pamphlet *Wortgottesdienst* (Regensburg, 1965) which first appeared in 1939 as *Die liturgische Feier* (Eng.: *Liturgical Worship* [New York, 1941]).

[4] Cf. I Cor, 14:17.

Cf. F. Probst, *Liturgie des 4. Jahrhunderts* 374.

well-recognized function of liturgical prayer are the exhortations to prayer and the introductory formulas which precede the actual prayers in so many liturgies.[1] Some liturgical formularies go so far in this direction that even their prayer can be all too like a homily.[2]

Though a certain element of instruction is inseparable from liturgical prayer, it is not the fine theological distinctions, the ultimate conclusions of the speculative analysis of the deposit of faith that can be the lodestars for the prayers of the community. Only the great outlines that permit us to survey the total riches of divine revelation, 'the truth in all its fulness', are suited to this.[3] In the contentious times of the fourth century, Basil warned against 'mythologizing' in the eucharistic prayer.[4] He seems to have had in mind the flooding of the prayer with anti-heretical phrases. Nor was he in favour of describing the benefits of the creation in too much detail; rather, God should be thanked for the greater good, the redemption, for 'the everlasting God having conquered death through the flesh'.[5]

The character of the liturgical assembly points in the same direction. Whether it be a Sunday assembly or a feast to be celebrated, in every case it is an assembling of the community in the presence of God. As the festal address differs not only in form but also in the dimensions of its subject-matter, and in its wider viewpoint, from the intimate talk with its chance theme, so also the liturgical *oratio*, *praefatio*, and *praedicatio*[6] differ from private prayer with its narrow purview. Thus it is only the great basic doctrines that can be put into words in liturgical prayer, the guiding thoughts of the Christian life which determine our relation to God; above all,

---

[1] Cf. above, pp. 12, 18 etc. (exclamation of the Eastern deacon), 93, 96 f. In the Roman liturgy: 'Oremus', 'Orate fratres', 'Dominus vobiscum', 'Sursum corda', 'Gratias agamus'.

[2] Cf. above, pp. 48 ff., 101, 113 f.

[3] Cf. R. Guardini, *Vom Geist der Liturgie* (Ecclesia Orans I), Freiburg 1918, p. 6 ff.: *The Church and the Catholic—The Spirit of the Liturgy* (tr. Ada Lane) (London, 1935), p. 126 ff.

[4] *Constitutiones Asceticae* c. 1, 2 (PG 31, 1329).

[5] Cf. F. Probst, *Liturgie des 4. Jahrhunderts* 132 ff., 137.

[6] The expression *praedicatio* is used for the Canon of the Mass in the Liber pontificalis (Duchesne I, 127): 'Hic (*scil.* Alexander I) passionem Domini miscuit in praedicatione sacerdotum, quando missae celebrantur.'

those with which the Apostles went out into the world: there is one God, who has made everything, and Jesus Christ, his only Son, has reconciled us sinners with him. If only these two doctrines, the second as well as the first, are not only believed but inwardly grasped, a good part of religious education is already accomplished. For the thought of the Mediator who has made us children of God brings the characteristics of fatherhood into our conception of God and teaches us courage and trust, gratitude and love—in short, true Christian virtue.[1] But these two pillars of Christian thought are manifest in every prayer addressed to God through Christ.

On liturgical days in the full sense—Sundays and feast-days— the prayer-address to God is suggested by the purpose of the assembly. This is not the time to follow any pious impulse of the heart, to give rein to any mysticism, or to seek help from *any* sort of heavenly power; it is the time to fulfil the first duty of man, to practise the virtue of religion. The creature must pay homage to the creator. It is natural therefore that in its form of address as well as in its content the solemn prayer be directed expressly to God the almighty Lord of all things, or that at all events this predisposition be the governing motive of the prayer. Here one day every path will find its goal, every stream will flow into the sea of eternity, where it may find its rest.

It is then in the Christian sacrifice, St Augustine's *sacrificium mediatoris*,[2] that the community in assembly worships God. Christ, 'our atonement', is the sacrificial gift which (obeying his instruction) we offer to the Lord God, as he himself did on the Cross. It is therefore supremely fitting not only that the accompanying words of prayer should be addressed to the highest Lord himself but also that they should appeal to the divine and human Mediator, who has

[1] More than once F. Probst has pointed out that 'the content of the apostolic missionary sermon and that of the liturgical eucharistic prayer are identical; the difference has been shown to be one of form only'. (*Liturgie des 4. Jahrhunderts* 60 f., 114. Cf. *Lehre und Gebet in den drei ersten christlichen Jahrhunderten*, Tübingen 1871, p. 57 ff.). Similarly he stresses the great practical importance of the liturgy in the early days of the Church: 'It was the heart of prayer and of pious living in general. Within it every religious lesson was imparted; from it private devotion drew its nourishment; into it flowed the stream of grace for a godly way of life.' (*Liturgie des 4. Jahrhunderts* 42).

[2] *Enchiridion* c. 110 (PL 40, 283).

conquered death and won life for us and who himself lives with the Father as the new Adam of redeemed mankind.

When these monumental themes of Christianity determine the broad outlines of the liturgical structure within and without the Mass, there is room enough in its spacious halls for the harmonious insertion of the smaller sanctuaries, before which the piety of the different generations, as they come and go, is more readily enkindled; in which the tongues of pious devotion are more easily loosened, so that all the over- and undertones of the variously attuned souls and generations blend together in the great hymn which rises up unceasingly from the holy Church of Christ to God.

Since the days of Pius X we have been witnessing a reform in the Roman liturgy which aims at freeing the old basic laws of liturgical prayer from the proliferation of feasts and forms of a secondary nature. The old formularies of the Sundays and of Lent have regained their favoured positions; and we may include in this development the enrichment of the Prefaces, the central eucharistic prayer. The communion decrees of Pius X seek to recreate in the Christian people the practical recognition of that conception of the Eucharist which has always been presupposed in the liturgical formulas and which in more recent times, too, has been repeatedly advocated by liturgical instructions as the happy medium between timid reverence and confident familiarity. As A. Baumstark rightly says, 'Even now that it has become a universal liturgy, the liturgy of Rome continues in a way hitherto unknown to the East to take thought about itself and its old essential traits'.[1]

Other liturgies show many beauties and justifiable differences; nevertheless, so far as the type of prayer is concerned, we may regard the Roman liturgy with grateful pride and rejoice in it—in its venerable age and its imperishable youth, so that it is still our best teacher of prayer, the safest guide that untiringly leads us by the one everlasting way—through Christ to God.[2]

[1] *Vom geschichtlichen Werden* 131.
[2] It is clear that these words, written in 1925, could be said with even more confidence since the *Constitutio de Sacra Liturgia* of 4 December 1963 of the second Vatican Council.

# INDEX

279

Paul St (*cont.*)
  and Christ as Mediator 134–5,
    135n, 136, 160, 197 and n
  and the expression 'in the Holy
    Spirit' 150n, 151
  and God's salvific decree in Christ
    153
  use of the formula 'through Christ'
    177
  and the phrase *unitatem spiritus* 203–4
  intercessory prayer to 264
Paulinus of Antioch 178
Pelagius II 108n
Penance
  sacrament of 241n
Penitence 47 and n
Pentecost, feast of
  prefaces for 108
  Mass for (Mozarabic) 221n
Peter, St
  collects for 117–18
  prayers for 131
  his community prayers 133
  and work 'through Christ' 134
  and the priesthood of the faithful
    149
  intercessory prayers to 264
Peter, Acts of St (apocryphal)
  its Christ-addressed prayers 170
  and the expression 'per te Deus'
    220n
Philo (c. 20 B.C.–c. A.D. 50) 243
  Origen and 158
Philostorgius (c. 368–c. 439)
  and the doxology 176n
Photius (c. 810–95) Patriarch of Constantinople
  and the apocryphal *Acts* 168, 170
Pius V, Pope (1566–72) 106
  his missal 222n
Pius X, Pope (1903–14)
  and the Missal 116n
  and frequent communion 263n
  his reforms in the liturgy 278
Polycarp, St (c. 69–c. 155), Bishop of
  Smyrna
  his prayers 147 and n
Pontifical
  and Christ's Passion 223

Pontificale Romanum 117
Port Royal
  nuns of and the adoration of the
    sacrament 263n
Postcommunions 114n, 116n, 117,
  118, 119n, 123
Post-sanctus
  in the Mozarabic liturgy 97–8,
    100 and n
  in St Mark liturgy 187n
Praedicatio Petri
  and Christ-addressed prayers 171n
Prayer, intercessory 33 and n, 40n,
  44, 54, 59, 63, 72, 82 and n, 102
  to the Virgin Mary 50, 54, 67, 68
    and n, 80, 81, 270
  replaced by Sedro-prayers 67
  for saints and martyrs 264–5, 265n,
    268–70
  nature of 265–7
Prayer, liturgical
  its varying nature xvii–xviii
  the idea of Christ and xviii, xix, xx
  its early freedom 3
  Christ's teaching on its nature
    127–8
  salvation its subject matter 132
  its priestly character 136n
  and mediation 136–43
  retains its christological formula in
    the 4th century 144–5, 164–5,
    170–1
  inclusion of the phrase Holy Church
    152–3
  its trinitarian development 153–6,
    161
  Origen and 156–7, 159
  Serapion and 162–3
  rejection of outworn element 194
  poetical additions to 214 and n
  and personification 214n
  effect of religious struggles on 222
  the Syrian Jacobite movement and
    230–4
  element of fear in 246–51
  and the veneration of the Saints
    267ff
  arrangements of 273–5
  functions of 275–8